MANAGING ELECTRONIC RECORDS

WILEY CIO SERIES

Founded in 1807, John Wiley & Sons is the oldest independent publishing company in the United States. With offices in North America, Europe, Asia, and Australia, Wiley is globally committed to developing and marketing print and electronic products and services for our customers' professional and personal knowledge and understanding.

The Wiley CIO series provides information, tools, and insights to IT executives and managers. The products in this series cover a wide range of topics that supply strategic and implementation guidance on the latest technology trends, leadership, and emerging best practices.

Titles in the Wiley CIO series include:

The Agile Architecture Revolution: How Cloud Computing, REST-Based SOA, and Mobile Computing Are Changing Enterprise IT by Jason Bloomberg

Big Data, Big Analytics: Emerging Business Intelligence and Analytic Trends for Today's Businesses by Michele Chambers, Ambiga Dhiraj, and Michael Minelli

The Chief Information Officer's Body of Knowledge: People, Process, and Technology by Dean Lane

CIO Best Practices: Enabling Strategic Value with Information Technology by Joe Stenzel, Randy Betancourt, Gary Cokins, Alyssa Farrell, Bill Flemming, Michael H. Hugos, Jonathan Hujsak, and Karl D. Schubert

The CIO Playbook: Strategies and Best Practices for IT Leaders to Deliver Value by Nicholas R. Colisto

Enterprise IT Strategy, + Website: An Executive Guide for Generating Optimal ROI from Critical IT Investments by Gregory J. Fell

Executive's Guide to Virtual Worlds: How Avatars Are Transforming Your Business and Your Brand by Lonnie Benson

Innovating for Growth and Value: How CIOs Lead Continuous Transformation in the Modern Enterprise by Hunter Muller

IT Leadership Manual: Roadmap to Becoming a Trusted Business Partner by Alan R. Guibord

Managing Electronic Records: Methods, Best Practices, and Technologies by Robert F. Smallwood

On Top of the Cloud: How CIOs Leverage New Technologies to Drive Change and Build Value Across the Enterprise by Hunter Muller

Straight to the Top: CIO Leadership in a Mobile, Social, and Cloud-based (Second Edition) by Gregory S. Smith

Strategic IT: Best Practices for IT Managers and Executives by Arthur M. Langer

Strategic IT Management: Transforming Business in Turbulent Times by Robert J. Benson

Transforming IT Culture: How to Use Social Intelligence, Human Factors and Collaboration to Create an IT Department That Outperforms by Frank Wander

Unleashing the Power of IT: Bringing People, Business, and Technology Together by Dan Roberts

The U.S. Technology Skills Gap: What Every Technology Executive Must Know to Save America's Future by Gary Beach

MANAGING ELECTRONIC RECORDS

METHODS, BEST PRACTICES, AND TECHNOLOGIES

Robert F. Smallwood

WILEY

Published by John Wiley & Sons, Inc., Hoboken, New Jersey.
Published simultaneously in Canada.

Library of Congress Cataloging-in-Publication Data:

Smallwood, Robert F., 1959-
 Managing electronic records : methods, best practices, and technologies / Robert F. Smallwood.
  pages cm
 Includes bibliographical references and index.
 ISBN 978-1-118-21829-7 (cloth);   ISBN 978-1-118-28483-4 (ebk);
 ISBN 978-1-118-28290-8 (ebk);   ISBN 978-1-118-28238-0 (ebk)
 1. Electronic records — Management. 2. Records —Management. I. Title.
 CD974.4.S63 2013
 025.04—dc23   2012045105

Printed in the United States of America

10 9 8 7 6 5 4 3 2 1

For my dearly departed brothers:

William Scott Smallwood
David Bruce Smallwood

CONTENTS

FOREWORD

This book is timely: There continues to be a strong need for comprehensive resources addressing the diverse issues and challenges of managing electronic records.

This need has grown over the twenty-plus years I have co-chaired the only national conference focusing exclusively on electronic records management (ERM). I am pleased to welcome and applaud Robert Smallwood's comprehensive book on managing electronic records as an excellent, profound information resource.

The need for this book is founded in the "sea change" that the management of electronic records has undergone—and continues to undergo—as society and business have moved full on into the digital age.

Consider just five of the component changes:

1. The historic function has evolved from materials management to risk mitigation.
2. An increasing focus on the broader tenets of information governance (IG).
3. The very nature of what constitutes records has expanded greatly to include metadata, e-mail, messaging, social media, cloud use—and it continues to evolve.
4. The volume of records being created and needing to be managed has grown exponentially.
5. The use of records to resolve legal disputes has expanded from primarily "proving the positive" to "proving the negative."

Bottom line: The sea change resulting in the digitization of business records has created a whole new world regarding what is managed, why it is managed, how it is managed, and who is responsible for the management process. And increasingly, as the goal of managing records has become more focused on risk mitigation, the sphere of solution buyers has expanded to include project managers and professionals in risk management, compliance, IG, and law.

From all these manifestations of change, Robert Smallwood, in collaboration and consultation with a number of leading practitioners, has come forward with a comprehensive and authoritative resource on the management of electronic records never before available. Robert's book is a pioneering resource with focus and quality. It presents not only a "big picture" perspective of the issues and problems but also quite specific recommendations from an operational perspective—providing insights and assistance not only for students, young professionals, and newly assigned project leaders, but also for seasoned records management, risk, legal, and compliance professionals.

This book is a huge undertaking that few have both the vision to take on and the perseverance to make a reality. It is a much-needed resource that will facilitate education on electronic records management issues and help in achieving the implementation of successful solutions. Bravo!

Robert F. Williams
Cohasset Associates

PREFACE

After more than five years of e-records research, and an intensive year of detailed research, consultation, collaboration, writing, and editing, this book has come to fruition. It represents a truly collaborative effort by a number of experts and highly skilled practitioners in electronic records management (ERM) and the broader information governance (IG) field. I am fortunate to know them: Some of the contributors I have known for decades; and this is a lesson for students and young professionals—that lasting business relationships are a vital resource that can yield career rewards over the long term, but also offer lasting friendships that are a reward in themselves. This is only possible if you immerse yourself in your chosen field and strive for excellence day after day, year after year, and hold respect for your work and the work of your colleagues. No one can know everything, but if you know key people who have specific expertise, you can always find the answers you need. Of course, you will also need to be able to return the favor.

We strove to extensively document our work so that researchers, analysts, practitioners, teachers, and students wishing to delve further into particular topics will have a head start in knowing where to find additional information. This was a difficult and tedious process, which yielded over 600 citations. We tried to distill the massive amount of information into clear, understandable, actionable terms. We also to confirm and document methods, best practices, standards, and technical information from a variety of sources, both public and private, from books, blogs, magazines, interviews, government portals, and consulting work product; and also, to include expertise from around the world to make this book truly a global resource.

Writing it was a challenging series of research and analysis tasks undertaken and represents a collective mountain of effort—and many, many mornings of waking before dawn to study, consult, collaborate, and write. It would have been easier and less stressful to give up, but we pressed on.

The result is the most comprehensive and current resource on the topic of ERM ever produced, which will hopefully afford those relying on this information an easier road as they implement ERM and IG programs.

This book will assist records managers, CIOs, IT managers, compliance and risk managers, and others involved in records management and information governance to make intelligent, informed decisions. For those seeking to implement an information governance program that includes electronic records management, bulk pricing for the book and e-book are available. Please visit: www.electronic-records-management.com.

— Robert F. Smallwood

ACKNOWLEDGMENTS

I would like to sincerely thank my colleagues for their support and generous contribution of their time and expertise, which made this book possible, and improved it greatly:

Many thanks to Lori Ashley, Barb Blackburn, Barclay Blair, Charmaine Brooks, Ken Chasse, Monica Crocker, Charles M. Dollar, Seth Earley, Marc Fresko, Steve Goodfellow, Gordon Hoke, Ulrich Kampffmeyer, John W. Orth, Bud Porter-Roth, Jon Pyke, Paula Lederman, Craig Rhinehart, and Robert F. Williams.

I am truly honored to include their work and owe them a great debt of gratitude.

MANAGING
ELECTRONIC
RECORDS

PART ONE
E-Records
Concepts

CHAPTER 1

E-Records Definitions, Business Drivers, and Benefits

First, some basic definitions of core terms used in this text: The International Organization for Standardization (ISO) defines (business) **records** as "information created, received, and maintained as evidence and information by an organization or person, in pursuance of legal obligations or in the transaction of business."[1] It further defines **records management** as "[the] field of management responsible for the efficient and systematic control of the creation, receipt, maintenance, use, and disposition of records, including the processes for capturing and maintaining evidence of and information about business activities and transactions in the form of records."[2]

The U.S.-based Association of Records Managers and Administrators (ARMA), defines a record as "evidence of what an organization does. They capture its business activities and transactions, such as contract negotiations, business correspondence, personnel files, and financial statements. . . ."[3]

Electronic records management (ERM) has moved to the forefront of business issues with the increasing automation of business processes, and the vast growth in the volume of electronic documents and records that organizations create. These factors, coupled with expanded and tightened reporting laws and compliance regulations, have made ERM increasingly essential for most enterprises—especially highly regulated and public ones—over the past decade.

ERM follows generally the same principles as traditional paper-based records management, that is, there are **classification** and **taxonomy** needs to group and organize the records; and there are **retention** and **disposition** schedules to govern the length of time a record is kept, and its ultimate disposition, whether it is destruction, transfer, or long-term archiving. Yet e-records must be handled differently and they contain more detailed data about their contents and characteristics, known as **metadata.** (This book discusses these detailed topics in more depth in later chapters.)

E-records are also subject to changes in **information technology** (IT) that may make them difficult to retrieve and view and therefore render them obsolete. These issues can be addressed through a sound ERM program that includes **long-term digital preservation (LTDP)** methods and technologies.

ERM is primarily the organization, management, control, monitoring, and auditing of formal business records that exist in electronic form. But automated ERM systems also track paper-based and other physical records. So ERM goes beyond simply managing electronic records; it is *the management of electronic records and the electronic*

> E-records management has become much more critical to enterprises with increased compliance legislation and massively increasing volumes of electronic information.

management of nonelectronic records (e.g., paper, CD/DVDs, magnetic tape, audio-visual, and other physical records).

Most electronic records, or "e-records," originally had an equivalent in paper form, such as memos (now e-mail), accounting documents (e.g., purchase orders, invoices), personnel documents (e.g., job applications, resumes, tax documents), contractual documents, line-of-business documents (e.g., loan applications, insurance claim forms, health records), and required regulatory documents (e.g., material safety data sheets, MSDS). In the past, many of these documents were first archived to microfilm or microform/microfiche, before e-document software began to mature in the 1990s.

Not all documents rise to the level of being declared a formal business record that needs to be retained; that definition depends on the specific regulatory and legal requirements imposed on the organization, and the internal definitions and requirements the organization imposes on itself, through internal **information governance** (IG) measures and business policies. IG *is the policies, processes, and technologies used to manage and control information throughout the enterprise to meet internal business requirements and external legal and compliance demands.*

ERM is a component of enterprise content management (ECM), just as document management, web content management, digital asset management, enterprise report management, and several other technology sets. ECM encompasses *all* an organization's unstructured digital content, (which means it excludes structured data i.e., databases). ECM includes the vast majority—over 90 percent—of an organization's overall information, which must be governed and managed.

ERM extends ECM to provide control and to manage records through their lifecycle—from creation to archiving or destruction. ERM is used to complete the lifecycle management of information, documents, and records.

ERM adds the functionality to complete the management of information and records by applying business rules to manage the maintenance, security, integrity and disposition of records. Both ERM and ECM systems will aid in locating and managing the records and information needed to conduct business efficiently, to comply with legal and regulatory requirements, and effectively destroy (paper) and delete (digital) records that have met their retention policy timeframe requirement, freeing up valuable space, physical and digital, and eliminating records that could be a liability if kept.

> E-records management follows the same basic principles as paper-based records management.

E-records management includes the management of electronic and nonelectronic records, like paper and other physical records.

Records Management Business Rationale

Historically, highly regulated industries, such as banking, energy, and pharmaceuticals, have had the greatest need to implement records management programs, due to their compliance and reporting requirements.[4] However, over the past decade or so, increased regulation and changes to legal statutes and rules have made records management a business necessity for nearly every enterprise (beyond very small businesses).

Notable industry drivers include:

- **Increased government oversight and industry regulation.** It is a fact that government regulations that require greater reporting and accountability were early business drivers that fueled the implementation of formal records management programs. This is true at the federal and state or provincial level. There are a number of laws and regulations related to records management that have been added in the past 10 to 15 years. In the United States, the Sarbanes-Oxley Act of 2002 (SOX) created and enhanced standards of financial reporting and transparency for the boards and executive management of public corporations and accounting firms. It also addressed auditor independence and corporate governance concerns. SOX imposes fines or imprisonment penalties for noncompliance, and requires that senior officers sign off on the veracity of financial statements. It states clearly that pertinent business records cannot be destroyed during litigation or compliance investigations. Since SOX, other countries, such as Japan, Australia, Germany, France, and India, have adopted stricter "'SOX-like" governance and financial reporting standards.
- **Changes in legal procedures and requirements during civil litigation.** In 2006, the need to amend the U.S. Federal Rules of Civil Procedure (FRCP) to contain specific rules for handling electronically generated evidence was addressed. The changes included processes and requirements for legal discovery of electronically stored information (ESI) during civil litigation. *Today, e-mail is the leading form of evidence requested in civil trials.* The changes to the U.S. FRCP had a pervasive impact on American enterprises and required them to gain control over their ESI and implement formal records management and electronic discovery ("e-discovery") programs to meet new requirements. Although they have been ahead of the U.S. in their development and maturity of records management practices, Canadian, British, and Australian law is closely tracking that of the United States in legal discovery. The U.S. is simply a more litigious society so this is not unexpected.
- **Information governance awareness.** *IG, in short, is the set of rules, policies, and business processes used to manage and control the totality of an organization's information.* Monitoring technologies are required to enforce and audit IG compliance. Beginning with major legislation like SOX in 2002, and continuing

A number of factors provide the business rationale for ERM, including facilitating compliance, supporting information governance (IG), and providing **backup** capabilities in the event of a disaster.

with the massive U.S. FRCP changes in 2006, enterprises have become more "IG aware" and have ramped up efforts to control, manage, and secure their information. *A significant component of any IG program is implementing a records management program that specifies the retention periods and disposition (e.g., destruction, transfer, archive) of formal business records.* This, for instance, allows enterprises to destroy records once their required retention period (based on external regulations, legal requirements, and internal IG policies) has been met, and allows the enterprise to legally destroy records with no negative impact or lingering liability.

■ **Business continuity concerns.** In the face of real disasters, such as the 9/11 terrorist attacks, Hurricane Katrina, and in 2012, Superstorm Sandy, executives now realize that disaster recovery and business resumption is something they must plan and prepare for. Disasters really happen and businesses do fail if they are not well-prepared. The focus is on **vital records** (more details on this topic in subsequent chapters), which are necessary to resume operations in the event of a disaster, and managing vital records is a part of an overall records management program.

Why Is Records Management So Challenging?

With these business environment, regulatory, legal, and IG influences and changes comes increased attention to records management as a driver for **corporate compliance.** For most organizations, a lack of defined policies and the enormous and growing volumes of e-documents (e.g., e-mail messages) make implementing a formal records management program challenging and costly. Some reasons for this include:

■ **Changing and increasing regulations.** Just when records and compliance managers have sorted through the compliance requirements of federal regulations, new ones at the state or provincial level are created or tightened down.

■ **Maturing information governance requirements within the organization.** As senior managers become increasingly aware of information governance—the rules, policies, and processes that control and manage information—they promulgate more reporting and auditing requirements for the management of formal business records.

■ **Managing multiple retention and disposition schedules.** Depending on the type of record, retention requirements vary, and they may vary for the same type of record based on state and federal regulations. Further, internal information governance policies may extend retention periods and may fluctuate with management changes.[5]

Implementing ERM is challenging because it requires user support and compliance, adherence to changing laws, and support for new information delivery platforms like mobile and cloud computing.

- **Compliance costs and requirements with limited staff.** Records management and compliance departments are notoriously understaffed, since they do not generate revenue. Departments responsible for executing and proving compliance with new and increasing regulatory requirements must do so expediently, often with only skeletal staffs. This leads to expensive outsourcing solutions, or staff increases. The cost of compliance must be balanced with the risk of maintaining a minimum level of compliance.
- **Changing information delivery platforms.** With cloud computing, mobile computing, Web 2.0, social media and other changes to information delivery and storage platforms, records and compliance managers must stay apprised of the latest information technology trends and provide records on multiple platforms – while maintaining the security and integrity of organizational records.
- **Security concerns.** Protecting and preserving corporate records is of paramount importance, yet users must have reasonable access to "official" records to conduct everyday business. "Organizations are struggling to balance the need to provide accessibility to critical corporate information with the need to protect the integrity of corporate records."[6]
- **Dependence on the information technology (IT) department or provider.** Since tracking and auditing use of formal business records requires IT, and records and compliance departments are typically understaffed, they must rely on assistance from their IT department or outsourced IT provider—which often do not have the same perspective and priorities as the departments they serve.
- **User assistance and compliance.** Users often "go their own way" with regard to records, ignoring directives from records managers to stop storing "shadow" files of records on their desktop (for their own convenience), and inconsistently following directives to classify records as they are created. Getting users across a range of departments in the enterprise to comply uniformly with records and compliance requirements is a daunting and unending task that requires constant attention and reinforcement.[7] But it can be done through methodical steps.

Benefits of Electronic Records Management

There are a number of business drivers and benefits that combine to create a strong case for implementing an enterprise ERM program. Most are tactical, such as cost savings, time savings, and building space savings. *But some drivers can be thought of as strategic*, in that they proactively give the enterprise an advantage. One example may be the advantages gained in litigation by having more control and ready access to complete business records, which yields more accurate results, and more time for corporate attorneys to develop strategies—while the opposition is wading through reams of

An investment in ERM is an investment in business process automation and yields document control, document integrity, and security benefits.

information, never knowing if they have found the complete set of records they need. Another example of a strategic benefit is more complete and better information for managers to base decisions upon.

Implementing ERM represents a significant investment. *An investment in ERM is an investment in business process automation and yields document control, document integrity, and security benefits.* The volume of records in organizations has often exceeded the employees' ability to manage them. ERM systems do for the information age what the assembly line did for the industrial age. The cost/benefit justification for ERM is sometimes difficult to determine, although there are real labor and cost savings. Also, many of the benefits are intangible or difficult to calculate, but help to justify the capital investment. There are many ways in which an organization can gain significant business benefits with ERM.

More detail on business benefits is provided in Chapter 20, Building the Business Case, but hard, calculable benefits (when compared to storing paper files) include office space savings, office supplies savings, cutting wasted search time, and reduced office automation costs (e.g., fewer printers, copiers, cutting automated filing cabinets).

In addition, implementing ERM will provide the organization with improved capabilities for enforcing IG over business documents and records, and improved, more complete, and more accurate searches; improved knowledge worker productivity; reduced risk of compliance actions or legal consequences; improved records security; improved ability to demonstrate legally defensible records management practices; and increased working confidence in making searches, which should improve decision-making.

Additional Intangible Benefits

The U.S. Environmental Protection Agency (EPA), a pioneer and leader in e-records implementation in the federal sector, lists some additional benefits[8] of implementing ERM:

1. **To Control the Creation and Growth of Records.** Despite decades of using various nonpaper storage media, the amount of paper in our offices continues to escalate. An effective records management program addresses both creation control (limits the generation of

ERM benefits are both tangible and intangible or difficult to calculate.

Improved professionalism, preserving corporate memory, and support for better decision-making are key intangible benefits of ERM.

records or copies not required to operate the business) and records retention (a system for destroying useless records or retiring inactive records), thus stabilizing the growth of records in all formats.

2. **To Assimilate New Records Management Technologies.** A good records management program provides an organization with the capability to assimilate new technologies and take advantage of their many benefits. Investments in new computer systems don't solve filing problems unless current manual recordkeeping systems are analyzed (and occasionally, overhauled) before automation is applied.

3. **To Safeguard Vital Information.** Every organization, public or private, needs a comprehensive program for protecting its vital records and information from catastrophe or disaster, because every organization is vulnerable to loss. Operated as part of the overall records management program, vital records programs preserve the integrity and confidentiality of the most important records and safeguard the vital information assets according to a "Plan" to protect the records.

4. **To Preserve the Corporate Memory.** An organization's files contain its institutional memory, an irreplaceable asset that is often overlooked. Every business day, you create the records that could become background data for future management decisions and planning. These records document the activities of the Agency that future scholars may use to research the workings of the Environmental Protection Agency.

5. **To Foster Professionalism in Running the Business.** A business office with files askew, stacked on top of file cabinets and in boxes everywhere, creates a poor working environment. The perceptions of customers and the public, and "image" and "morale" of the staff, though hard to quantify in cost-benefit terms, may be among the best reasons to establish a good records management program.[9]

So there are a variety of tangible and intangible benefits derived from ERM programs, yet the business rationale that fits for your organization depends on its specific needs and business objectives.

CHAPTER SUMMARY: **KEY POINTS**

■ According to ISO, a record is "information created, received, and maintained as evidence and information by an organization or person, in pursuance of legal obligations or in the transaction of business."[10]

(Continued)

(Continued)

- Records management is "[the] field of management responsible for the efficient and systematic control of the creation, receipt, maintenance, use, and disposition of records, including the processes for capturing and maintaining evidence of and information about business activities and transactions in the form of records."[11]

- Electronic records management (ERM) includes the management of electronic and nonelectronic records, like paper and other physical records.

- ERM has become much more critical to enterprises with increased compliance legislation and massively increasing volumes of electronic information.

- ERM follows the same basic principles as paper-based records management.

- A number of factors provide the business rationale for ERM, including facilitating compliance, supporting information governance (IG), and providing backup capabilities in the event of a disaster.

- Implementing ERM is challenging since it requires user support and compliance, adherence to changing laws, and support for new information delivery platforms like mobile and cloud computing.

- ERM benefits are both tangible and intangible or difficult to calculate. Tangible benefits include space savings, office automation and supplies savings, and search time reduction.

- Improved professionalism, preserving corporate memory, support for better decision-making, and safeguarding vital records are key intangible benefits of ERM.

Notes

1. International Organization for Standardization, "Information and Documentation—Records Management. Part 1: General," ISO 15489-1:2001 section 3.15 (Geneva: ISO, 2001).
2. International Organization for Standardization, "Information and Documentation—Records Management. Part 1: General," ISO 15489-1:2001, section 3.16 (Geneva: ISO, 2011).
3. ARMA.org, "What Is Records Management?" 2009, www.arma.org/pdf/WhatIsRIM.pdf.
4. www.microsoft.com/en-us/download/details.aspx?id=15932, "Records Management with Office SharePoint Server," Microsoft White Paper, 2007. Used with permission from Microsoft.
5. Ibid.
6. Ibid.
7. "Records Management with Office SharePoint Server."
8. EPA, "Why Records Management? Ten Business Reasons," updated March 8, 2012, www.epa.gov/records/what/quest1.htm.
9. Ibid.
10. International Organization for Standardization, "Information and Documentation—Records Management. Part 1: General," ISO 15489-1:2001, section 3.15 (Geneva: ISO, 2001).
11. International Organization for Standardization, "Information and Documentation—Records Management. Part 1: General," ISO 15489-1:2001, section 3.16 (Geneva: ISO, 2011).

CHAPTER 2

Information Governance

The Crucial First Step

nformation governance (IG) is a sort of "super discipline" that has emerged as a result of new and tightened legislation governing businesses, and the recognition that multiple overlapping disciplines were needed to address today's information management challenges in an increasingly regulated and litigated business environment.[1]

IG includes key concepts from corporate governance, records management, content management, IT and data governance, information security, data privacy, risk management, litigation readiness, regulatory compliance, and even business intelligence. This also means that it includes related technology and discipline subcategories such as document management, enterprise search, knowledge management, business continuity, and disaster recovery.

Practicing good IG is the essential foundation for building a *legally defensible* records management program; it provides the basis for consistent, reliable methods for managing documents and records. Having trusted and reliable records, reports, and databases allow managers to make key decisions with more confidence.[2] And accessing that information and business intelligence in a timely fashion can yield a long-term sustainable competitive advantage, creating more agile enterprises.

To do this, organizations must standardize and systematize their handling of information, and most especially their formal business records. They must analyze and optimize how information is accessed, controlled, managed, shared, stored, preserved, and audited. They must have complete, current, and relevant policies, processes, and technologies to manage and control information, including *who is able to access which information*, and *when*, to meet external legal and regulatory demands and internal governance requirements. This, in short, is **information governance** (IG).

IG is not a project but rather an ongoing program that provides an umbrella of rules and policies, monitored and enforced by information technologies, to manage and control information output and communications. Since technologies change so quickly, it is necessary to have overarching policies that can manage the various information technology (IT) platforms that an organization may use.

Compare it to a workplace safety program; every time a new location, team member, piece of equipment, or toxic substance is acquired by the organization, the workplace safety program should dictate how that is handled and, if it doesn't, the workplace safety policies/procedures/training that are part of the workplace safety program need to be updated. And you conduct regular reviews to ensure the program is being followed and make adjustments based on your findings. *The effort never ends.*[3] The same is true for IG.

IG is the necessary underpinning for developing an electronic records management strategy that maximizes productivity, while minimizing risk and costs.

IG is a multidisciplinary program that requires an ongoing effort.

First, Better Policies; Then, Better Technology for Better Enforcement

Typically, some policies governing the use and control of information and records may have been established for financial and compliance reports, and perhaps e-mail, but they are often incomplete and out-of-date, and have not been adjusted for changes in the business environment, such as new technology platforms (e.g., Web 2.0, social media), changing laws (e.g., U.S. FRCP 2006 changes), and additional regulations.

Further adding to the challenge is the rapid proliferation of mobile devices like tablets and smartphones used in business—information can be more easily lost or stolen, especially in a "bring-your-own-device" (BYOD) environment—so IG efforts must be made to preserve and protect the enterprise's information assets.

Proper IG requires that policies are flexible enough not to hinder the proper flow of information in the heat of the business battle, yet strict enough to control and audit for misuse, policy violations, or security breaches. This is a continuous iterative policy-making process, which must be monitored and fine-tuned. Even with the absolute best efforts, some policies will miss the mark and need to be reviewed and adjusted.

Getting started with IG awareness is the first step. It may have popped up on an executive's radar at one point or another and an effort might have been made, but many organizations leave these policies on the shelf and do not revise them regularly, so, when new platforms like cloud computing or social media arrive, they may find themselves on their heels and in the throes of new policy-making and enforcement efforts.

This reactive, tactical *project* approach is not the way to go about it—haphazardly swatting at technological, legal, and regulatory flies. A proactive, strategic *program*, with a clear, accountable sponsor, an ongoing plan, and regular review process is the only way to continuously adjust IG policies to keep them current so that they best serve the organization's needs.

The information and business records that companies are busy generating, collecting, and mining offers a wealth of potential benefits; however, their use also carries substantial risks. As a result, some organizations have created formal governance bodies to establish strategies, policies, and procedures surrounding the distribution of information inside and outside the enterprise. These governance bodies, steering committees, or teams may include members from many different functional areas, since proper IG necessitates input from a variety of stakeholders. Representatives from information technology (IT), records management, corporate/organizational archiving, risk management, compliance, operations, security, legal, finance, and

Information governance is a subset of corporate governance.

> IG is an all-encompassing term for how an organization manages the totality of its information.

perhaps knowledge management are typically a part of IG teams. Often these efforts are jumpstarted and organized with third-party consulting resources that specialize in IG efforts.

Defining Information Governance

What is information governance? According to "The Rise of Information Governance" by The 451 Group, "There's no single answer to that question. At a high level, information governance encompasses the policies and leveraged technologies meant to dictate and manage what corporate information is retained, where and for how long, and also how it is retained (e.g., protected, replicated, and secured). Information governance spans retention, security and lifecycle management issues."[4]

Information governance is a subset of corporate governance, which has been around as long as corporations have existed. IG is a rather new multidisciplinary field that is still being defined, but has gained traction in the past several years. The focus on IG comes not only from compliance, legal, and records management functionaries, but also from executives who understand they are accountable for the governance of information, and that theft, misuse, or erosion of information assets has real costs and consequences.

IG is an all-encompassing term for *how an organization manages the totality of its information.*

IG is more than simply the governance of IT. It goes much further than controlling and managing IT and its development; IG focuses on the output, the *result* of applying IT. That means it focuses on the actual documents, reports, and records (created from raw data and applications), and controlling their use and security.

IG is a hybrid field, using a set of multidisciplinary methods and technologies to support an organization's operational and compliance requirements.

IG includes the set of policies, processes, and controls to manage information in compliance with external regulatory requirements and internal governance frameworks. Specific policies apply to specific document types, records series, and other business information such as e-mail and reports. Simply put, IG is "the way in which an organization handles, uses, and manages its information in an efficient, effective, and secure manner to all the appropriate ethical, legal, and quality standards."[5]

> Information governance is more than governing IT—rather it focuses more on managing and controlling the output of IT.

> Information governance is how an organization maintains security, complies with regulations, and meets ethical standards when managing information.

Industry thought leader Barclay T. Blair explains that IG is a "relatively new term for which the precise meaning is still being shaped by the market and those that promote its use."[6]

Essentially, information governance is "a quality-control discipline for managing, using, improving, and protecting information."[7]

Stakeholder Consultation Is Key

IG requires inclusion and consultation with stakeholders, and a holistic thought process to improve the quality and security of information throughout its lifecycle. The result is not only more secure information, but also better information to base decisions on, and closer adherence to regulatory and legal demands.[8]

As previously stated, IG is a part of corporate governance and it draws on IT governance, but it goes much further. IG is expansive and amorphous and difficult to get one's arms around to understand, but the key is that *IG involves creating, maintaining, monitoring, and enforcing policies for the use of information*—including unstructured information such as electronic documents—*to meet external compliance demands and internal governance controls.*

The scope of this book is in developing and leveraging IG in the narrower context of managing electronic records and documents.

Accountability Is Key

According to Debra Logan at Gartner Group, *none of the proffered definitions of IG include "any notion of coercion, but rather ties governance to accountability* [italics added] that is designed to encourage the right behavior. . . . The word that matters most is *accountability* [italics in the original]." The root of many problems with managing information is the "fact that there is no accountability for information as such."[9]

Establishing policies, procedures, processes, and controls to ensure the quality, integrity, accuracy, and security of business records are the fundamental steps needed to reduce the organization's risk and cost structure for managing these records. Then, it is essential that IG efforts are supported by information technologies (IT). The auditing, testing, maintenance, and improvement of IG is enhanced by using electronic records management (ERM) and e-document management software, along with other complementary technology sets such as workflow and business process management suite (BPMS) software (see Chapters 9 and 10 for discussions on business process improvement, workflow, and BPMS software) document lifecycle security (DLS) tools, and digital signatures.

Why IG Is Good Business

IG is a tough sell. It can be difficult to make the business case for it, unless there has been some major compliance sanction, fine, legal loss, or colossal data breach. In fact, *the largest impediment to IG adoption is simply identifying its benefits and costs*, according to The Economist Intelligence Unit. Sure, the enterprise needs better control over its information, but how much better? At what cost? What is the payback period and the return on investment (ROI)?[10]

It is challenging to make the business case for IG, yet making that case is fundamental to getting IG efforts off the ground.

Here are eight reasons why IG makes good business sense, from Barclay Blair:

1. **We can't keep everything forever.** IG makes sense because it enables organizations to get rid of unnecessary information in a [legally] defensible manner. Organizations need a sensible way to dispose of information in order to reduce the cost and complexity of the IT environment. Having unnecessary information around only makes it more difficult and expensive to harness information that has value.

2. **We can't throw everything away.** IG makes sense because organizations can't keep everything forever, nor can they throw everything away. We need information—the right information, in the right place, at the right time. Only IG provides the framework to make good decisions about what information to keep.

3. **E-discovery.** IG makes sense because it reduces the cost and pain of discovery. Proactively managing information reduces the volume of information exposed to e-discovery and simplifies the task of finding and producing responsive information.

4. **Your employees are screaming for it—just listen.** IG makes sense because it helps knowledge workers separate "signal" from "noise" in their information flows. By helping organizations focus on the most valuable information, IG improves information delivery and improves productivity.

5. **It ain't gonna get any easier.** IG makes sense because it is a proven way for organizations to respond to new laws and technologies that create new requirements and challenges. The problem of IG will not get easier over time, so organizations should get started now.

6. **The courts will come looking for IG**. IG makes sense because courts and regulators will closely examine your IG program. Falling short can lead to fines, sanctions, loss of cases, and other outcomes that have negative business and financial consequences.

7. **Manage risk: IG is a big one**. Organizations need to do a better job of identifying and managing risk. The risk of information management failures is a critical risk that IG helps to mitigate.

8. **E-mail: Reason enough**. IG makes sense because it helps organizations take control of e-mail. Solving e-mail should be a top priority for every organization.[11]

Impact of a Successful IG Program

When making the business case for IG, and articulating its benefits, it is useful to focus on its central impact. *Putting cost-benefit numbers to this may be difficult, unless you also consider the worst-case scenario of loss or misuse of corporate or agency records.* What is losing the next big lawsuit worth? How much are confidential merger and acquisition (M&A) documents worth? How much are customer records worth? Frequently, executives and managers do not understand the value of IG until it is a crisis, an expensive legal battle is lost, heavy fines are imposed for noncompliance, or executives go to jail.

There are some key outputs from implementing an IG program. A successful IG program should enable organizations to:

- **Use common terms across the enterprise.** This means that departments must agree on how they are going to classify document types, which relies on a cross-functional effort. With common enterprise terms, searches for information are more productive and complete. This begins with developing a standardized corporate taxonomy, which defines the terms (and substitute terms in a custom corporate thesaurus), document types, and their relationships in a hierarchy.
- **Map information creation and usage.** This effort can be buttressed with the use of technology tools such as **data loss prevention (DLP)**, which can be used to discover the flow of information within and outside of the enterprise. You must first determine *who* is accessing *which* information *when*, and *where* it is going. Then these information flows can be monitored and analyzed. The goal is to stop the erosion or misuse of information assets, and to stem data breaches with monitoring and security technology.
- **Obtain "information confidence."** That is, the assurance that information has integrity, validity, accuracy, and quality; this means being able to *prove* that the information is reliable, and its access, use, and storage meets compliance and legal demands.
- **Harvest and leverage information.** Using techniques and tools like data mining and business intelligence, new insights may be gained that provide an enterprise with a sustainable competitive advantage over the long term, since managers will have more and better information as a basis for business decisions.[12]

Critical Factors in an IG Program

When presenting a proposed IG program, it is helpful to clarify the keys to making it successful. Listed below are the most important factors of a successful IG program, adapted from the MIKE2.0 open framework for information management, created by the consulting firm BearingPoint. This definition provides the "target scope" for an IG solution offering:[13]

- **Accountability.** Because of the ways in which information is captured—and how it flows across the enterprise, *everyone* has a role to play in how it is governed. Many of the most important roles are played by individuals who are fairly junior in the organization. They typically play a key role in the data capture stage and often cause—or see—errors on a first-hand basis. Certain key individuals need to be dedicated to IG. These roles are filled by senior executives such as the CIO, Information Architects, and Data and Content Stewards.

- **Efficient operating models.** The IG approach should define an organizational structure that most effectively handles the complexities of both integration *and* information management (IM) across the whole of the organization. Of course, there will typically be some degree of centralization as information flows across the business. However, this organizational model need not be a single, hierarchical team. The common standards, methods, architecture, and collaborative techniques so central to IG allow this model to be implemented in a wide variety of models: physically central, cloud or virtual, or offshore. *Organizations should provide assessment tools and techniques to progressively refine these new models over time.*

- **A common methodology.** An IG program should include a common set of activities, tasks, and deliverables. Doing so builds specific IM [information management]-based competencies. This enables greater reuse of artifacts and resources, not to mention higher productivity out of individuals. It also manifests the commonalities of different IM initiatives across the organization.

- **Standard models.** A common definition of terms, domain values, and their relationships is one of the fundamental building blocks of IG. This should go beyond a traditional data dictionary. It should include a lexicon of unstructured content. Defining common messaging interfaces allows for easy inclusion of "data in motion." Business and technical definitions should be represented and, just as important, the lineage between them easy to navigate.

- **Architecture.** An IM (Information Management) architecture should be defined for the current-state, transition points, and target vision. The inherent complexity of this initiative will require the representation of this architecture through multiple views. This is done in Krutchen's Model. Use of architectural design patterns and common component models are key aspects of good governance. This architecture must accommodate dynamic and heterogeneous technology environments that, invariably, will quickly adapt to new requirements.

- **Comprehensive scope.** An IG approach should be comprehensive in its scope, covering structured data *and* unstructured content. It should also include the entire lifecycle of information. This begins with its initial creation, including integration across systems, archiving, and eventual destruction. This comprehensive scope can only [be] achieved with an architecture-driven approach and well-defined roles and responsibilities.

- **Information value assessment (IVA).** Organizations (should) place a very high value on their *information assets*. As such, they will view their organization as significantly devalued when these assets are unknown—or poorly defined. An IVA assigns an economic value to the information assets held by an organization. The IVA also [shows] how IG influences this value. It must also measure whether the return outweighs the cost, as well as the time required to attain this return. In this vein, current methods are particularly immature, although some rudimentary models do exist. In this case, industry models must greatly improve, much like what has occurred in the past ten years in the infrastructure space.

- **Senior leadership.** *Senior leaders need to manage their information*, and deal with related issues. CIOs, for example, must face a host of business users who increasingly demand relevant, contextual information. At this same time, leadership teams often blame failures on "bad data." In the post-Sarbanes-Oxley environment, CFOs are asked to sign off on financial statements. To this end, *the quality of data and the systems that produce that data are being scrutinized now more than ever before.* CMOs are being asked to grow revenues with less human resources. New regulations around the management of information have prevented many organizations from being effective. Senior leaders must work towards a common goal of improving information while concurrently appreciating that IM is still immature as a discipline. The bottom line is that there will be some major challenges ahead.

- **Historical quantification.** In the majority of cases, the most difficult aspect of IM [and information governance] can be stated very simply: most organizations are trying to fix decades of "bad behavior." The current-state is often unknown, even at an architectural or model level. The larger the organization, the more complex this problem typically becomes. Historical quantification through common architectural models and quantitative assessments of data and content are key aspects of establishing a known baseline. Only then can organizations move forward. For such a significant task, this assessment must be conducted progressively—not all at once.

- **Strategic approach.** An IG program will need to address complex issues across the organization. Improvements will typically be measured over months and years, not days. As a result, a strategic approach is required. A comprehensive program can be implemented over long periods of time through multiple release cycles. The strategic approach will allow for flexibility to change. However, the level of detail will still be meaningful enough to effectively deal with complex issues.

- **Continuous improvement.** It is not always cost-effective to fix all issues in a certain area. Sometimes, it is best instead to follow the 80/20 rule. An IG program should explicitly plan to revisit past activities. It should build on a working baseline through audits, monitoring, technology re-factoring, and personnel training. Organizations should look for opportunities to "release early, release often." At the same time, though, they should remember what this means from planning and budgeting perspectives.

- **Flexibility for change.** While an IG program involves putting standards in place, it must utilize its inherent pragmatism and flexibility for change. A strong governance process does *not* mean that exceptions can't be granted. Rather, key individuals and groups need to know exceptions are occurring—and why. The continuous improvement approach grants initial workarounds. These then have to be re-factored at a later point in order to balance short-term business priorities.

- **Governance tools.** Measuring the effectiveness of an IG program requires tools to capture assets and performance. Just as application development and service delivery tools exist, organizations need a way to measure information assets, actions, and their behaviors.[14]

By focusing an IG program proposal on its resultant impact, senior managers can more readily understand the business case to implement and its crucial benefits.

Who Should Determine IG Policies?

When forming an information governance steering committee or board, it is essential to include representatives from cross-functional groups, and at differing levels of the organization. It must be driven by an executive sponsor (see later chapter on securing and managing executive sponsorship), and include active members from key business units, as well as other departments including IT, finance, risk, compliance, records management, and legal. Then, corporate training/education and communications must be involved to keep employees trained and current on IG policies. This function may be performed by an outside consulting firm if there is no corporate education staff.

Knowledge workers, those who work with records and sensitive information in any capacity, best understand the nature and value of the records they work with as they perform their day-to-day functions. IG policies must be developed, and also communicated clearly and consistently. *Policies are worthless if people do not know or understand them, or how to comply.* And training is a crucial element that will be examined in any compliance hearing or litigation that may arise. "Did senior management not only create the policies, but provide adequate training on them, on a consistent basis?" This will be a key question raised. So a training plan is a necessary piece of IG and education should be heavily emphasized.[15]

The need for IG is increasing due to increased and tightened regulations, increased litigation, and the increased incidence of theft and misuse of internal documents and records. *Organizations that do not have active IG programs should reevaluate IG policies and their internal processes following any major loss of records, the inability to produce accurate records in a timely manner, or any document security breach or theft.* If review boards include a broad section of critical players on the IG committee and leverage executive sponsorship, they will be better preparing the organization for legal and regulatory rigors.

CHAPTER SUMMARY: **KEY POINTS**

- Information governance is how an organization maintains security, complies with regulations and laws, and meets ethical standards when managing information.

- IG is a multidisciplinary program requiring representatives from a broad cross-section of the organization that requires an ongoing effort.

- IG is a subset of corporate governance, and encompasses the policies and leveraged technologies meant to manage what corporate information is retained, where, and for how long, and also how it is retained.

(Continued)

(Continued)

■ A solid IG underpinning is required for a successful ERM strategy.

■ Information governance is more than governing IT—rather it focuses more on managing and controlling the output of IT.

■ The output of a successful IG program will yield: Use of common terms across the enterprise, information creation and usage mapping, information confidence, and harvesting and leveraging information.

■ Training and communications are key components of an IG program. Knowledge workers must be apprised of the value and risks of proprietary information so they can actively support IG efforts daily.

Notes

1. Monica Crocker, e-mail to author, June 21, 2012.
2. The Economic Intelligence Unit, "The Future of Information Governance," www.emc.com/leadership/business-view/future-information-governance.htm (accessed February 10, 2013).
3. Monica Crocker, e-mail to author, June 21, 2012.
4. Kathleen Reidy, "The Rise of Information Governance," *Too Much Information: The 451 Take on Information Management* (blog), August 5, 2009, http://blogs.the451group.com/information_management/2009/08/05/the-rise-of-information-governance.
5. "Information Governance Framework," *Adventures in Records Management*, posted November 12, 2007, http://adventuresinrecordsmanagement.blogspot.com/2007/11/information-governance-framework.html.
6. Via Lumina, "What Is Information Governance?" http://vialumina.com/our-services/what-is-information-governance (accessed July 15, 2011).
7. Arvind Krishna, "Three Steps to Trusting Your Data in 2011," CTO Edge, posted March 9, 2011, www.ctoedge.com/content/three-steps-trusting-your-data-2011.
8. Ibid.
9. Debra Logan, "What Is Information Governance? And Why Is It So Hard?" posted January 11, 2010, http://blogs.gartner.com/debra_logan/2010/01/11/what-is-information-governance-and-why-is-it-so-hard.
10. Barclay T. Blair, "Making the Case for Information Governance: Ten Reasons IG Makes Sense," ViaLumina Ltd, 2010. Online at http://barclaytblair.com/making-the-case-for-ig-ebook.
11. Barclay T. Blair, "8 Reasons Why Information Governance (IG) Makes Sense," posted June 29, 2009, http://aiim.typepad.com/aiim_blog/2009/06/8-reasons-why-information-governance-ig-makes-sense.html.
12. Arvind Krishna, "Three Steps to Trusting Your Data in 2011," CTO Edge, posted March 9, 2011, www.ctoedge.com/content/three-steps-trusting-your-data-2011.
13. MIKE2.0, "Information Governance Solution Offering," http://mike2.openmethodology.org/wiki/Information_Governance_Solution_Offering.
14. Ibid.
15. "Governance Overview (SharePoint Server 2010)," http://technet.microsoft.com/en-us/library/cc263356.aspx (accessed April 19, 2011).

CHAPTER 3
Generally Accepted Recordkeeping Principles®

Charmaine Brooks, CRM

Records and recordkeeping are inextricably linked with any organized business activity. Through the information that an organization uses and records, creates or receives in the normal course of business, it knows what has been done and by whom—if records management best practices and information governance (IG) policies are followed. This allows the organization to effectively demonstrate compliance with applicable standards, laws, and regulations, as well as plan what it will do in the future to meet its mission and strategic objectives.

Standards and principles of recordkeeping have been developed by **records and information management** (RIM) practitioners to establish benchmarks for how organizations of all types and sizes can build and sustain compliant, legally defensible **records management** (RM) programs.

The Principles

In 2009 ARMA International published a set of eight Generally Accepted Recordkeeping Principles®, known as "GAR Principles" or "The Principles",[1] to foster awareness of good recordkeeping practices. These principles and associated metrics provide an IG framework that can support continuous improvement.

The eight Generally Accepted Recordkeeping Principles are:

1. **Accountability.** A senior executive (or person of comparable authority) oversees the recordkeeping program and delegates program responsibility to appropriate individuals. The organization adopts policies and procedures to guide personnel, and ensure the program can be audited.

2. **Transparency.** The processes and activities of an organization's recordkeeping program are documented in a manner that is open and verifiable and is available to all personnel and appropriate interested parties.

3. **Integrity.** A recordkeeping program shall be constructed so the records and information generated or managed by or for the organization have a reasonable and suitable guarantee of authenticity and reliability.

4. **Protection.** A recordkeeping program shall be constructed to ensure a reasonable level of protection to records and information that are private, confidential, privileged, secret, or essential to business continuity.

5. **Compliance.** The recordkeeping program shall be constructed to comply with applicable laws and other binding authorities, as well as the organization's policies.

6. **Availability.** An organization shall maintain records in a manner that ensures timely, efficient, and accurate retrieval of needed information.

7. **Retention.** An organization shall maintain its records and information for an appropriate time, taking into account legal, regulatory, fiscal, operational, and historical requirements.

8. **Disposition.** An organization shall provide secure and appropriate disposition for records that are no longer required to be maintained by applicable laws and the organization's policies.[2]

The Generally Accepted Recordkeeping Principles apply to all sizes of organizations, in all types of industries, and in both the private and public sectors, and can be used to establish consistent practices across business units. The GAR Principles are an IG maturity model and this is used as a preliminary evaluation of recordkeeping programs and practices.

Interest and the application of GAR Principles for assessing an organization's recordkeeping practices have steadily increased since its establishment. It is an accountability framework that includes the processes, roles, standards, and metrics that ensure the effective and efficient use of records and information in support of an organization's goals and business objectives.

As shown in Table 3.1, the Generally Accepted Recordkeeping Principles Maturity Model associates characteristics that are typical in five levels of recordkeeping capabilities that range from 1 (substandard) to 5 (transformational). The levels are both descriptive and (can be) color-coded for ease of understanding. The eight principles and levels (metrics) are applied to the current state of an organization's recordkeeping capabilities and can be cross-referenced to the policies and procedures. *While it is not unusual for an organization to be at differing levels of maturity in the eight principles, the question "How good is good enough?" must be raised and answered*; a rating of less than "transformational" may be acceptable, depending on the organization's tolerance for risk and an analysis of the costs and benefits of moving up each level.

The maturity levels define the characteristics of evolving and maturing records management programs. The assessment should reflect the current RM environment and practices. The principles and maturity level definitions, along with improvement recommendations (roadmap), outline the tasks required to proactively approach addressing systematic records management practices and reach the next level of maturity for each principle. While the Generally Accepted Recordkeeping Principles are broad in focus, they illustrate the requirements of good records management practices. The GAR

The Generally Accepted Recordkeeping Principles consists of eight principles that provide an information governance (IG) framework that can support continuous improvement.

Table 3.1 Generally Accepted Recordkeeping Principles Levels

Level 1 Substandard	Characterized by an environment where recordkeeping concerns are either not addressed at all or are addressed in an ad hoc manner.
Level 2 In Development	Characterized by an environment where there is a developing recognition that recordkeeping has an impact on the organization, and the organization may benefit from a more defined information governance program.
Level 3 Essential	Characterized by an environment where defined policies and procedures exist that address the minimum or essential legal and regulatory requirements, but more specific actions need to be taken to improve recordkeeping.
Level 4 Proactive	Characterized by an environment where information governance issues and considerations are integrated into business decisions on a routine basis, and the organization consistently meets its legal and regulatory obligations.
Level 5 Transformational	Characterized by an environment that has integrated information governance into its corporate infrastructure and business processes to such an extent that compliance with program requirements is routine.

Source: Used with permission from ARMA.

Principles Assessment can also be a powerful communication tool to promote cross-functional dialogue and collaboration among business units and staff.

Accountability

The principle of **accountability** covers the assigned responsibility for RM at a senior level to ensure effective governance with the appropriate level of authority. A senior-level executive must be high enough in the organizational structure to have sufficient authority to operate the records management program effectively. The primary role of the senior executive is to develop and implement records management policies, procedures and guidance, and to provide advice on all record-keeping issues. The direct responsibility for managing or operating facilities or services may be delegated.

The senior executive must possess an understanding of the business and legislative environment within which the organization operates; business functions and activities; and the required relationships with key external stakeholders, to understand how records management contributes to achieving the corporate mission, aims, and objectives.

It is important for top-level executives to take ownership of the records management issues of the organization; and to identify corrective actions required for mitigation or ensure resolution of problems and recordkeeping challenges. An executive sponsor should identify opportunities to raise awareness of the relevance and importance of RM and effectively communicate the benefits of good records management to staff and management.

> The Generally Accepted Recordkeeping Principles maturity model measures recordkeeping maturity in five levels.

The regulatory and legal framework for records management must be clearly identified and understood. The senior executive must have a sound knowledge of the organization's information and technological architecture and actively participate in strategic decisions for information technology systems acquisition and implementation.

The senior executive is responsible for ensuring the processes, procedures, governance structures, and related documentation are developed. The policies should identify the roles and responsibilities at all levels of the organization.

An audit process must be developed to cover all aspects of RM within the organization, including substantiating that sufficient levels of accountability have been assigned and accountability deficiencies are identified and remedied. Audit processes should include compliance with the organization policies and procedures for all records, regardless of format or media. Accountability audit requirements for electronic records include employing appropriate technology to audit the information architecture and systems. Accountability structures must be updated and maintained as changes occur in the technology infrastructure.

The audit process must reinforce compliance and hold individuals accountable. The results should be constructive, encourage continuous improvement, but not be used as a means of punishment. *The audit should contribute to records program improvements in risk mitigation, control, and governance issues, and have the capacity to support sustainability.*

Transparency

Policies are broad guidelines for the operation of the organization and provide a basic guide to action that prescribes the boundaries within which business activities are to take place. They state the course of action to be followed by the organization, business unit, department, and employees.

Transparency of recordkeeping practices includes documenting processes and promoting an understanding of the roles and responsibilities of all stakeholders. *To be effective policies must be formalized and integrated into business processes.* Business rules and recordkeeping requirements need to be communicated and socialized at all levels of the organization.

Senior management must recognize that transparency is fundamental to IG and compliance. Documentation must be consistent, current, and complete. A review and approval process must be established to ensure the introduction of new programs or changes can be implemented and integrated into business processes.

Employees must have ready access to RM policies and procedures. They must receive guidance and training to ensure they understand their roles and requirements for records management. Recordkeeping systems and business processes must be designed and developed to clearly define the records lifecycle.

An audit process must be developed to cover all aspects of RM in the organization.

> To be effective, policies must be formalized and integrated into business processes.

In addition to policies and procedures, the development of guidelines and operational instructions, diagrams and flowcharts, system documentation, and user manuals must include clear guidance on how records are to be created, retained, stored, and dispositioned. The documentation must be readily available and incorporated in communications and training provided to staff.

Integrity

Record generating systems and repositories must be assessed to determine recordkeeping capabilities. *A formalized process must be in place for acquiring or developing new systems, including requirements for capturing the metadata required for lifecycle management of records in the systems.* In addition, the record must contain all the necessary elements of an official record, including structure, content, and context. **Records integrity**, reliability, and trustworthiness are confirmed by ensuring that a record was created by a competent authority according to established processes.

Maintaining the integrity of records means that they are complete and protected from being altered. The authenticity of a record is ascertained from internal and external evidence, including the characteristics, structure, content, and context of the record to verify they are genuine and not corrupted or altered. In order to trust that a record is authentic, organizations must ensure that recordkeeping systems that create, **capture**, and manage electronic records are capable of protecting records from accidental or unauthorized alteration or deletion while the record has value.

Protection

*Organizations must insure the **protection** of records and ensure they are unaltered through loss, tampering, or corruption.* This includes technological change or the failure of digital storage media and protecting records against damage or deterioration.

This principle applies equally to physical and electronic records, each having unique requirements and challenges.

Access and security controls need to be established, implemented, monitored, and reviewed to ensure business continuity and minimize business risk. Restrictions on access and disclosure include the methods for protecting personal privacy and proprietary information. Access and security requirements must be integrated into the business systems and processes for the creation, use, and storage of records.

Long-term digital preservation (LTDP) is a series of managed activities required to ensure continued access to digital documents and information for as long as necessary. Electronic records requiring long-term retention may require conversion to a medium and format suitable to ensure long-term access and readability.

Compliance

Records management programs include the development and training of the fundamental components, including **compliance monitoring** to ensure sustainability of the program.

Monitoring for compliance involves reviewing and inspecting the various facets of records management, including ensuring records are being properly created and captured, implementation of user permissions and security procedures, workflow processes through sampling to ensure adherence to policies and procedures, ensuring records are being retained following disposal authorities, and documentation of records destroyed or transferred to determine whether destruction/transfer was authorized in accordance with disposal instructions.

Compliance monitoring can be carried out by an internal audit, external organization, or records management and must be done on a regular basis.

Availability

Organizations should evaluate how effectively and efficiently records and information are stored and retrieved using present equipment, networks, and software. The evaluation should identify current and future requirements and recommend new systems as appropriate. Certain factors should be considered before upgrading or implementing new systems. These factors are practicality, cost, and effectiveness of new configurations.

A major challenge for organizations is ensuring that timely and reliable access to and use of information and records are accessible and usable for the entire length of the retention period. Rapid changes and enhancements to both hardware and software compound this challenge.

Retention

Retention is the function of preserving and maintaining records for continuing use. The retention schedule identifies the actions needed to fulfill the requirements for the retention and disposal of records and provides the authority for employees and systems to retain, destroy, or transfer records. The records retention schedule documents the recordkeeping requirements and procedures, identifying how records are to be organized and maintained, what needs to happen to records and when, who is responsible for doing what, and who to contact with questions or guidance.

Organizations must identify the scope of their recordkeeping requirements for documenting business activities based on regulated activities and jurisdictions that impose control over records. This includes business activities regulated by the government for every location or jurisdiction in which you do business. Other considerations for determining retention requirements include operational, legal, fiscal, and historical.

Records appraisal is the process of assessing the value and risk of records to determine their retention and disposition requirements. Legal research is outlined in appraisal reports. This may be accomplished as a part of the process of developing the records retention schedules, as well as conducting a regular review to ensure that citations and requirements are current.

*The **record retention period** is the length of time that records should be retained and the actions taken for them to be destroyed or preserved.* The retention periods for different records should be based on legislative or regulatory requirements as well as on administrative and operational requirements.

It is important to document the legal research conducted and used to determine whether the law or regulation has been reasonably applied to the recordkeeping practices and provide evidence to regulatory officials or courts that due diligence has been conducted in good faith to comply with all applicable requirements.

Disposition

Disposition is the last stage in the life cycle of records. When the retention requirements have been met and they no longer serve a useful business purpose, records may be destroyed. Records requiring long-term or permanent retention should be transferred to an **archive** for preservation. The timing of the transfer of physical or electronic records should be determined through the records retention schedule process. Additional methods are often required to preserve electronic records, which may include migration or conversion.

Records must be destroyed in a controlled and secure manner and in accordance with authorized disposal instructions. The destruction of records must be clearly documented to provide evidence of destruction according to an agreed-on program.

Destruction of records must be undertaken by methods appropriate to the confidentiality of the records and in accordance with disposal instructions in the records retention schedule. An audit trail documenting the destruction of records should be maintained and certificates of destruction obtained for destruction undertaken by third parties. In the event disposal schedules are not in place, the written authorization should be obtained prior to destruction. Procedures should specify who must supervise the destruction of records. Approved methods of destruction must be specified for each media type to ensure that information cannot be reconstructed.

Disposition is not synonymous with destruction, though destruction may be one disposal option. Destruction of records must be carried out under controlled, confidential conditions by shredding or permanent disposition. This includes the destruction of confidential microfilm, microfiche, computer cassettes, and computer tapes, as well as paper.

Methods of Disposition

- **Discard.** The standard destruction method for nonconfidential records. If possible, all records should be shredded prior to recycling. Note that transitory records can also be shredded.
- **Shred.** Confidential and sensitive records should be processed under strict security. This may be accomplished internally or by secure on-site shredding by a third party vendor who provides certificates of secure destruction. The shredded material is then recycled.

Disposition is the last stage in the life cycle of records. Disposition is not synonymous with destruction, though destruction may be one disposal option.

- **Archive.** This designation is for records requiring long-term or permanent preservation. Records of enduring legal, fiscal, administrative, or historical value are retained.
- **Imaging.** Physical records converted to digital images, after which the original paper documents are destroyed.
- **Purge.** This special designation is for data, documents, or records sets that need to be purged by removing material based on specified criteria. This often applies to structure records in databases and applications.

Assessment and Improvement Roadmap

The Generally Accepted Recordkeeping Principles maturity model can be leveraged to develop a current state assessment of an organization's recordkeeping practices and resources, identify gaps and assess risks, and develop priorities for desired improvements.

The GAR Principles were developed by ARMA International to identify characteristics of an effective recordkeeping program. Each of the eight principles identifies issues and practices that, when evaluated against the unique needs and circumstances of an organization, can be applied to improvements for a recordkeeping program that meets recordkeeping requirements. The GAR Principles identify requirements and can be used to guide the incremental improvement in the management and governance of the creation, organization, security, maintenance, and other activities over a one- to five-year period. Fundamentally, records management and information governance are business disciplines that must be tightly integrated with operational policies, procedures, and infrastructure.

GAR Principles can be mapped to the four improvement areas in Table 3.2.

As an accepted industry guidance maturity model, GAR Principles provide a convenient and complete framework for assessing the current state of an organization's record keeping and developing a roadmap to identify improvements that will bring the organization into compliance. An assessment/analysis of the current record management practices, procedures, and capabilities together with current and future state practices provides two ways of looking at the future requirements of a complete RM (see Table 3.3).

Table 3.2 Improvement Areas for Generally Accepted Recordkeeping Principles

Improvement Area	Accountability	Transparency	Integrity	Protection	Compliance	Availability	Retention	Disposition
Roles and responsibilities	◊				◊		◊	
Policies and procedures	◊	◊	◊	◊	◊	◊	◊	◊
Communication and training	◊	◊		◊	◊		◊	
Systems and automation	◊			◊	◊	◊	◊	◊

Table 3.3   Assessment Report and Roadmap

Principle	Level	Findings	Requirements to Move to the Next Step
Accountability	Level 1 Substandard	▪ No senior executive (or person of comparable authority) is responsible for the records management program. ▪ The records manager role is largely nonexistent or is an administrative and/or clerical role distributed among general staff.	1. Assign records management responsibilities to senior executive. 2. Hire or promote records manager.
Transparency	Level 1 Substandard	▪ It is difficult to obtain information about the organization or its records in a timely fashion. No clear documentation is readily available. ▪ There is no emphasis on transparency. ▪ Public requests for information, discovery for litigation, regulatory responses, or other requests (e.g., from potential business partners, investors, or buyers) cannot be readily accommodated. ▪ The organization has not established controls to ensure the consistency of information disclosure. ▪ Business processes are not well defined.	1. Develop policies and procedures. 2. Develop training for all levels of staff. 3. Identify requirements for records findability and accessibility. 4. Define business processes.
Integrity	Level 1 Substandard	▪ There are no systematic audits or defined processes for showing the origin and authenticity of a record. ▪ Various organizational functions use ad hoc methods to demonstrate authenticity and chain of custody, as appropriate, but their trustworthiness cannot easily be guaranteed.	1. Develop audit process. 2. Identify business activities for creation and storage of records.
Protection	Level 1 Substandard	▪ No consideration is given to record privacy. ▪ Records are stored haphazardly, with protection taken by various groups and departments with no centralized access controls. ▪ Access controls, if any, are assigned by the author.	1. Assess security and access controls. 2. Develop access and security control scheme.
Compliance	Level 3 Essential	▪ The organization has identified all relevant compliance laws and regulations. ▪ Record creation and capture are systematically carried out in accordance with records management principles.	1. Implement systems to capture and protect records. 2. Develop metadata scheme. 3. Develop remediation plan and implement corrective actions.

(continued)

Table 3.3 (*Continued*)

Principle	Level	Findings	Requirements to Move to the Next Step
Compliance	Level 3 Essential	■ The organization has a strong code of business conduct which is integrated into its overall information governance structure and recordkeeping policies. ■ Compliance and the records that demonstrate it are highly valued and measurable. ■ The hold process is integrated into the organization's information management and discovery processes for the "most critical" systems. ■ The organization has defined specific goals related to compliance.	
Availability	Level 2 In Development	■ Record retrieval mechanisms have been implemented in certain areas of the organization. ■ In those areas with retrieval mechanisms, it is possible to distinguish between official records, duplicates, and nonrecord materials. ■ There are some policies on where and how to store official records, but a standard is not imposed across the organization. ■ Legal discovery is complicated and costly due to the inconsistent treatment of information.	1. Develop enterprise classification scheme. 2. Identify user search and retrieval requirements. 3. Develop standards for managing the lifecycle of records.
Retention	Level 2 In Development	■ A retention schedule is available, but does not encompass all records, did not go through official review, and is not well known around the organization. ■ The retention schedule is not regularly updated or maintained. ■ Education and training about the retention policies are not available.	1. Develop enterprise wide functional retention schedule. 2. Map retention schedule to classification scheme. 3. Implement an annual review process for record series and legal research. 4. Develop training for classification scheme and retention schedule.
Disposition	Level 2 In Development	■ Preliminary guidelines for disposition are established. ■ There is a realization of the importance of suspending disposition in a consistent manner, repeatable by certain legal groupings. ■ There may or may not be enforcement and auditing of disposition.	1. Develop procedures for disposition of records. 2. Implement disposition processes. 3. Develop audit trails for records transfers and destruction.
Overall	Level 1 Substandard		

Generally Accepted Recordkeeping Principles® Benchmarks

The Generally Accepted Recordkeeping Principles maturity model sets forth the characteristics of an effective recordkeeping program. The eight principles outline issues of general applicability and general considerations that, when combined with the unique needs and circumstances of an organization can be applied to the development of a customized recordkeeping solution.

IMERGE Consulting, Inc. has developed a RM toolkit based on the GAR Principles to identify the constraints, demands, necessities, needs, or parameters that must be met or satisfied for the creation and maintenance of records. This toolkit is part of the assessment process used with their clients and provides a sufficient sampling of Generally Accepted Recordkeeping Principles® scores to be considered a benchmark.

Table 3.4 lists nine organizations and their Generally Accepted Recordkeeping Principles levels of maturity. A brief description of the companies follows.

Companies 1 and 2 are large global manufacturing companies. Company 2 had, at one time a records program for physical records, but the records management staff was reduced through attrition and vacant positions were not filled. Neither company had a records manager, records management policies, or procedures. Retention was at the discretion of the departments and records were rarely destroyed. Both companies were moving to new locations with limited space for records storage. Company 2 had large volumes of physical records in unused factory space. Electronic records were backed up and retained "forever" without retention or disposition rules. One company hired a records manager and is in the process of developing their records program. The other company still retains the legacy records in hardcopy in the warehouse.

Company 3 had a robust records program for physical records, but when the company was split apart in the late 1990s the records group transferred to the divested company. The records manager title was assigned to the Information Security officer, but took a back seat to IT security in this heavily regulated utility. The preexisting record retention schedule was posted on the intranet, but it was not function based and employees were not trained. The organization was planning to implement ECM in a select department.

Company 4 is a financial institution in the United States. The new records manager needed assistance in developing a records retention schedule and classification scheme as a framework for the planned SharePoint deployment. The business processes were well defined and controlled with an established records program for physical records.

Company 5 is a large manufacturer with divisions in four states and Canada. The company has a strong records management department and established records officers in each of the eleven divisions. Records management policies and records retention schedule including defined disposition processes were in place and formal RM training was active. The records manager is at a middle management level and has difficulty obtaining resources for further advancement of the records program.

Company 6 is a large city in the United States. The IT department recognized the need for a functional classification after attempts to apply the records retention schedule to electronic records. The records management position is not at an executive level, but the city does have an extensive network of records coordinators. The policies, procedures, and business process mapping are in need of improvement.

Table 3.4 Generally Accepted Recordkeeping Principles Levels of Maturity

Principle	Company 1	Company 2	Company 3	Company 4	Company 5	Company 6	Company 7	Company 8	Company 9	Average
Accountability	1	1	2	3	2	3	2	3	3	2.22
Transparency	1	1	1	2	2	1	1	1	1	1.22
Integrity	1	2	2	2	2	2	2	2	1	1.78
Protection	1	1	1	3	3	1	2	1	1	1.56
Compliance	3	1	1	2	3	2	1	1	2	1.78
Availability	2	2	2	3	4	4	4	4	3	2.78
Retention	2	2	2	2	5	4	3	3	2	2.78
Disposition	2	2	1	2	5	2	2	2	3	2.33
Overall	**1**	**1**	**2**	**3**	**3**	**2**	**2**	**2**	**2**	**2.00**

Company 7 is a large provincial agency in Canada with a strong records management program for physical records. The RM department uses the ECM as the repository for final records only. Users have difficulty locating records. The classification scheme and retention schedule are subject based making it difficult to apply to electronic records and the ECM. Policies and procedures also require updating for electronic records management.

Company 8 is the public works division of a large county located in the United States. A records assessment and inventory was conducted and an ECM/RM was acquired. The state records retention schedule was used, but the division needed a file plan for the ECM. The classification scheme mapped to the retention schedule was the foundation for the file plan for the ECM implementation. The division had multiple policies for managing records requiring consolidation and updating for simplicity and to include electronic records management.

Company 9 is an association with an existing ECM that was being used by staff for inactive records only. The ECM functionality for capturing records at receipt or creation, workflow, versioning, accessibility and search, and so on was not well understood by the IT staff or ECM administrators. Staff retained duplicate records on shared drives and retention was not integrated into the system. The records management program was primarily paper-based and in need of updating for electronic records.[3]

CHAPTER SUMMARY: **KEY POINTS**

- The Generally Accepted Recordkeeping Principles ("GAR Principles") consist of eight principles that provide an IG framework that can support continuous improvement.

- The Principles Maturity Model measures recordkeeping maturity in five levels.

- An audit process must be developed to cover all aspects of RM in the organization to meet the GAR Principles. Monitoring for compliance involves reviewing and inspecting the various facets of records management.

- To be effective, policies must be formalized and integrated into business processes.

- Records appraisal is the process of assessing the value and risk of records to determine their retention and disposition requirements.

- Retention is the function of preserving and maintaining records for continuing use.

- Long term digital preservation (LTDP) is a series of managed activities required to ensure continued access to digital materials for as long as necessary.

- Disposition is the last stage in the life cycle of records. Disposition is not synonymous with destruction, though destruction may be one disposal option.

- The Generally Accepted Recordkeeping Principles were developed by ARMA International to identify characteristics of an effective recordkeeping program.

Notes

1. ARMA International, Generally Accepted Recordkeeping Principles, www.arma.org/garp/copyright .cfm (accessed May 8, 2012).
2. ARMA International, Information Governance Maturity Model, www.arma.org/garp/Garp%20 maturity%20Model%20Grid%20(11×23).pdf (accessed June 12, 2012).
3. ARMA International and the Generally Accepted Recordkeeping Principles: ARMA International (www.arma.org) is a not-for-profit professional association and the authority on managing records and information. Formed in 1955, ARMA International is the oldest and largest association for the information management profession with a current international membership of more than 10,000. It provides education, publications, and information on the efficient maintenance, retrieval, and preservation of vital information created in public and private organizations in all sectors of the economy. It also publishes *Information Management* magazine, and the Generally Accepted Recordkeeping Principles. More information about The Principles can be found at www.arma.org.

CHAPTER 4

Managing E-Documents and Records

This chapter provides an overview of the types of software applications that manage electronic documents and records to afford a basic understanding of the fundamentals of automating document-based business processes and records management.

Electronic documents and records can be managed by a few different types of software applications, which overlap in functionality, and are often implemented in more than one instance in an organization.

Enterprise Content Management

Enterprise content management (ECM) software (sometimes referred to as content management systems, or CMS) has the capability to manage the totality of an organization's content, from web content to internal e-documents, reports, and business records. So, when a document is rendered in various forms (e.g., web, electronic, print), only one file of the content is needed, and it is rendered consistently. This one file is kept up-to-date for access across departments or the entire enterprise.

ECM can manage all types of content in the enterprise as objects, although in practice its focus is on managing unstructured content, while databases manage structured content. Structured content consists of numbers in rows and columns that can be manipulated arithmetically in calculations. This data is primarily financial and is often used in financial reports and business intelligence (BI) applications. Unstructured content is everything else—*and by most estimates accounts for over 90 percent of an organization's total information*—including those e-documents, e-records, e-mail, and other content that is not expressed in numbers but exists as digital files. This may include scanned copies of documents like contracts or customer letters, loan or insurance applications, bills of lading, and land deeds, or internally created documents, like

> ECM systems manage unstructured content like e-mail, scanned documents, spreadsheets, and presentations. Unstructured content makes up over 90 percent of an organization's information.

letters and memos, spreadsheets, audiovisual presentations, and other common business outputs.

Beginning with basic document imaging software commercially pioneered by Wang Laboratories in the late 1980s, this author was a part of that organization and we collectively felt this technology would change the business world. But it was a tough sell. Systems were sold and installed, and demonstrated good investment payback, *but the greatest resistance came from the required redesign of business processes and change management efforts to convince and train users on new ways of working.*

Document imaging started as a sort of electronic filing cabinet—a very expensive one—and the technology did not really take off until the 1990s, when **workflow** capabilities were added to move folders and documents through worksteps in an automated way, capturing statistics along the way. Graphical workflow capabilities made designing the work process steps much easier. Some dedicated or "pure play" workflow software companies emerged.

But imaging and workflow software did not yet manage other types of e-documents, only images, so soon a market for document management products opened up and those companies were soon swallowed by the big document imaging players like Wang, FileNet, and IBM. They also purchased report output and management software companies, at the time called computer output to laser disk (COLD) and later renamed ERM (enterprise report management). So document imaging evolved into document management and included report management. Then, the need for **electronic records management** (*another* ERM) capability became apparent. This was the marketplace's response to organizations demanding complete information management solutions.

The major software firms in this marketplace developed complementary technology sets that became an integrated suite of ECM applications, which includes:[1]

- *Document imaging*: scanning and digitizing paper documents.
- *Document management*: including versioning, renditioning, check-in/check-out of documents, and search capabilities.
- *Records management*: formally declaring documents as business records and track records according to retention and disposition schedules.
- *Collaboration*: working in team workspaces, creating, sharing, and editing documents with physically remote users.
- *Web content management*: maintaining one copy of content and publishing it in multiple places across the web and on intranets.
- *Digital asset management*: managing graphic files such as logos, artwork, advertisements, marketing collateral, and other digital assets.
- *Enterprise report management/COLD*: creating, publishing, and managing reports across the enterprise (which were formerly printed).
- *Workflow*: automated routing through worksteps of the business process helps to speed approval and other decision processes, and workflow capabilities are often included in ECM suites or as add-ons.

ECM systems now provide powerful document management support for versioned e-documents, and ensure that users can easily retrieve the latest versions, while tracking revisions. *But many users will still have a tendency to use out-of-date versions they have stored locally, outside the repository* (e.g., from their desktop PC, tablet, or smart-

ECM suites include document imaging, document management, collaboration, web content management, digital asset management, report management, and workflow.

phone, or in their e-mail inbox). This can result in costly errors, wasted work, and, most important, failure to comply with current regulations and operating procedures.

Information governance (IG) measures and additional technology are needed to find those errant e-documents that are scattered about the enterprise. In addition, e-documents and other content are no longer secure once they are accessed by authorized users, so protections must be added to the e-documents directly, to maintain persistent security wherever they are routed.

The glaring weakness of ECM systems is that, by and large, once a document is accessed by an authorized user it has no protections at all outside the repository to track and secure it. Another layer of information technology, such as information rights management (IRM—also known as enterprise rights management—one more "ERM"—enterprise digital rights management or E-DRM)) is necessary.

Document Management Principles

Document management is a subset and component of the broader discipline of ECM and is related to document imaging (scanning paper to digital), collaboration, workflow, records management (RM), and digital asset management (DAM).

To develop a proper IG approach, it is essential to have an understanding of the **document lifecycle**, the entire span of use of e-documents, from creation to final disposition (i.e., archiving, transfer, or destruction), and how they are controlled through those processes.

Document lifecycle management (DLM) is a subset of **information lifecycle management** (ILM), *which is the concept that a document must be managed through its entire cycle of use, from its original creation (or delivery to the enterprise) to final disposition.*

This seems obvious. Of course documents must be managed as they are used throughout the organization. But the *management* part of DLM includes specific actions or processes that are invoked automatically as the document works its way through its lifecycle.

For instance, when a document's *draft* state is complete, it may be automatically routed for approval to the next level employee responsible. Once it is approved, it becomes a *final* document, and that may invoke an automatic routing of a copy to the document management repository. If it is an actual business record (as defined by laws, regulations, and also the organization itself), it may be routed to the ERM system repository.[2]

Once a document is in the ERM system, a record retention schedule will be applied, based on its document type, and all business, legal, and regulatory requirements. As the document reaches the end of its required retention period, a decision is made as to whether to archive it permanently or to destroy it, based on the disposition schedule (arguably, this decision should be made when the document is created). This routing and these

A record retention schedule is applied to documents that become records based on document type, and all business, legal, and regulatory requirements.

decisions can be completely automated, or can allow for human review between steps. In any case, it is best if this document routing and processing is performed transparently, so the knowledge workers who create and use these e-documents may work unimpeded.

But the policies on how the document is routed, handled, stored, and ultimately archived or destroyed must first be developed, and they must be fine-tuned and improved and kept up to date. This is the hard part of IG.

Electronic Document Management Systems

An **electronic document management system** (EDMS or DMS) is software designed to store and track electronic documents. It manages electronic documents such as word processing and spreadsheet files, digital report files, and scanned images of paper documents. Often an EDMS has records management capabilities and is referred to as an **electronic document and records management system** (EDRMS).

"Document management [software] controls the lifecycle of documents in your organization—how they are created, reviewed, and published, and how they are ultimately disposed of or retained."[3]

A well-designed EDMS/EDRMS allows knowledge workers to more easily find and share documents. First, it organizes documents in a logical way, by using standardized terms in a corporate taxonomy, making them easier to search; standardized metadata fields describe the document's characteristics, like author, creation date, subject, and number of pages. Second, an EDMS standardizes e-document creation and its presentation across an enterprise. Such standardization components must be worked out ahead of time in an initial document governance plan. This plan should lay out which types of documents will be managed, which file types will be accepted, what restrictions will be placed on file size, and other parameters of the DMS's operation.

This standardization and organization makes it easier to meet required legal and compliance obligations, while reducing the cost of doing so. In following standardized policies, the organization builds processes that are *legally defensible*, since they are documented and consistent. Documents requested by legal counsel or regulators can be searched for and found faster, and at a lower cost. Knowledge workers can be confident that the documents they are working on are the most current, and their searches

Document management software is used to track and store electronic documents throughout their lifecycle.

for documents are complete and thorough. And having an efficient document management system in place can be strategic in that it helps feed other high-level business activities that can give an organization a competitive edge.[4]

According to TechNet:

An effective document management solution specifies:

- What types of [electronic] documents and other content can be created within an organization.
- What templates to use for each type of document.
- What metadata [descriptive information] to provide for each type of document.
- Where to store documents at each stage of a document's life cycle.
- How to control access to a document at each stage of its life cycle.
- How to move documents within the organization as team members contribute to the documents' creation, review, approval, publication, and disposition.
- What policies to apply to documents so that document-related actions are audited, documents are retained or disposed of properly, and content important to the organization is protected.
- How documents are converted as they transition from one stage to another during their life cycles.
- How [electronic] documents are treated as corporate records, which must be retained according to legal requirements and corporate guidelines.[5]

As with ECM systems, the vulnerability that document management systems have is that once a document is legitimately accessed by an authorized user, it has few, if any protections to track and secure it. So, if a document is checked out from the corporate electronic document library or SharePoint system, and is outside the confines of the document management system, it is exposed to not only malicious threats, but also accidental or unintentional loss or misuse. Additional IG policies and additional layers of technology are needed in order that the documents may be secured, wherever they may be.

Some may believe that document encryption is the simple answer: The problem with encrypting documents is that this eliminates the ability to conduct full-text searches of electronic documents and records. But there are workarounds. So more analysis and thought have to go into securing documents and balancing user needs.

Electronic Records Management

Electronic records management (ERM) software—often also referred to by the newer, expanded moniker, **electronic document and records management system** (EDRMS)—manages all business records and documents regardless of their physical form. This means that both paper and electronic records are tracked in an ERM/EDRMS. Electronic forms of records can be e-documents, e-forms, video files, voice files, CDs, DVDs, audiotapes, or any other type of electronic record. In sum, a true ERM system tracks all records in any form.

ERM systems enforce record retention and disposition policies according to established retention schedules (e.g., ensuring that critical business records are retained for seven years), during which time they cannot be modified, and after which they can be archived or deleted so that they are no longer subject to the risk of legal discovery during a potential litigation. *But deleting records from a records management repository will often still leave dozens of copies scattered around internal and external servers and desktops.* This creates a liability for the organization and exposes it to potential misuse of confidential information assets.

So again, further IG measures and additional technology are necessary to ensure full compliance when destruction of a record is called for at the end of its lifecycle. Those errant, unfiled, or misfiled records can be easily found using modern enterprise search and data-mapping tools.

Records Management Principles

Not all documents are records. In business, a *record* is a document or other physical or electronic item that serves as evidence of a transaction or business activity performed by the organization. ISO 15489, "Information and Documentation—Records Management," defines a record as *"Information created, received, and maintained as evidence and information by an organization or person, in pursuance of legal obligations or in the transaction of business."*[6]

Records management is the process by which an organization determines what types of information are records, how to manage them through their retention periods, and how to ultimately destroy or archive them. The same basic principles that apply in records management apply in the management of electronic records, *but e-records have their own unique management needs and requirements,* due to their nature. This is particularly true when implementing disposition policies, such as complete destruction of electronic files, and also when preserving e-records over the long term, using **long-term digital preservation** (LTDP) techniques (see Chapter 17 for more detail) that are much more complex than they are for managing paper files, due to the interaction of application software, operating systems, and computer hardware.

ERM Principles in Detail

The basic principles of ERM and capabilities ERM systems are spelled out in this section.[7]

Accessibility and Readability over Time

Computer technology is one of the fastest-changing areas of technological change. It's been said that if the automobile industry innovated at the pace the computer industry does, we could all drive a Rolls Royce for the price of a VW Beetle. There are continual changes and improvements in computer technology components that add to

ERM systems enforce record retention and disposition policies according to established retention schedules and IG policies.

the challenge of maintaining records access and readability as time progresses. Software isn't just developed and released—no matter how good the quality assurance (QA) process is, there are always some glitches or things that don't work exactly as the design intended, which are "bugs" that need to be fixed, and, over time, software is usually updated and improved to stay competitive and address user needs. There may also be changes in file formats for storage and display, either by vendors improving their proprietary formats or from industry standards that emerge. Changes in compression algorithms to reduce storage and communications bandwidth requirements also occur. The operating system environments that application software operates within are more stable but they too require fixes, security updates, and improvements. New computer hardware models come out every year, sometimes several times a year. And there continue to be improvements and innovations in storage capacity and techniques.

The intermixture and interaction of these variables make maintaining the authenticity and integrity of electronic records stored in ERM systems more challenging, particularly over the long term.[8]

Although the national legislation of a particular country may not require that records be transferred to "archival custody" for 10 or 20 years, there are steps that must be taken in the interim to test and assure that records are readable and have not been corrupted or degraded over time, or completely erased or rendered unreadable due to mishandling or malicious intent. This is all part of the LTDP process, which must be governed by strong IG policies.

Preserving records over time does not require that all the hardware and software they were originally created on be kept and maintained.[9] There are steps that can be taken to **migrate** records to new computing platforms, or to copy stored e-records to new copies of the same media, which is termed *refreshment*.

See Chapter 17, Long-Term Digital Preservation, for more detail regarding the policies, processes, and techniques that are required to ensure preservation of records over the long term.

Appraisal of Records

Records have different types of values, such as legal, financial, administrative, or historical. Once this appraisal has been made, decisions as to the final disposition of records—destroy, transfer, or archive—may be carried out in a consistent, complete, and systematic way. (Records appraisal will be discussed in Chapter 5, Inventorying E-Records, and more details in Chapter 7, Developing Retention Schedules for E-Records). The goal is to optimize the disposition process: to keep only what is needed and discard what is not, as maintaining unneeded or obsolete records carries additional capital and labor costs, and "old" records that should have been destroyed can pose a legal liability in the future, as they may be requested during legal discovery. Also, wrongfully or prematurely destroying records (due to, for instance, pending legal action) is illegal and can cause fines, sanctions, or even jail time to be levied.

In the records appraisal process, records can be deemed to have legal, financial, administrative, or historical value.

In the public sector, it is unilaterally against the law to destroy e-records without the prior written approval of the Chief Archivist or similar authority ultimately accountable for maintaining an organization's records.[10]

Audit Trail

One of the key benefits of moving to an ERM environment is that the system will capture a lot of document and records usage and routing data that can be analyzed to further improve processes and optimize workloads. Another benefit of this capability is that a complete electronic audit trail of *which* records were accessed *by whom, when*, and for *how long* will be generated. "An audit trail is required to keep an unalterable history of system events."[11] This is key to proving records are authentic and reliable. The audit trail can also keep track of print requests, and any attempts to modify or move a folder, document, or record. This is an expected capability in ERM systems. This is crucial to enforcing IG policies and maintaining record integrity. The audit trail must be kept secure and intact for future potential legal and regulatory challenges. That means that it must be managed as a record, too, preserved instantly upon creation to permanent uneditable media, such as write-once-read-many (WORM) discs, and it should be accessed only by authorized personnel and auditors, per IG policy.

Taking audit trail capabilities a step further, some newer **document analytics** capabilities that can be overlaid provide granular detail that can actually alert a system administrator or supervisor immediately if a person is suddenly printing an inordinate amount of documents, or if they are spending an inordinate amount of time viewing records, particularly records outside of their normal purview, and additional data.

It is important to note that audit trail capability in an ERM/EDRMS allows for some flexibility in how they are set up, and what data they track. They can track all the way down to someone making a minor change to a metadata field, which can affect the standing of the record in question in court or regulatory proceedings. *So be mindful that all audit trails are not equal, and that in order to fully track all system activities that your organization may require through its IG policies, they must be configured to meet your business needs.*

> [Various authorities] . . . recommend that as a minimum requirement audit trail information should be captured for
>
> - The file plan
> - Groups of electronic folders
> - Individual electronic folders
> - Electronic volumes
> - Electronic records
> - Metadata associated with any of the above
>
> and that the following events should be captured:
>
> - The type of action which is being carried out, for example:
>   - Relocation of an electronic record to another electronic folder, identifying both source and destination folders

An audit trail provides critical proof that records are unaltered and should capture, at a minimum, information on the file plan, groups and individual files and folders, and their associated metadata.

- Relocation of an electronic folder to a different series, identifying both source and destination series
- Reallocation of a disposal schedule to an object, identifying both previous and reallocated schedules
- Placing of a disposal hold on a folder
- The date and time of a change made to any metadata associated with electronic folders or electronic records
- Changes made to the allocation of access control markings to an electronic folder, electronic record or user
- Export actions carried out on an electronic folder
- Attempts to edit a record
- The user carrying out the action
- The date and time of the event

It must at all times be possible to prove that the system was tamperproof at the time the records were created and stored. It is therefore imperative that the system should log all attempts to access it, and that it captures the identity of a user and the time edits were made.[12]

Authenticity

Most developed countries now recognize the acceptance of e-records as legitimate records by law, so long as they can be proven to be authentic, unaltered, and accurate. Authenticity provides users of records with the knowledge and confidence that the records are true and authentic. This can be proven by following the chain of custody of the record from its creation and though its lifecycle. Having IG controls and auditing checkpoints in place help to prove that a record is authentic and reliable.[13]

Business Classification Schemes

Records should be classified upon creation, and records series categories should be based on the business functions of its users. **Classification** "refers to the process whereby electronic records stored in the electronic repository are assigned subjects in the classification system that matches the document's [record's] subject."[14] A primary goal of IG efforts is to standardize and systematize the classification of records across the enterprise so that common terms are used and records are more easily searched for and retrieved. If classification schemes are consistent, then the retention and disposal of records series or systems will be consistent, and legally defensible.

Consistency is the hallmark of successful IG efforts.

A **business classification scheme** (BCS) is the overall structure an organization uses for organizing, searching, retrieving, storing, and managing documents and records in ERM. The BCS must be developed based on the business functions and activities. A **file plan** is a graphic representation of the BCS, usually a "hierarchical structure consisting of headings and folders to indicate where and when records should be created during the conducting of the business of an office. In other words *the file plan links the records to their business context*."[15] The file plan shows business functions and records and links the two, showing the records that specific business functions generate.

Central Repository

The approach of maintaining records in a central repository is the standard architecture of nearly all of today's ERM vendors. The system may be located across multiple networked servers, but users can conduct federated searches across them and they appear as a central repository to users.[16] This conceptually mimics the central fileroom approach of the hardcopy, paper folder days, so it is easy to understand. Its purpose is to provide centralized control over records. This makes IG, compliance, and legal responses straightforward, and it is easier to follow the path of the lifecycle of a record when it is controlled and managed centrally.

However, this is not the only way an ERM system can be designed. Newer approaches are evolving and newer structures, newer ways of architecting ERM systems are being presented. For instance, the European MoReq2010 standard allows for records to be "aggregations" of progressive versions and for records management to occur within business applications and for records to be managed in a decentralized way.

Collaboration

Having collaboration capabilities helps groups or teams of knowledge workers improve productivity when working with records.[17] Collaboration is not always a part of ERM systems, but it provides efficiency benefits and collaboration is increasingly being included in ERM systems, and now those collaborative features are being offered as integrated cloud services.

Disposition: Transfer, Destruction, Preservation

Records deemed of enduring value in the records appraisal process are transferred to be archived when they meet the end of their lifecycle. Some will remain there for several years and some will remain in archival storage for decades, which requires detailed preservation, testing, and auditing measures. The appraisal process, which takes place proactively, helps to determine which records series need to be archived and how long they should be preserved.

> A BCS is the overall structure an organization uses for organizing files, which is graphically represented by the file plan.

Records don't always stay in the same place. At times, they must be moved to a new, larger facility, or under the control of a business unit that is given responsibility for them. This transfer process has to be carefully monitored, controlled, and documented. Following the records transfer process, there must be a way to *certify* that the records have, in fact, been transferred, and an unbroken chain of custody can be proven between the transferring entity and the new custodian, maintaining the validity of the **authenticity of records**. The records export, the authority to transfer, an actual inspection to verify the records' content, the import of the records to a new system, the authenticity of the record creator, and the audit trail and metadata *must all be verified to be accurate and then documented.*

The receiving or importing custodian should implement controls to ensure the integrity of the transferred records while they are accessed from the new system. Controls may include access credentials, controls on editing or printing records, steps to ensure that alteration, corruption, replacement, or deletion of e-records do not take place and that the media the records are stored on are tested, and then migrated, rotated, or replaced to guard against media failure, corruption, or technological obsolescence.

Destruction of records following their useful life is another important issue: the destruction must be carried out properly and documented correctly or there is a risk that the destruction could be viewed as criminal (obstruction of justice). Also, records must not only be destroyed, but they must be destroyed systematically, consistently and *completely*, so that the disposition program is legally defensible. *In an electronic environment, this is more difficult than simply shredding paper files.* Certain controls must be in place to ensure that all traces of an electronic record are obliterated in the destruction process. No traces of metadata or content should be left on the hard drive, optical disc, or other media the records were stored on. Solid state drives are becoming more popular and they are more easily erased completely than other electronic storage media.

In cases where a hold has been placed on the destruction of a record, then it must be documented who requested, authorized, and reviewed the destruction hold.

Once the destruction of a record is complete, a **destruction certificate** verifying that it has taken place should be issued and filed.

If an e-record is scheduled for long-term archival and has been appraised to be in need of LTDP, which is typically over five years, the strategy for its preservation will be dependent on its total retention period, the media it is stored on, and related technology issues. E-records may be migrated to newer technology platforms so that they remain readable, but this strategy must be carefully planned and documented to ensure the authenticity of the records. Information technology (IT) will continue to change and the challenge is to continue to keep e-records intact and readable over the long term.[18]

Document Scanning

In ERM, paper documents must be able to be digitally scanned and captured in electronic format, which is called **document imaging**. This is accomplished via desktop scanners or standalone, high-speed scanners, although it can be accomplished remotely via fax. One of the key benefits of an ERM system is providing faster access to records and controlling them through their lifecycle, and this often begins with externally generated letters, contracts, or other documents that must be scanned to be ingested into the ERM system.[19] Document scanning can occur with individual documents, or in large batches, broken up by separator pages.

File Formats

Most software providers utilize their own proprietary file formats and compression algorithms to store, transfer, and display digital images of records and documents. That may use parts of some industry standard components, such as tagged image file format (TIFF) for images, and Group IV (G4) fax compression, but there are usually nuances that set each vendor's format apart. Maybe it is in the file header, maybe it is in the metadata structure. Part of the vendor strategy historically has been to get the customers' content into the vendor's format and, in essence, to "lock them in" to the vendor's technology. The software vendors have not made it very easy to convert files from one competitive system to another—there have typically been those bits of proprietary software that encode the documents and records in a way unique to the vendor. There have been standardization efforts aimed at providing e-document interchangeability, and they have demonstrated this capability in test settings, but they have largely failed in practice.

It is best to limit the use of proprietary formats, but standard formats have issues too. If you convert files to industry standard ASCII or rich text format (RTF) there is a loss of "structure and functions" and it may bring the authenticity of records into question. With pushback from customers, and progress in standards, there have been a couple of formats that have gained in preference for storing records over time. *First, and primarily, Adobe portable document format (PDF) has gained prominence for storing records.* Adobe released control of its archival version of its PDF, called PDF/A, based on PDF 1.4, which has become the international standard ISO 19005-1:2005, which applies to e-documents that may contain raster or vector graphics, and character data.[20]

For text-based documents, eXtensible Markup Language (XML) has risen to become the preferred format for archival storage.

There are still no perfect and stable long-term solutions for all document and records stored, since systems, formats, and standards continue to change and evolve. Format migration is still a decision that needs to be studied for your particular business records scenario, so that records are able to be preserved over the long term.[21]

Yet using PDF/A for e-records follows the standard ISO 19005-1: "Document Management Applications—Electronic Document File Format for Long Term Preservation—Part 1: Use of PDF 1.4 (PDF/A-1)," and plans are to continue down the PDF/A path to support newer PDF versions, such as PDF 1.7, and so on. But the only guarantee is that standards change and evolve.

Metadata

Discussions about metadata can get complex, but metadata for e-records are the data fields that are associated with the record that contain defining and descriptive

PDF/A is the ISO standard for archiving documents as records.

Metadata are the data fields that are associated with the record that contain defining and descriptive information about its characteristics.

information about its characteristics, such as creator, date, record type, department, and length of the document.

According to ISO 15489, the international records management standard, metadata is "Data describing context, content, and structure of records, and their management through time."[22]

When users perform searches for records, they are searching metadata fields. That is why it is important to have IG policies in place that standardize these metadata fields so users can find what they are looking for. It is also important for legal and regulatory reasons, so that the metadata fields can be used to create a records retention schedule for managing records according to established policies that are legally defensible.

Metadata is used to map the Records Retention Schedule to the documents and records to apply retention and disposition rules.

Physical Records Management

ERM systems must be able to track not only e-records, but also hardcopy and physical records, which may be located in filing cabinets and file rooms in order to provide complete records management application (RMA) functionality.[23]

Retention Scheduling

Records retention scheduling is a core ERM concept. Records must be able to be assigned a retention schedule for its lifecycle, and certain actions are indicated when it completes its lifecycle. Some records are automatically archived, others are retained for a specified period and then destroyed.[24] Others may be scheduled for destruction but are queued up for an authorized person to approve or deny the destruction of the record. Retention scheduling is a basic concept of records management, but it can get complex with the myriad of legal and regulatory requirements, some of which may apply to different parts of a particular record.

Search and Retrieval

ERM systems must provide basic and complex search capabilities to enable users to find records they are looking for. Also, the search capability should be robust enough for users to browse the records repository and also to suggest terms and concepts when users are not quite sure what records might exist as they conduct their research.

Records retention scheduling is a core ERM concept.

Searches should be able to find *all* relevant records, whether they be electronic or physical. In an EDRMS, searches should be able to span across all documents and records in the repository.[25]

Security and Access Control

Part of an IG policy framework includes technologies to control *and govern* who has the right to access the ERM system. Security and access control help to prove that records have not been inappropriately accessed, created, amended or edited, transferred, or deleted entirely. This supports the credibility of e-records as authentic.

Individuals, such as the corporate records manager, can be given access to the ERM system, or they may be allowed to view and interact with only the records pertaining to their area of responsibility. For larger organizations, those individuals in certain roles requiring records access are provided it through a designated **access control list** (ACL). The ACL will also authorize access rights, such as right to view, amend, transfer, or even delete—with proper IG controls. These controls extend to the actual metadata too, which is critical to successful searches. In other words, the record may be there, but there is no way of finding it if its metadata indices have been deleted or changed.

Controlling and updating the ACL is crucial to maintaining the integrity of electronic records. Without it, no assurance of the unaltered veracity of records can be proven. And beyond that, an ACL helps keep sensitive records from prying, unauthorized eyes.

ACLs can become complex and challenging to manage as the list grows, and employees move to different areas and assignments, so an ACL is best suited for governing access for a limited number of employees, and IG processes must be in place and enforced to provide effective access and security control.[26]

Storage Media

In the early days (1990s) the storage size requirements for scanned images required that document imaging systems stored digitized images on 12-inch or even 14-inch optical disc (OD) platters using WORM technology that assured the images—or records—could never be erased (although the index to them could, making them nearly impossible to find). To accommodate the large amounts of data that storing images required, these OD platters were mounted in a "jukebox" filled with OD platters and robotic arms to pick, insert, remove, and replace the OD. Some are still in use today, although they have largely been phased out and images have been migrated to newer media.

The OD jukebox storage and retrieval process was very slow, especially when compared to the response time users were accustomed to for retrieving data from magnetic disk storage. Adding to the slowness was the large file sizes of images being

Access control lists contain named, authorized users and their access rights such as right to view, amend, transfer, or even delete records.

transported over networks, which have been described as like "a pig in a python" since they were so large. Users could be waiting for 30 seconds or even a minute or two to get their requested record image. This was faster than going to the file room to get a folder, but it was unacceptable and improvements were needed.

There are still plenty of these large ODs around filled with images, although response times sped up and reliability improved as storage technology improved. Many vendors moved to smaller (5.25 inch) CD-WORM or DVD-WORM storage media. This made jukeboxes faster. Other vendors moved to stacks of online CD or DVD drives that did not use the jukebox picking mechanism and were online all the time and retrieved images even faster yet.

To address the problem of extended seek times, technology was developed to retrieve data based on like, fixed content (records), rather than its storage location, called content-addressable storage (CAS).

Response times for retrieving images of records have continued to improve with the use of magnetic storage with WORM emulation capabilities.

Consideration of storage media is critical when planning for e-records archiving, especially in the LTDP process.

Version Control

It is essential to have the latest, certifiable, original record for legal and compliance purposes, and records often go through multiple revisions, so strong version control is a key feature of ERM/EDRMS systems. Also, a "check-out/check-in" feature, originally a part of electronic document management systems (EDMS), is essential. Think of it as similar to checking out a book from a library electronically, reading it, and checking it back in, only in this case e-records are being checked out by users. But still, "Electronic records can be located in various places at the same time, for example, in a centralized database, in shared network filing spaces, on local hard drives, in e-mail systems in the inbox, outbox, and deleted items, and on a variety of storage media. This makes it more difficult to manage the creation, revision, and deletion of records and to identify the authoritative record. If the creation of records is not managed properly someone may accidentally use the wrong version of an electronic record or records that should have been kept may accidentally be destroyed."[27]

If your organization finds it has multiple (nonoriginal) copies of the same record involved in your business processes, you must further develop and enforce your IG policies so that there is only one authentic, identifiable original record, (and backup copies are kept off-site in the event of a disaster).

Vital Records

Vital records are those that an organization must have to resume its business in the case of a disaster. Typically, they make up a subset of approximately 3 to 5 percent of an organization's records. These are the high-value records that an organization must protect most, by using disaster recovery/business continuity measures to ensure that multiple copies are stored safely in multiple geographic locations so that in the event of a disaster the organization can reinstate its operations.

An ERM system must have the capability to allow users to identify, track, and backup vital records.

Workflow

Improvements in business process cycle times are gained by using workflow software technology to move documents and records from desk to desk, to route copies of files within folders for approval and then rendezvous them with the folder to update it, and to send working folders back through different routes based on conditional data. Workflow moves folders, documents, and records through a series of worksteps and captures statistics along the way that can provide insights into further business process improvements. Obviously, moving records at electronic speeds versus physically moving paper folders through an office has obvious benefits in speeding up processes, but even greater benefits are gained through increased control, and the ability to enforce IG policies.

CHAPTER SUMMARY: **KEY POINTS**

- Electronic documents and records can be managed by a few different types of software applications that overlap in functionality, and often are implemented in more than one instance in an organization. These include enterprise content management (ECM) systems, electronic document management systems (EDMS or DMS), electronic document and records management systems (EDRMS), and electronic records management (ERM) systems.

- Enterprise content management (ECM) systems manage unstructured content, from web content to internal documents, reports, and business records. Databases manage structured content that is expressed numerically in rows and columns.

- An electronic document management system (EDMS or DMS) is software designed to store and track electronic documents. An EDMS is used to track and store electronic documents such as word processing and spreadsheet files, digital report files, and scanned images of paper documents. Documents are vulnerable once outside the repository.

- ERM systems manage all business records and documents, regardless of their physical form. This means that both paper and electronic records are tracked in an ERM (or EDRMS).

- Metadata are the data fields that are associated with the records that contain defining and descriptive information about its characteristics.

- In the records appraisal process, records can be deemed to have legal, financial, administrative, or historical value.

(Continued)

(Continued)

- An audit trail provides critical proof that records are unaltered and should capture, at a minimum, information on the file plan, groups and individual files and folders, and their associated metadata.

- A Business Classification Scheme (BCS) is the overall structure an organization uses for organizing files, which is graphically represented by the file plan.

- PDF/A is the ISO standard for archiving documents as records.

- A record retention schedule is applied to documents that become records based on document type, and all business, legal, and regulatory requirements.

- ERM systems enforce record retention and disposition policies according to established retention schedules and IG policies.

- Access control lists contain named, authorized users and their access rights such as right to view, amend, transfer, or even delete records.

- Improvements in business process cycle times are gained by using workflow software technology to move documents and records through a series of worksteps.

Notes

1. Barry Murphy, "What Is Information Governance?," March 22, 2010, http://ediscoveryjournal.com/2010/03/what-is-information-governance/ .
2. Don Lueders, "The Information Lifecycle Model," October 21, 2009, http://sharepointrecordsmanagement.com/2009/10/21/the-information-lifecycle-model.
3. "Document Management Overview (SharePoint Server 2010)," May 12, 2010, http://technet.microsoft.com/en-us/library/cc261933.aspx. Used with permission by Microsoft.
4. "Document Management," Kofax, www.kofax.com/glossary/Document-Management (accessed October 6, 2011).
5. "Document Management Overview (SharePoint Server 2010)." Used with permission by Microsoft.
6. International Standards Organization, www.iso.org/iso/catalogue_detail?csnumber=31908 (accessed April 19, 2012).
7. "Managing Electronic Records in Governmental Bodies: Policy, Principles and Requirements," National Archives and Records Service of South Africa, April 2006, www.national.archives.gov.za/rms/NARS_DMLIB-4878-v1-Managing_electronic_records_Policy__principles_and_Requirements_April_2006 (PDF).
8. Ibid.
9. Ibid.
10. Ibid.
11. "Managing Electronic Records in Governmental Bodies."
12. Ibid.
13. Ibid.
14. Ibid.
15. Ibid.

16. Azad Adam, *Implementing Electronic Document and Record Management Systems* (Boca Raton, FL: Auerbach Publications, 2008), 17.
17. Ibid., 20.
18. "Managing Electronic Records in Governmental Bodies."
19. Adam, Implementing Electronic Document and Record Management Systems, 19–20.
20. International Organization for Standardization (ISO), ISO 19005-1:2005, www.iso.org/iso/catalogue_detail?csnumber=38920 (accessed May 29, 2012).
21. "Managing Electronic Records in Governmental Bodies."
22. Ibid.
23. Adam, Implementing Electronic Document and Record Management Systems, 18.
24. Ibid.
25. Ibid., 18–19.
26. "Managing Electronic Records in Governmental Bodies."
27. Ibid.

PART TWO

E-Records
Fundamentals

CHAPTER 5

Inventorying E-Records

According to the U.S. National Archives and Records Administration (NARA), "In **records management**, an **inventory** is a descriptive listing of each record series or system, together with an indication of location and other pertinent data. *It is not a list of each document or each folder but rather of each series or system.*"[1] (Italics added.)

Conducting an inventory of electronic records is more challenging than a physical records inventory, but the purposes are the same, which is to ferret out records management (RM) problems and to use the inventory as the basis for developing the retention schedule. Some of the RM problems that may be uncovered, "include inadequate documentation of official actions, improper applications of recordkeeping technology, deficient filing systems and maintenance practices, poor management of nonrecord materials, insufficient identification of vital records, and inadequate records security practices. When completed, the inventory should include all offices, all records, and all nonrecord materials. An inventory that is incomplete or haphazard can only result in an inadequate schedule and loss of control over records."[2]

So the first step in gaining control over an organization's records, and implementing information governance (IG) measures to control and manage them, is to complete an inventory of all groupings of business records, including electronic records,[3] *at the system or file series level.*

The focus of this book is on e-records, and when it comes to e-records, NARA has a specific recommendation: inventory *at the computer systems level.* This differs from advice given by experts in the past.

The records inventory is the basis for developing a **records retention schedule** that spells out how long different types of records are to be held, and how they will be archived or disposed of at the end of their lifecycle. But first you must determine where business records reside, how they are stored, how many exist, and how they are used in the normal course of business.

There are a few things to keep in mind when approaching the e-records inventorying process:

- Those who create and work with the records themselves are the best source of information about how the records are used. They are your most critical resource in the inventorying process.

NARA recommends, "Electronic records should be inventoried by information system, rather than by record series."

- Records management is something that everyone wants done but no one wants to do (although they will have an opinion on how to do it).
- The people working in business units are touchy about their records and it will take some effort to get them to trust a new records management approach.[4]

These knowledge workers are your best resource and can be your greatest ally or worst enemy when it comes to gathering accurate inventory data, developing a workable file plan, and keeping the records declaration, retention, and disposition process operating efficiently. A sound records management program will keep the records inventory accurate and up-to-date.

The Generally Accepted Recordkeeping Principles®

It may be useful to use a model or framework to guide your records inventorying efforts. Such frameworks could be the D.I.R.K.S. (Designing and Implementing Recordkeeping Systems) used in Australia, or the Generally Accepted Recordkeeping Principles® (or "GAR Principles"), which originated in the U.S. at **ARMA International**, which is a *"framework for managing records in a way that supports an organization's immediate and future regulatory, legal, risk mitigation, environmental, and operational requirements."*[5] (See Chapter 3, Generally Accepted Recordkeeping Principles, for more detail).

Special attention should be given to creating an accountable, open, inventorying process that can demonstrate integrity. The result of the inventory should help the organization adhere to records retention, disposition, availability, protection, and compliance aspects of the GAR Principles, and similar principles in other established record-keeping frameworks.

E-Records Inventory Challenges

If your organization has received a legal summons for e-records, and you do not have an accurate inventory, the organization is already in a compromising position: you do

What are the GAR Principles? Information management and governance of record creation, organization, security, maintenance, and other activities used to effectively support recordkeeping of an organization.

not know where the requested records might be, how many copies there might be, or the process and cost of producing them. Inventorying must be done sooner rather than later, and proactively, rather than reactively.

Electronic records present challenges beyond those of paper or microfilmed records, due to their (electronic) nature: (1) You cannot see or touch them without searching online, as opposed to simply thumbing through a filing cabinet or scrolling through a roll of microfilm; (2) they are not sitting in a central fileroom, but rather, they may be scattered about on servers, shared network drives, or on storage attached to mainframe or minicomputers; (3) they have metadata attached to them that may distinguish very similar-looking records; and (4) additional "shadow" copies of the e-records may exist and it is difficult to determine the true or original copy.[7]

Records Inventory Purposes

The completed records inventory contributes toward the pursuit of an organization's IG objectives in a number of ways: it supports the ownership, management, and control of records; helps to organize and prepare for the discovery process in litigation; reduces exposure to business risk; and provides the foundation for a disaster recovery/business continuity (DR/BC) plan.

There are at least eight additional benefits to completing the records inventory:[8]

1. Identifies records ownership and sharing relationships, both internal and external.
2. Determines which records are physical, electronic, or a combination of both.
3. Provides the basis for Retention and Disposition Schedule development.
4. Improves compliance capabilities.
5. Supports training objectives for those handling records.
6. Identifies vital and sensitive records needing added security and backup measures.
7. Assesses the state of records storage, its quality and appropriateness.
8. Supports the release of information for Freedom of Information Act (FOIA), Data Protection Act (DPA), and other mandated information release requirements for governmental agencies.

With respect to *e-records*, the purpose of the records inventory "should include the following objectives:[9]

- Provide a survey of the existing electronic records situation
- Locate and describe the organization's electronic record holdings
- Identify obsolete electronic records
- Determine storage needs for active and inactive electronic records
- Identify vital and archival electronic records, indicating need for their ongoing care
- Raise awareness within the organization of the importance of electronic records management
- Lead to electronic record keeping improvements that increase efficiency

- Lead to the development of a needs assessment for future actions
- Provide the foundation of a written records management plan with a determination of priorities and stages of actions, assuring the continuing improvement of records management practices."

Records Inventorying Steps

NARA's guidance on how to approach a records inventory applies to both physical and e-records; "the steps in the records inventory process are:

1. **Define the inventory's goals.** While the main goal is gathering information for scheduling purposes, other goals may include preparing for conversion to other media, or identifying particular records management problems.
2. **Define the scope of the inventory;** it should include all records and other materials.
3. **Obtain top management's support,** preferably in the form of a directive, and keep management and staff informed at every stage of the inventory.
4. **Decide on the information to be collected** (the elements of the inventory). Materials should be located, described, and evaluated in terms of use.
5. **Prepare an inventory form**, or use an existing one.
6. **Decide who will conduct the inventory**, and train them properly.
7. Learn **where the** agency's [or business'] **files are located**, both physically and organizationally.
8. **Conduct the inventory.**
9. **Verify and analyze the results.**[10] (bold added for emphasis)

Goals of the Inventory Project

The goals of the inventorying project must be set and conveyed to all stakeholders. At a basic level, the primary goal can be simply to generate a complete inventory for compliance and reporting purposes, and to update the Retention Schedule. It may focus on a certain business area or functional group, or the enterprise as a whole. An enterprise approach requires segmenting the effort into smaller, logically-sequenced work efforts, such as by business unit. *Perhaps the organization has a handle on their paper and microfilmed records, but e-records have been growing exponentially and spiraling out of control, without good policy guidelines or IG controls.* So a complete inventory of records and e-records by system is needed, which may include e-records generated by

> The completed records inventory contributes toward the pursuit of an organization's IG objectives in a number of ways.

> Whatever the business goals for the inventorying effort are, they must be conveyed to all stakeholders, and that message must be reinforced periodically and consistently, and through multiple means.

application systems, residing in e-mail, created in office documents and spreadsheets, or other potential business records. This is a tactical approach that is limited in scope.

The goal of the inventorying process may be more ambitious: to lay the groundwork for the acquisition and implementation of an electronic records management (ERM) system that will manage the retention, disposition, search, and retrieval of records. This will require more business process analysis and redesign, some rethinking of business classification schemes and file plans, and development of an enterprise-wide taxonomy. This will allow for more sharing of information and records; faster, easier, and more complete retrievals; and a common language and approach for knowledge professionals across the enterprise to declare, capture, and retrieve business records.

The plan may be still much greater in scope, and involve more challenging goals, that is, the inventorying of records may be the first step in the process of implementing an organization-wide IG program to manage and control information, by rolling out ERM and IG systems and new processes; to improve litigation readiness and prepare for e-discovery requests; and to demonstrate compliance adherence with business agility and confidence. This involves an entire cultural shift in the organization, and a long-term approach.

Whatever the business goals for the inventorying effort are, they must be conveyed to all stakeholders, and that message must be reinforced periodically and consistently, and through multiple means. It must be clearly spelled out in communications and presented in meetings as the overarching goal that will help the organization meet its business objectives. The scope of the inventory must be appropriate for the business goals and objectives it targets.

Scoping the Inventory

"With senior-level support, the records manager must decide on the scope of the records inventory. A single inventory could not describe every electronic record in an organization; *an appropriate scope might enumerate the records of a single program or division, several functional series across divisions, or records that fall within a certain time frame.*"[11] Most organizations have not deployed an "enterprise-wide records management system," which makes the e-records inventorying process an arduous and time-consuming task. It's just not very easy to find where all the electronic records reside—they are scattered all over the place, and on differing media. But impending (and inevitable) litigation and compliance demands require that it be done. And, again, sooner has been proven to be better than later. Since courts have ruled that if lawsuits have been filed against your competitors over a certain (industry-specific) issue, your organization should anticipate and prepare for litigation—which means conducting records inventories and placing a litigation hold on documents that might be relevant. Simply doing nothing and waiting on a subpoena is an avoidable business risk.

A methodical, step-by-step approach must be taken—it is the only way to accomplish the task. A plan that divides up the inventorying tasks into smaller, accomplishable

> An appropriate scope might enumerate the records of a single program or division, several functional series across divisions, or records that fall within a certain time frame.

pieces is the only one that will work. It has been said, "How do you eat an elephant?" And the answer is, "One bite at a time." So scope the inventorying process into segments, such as a business unit, division, or information system/application.

Management Support: Executive Sponsor

It is crucial to have management support to drive the inventory process to completion. There is no substitute for an executive sponsor. Asking employees to take time out for yet another survey or administrative task without having an executive sponsor will lose steam and will likely not work. Employees are more time-pressed than ever, and they will need a clear directive from above, along with an understanding of what role the inventorying process plays in achieving a business goal for the enterprise, if they are to take the time to properly participate and contribute meaningfully to the effort.

Information/Elements for Collection

"During the inventory you should collect the following information at a minimum:

- What kind of record it is—*contracts, financial reports, memoranda, etc.*
- What department owns it
- What departments access it
- What application created the record (e-mail, MS Word, Adobe PDF)
- Where it is stored, both physically (tape, server) and logically (network share, folder)
- Date created
- Date last changed
- Whether it is a vital record (mission-critical to the organization)
- Whether there are other forms of the record (for example, a document stored as a Word document, a PDF, and a paper copy) and which of them is considered the official record

Removable media should have a unique identifier and the inventory should include a list of records on the particular volume as well as the characteristics of the volume, e.g., the brand, the recording format, the capacity and volume used, and the date of manufacture and date of last update. (Italics added)"[12]

More Comprehensive Approach

NARA provides a more detailed list of "the data elements that should be collected in the inventorying process:[13]

Date prepared

The date the inventory was prepared.

Office maintaining the files

The name and symbol of the office maintaining the records. If the office received this series from another office, also indicate the name and symbol of that office and designate it as the "creating office."

Person conducting the inventory

Name, office, and telephone number.

Series location

Give the precise location of the series. If the series is located in more than one office, indicate multiple locations.

Series title

Give each series a title for brief reference or include the generally accepted title.

Inclusive dates

The earliest and most recent dates of the records in each series. These are needed to schedule records, and to determine when to cut off, or break them and transfer them to records centers or agency storage facilities.

Series description

A clear description of the series is basic to the success of the inventory and the schedule. It may also be needed to clarify the series title and should contain enough information to show the purpose, use, and subject content of the records.

Medium

Indicate whether the record medium is paper, microform, electronic, audiovisual, or a combination of these.

Arrangement

Indicate the arrangement, or filing system, used.

Volume

Express the volume of records in cubic feet, where possible. When inventorying audiovisual, microform, cartographic, and related records, also provide an item count (e.g., 1,200 prints, 3,500 negatives) where appropriate. Sampling may be necessary for large series or collections. NARA requires agencies to give volume figures for records proposed for permanent retention, as well as for nonrecurring records proposed for immediate destruction.

Annual accumulation

Based on information from the files custodian, estimate the annual rate of accumulation for each series if the records are current and continuing. If the records no longer accumulate, indicate "none." NARA requires agencies to furnish the rate of accumulation of those records proposed for permanent retention.[14]

Cutoff

To cut off records means to break, or end, them at regular intervals to permit their disposal or transfer in complete blocks to permit the establishment of new files. Indicate how often the records are cut off and when the last cutoff occurred. If they are not cut off, explain how inactive records are separated from active ones.

Reference activity

Rate the reference activity of a paper record series, after the regular cutoff, by placing it in one of three categories:

- Current, or active (used more than once a month)
- Semicurrent, or semiactive (used less than once a month)
- Noncurrent, or inactive (not used for current operations)

Vital records status

If the records qualify as vital records, specify whether they would be needed in an emergency (emergency-operating records) and whether they are needed to document legal or financial rights, or both. Also indicate whether they are the originals or duplicates. (See 36 CFR Part 1236 for requirements in managing vital records).

Duplication

Indicate duplication in form or content. It can exist in the following ways:

- Copies may be in the same organizational unit or elsewhere in the agency. The copies may contain significant differences or notations.
- Similar data or information may be available elsewhere in the agency, either physically duplicated or in summarized form.

Finding aids

Note the existence of any finding aids for the series, especially if the records are to be proposed for permanent retention. Indicate where the finding aid is located and note if it covers more than one series.

Restrictions on access and use

Indicate any restrictions on access to, and use of, the particular series. Such restrictions may result from statutes, executive orders, or agency directives. Common types of restrictions are:

- Privacy Act restrictions
- National security restrictions
- Freedom of Information Act restrictions
- Other applicable restrictions that may be specific to the agency

Condition of permanent records

During the inventory, take note of the physical condition of records that are actually or potentially permanent, especially those stored off-site. Identify threats to their preservation and security.

Disposition authority

If the series has an approved disposition authority, list the schedule and item number and then the retention period. If the series has no such authority, list the files as 'unscheduled,' make sure they are preserved, and ask the program office to recommend a suitable retention period."[15]

Additional Information Needed for E-Records Inventorying

[NARA recommends that] "besides the inventory information listed above, include the following in an inventory of electronic records and electronic records systems:[16]

- Name of the system
- Program or legal authority for creation of the system
- System control number
- Agency program supported by the system
- Purpose of the system
- Data input and sources
- Major outputs
- Informational content (include where applicable):
    - Description of data
    - Persons, places, or things that are the subject of the system and the information maintained on those subjects
    - Geographic coverage
    - Time span
    - Update cycle
    - Date that the system was initiated
    - Applications that the systems supports
    - How data are manipulated
    - Key unit of analysis for each file
    - Whether a public-use version is created
- Description of indexes, if any
- Hardware and software environment
- Name, office, telephone number, and location of the system manager
- Name, office, telephone number, and room number of the person with the documentation needed to read and understand system, including
- Codebooks
- File layouts
- Other (specify)
- Location and volume of any other records containing the same information"[17]

The IT Network Diagram

Laying out the overall topology of the IT infrastructure in the form of a network diagram is an exercise that is helpful in understanding where to target efforts, and to map information flows. Creating this "map" of the IT infrastructure is a crucial step in inventorying e-records. It graphically depicts how and where computers are connected to each other and the software operating environments of various applications that are in use. It should be a high-level diagram and it need not include every device, but rather, each type of device, and how it is used.

The IT staff will usually have a network diagram that can be used as a reference; perhaps after some simplification it can be put into use as the underpinning for inventorying electronic records. It does not need great detail, such as where network bridges

Additional information not included in inventories of physical records must be collected in any inventory of e-records.

and routers are located, but it should show which applications are utilizing the cloud or hosted applications to store and/or process documents and records.

In diagramming the IT infrastructure for purposes of the inventory, it is easiest to start in the central computer room where any mainframe or other centralized servers are located, and then follow the connections out into the departments and business unit areas, where there may be multiple shared servers and drives supporting a network of desktop personal computers or workstations.

Microsoft's SharePoint is a prevalent document and records management portal platform, and many organizations will have SharePoint servers to house and process electronic documents and records. Some utilities and tools may be available to assist in the inventorying process on SharePoint systems.

Mobile devices that are processing documents and records should also be represented, which may include tablets, smartphones, and other portable devices, including BYOD. And any e-records residing in cloud storage should also be included.

Creating a Records Inventory Survey Form

The form must suit its purpose. Do not collect data that is irrelevant, but be sure to collect all the needed data elements in conducting the survey. You can use a standard form but some customization is recommended. Table 5.1 shows a sample records survey form that is wide-ranging, yet succinct, that has been used successfully in practice.[18]

If conducting the e-records portion of the inventory, the sample form may be somewhat modified, as shown in Table 5.2.[19]

Table 5.1   Records Inventory Survey Form

Department Information

1. What is the reporting structure of the department?

2. Who is the department liaison for the records inventory?

3. Who is the IT or business analyst liaison?

Record Requirements

4. Are there any external agencies that impose guidelines, standards or other requirements?

5. Are their specific legislative requirements for creating or maintaining records? Please provide a copy.

6. Is there a departmental records retention schedule?

7. What are the business considerations that drive record keeping? Regulatory requirements? Legal requirements?

8. Does the department have an existing Records Management Policy? Guidelines? Procedures? Please provide a copy.

9. Does the department provide guidance to employees on what records are to be created?

10. How are policies, procedures and guidance disseminated to the employees?

11. What is the current level of awareness of employees their responsibilities for records management?

12. How are nonrecords managed?

13. What is the process for ensuring compliance with policies, procedures, and guidelines? When an employee changes jobs/roles or is terminated?

14. Does the department have a classification or file plans?

15. Are any records in the department confidential or sensitive?

Table 5.1 (*Continued*)

16. What information security controls does the department have for confidential or sensitive records?

17. Does the department have records in sizes other than letter (8 ½ × 11)

18. What is the cutoff date for the records?

  ☐ Fiscal Year   ☐ Calendar Year   ☐ Other

19. Have department vital records been identified?

20. Is there an existing Business or Disaster Recovery Policy?

21. Is the department subject to audits? Internal? External? Who conducts the audits?

22. Where and how are records stored?

  Online? Near Line? Offline? On-site? Off-site? One location? Multiple locations?

23. How does the department ensure that records will remain accessible, readable, and useable throughout their scheduled retention period?

Technology and Tools

24. Are any tools used to track active records? Spreadsheets, word documents, databases, and so forth?

25. Are any tools used to track inactive records? Spreadsheets, word documents, databases, and so forth?

26. Does the department use imaging, document management, and so forth?

Disposition

27. Are there guidelines for destroying obsolete records?

28. What disposition methods are authorized or required?

29. How does disposition occur? Paper? Electronic? Other?

30. What extent does the department rely on each individual to destroy records? Paper? Electronic? Other?

Records Holds

31. What principles govern decisions for determining the scope of records that must be held or frozen for an audit or investigations?

32. How is the hold or freeze communicated to employees?

33. How are records placed on hold protected?

Table 5.2   Electronic Records Inventory Survey Form

Identifying Information

1. Name of system?

2. Program or legal authority for system?

3. System identification or control number?

4. Person responsible for administering the system. Include e-mail, office address, and phone contact info.

5. Date system put in service.

6. Business unit or agency supported by system.

7. Description of system (what does the application software do?).

8. Purpose of system.

System Inputs/Outputs

9. Primary sources of data inputs.

10. Major outputs of system (e.g., specific reports).

(continued)

Table 5.2   (*Continued*)

11. Informational content (all applicable): Description of data; applicability of data (people, places, things); geographic information; time span; update cycle; applications the system supports; how data are manipulated; key unit analysis for each file; public use or not?

12. Hardware configuration.

13. Software environment, including revision levels, operating system, database, and so forth.

14. Indices or any classification scheme/file plan that is in place?

15. Duplicate records? Location and volume of any other records containing the same information.

Record Requirements

16. Are there any external agencies that impose guidelines, standards or other requirements?

17. Are their specific legislative requirements for creating or maintaining records? Please provide a copy.

18. Is there a departmental records retention schedule?

19. What are the business considerations that drive record keeping? Regulatory requirements? Legal requirements?

20. Does the department have an existing Records Management Policy? Guidelines? Procedures? If so, please provide a copy.

21. How are nonrecords managed?

22. Are any records in the department confidential or sensitive? How are they indicated or set apart?

23. What information security controls does the department have for confidential or sensitive records?

24. What is the cutoff date for the records?

      ☐ Fiscal Year   ☐ Calendar Year   ☐ Other

25. Have department vital records been identified?

26. Is there an existing Business or Disaster Recovery Policy?

27. Is the department subject to audits? Internal? External? Who conducts the audits?

28. Where and how are records stored?

      Online? Near line? Offline? On-site? Off-site? One location? Multiple locations?

29. How does the department ensure that records will remain accessible, readable, and useable throughout their scheduled retention period?

Disposition

30. Are there guidelines for destroying obsolete records?

31. What disposition methods are authorized or required?

32. How does disposition occur? Are electronic deletions verified?

33. What extent does the department rely on each individual to destroy e-records?

Records Holds

34. What principles govern decisions for determining the scope of records that must be held or frozen for an audit or investigations?

35. How is the hold or freeze communicated to employees?

36. How are records placed on hold protected?

Adapted from: www.archives.gov/records-mgmt/faqs/inventories.html and Charmaine Brooks, IMERGE Consulting.

An example of an Electronic Information System Inventory Survey form used by the U.S. Environmental Protection Agency (EPA) is shown in Table 5.3.[20]

Who Should Conduct the Inventory?

Typically, a records management project team is formed to conduct the survey, often assisted by resources outside of the business units. These may be records management and IT staff members, business analysts, members of the legal staff, outside specialized consultants, or a combination of these groups. The greater the cross-section from the organization, the better, and the more expertise brought to bear on the project, the more likely it will be completed thoroughly and on time.

Critical to the effort is that those conducting the inventory are trained in the survey methods and analysis, so that when challenging issues arise, they will have the resources and knowhow to continue the effort and get the job done.

Determine Where Records Are Located

The inventory process is, in fact, a surveying process, and it involves going physically out into the units where the records are created, used, and stored. So mapping out where the records are *geographically*, is a basic necessity. Which buildings are they located in? Which office locations? Computer rooms?

Also, the inventory team must look *organizationally* at where the records reside, that is, which departments and business units to target and prioritize in the survey process.

Conduct the Inventory

There are several approaches that can be taken to conduct the inventory, including these three basic methods:

1. Distributing and collecting surveys.
2. Conducting in-person interviews.
3. Direct observation.

Creating and distributing a survey form is the traditional and proven way to collect e-records inventory data. This is a relatively fast and inexpensive way to gather the inventory data. The challenge is getting the surveys completed, and completed in a consistent fashion. This is where a strong executive sponsor can assist. They can make the survey a priority, and tie it to business objectives, making the survey completion compulsory. The survey is a good tool, and it can be used to cover more ground in the data collection process. If following up with interviews, the survey form is a good starting point; responses can be verified and clarified, and more detail can be gathered.

There are three primary ways to conduct the inventory: surveys, interviews, and observation. Combining these methods yields the best results.

Table 5.3 Electronic Information System Inventory Survey Form

Name of System   Identify the system by its official title.

Acronym   Identify the short name, or acronym, for this database.

Contact Information: Name, Organization, Phone, E-Mail   Identify the person or persons who are responsible for the administration or maintenance of the system and who are familiar with the business practices for which the system is used (i.e., System Administrator, Information Management Official, Information Resource Steward). Include both phone numbers and e-mail addresses.

Hardware   Identify the environment on which this system resides, for example, stand-alone workstation/PC (non-network), server-based, mainframe.

Software   Identify software currently used to build, operate, store, and deliver the system.

Where is this system used?   For example, agency-wide, region, local office

What is the purpose or function of the system?   Provide a brief executive summary describing the type of information in the system; the primary uses made of the system; who adds data, and why.

What is the program and/or legal authority for the creation of this system?   List any statutes, regulations or other governing authority for the creation of the system.

What is the source of system input and how is it entered into the system?   Is the input keyed into the system, scanned, or migrated? Where does the data originate (e.g., states, regulated community)?

Does the system contain electronic signatures?   Are electronic signatures used for verification?

What are the major outputs (e.g., reports, publications)?   Describe (1) the kinds of searches that are routinely run on this system and any features of its search (filter) capabilities, and (2) the format(s) in which the data or results of searches of the data can be produced (e.g., comma-delimited, tab-delimited, hard copy, and so forth). Is there a preferred format? Does that format require the use of proprietary software? If so, is there an alternative format for production? Can the data be exported to a standard format such as comma delimited?

How are the data arranged or sorted?   Is there a primary key for sorting or analysis?

What are the system dates?   When was the system created, and what is the date range of the information in the system?

What are the update and/or backup processes?   For example, are you able to obtain "historical snapshots" of data as they existed in the system at any time in the past (i.e., once the system is updated, does it retain a file with the preexisting version of the data)? If yes, describe any limitations on the earlier versions that can be retrieved.

In the ordinary course of business, is there routine archiving, destruction, purging, overwriting or alteration of information in the system that could result in the loss of data as it currently exists?

Is the system linked to other systems, and if so, which systems?   For example, is data migrated to another system?

Does the system produce a public version of the data?   For example, is a public version of the data available on EPA's Internet site?

What kind of documentation is available?   For example, user manual, data dictionary.

Are there any restrictions on the data? Does transfer of this data in any format raise any security issues? Are the data encrypted?

What are the retention requirements for the data in the system?   Is there an existing NARA-approved *records schedule* for this system? If there isn't an existing records schedule, how long does the information need to be retained and why?

Source: EPA, www.epa.gov/records/tools/toolkits/6step/6step-02.htm (accessed February 10, 2013).

Some issues may not be entirely clear initially, so following up with scheduled in-person interviews can dig deeper into the business processes where formal records are created and used. A good approach is to have users walk you through their typical day and how they access, use and create records—but be sure to interview managers too, as managers and users have differing needs and uses for records.[21]

You will need some direction to conduct formal observation, likely from IT staff or business analysts familiar with the recordkeeping systems and associated business processes. They will need to show you where business documents and records are created and stored. If there is an existing electronic records management (ERM) system or other automated search and retrieval tools available, they may be employed to speed the inventorying process.

When observing and inventorying e-records, starting in the server room and working outward toward the end user is a logical approach. Begin by enumerating the e-records created by enterprise software applications (such as accounting, enterprise resource planning [ERP], or customer relationship management [CRM] systems), and work your way to the departmental or business unit applications, on to shared network servers and then finally, out to individual desktop and laptop PCs, and other mobile devices. With today's smartphones, this can be a tricky area, due to the variety of platforms, operating systems, and capabilities. In a bring-your-own-device (BYOD) environment, records should not be stored on personal devices, but if they must be, they should be protected with technologies like encryption or information rights management (IRM).

There are always going to be thorny areas when attempting to inventory e-records to determine what files series exist in the organization. Mobile devices and removable media may contain business records. These must be identified, isolated, and any records on these media must be recorded for the inventory. Particularly troublesome are thumb or flash drives, which are compact yet can store 20 gigabytes of data or more. If your IG measures call for excluding these types of media, the ports they use can be blocked on PCs, tablets, smartphones, and other mobile computing devices. A sound IG program will consider the proper use of removable media and the potential impact on your records management program.[22]

The best approach for conducting the inventory is to combine the available inventorying methods, where possible. Begin by observing, distribute surveys, collect and analyze them, and then target key personnel for follow up interviews and walk-throughs. Utilize whatever automated tools that are available along the way. This approach is the most complete. *Bear in mind the focus is not on individual electronic files, but rather, the file series level for physical records, and at either the file series or system level for e-records (preferably the latter, according to guidance from NARA).*

Interviewing Programs/Service Staff

Interviews are a very good source of records inventory information. Talking with actual users will help the records lead or inventory team to better understand how documents and records are created and used in everyday operations. They can also report why they are needed; an exercise that can uncover some obsolete or unnecessary processes and practices. This is helpful in determining where e-records reside and how they are grouped in records series or by system, and ultimately, the proper length of their retention period and whether or not they should be archived or destroyed at the end of their useful life.[23]

Since interviewing is a time-intensive task, it is crucial that some time is spent in determining the key people to interview: it takes not only your time but theirs as well, and the surest way to lose momentum on an inventorying project is to have stakeholders believe you are wasting their time. "You need to interview representatives from all functional areas and levels of the program or service, including:

- Managers
- Supervisors
- Professional/technical staff
- Clerical/support staff

The people who work with the records can best describe to you their use. They will likely know where the records came from, if copies exist, who needs the records, any computer systems that are used, how long the records are needed and other important information that you need to know to schedule the records."[24]

Selecting Interviewees

As stated earlier, it is wise to include a cross-section of staff, managers, and "front line" employees to get a rounded view of how records are created and used. Managers have a different perspective and may not know the details of how staff workers utilize electronic records in their everyday operations.

A good lens to use is to focus on those who make decisions based on information contained in the electronic records, and to follow those decision-based processes through to completion, observing and interviewing at each level.

"For example, an application is received (mail room logs date and time), checked (clerk checks the application for completeness and enters into a computer system), verified (clerk verifies that the information on the application is correct), and approved (supervisor makes the decision to accept the application). These staff members may only be looking at specific pieces of the record and making decisions on those pieces."[25]

Interview Scheduling and Tips

One Golden Rule to consider is this: be considerate of other people's work time. Since they are probably not getting compensated for participating in the records inventory, the time you take to interview them is time taken away from compensated tasks they are evaluated on. So, once the interviewees are identified, provide as much advance notice as possible, follow up to confirm appointments, and stay within the scheduled time. Interviews should be kept to 20 to 60 minutes. Most of all—*never be late!*

Before starting any interviews, be sure to restate the goals and objectives of the inventorying process, and how the resulting output will benefit people in their jobs.

In some cases it may be advisable to conduct interviews in small groups, not only to save time, but to generate a discussion of how records are created, used, and stored. Some new insights may be gained.

Try to schedule interviews that are as convenient as possible for participants. That means providing them with questions in advance and holding the interviews as close to their work area as possible. Do not schedule interviews back-to-back with no time for a break between. You will need time for consolidating your thoughts and notes, and at times, interviews may exceed their planned time if a particularly enlightening line of questioning takes place.

If you have some analysis from the initial collection of surveys, share that with the interviewees so they can validate or help clarify the preliminary results. Provide it in advance, so they have some time to think about it and discuss it with their peers.[26]

Sample Interview Questionnaire

You'll need a pre-planned guide to structure the interview process. A good starting point is the sample questions presented in the questionnaire shown in Table 5.4. It is a useful tool that has been used successfully in actual records inventory projects.[27]

Table 5.4 Sample Interview Questionnaire

What is the mandate of the office?

Reporting structure of the department?

Who is the department liaison for the records inventory?

Are there any external agencies that impose guidelines, standards, or other requirements?

Is there a departmental records retention schedule?

Are their specific legislative requirements for creating or maintaining records?
Please provide a copy.

What are the business considerations that drives record keeping? Regulatory requirements? Legal requirements?

Does the department have an existing records management policy? Guidelines? Procedures?
Please provide a copy.

Does the department provide guidance to employees on what records are to be created?

What is the current level of awareness of employees about their responsibilities for records management?

How are nonrecords managed?

Does the department have a classification or file plans?

What are the business drivers for creating and maintaining records?

Where are records stored? Onsite? Offsite? One location? Multiple locations?

(continued)

Table 5.4   (*Continued*)

Does the department have records in sizes other than letter (8½ × 11)
What is the cutoff date for the records? Fiscal Year _____? Calendar Year? Other _____?
Are any tools used to track active records? Excel, Access, and so forth . . .
Does the department use imaging, document management, and so forth . . .
Is the department subject to audits? Internal? External?
Who conducts the audits?
Are any records in the department confidential or sensitive?
Are there guidelines for destroying obsolete records?
What disposition methods are authorized or required?
How does disposition occur? Paper? Electronic? Other?
What extent does the department rely on each individual to destroy records? Paper? Electronic? Other?
What principles govern decisions for determining the scope of records that must be held or frozen for an audit or investigations?
How is the hold or freeze communicated to employees?

Source: Charmaine Brooks, IMERGE Consulting, e-mail to author, March 20, 2012.

Analyze and Verify the Results

Once collected, there will be some required follow-up to verify and clarify responses. Often, this can be effectively done over the telephone. For particularly complex and important areas, a follow-up in person visit can clarify the responses and gather insights.

Once the inventory draft is completed, a good practice is to go out into the business units and/or system areas and verify the findings of the survey. Once presented with findings in black and white, key stakeholders may have additional insights that are relevant to consider before finalizing the report. Do not miss out on the opportunity to allow "power users" and other key parties to provide valuable input.

Be sure to tie the findings in the final report of the records inventory to the business goals that launched the effort. This helps to underscore the purpose and importance of the

Be sure to tie the findings in the final report of the records inventory to the business goals that launched the effort.

effort, and will help in getting that final signoff from the executive sponsor that states the project is complete and there is no more work to do.

Depending on the magnitude of the project, it may (and *should*) turn into a formal IG program that methodically manages records in a consistent fashion in accordance with internal governance guidelines and external compliance and legal demands.

UK Approach to the Records Inventorying Process

There are multiple ways to frame the effort for records inventorying and to provide a planning tool to guide you through the process. In the United Kingdom, the Scottish government has published its approach to inventorying records, broken out by six stages.[28]

Stage 1: Creating a Project Schedule and Plan

Due to the fact that conducting, compiling, and completing a records inventory is a complex and far-reaching task that requires a cross-section of participants, *planning is essential*. Progress may be slow but it must be methodical, and it requires the force of an executive sponsor to drive it to completion. It will span multiple systems and locations and staff commitment is needed to bring the project to completion. A plan and schedule including milestones must be laid out, and a tailored records survey form must be developed and distributed. It is unwieldy to attempt to survey the entire enterprise at once. "A practical way to compile an inventory is to do it in steps or stages, for example, by targeting specific directorates, departments, or locations until all records have been covered."[29]

Stage 2: Clear Communication of Business Objectives and Scope

The inventory process is a tough sell, and a long haul. Users may not perceive any benefit, since it is "not their job." So the end *results* should be focused on, that is, users will be able to find information and records faster and more easily, and they will be able to have more confidence in the information and records they retrieve. All stakeholders should be clear on the business objectives and purpose of the inventorying process, and its scope. They must understand the big picture, that this inventorying process is a part of information governance; and they must understand the details, down to the specific directions for completing the survey inventory form, when it is due, and who is to fill it out. Beyond the inventory, stakeholders must be clear on the going-forward process for keeping the records inventory up-to-date.

Stage 3: Tailoring the Records Inventory Survey

The survey form itself is crucial. It must be tailored to the specific organization and comprehensive enough to gather all required information, yet it must not be excessively long or elaborate (increasing the likelihood that it will be ignored or de-layed). Training and/or explanatory notes will help ensure compliance and consistency in responses. There are differing approaches to records inventory survey distribution. Sometimes there are only the resources to distribute and collect the survey forms, and compile the results. This is relatively fast and inexpensive. Sometimes a dedicated team can be dispatched to conduct in-depth observation and interviews. This takes more time, is more costly, but more thorough. When possible, perhaps the best approach is a blended one, which consists of surveys, interviews, observations, and utilizing any automated tools available to search and retrieve records. "The appropriate method will depend upon the resource available and the level of understanding and commitment available from directorate and departmental staff."[30]

The challenge in using the survey only approach is getting the individual director-ates and departments to properly and expediently complete the survey.

Stage 4: Inventory Form Fulfillment

All target areas should be sent the records inventory survey form, with any available detailed notes and instructions that may pertain to that business area. Participants should be clear on the deadline and how to contact the records inventory team leader or lead consultant with any questions or issues.

Stage 5: Records Inventory Tabulation and Documentation

The records inventory team may set up a spreadsheet or database to record and compile the responses. Each inventory form response should be tracked with its own unique identification number. Then some analysis needs to be done to determine where some consolidations or improvements can be made, or where duplications may exist." It depends on the objectives of the inventory, and how far the revamping and organiza-tion of the records is intended to progress. If developing an enterprise-wide taxonomy is the goal, then more analysis must go into the compilation of the results to see how some new thinking regarding the classification of records may benefit the enterprise. In general, larger groupings or 'buckets' are going to make it easier to include more records, so searches should be faster and more complete. The level of granularity is an issue that would need further discussion during the project.

Stage 6: Ongoing Inventorying Program Requirements

Although the initial inventory is a project, maintaining the inventory on an ongoing basis is a *program*. It is a program that requires information governance (IG) policies, moni-toring, and periodic tests, checks or audits. Once in place, the new "system"—including policies, processes, and technologies—should keep the records inventory current.[31]

Appraising the Value of Records

Part of the process of determining the retention and disposition schedule of records is to appraise their value. Records can have value in different ways, which affects retention decisions. "**Records appraisal** is an analysis of all records within an agency [or

Records appraisal is based upon the information contained in the records inventory.

business] to determine their administrative, fiscal, historical, legal, or other archival value.[32] The purpose of this process is to determine for how long, in what format, and under what conditions a record series ought to be preserved. *Records appraisal is based upon the information contained in the records inventory.* Records series shall be either preserved permanently or disposed of when no longer required for the current operations of an agency or department, depending upon:

- *Historical value* or the usefulness of the records for historical research, including records that show an agency [or business] origin, administrative development, and present organizational structure.
- *Administrative value* or the usefulness of the records for carrying on [a business or] an agency's current and future work, and to document the development and operation of that agency over time.
- *Regulatory and statutory* [value to meet] requirements.
- *Legal value* or the usefulness of the records to document and define legally enforceable rights or obligations of [business owners, shareholders, or a] government and/or citizens.
- *Fiscal value* or the usefulness of the records to the administration of [a business or] an agency's current financial obligations, and to document the development and operation of that agency over time
- Other archival value as determined by the State [or corporate] Archivist."[33] (italics added)

Ensuring Adoption and Compliance of RM Policy

The inventorying process in not a one-shot deal: It is only useful if the records inventory is kept up-to-date, so it should be reviewed, at least annually. A process should be put in place so that business unit or agency heads notify the records management head/lead if a new file series or system has been put in place and new records collections are created.[34]

The following five tips can help ensure that a records management program achieves its goals:

1. **Records management is everyone's role**: The volume and diversity of business records, from e-mail to reports to tweets, means that the person who creates or receives a record is in the best [position] to classify it. Everyone in the organization needs to adopt the records management program.
2. **Don't micro-classify**: Having hundreds, or possibly thousands of records classification categories may seem like a logical way to organize the multitude of different records in a company. However, the

average information worker, whose available resources are already under pressure, does not want to spend any more time than necessary classifying records. Having a few broad classifications makes the decision process simpler and faster.

3. **Talk the talk from the top on down**: A culture of compliance starts at the top. Businesses should establish a senior-level steering committee comprised of executives from legal, compliance, and information technology (IT). A committee like this signals the company's commitment to compliant records management and ensures enterprise adoption.

4. **Walk the walk, consistently**: For compliance to become second nature, it needs to be clearly communicated to everyone in the organization, and policies and procedures must be accessible. Training should be rigorous and easily available, and organizations may consider rewarding compliance through financial incentives, promotions and corporate-wide recognition.

5. **Measure the measurable**: The ability to measure adherence to policy and adoption of procedures should be included in core business operations and audits. Conduct a compliance assessment, including a gap analysis, at least once a year, and prepare an action plan to close any identified holes.

The continuing growth of data challenges an organization's ability to use and store its records in a compliant and cost-effective manner. Contrary to current practices, the solution is not to hire more technology services vendors or to adopt multiple technologies. The key to compliance is consistency, with a unified enterprise-wide approach for managing all records, regardless of their format or location.[35]

So a steady and consistent IG approach that includes controls, audits, and clear communication is key to maintaining an accurate and current records inventory.

CHAPTER SUMMARY: **KEY POINTS**

- NARA recommends that e-records are inventoried by information system, versus file series, which is the traditional approach for physical records.

- Generally Accepted Recordkeeping Principles or "GAR Principles" or "The Principles" are "information management and governance of record creation, organization, security, maintenance and other activities used to effectively support recordkeeping of an organization."

- It may be helpful to use a recordkeeping methodology such as the GAR Principles or D.I.R.K.S. to guide inventorying efforts.

(Continued)

(*Continued*)

- Perhaps the organization has a handle on their paper and microfilmed records, but e-records have been growing exponentially and spiraling out of control.

- Whatever the business goals for the inventorying effort are, they must be conveyed to all stakeholders, and that message must be reinforced periodically and consistently, and through multiple means.

- An appropriate scope might enumerate the records of a single program or division, several functional series across divisions, or records that fall within a certain time frame, versus an entire enterprise.

- The completed records inventory contributes toward the pursuit of an organization's IG objectives in a number of ways.

- There are basic three ways to conduct the inventory: surveys, interviews, and observation. Combining these methods yields the best results.

- Additional information not included in inventories of physical records must be collected in any inventory of e-records.

- Be sure to tie the findings in the final report of the records inventory to the business goals that launched the effort.

- Records appraisal is based upon the information contained in the records inventory.

- Records can have different types of value to organizations: historical, administrative, regulatory and statutory, legal value, fiscal value, or other archival value as determined by an archivist.

- Consistency in managing records across an enterprise, regardless of media, format or location, is the key to compliance.

Notes

1. "Disposition of Federal Records: A Records Management Handbook," The U.S. National Archives and Records Administration, 2000, web edition, www.archives.gov/records-mgmt/publications/disposition-of-federal-records/chapter-3.html.
2. Ibid.
3. State and Consumer Services Agency Department of General Services, "Electronic Records Management Handbook," State of California Records Management Program, February 2002, www.documents.dgs.ca.gov/osp/recs/ermhbkall.pdf.
4. U.S. Environmental Protection Agency, "Six Steps to Better Files," updated March 8, 2012, www.epa.gov/records/tools/toolkits/6step/6step-02.htm.
5. Margaret Rouse, "Generally Accepted Recordkeeping Principles," updated March 2011, http://searchcompliance.techtarget.com/definition/Generally-Accepted-Recordkeeping-Principles-GARP (accessed March 19, 2012).

6. Ibid.
7. Ibid.
8. Public Record Office, "Guidance for an Inventory of Electronic Record Collections: A Toolkit," September 2000, www.humanrightsinitiative.org/programs/ai/rti/implementation/general/guidance_for_inventory_elect_rec_collection.pdf, pp. 5–6.
9. Public Record Office, "Guidance for an Inventory of Electronic Record Collections: A Toolkit."
10. National Archives, "Frequently Asked Questions about Records Inventories," updated October 27, 2000, www.archives.gov/records-mgmt/faqs/inventories.html.
11. William Saffady, Managing Electronic Records, 4th ed., *Journal of the Medical Library Association*, 2009, www.ncbi.nlm.nih.gov/pmc/articles/PMC2947138/.
12. Jesse Wilkins, "The First Step: Inventory Your Electronic Records," IMERGE Consulting, http://pr1vacy.blogspot.mx/2005/11/first-step-inventory-your-electronic.html (accessed October 11, 2012).
13. National Archives, "Frequently Asked Questions about Records Inventories."
14. Ibid.
15. Ibid.
16. Ibid.
17. Ibid.
18. Charmaine Brooks, e-mail to author, March 20, 2012.
19. www.archives.gov/records-mgmt/faqs/inventories.html (accessed April 9, 2012).
20. U.S. Environmental Protection Agency, "Six Steps to Better Files," updated March 8, 2012, www.epa.gov/records/tools/toolkits/6step/6step-02.htm.
21. Wilkins, "The First Step: Inventory Your Electronic Records."
22. Ibid.
23. Government of Alberta, Records and Information Management, www.im.gov.ab.ca/index.cfm?page=imtopics/Records.html.
24. Ibid.
25. Ibid.
26. Ibid.
27. Charmaine Brooks, e-mail to author, March 20, 2012.
28. The Scottish Government, "Compiling a Records Inventory," updated April 22, 2010, www.scotland.gov.uk/Publications/2010/04/22093418/5 .
29. Ibid.
30. Ibid.
31. Ibid.
32. Maryland State Archives, "Retention Schedule Preparation," June 1, 2012, www.msa.md.gov/msa/intromsa/html/record_mgmt/retention_schedule.html.
33. Ibid.
34. NHS Connecting for Health, www.connectingforhealth.nhs.uk (accessed April 10, 2012).
35. Wortzman Nickle Professional Corporation, "Effective Records Management—Part 4—Ensuring Adoption and Compliance of RM Policy," 2009, www.wortzmannickle.com/ediscovery-blog/2011/12/14/rmpart4 (accessed April 12, 2012).

CHAPTER 6

Taxonomy Development for E-Records

Barb Blackburn, CRM, with Robert Smallwood;
edited by Seth Earley

The creation of electronic documents and records is exploding exponentially, multiplying at an increasing rate, and sifting through all this information results in a lot of wasted, unproductive (and expensive) knowledge-worker time. This has real costs to the enterprise. According to the study, "The High Cost of Not Finding Information," an IDC report, "knowledge workers spend at least 15 to 25 percent of the workday searching for information. Only half the searches are successful."[1] *Experts point to poor* **taxonomy** *design as being at the root of these failed searches and lost productivity.*

Taxonomies are at the heart of the solution to harnessing and governing information. *Taxonomies are hierarchical classification structures* used to standardize the naming and organization of information, and their role and use in managing electronic records cannot be overestimated.

Although the topic of taxonomies can get complex, in **electronic records management** (ERM), they are a sort of online card catalog that is cross-referenced with hyperlinks that is used to organize and manage records and documents.[2]

According to Forrester Research, taxonomies "represent agreed-upon terms and relationships between ideas or things and serve as a glossary or knowledge map helping to define how the business thinks about itself and represents itself, its products and services to the outside world."[3]

Gartner Group researchers warn that "to get value from the vast quantities of information and knowledge, enterprises must establish discipline and a system of governance over the creation, capture, organization, access, and utilization of information."[4]

Over time, organizations have implemented taxonomies to attempt to gain control over their mounting masses of information, creating an orderly structure to harness unstructured information (such as e-documents, e-mail messages, scanned records, and other digital assets), and to improve searchability and access.[5]

Taxonomies for electronic records management (ERM) standardize the vocabulary used to describe records, making it easier and faster for searches and retrievals to be made.

> Knowledge workers spend at least 15 to 25 percent of the workday searching for information with only half the searches being successful.

Search engines are able to deliver faster and more accurate results from good taxonomy design by limiting and standardizing terms. A robust and efficient taxonomy design is the underpinning that indexes collections of documents uniformly and helps knowledge workers find the proper files to complete their work. The way a taxonomy is organized and implemented is critical to the long-term success of any enterprise, as it directly impacts the quality and productivity of knowledge workers who need organized, trusted information to make business decisions.

It doesn't sound so complicated, simply categorizing and cataloguing information, yet most enterprises have had disappointing or inconsistent results from the taxonomies they use to organize information. *Designing taxonomies is hard work.* Developing an efficient and consistent taxonomy is a detailed, tedious, labor-intensive team effort on the front end, and its maintenance must be consistent and regular and follow established **information governance** (IG) guidelines, in order to maintain its effectiveness.

Once a taxonomy is in place, it requires systematic updates and reviews, to ensure that guidelines are being followed and new document and record types are included in the taxonomy structure. Technology tools like **text mining, social tagging,** and **auto-classification** can help uncover trends and suggest candidate terms. (More on these technologies later in this chapter.)

When done correctly, the business benefits of good taxonomy design go much further than speeding search and retrieval; an efficient, operational taxonomy also is a part of IG efforts that help the organization to manage and control information so that it may efficiently respond to litigation requests, comply with governmental regulations, and meet customer needs (both external and internal).

Taxonomies are crucial to finding information and optimizing knowledge worker productivity, yet some surveys estimate that nearly half of organizations do not have a standardized taxonomy in place.[6]

According to the Montague Institute, "The way your company organizes information (i.e., its taxonomy) is critical to its future. A taxonomy not only frames the way people make decisions, but also helps them find the information to weigh all the alternatives. *A good taxonomy helps decision makers see all the perspectives, and 'drill down' to get details from each, and explore lateral relationships among them*" (italics added).[7] Without it, your company will find it difficult to leverage intellectual capital, engage in electronic commerce, keep up with employee training, and get the most out of strategic partnerships.

With the explosion in growth of electronic documents and records, a standardized classification structure that a taxonomy imposes optimizes records retrievals for daily business operations and also legal and regulatory demands.[8]

Since end-users can choose from topic areas, subject categories, or groups of documents, rather than blindly typing word searches, *taxonomies narrow searches and speed search time and retrieval.*[9]

> To maximize efficient and effective retrieval of records for legal, business, and regulatory purposes, organizations must develop and implement taxonomies.

Taxonomies speed up the process of retrieving records because end-users can select from subject categories or topics.

"The link between taxonomies and usability is a strong one. The best taxonomies efficiently guide users to exactly the content they need. Usability is judged in part by how easily content can be found," according to the Montague Institute.[10]

Importance of Navigation and Classification

Taxonomies need to be considered from two main perspectives: Navigation and Classification. *Most people consider the former, but not the latter.* The navigational construct that is represented by a taxonomy is evident in most file structures and file shares—the nesting of folders within folders—and in many web applications where users are navigating hierarchical arrangements of pages or links. However, classification is frequently behind the scenes. A document can "live" in a folder that the user can navigate to. *But within that folder, the document can be classified in different ways through the application of metadata.* (See Chapter 16, Metadata Governance, Standards, and Strategies, for more detail.) Metadata are descriptive fields that delineate a (document or) record's characteristics, such as author, title, department of origin, date created, length, number of pages or file size, and so forth. The metadata is also part of the taxonomy or related to the taxonomy. In this way, usability can be impacted by giving the user *multiple ways* to retrieve their information.[11]

When Is a New Taxonomy Needed?

In some cases, organizations have existing taxonomy structures but they have gone out of date or have not been maintained. They may not have been developed with best practices in mind or with correct representation of user groups, tasks, or applications. There are many reasons why taxonomies no longer provide the full value that they can provide. There are certain situations that clearly indicate that the organization needs a refactored or new taxonomy.[12]

If knowledge workers in your organization regularly conduct searches and receive hundreds of pages of results, then you need a new taxonomy. If you have developed a vast knowledge base of documents and records, and designated **subject matter experts** (SME), yet employees struggle to find answers, you need a new taxonomy. If

Taxonomies need to be considered from two main perspectives: navigation and classification.

Poor search results, inconsistent or conflicting file plans, and the inability to locate information on a timely basis are indications taxonomy work is needed.

there is no standardization of the way content is classified and catalogued, or there is conflict between how different groups or business units classify content, you need a new taxonomy. And if your organization has experienced delays, fines, or undue costs in producing documentation to meet compliance requests or legal demands, your organization needs to work on a new taxonomy.[13]

Taxonomies Improve Search Results

Taxonomies can improve a search engine's ability to deliver results to user queries in finding documents and records in an enterprise. The way the digital content is indexed (e.g., spidering, crawling, rule sets, algorithms) is a separate issue, and a good taxonomy improves search results regardless of the indexing method.[14]

Search engines struggle to deliver accurate and refined results since the wording in queries may vary and also words can have multiple meanings. A taxonomy addresses these problems since the terms are set and defined in a **controlled vocabulary**.

Metadata, which, as stated earlier, are data fields that describe content, such as document type, creator, date of creation, and so forth, *must be leveraged in the taxonomy design effort.*

A formal definition of metadata is "standardized administrative or descriptive data about a document [or record] that is common for all documents [or records] in a given repository." Standardized metadata elements of e-documents should be utilized and supported by including them in controlled vocabularies when possible.[15]

The goal of a taxonomy development effort is to help users find the information they need, in a logical and familiar way, even if they are not sure what the correct search terminology is. *Good taxonomy design makes it easier and more comfortable for users to browse topics and drill down into more narrow searches to find the documents and records they need.* Where it really becomes useful and helps contribute to productivity is when complex or compound searches are conducted.

Taxonomies improve search results by increasing accuracy and also improving the user experience.

Metadata, which are the characteristics of a document expressed in data fields, must be leveraged in taxonomy design.

On a continuing basis, text mining can be conducted on documents to learn of emerging potential taxonomy terms. Text mining is basically performing detailed full-text searches on the content of a document to determine patterns and trends. And with more sophisticated tools like neural computing and artificial intelligence (AI), *concepts*, not just key words, can be discovered and leveraged for improving search quality for users.

Another tool is the use of **faceted search** (sometimes referred to as faceted navigation or faceted browsing) where, for instance, document collections are classified in multiple ways, rather than in a single, rigid taxonomy. Knowledge workers may apply multiple filters to search across documents and records and find better and more complete results. And when they are not quite sure what they are looking for, or if it exists, then a good taxonomy can help suggest terms, related terms, and associated content, truly contributing to enterprise **knowledge management** (KM) efforts, adding to corporate memory, and increasing the organizational knowledge base.[16] Good KM helps to provide valuable training content for new employees and helps to reduce the impact of turnover and retiring employees.

Search is ultimately about metadata—whether your content has explicit metadata or not. The search engine creates a forward index and determines what words are contained in the documents being searched. It then inverts that index to provide the documents that words are contained in. This is effectively metadata about the content. A taxonomy can be used to enrich that search index in various ways. This does require configuration and integration with search engines, but the result is the ability to increase both precision and recall of search results. Search results can also be grouped and clustered using a taxonomy. This allows large numbers of results to be more easily scanned and understood by the user. Many of these functions are determined by the capabilities of search tools and document and records management systems. As search functionality is developed, don't miss this opportunity to leverage the taxonomy.

Records Grouping Rationale

The primary reasons that records are grouped together are:

- They tie together documents with like content, purpose, or theme.
- To improve search and retrieval capabilities.
- To identify content creators, owners, and managers.

Text mining is basically performing detailed full-text searches on the content of a document to determine patterns and trends.

- To provide an understandable context.
- For retention and disposition scheduling purposes.[17]

Taxonomies group records with common attributes. The groupings are constructed not only for records management classification and functions, but also to support end users in their search and retrieval activities. Associating documents of a similar theme enables users to find documents when they do not know the exact document name. Choosing the theme or topic enables the users to narrow their search to find the relevant information.

The theme or grouping also places the document name into context. Words have many meanings and adding a theme to them further defines them. For example, the word "article" could pertain to a newspaper article, an item or object, or a section of a legal document. If it were grouped with publications, periodicals, and so on the meaning would be clear. The challenge here is when to choose to have a separate category for "article" or to group "article" with other similar publications. Some people tend to develop finer levels of granularity in classification structures. These people can be called the "splitters." Those who group things together are "lumpers." *But there can be clear rules for when to lump versus split.* Experts recommend splitting into another category when business needs demand that we treat the content differently or users need to segment the content for some purpose. This rule can be applied to many situations when trying to determine whether a new category is needed.[18]

Management, security, and access requirements are usually based on a user's role in a process. Grouping documents based on processes makes the job of assigning the responsibilities and access easier. For example, documents used in financial processes can be sensitive and there is a need to restrict access to only those users that have the role in the business with a need to know.

Records retention periods are developed to be applied to a series (or group) of documents. When similar documents are grouped, it is easier to apply retention rules. However, when the grouping for retention is not the same as the grouping for other user views, a cross-mapping (**file plan**) scheme must be developed and incorporated into the taxonomy effort.

Business Classification Scheme, File Plans, and Taxonomy

In its simplest definition a **business classification scheme** (BCS) is a hierarchical conceptual representation of the business activity performed by an organization.[19] The highest level of a BCS is called an *Information Series*, which signifies "high-level business functions" of a business or governmental agency, and the next level is *Themes*, which represent the specific activities that feed into the high-level functions at the information series level. These two top levels are rarely changed in an organization.[20]

A BCS is often viewed as synonymous with the term *file plan*, which is the shared file structure in an Electronic Records Management (ERM) System, but it is *not a direct file plan*.

Yet, a file plan can be developed and mapped back to the BCS, and automated through an electronic document and records management system (EDRMS) or electronic records management (ERM) system.[21]

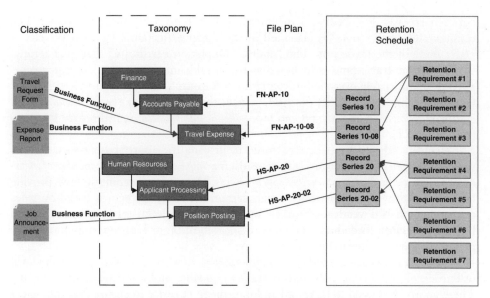

Figure 6.1   Mapping the Records Retention Schedule to the Taxonomy
Source: Blackburn Consulting.

A BCS is required by ISO 15489, the international records management standard, and, together with the folders and records it contains, comprises what in the paper-based environment was called simply a "Fileplan." A BCS is therefore a full representation of the business of an organization.

Classification and Taxonomy

Classification of records extends beyond the categorization of records in the taxonomy. It also must include the application of retention requirements. These are legal and business requirements that specify the length of time a record must be maintained. A **Records Retention Schedule** is a document that specifies the periods for which an organization's records should be retained to meet its operational needs and to comply with legal and other requirements. *The Records Retention Schedule groups documents into records series that relate to specific business activities.* This grouping is performed because laws and regulations are mainly based on the business activity that creates the documents. These business activities are not necessarily the same as the activities described in the hierarchy of the taxonomy. Therefore, there must be a method to map the Records Retention Schedule to the Taxonomy. This is accomplished with a File Plan. The File Plan facilitates the application of retention rules during document categorization without requiring a user to know or understand the Records Retention Schedule (see Figure 6.1).

Metadata and Taxonomy

One potential limitation of a purely hierarchical taxonomy is the lack of association between tiers (or nodes). There are often one-to-many or many-to-many associations between records. For example, an employee travels to a certification course. The resultant "expense report" is classified in the Finance/Accounts Payable/Travel Expense node of the taxonomy. The "course completion certificate" that is generated from the same travel (and is included as backup documentation for the expense report) is appropriately classified in the Human Resources/Training and Certification/Continuing Education node. *For ERM systems that don't provide the functionality for a multifaceted taxonomy, metadata is used to provide the link between the nodes in the taxonomy* (see Figure 6.2).

Metadata schema must be structured to provide the appropriate associations as well as meet the users' keyword search needs. *It is important to limit the number of metadata fields that a user must manually apply to records.* Most recordkeeping systems provide the functionality to automatically assign certain metadata to records based on rules that are established in advance and set up by a system administrator (referred in this book as **inherited metadata**). The record's classification or location in the taxonomy is appropriate for inherited metadata.

Metadata can also be applied by autocategorization software. This can reduce the level of burden placed on the user and increase the quality and consistency of metadata. These approaches need to be tested and fine-tuned in order to ensure that they meet the needs of the organization.[22]

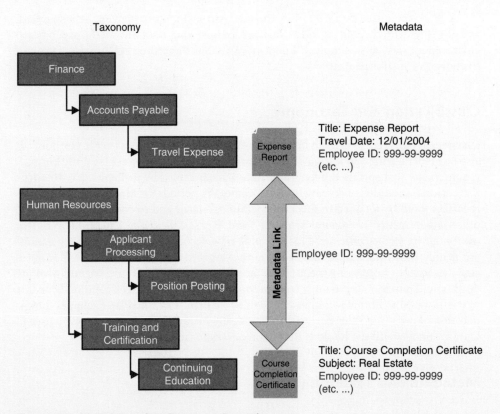

Figure 6.2   Metadata Link to Taxonomy Example
Source: Blackburn Consulting.

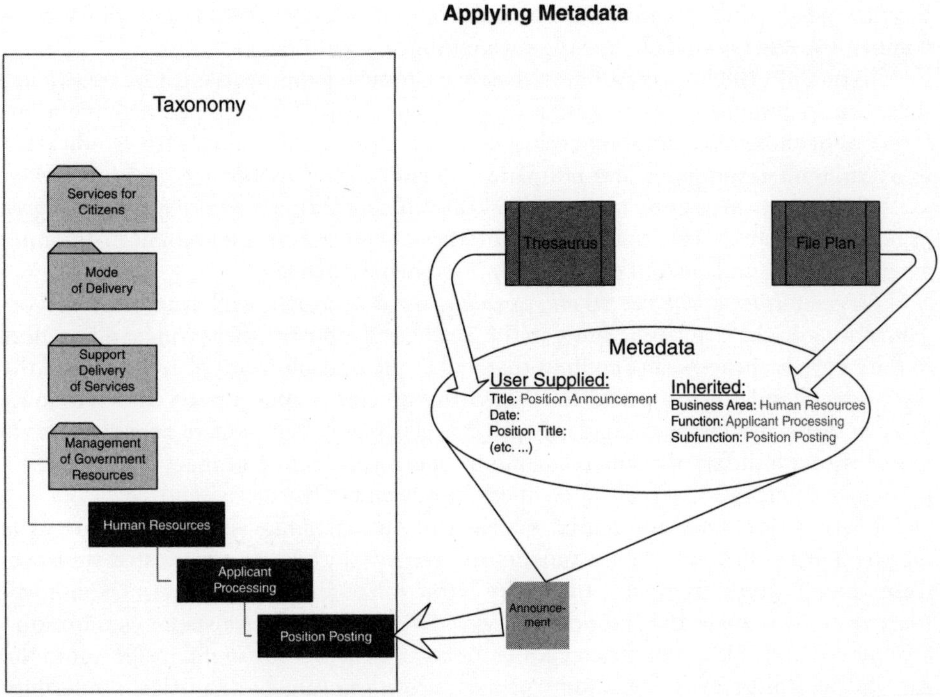

Applying Metadata

Figure 6.3   Application of Metadata to Taxonomy Structure

The File Plan will provide the necessary data to link the taxonomy to the document via inherited metadata. In most systems, this metadata is applied by the system and is transparent to the users. Additional metadata will need to be applied by the user. To maintain consistency, a **thesaurus**, which contains all synonyms and definitions, is used to enforce naming conventions (see Figure 6.3).

Prebuilt versus Custom Taxonomies

Taxonomy templates for specific vertical industries (e.g., law, pharmaceuticals, aerospace) are provided by ECM, ERM/EDRMS, KM, and enterprise search vendors, and trade associations. These prebuilt taxonomies use consistent terminology, have been tried and tested, and incorporate industry best practices, where possible. They can provide a jump-start and faster implementation at a lower cost than developing a custom taxonomy in-house or with external consulting assistance.

There are advantages and disadvantages to each approach. A prebuilt taxonomy will typically have some parameters that are able to be configured to better meet the business needs of an organization, yet compromises and trade-offs will have to be made. It may also introduce unfamiliar terminology that knowledge workers will be forced to adapt to, increasing training time and costs, and reducing its overall effectiveness. These considerations must be factored into the "build or buy" decision. Using the custom-developed approach, a taxonomy can be tailored to meet the precise business needs of an organization or business unit, and can include nuances such as company-specific nomenclature and terminology.[23]

Frequently, the longer and more costly customized approach must be used, since there are no prebuilt taxonomies that fit well. This is especially the case with niche enterprises or those operating in developing or esoteric markets. For mature industries, more prebuilt taxonomies and template choices exist. *Attempting to tailor a prebuilt taxonomy can actually end up taking longer than building one from scratch if it is not a good fit in the first place,* so best practices dictate that organizations use prebuilt taxonomies where practical, and custom design taxonomies where needed.

There really is no "one size fits all" when it comes to taxonomy. And even when two organizations do the exact same thing in the exact same industry, there will be differences in their culture, process, and content that will require customization and tuning of the taxonomy. Standards are useful for improving efficiency of a process and taxonomy projects really are internal standards projects. However, competitive advantage is attained through differentiation. A taxonomy specifically tuned to meet the needs of a particular enterprise is actually a competitive advantage.[24]

There is one other alternative, which is to "autogenerate" a taxonomy from the metadata in a collection of e-documents and records, by using sophisticated statistical techniques like term frequency and entity extraction to attempt to create a taxonomy.[25] It seems to be perhaps the "best of both worlds" in that it offers instant customization at a low cost, but, although these types of tools can help provide useful insights into the data on the front end of a taxonomy project, providing valuable statistical renderings, the only way to focus on user needs is to interview and work with users to gain insights into their business process needs and requirements, while considering the business objectives of the taxonomy project. This cannot be done with mathematical computations—the human factor is key.

In essence, these auto-generated taxonomy tools can determine which terms and documents are used frequently, but they cannot assess the *real value* of information being used by knowledge workers and *how* they use the information. That takes consultation with stakeholders, studied observation, and business analysis.[26] *Machine-generated taxonomies look like they were generated by machines*—which is to say they are not very usable by humans.[27]

Controlled Vocabularies and Hierarchical Taxonomies

A controlled vocabulary "is simply a restricted list of words or terms for some specialized purpose, usually for indexing, labeling, or categorizing."[28] The terms are controlled in that only those terms may be used to index and categorize business documents and records, and the addition or changing of terms is also restricted, tracked, and controlled, under the umbrella of IG. A controlled vocabulary forces consistency

Best practices dictate that taxonomy development includes designing the taxonomy structure and heuristic principles to align with user needs.

in the use of "index terms, tags, or labels to avoid ambiguity and the overlooking of information."[29]

Often, synonyms must be used in controlled vocabularies so that similar terms to describe the same records series are incorporated so that search results are more complete and accurate. A **synonym ring** (or **synset)** denotes that no synonym is preferred and all have equal weight. For instance, "human resources" may be the same term as "personnel." Various (agreed-on) synonyms may be displayed to the user when making searches in the ERM/EDRMS system. The taxonomist or taxonomy team may designate a "preferred" term among synonyms.

Thesaurus Use in Taxonomies

A **thesaurus** in the use of taxonomies contains the agreed-on synonyms and similar names for terms used in a controlled vocabulary. So, "invoice" may be listed as the equivalent term for "bill" when categorizing records. The thesaurus goes further and lists "information about each term and their relationships to other terms within the same thesaurus."

A thesaurus is similar to a hierarchical taxonomy but also includes "associative relationships."[30] An associative relationship is a conceptual relationship. *It is the "see also" that we may come across in the back of the book index.* But the question is, Why do we want to see it? Associative relationships can provide a linkage to specific classes of information of interest to users and for particular processes. Use of associative relationships can provide a great deal of functionality in content and document management systems and needs to be considered in records management applications.[31]

There are international standards for thesauri creation from the International Organization for Standardization (ISO), American National Standards Institute (ANSI), and the British Standards Institution (BSI).[32]

ISO 25964, "Information and Documentation—Thesauri and Interoperability with Other Vocabularies," "will draw on [the British standard, BS 8723] but reorganize the content to fit into two parts." Part 1, "Thesauri for Information Retrieval," of the standard ISO 25964 was published in August 2011. Part 2, "Interoperability with Other Vocabularies," is in development and should be approved in 2013.[33]

Taxonomy Types

Taxonomies used in ERM systems are usually hierarchical where categories (nodes) in the hierarchy progress from general to specific. Each subsequent node is a subset of the higher level node. There are three basic types of hierarchical taxonomies: subject, business-unit, and functional.[34]

A *subject* taxonomy uses controlled terms for subjects. The subject headings are arranged in alphabetical order by the broadest subjects, with more precise subjects listed under them. An example is the Library of Congress subject headings (LCSH) used to categorize holdings in a library collection (see Figure 6.4). Even the Yellow Pages could be considered a subject taxonomy.

```
...
H — SOCIAL SCIENCES
J — POLITICAL SCIENCE
K — LAW
L — EDUCATION
M — MUSIC AND BOOKS ON MUSIC
N — FINE ARTS
P — LANGUAGE AND LITERATURE
Q — SCIENCE
R — MEDICINE
–   Subclass RA Public aspects of medicine
–   Subclass RB Pathology
–   Subclass RC Internal medicine
    –  RC31-1245 Internal medicine
    –  RC49-52 Psychosomatic medicine
    –  RC251 Constitutional diseases (General)
    –  RC254-282 Neoplasm. Tumors. Oncology
...
```

Figure 6.4   Library of Congress Subject Headings

It is difficult to establish a universally recognized set of terms in a subject taxonomy. If users are unfamiliar with the topic, they may not know the appropriate term heading with which to begin their search. For example, say a person is searching through the Yellow Pages for a place to purchase eyeglasses. They begin their search alphabetically by turning to the E's and scanning for the term eyeglasses. Since there are no topics titled "eyeglasses," the person consults the Yellow Pages index, finds the term *eyeglasses*, and this provides a list of preferred terms or "see alsos" that direct the person to "Optical—Retail" for a list of eyeglass businesses (see Figure 6.5).[35]

In both examples (LCSH and Yellow Pages), the subject taxonomy is supported by a thesaurus. Again, a thesaurus is a controlled vocabulary that includes synonyms, related terms, and preferred terms. In the case of the Yellow Pages, the index functions as a basic thesaurus.

In a *business-unit*-based taxonomy the hierarchy reflects the organizational charts (e.g., Department/Division/Unit). Records are categorized based on the business unit that manages them. Figure 6.6 shows the partial detail of one node of a business-unit based taxonomy that was developed for a county government.[36]

One advantage of a business-unit-based taxonomy is that it mimics most existing paper-filing system schemas. Therefore, users are not required to learn a "new" system. However, conflicts arise when documents are managed or shared among multiple business units. As an example, for the county government referenced earlier,

There are three basic types of hierarchical taxonomies: subject, business-unit, and functional.

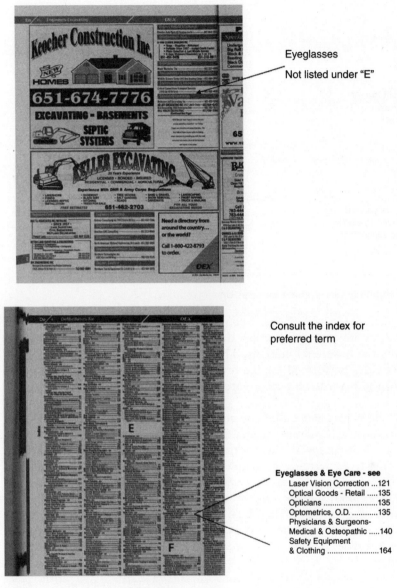

Eyeglasses
Not listed under "E"

Consult the index for
preferred term

Eyeglasses & Eye Care - see
Laser Vision Correction ...121
Optical Goods - Retail 135
Opticians 135
Optometrics, O.D. 135
Physicians & Surgeons-
Medical & Osteopathic 140
Safety Equipment
& Clothing 164

Figure 6.5   Yellow Pages Example

a property transfer document called the "TD1000" is submitted to the Recording Office for recording and then forwarded to the Assessor for property tax evaluation processing. This poses a dilemma as to where to categorize the TD1000 in the taxonomy.[37]

Another issue arises with organizational changes. When the organizational structure changes, so must the business-unit based taxonomy.

In a *functional* taxonomy records are categorized based on the functions and activities that produce them (function/activity/transaction). The organization's

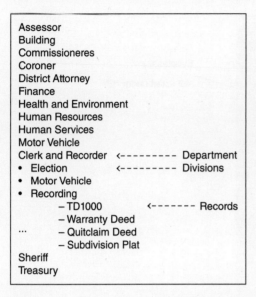

```
Assessor
Building
Commissioneres
Coroner
District Attorney
Finance
Health and Environment
Human Resources
Human Services
Motor Vehicle
Clerk and Recorder   <--------- Department
•  Election          <--------- Divisions
•  Motor Vehicle
•  Recording
       – TD1000           <------- Records
       – Warranty Deed
...    – Quitclaim Deed
       – Subdivision Plat
Sheriff
Treasury
```

Figure 6.6   Community Government Business-Unit Taxonomy

business processes are used to establish the taxonomy. The highest or broadest level represents the business functions. The next level down the hierarchy constitutes the activities performed for the function. The lowest level in the hierarchy consists of the records that are created as a result of the activity (a.k.a. the *transactions*).

Figure 6.7 shows partial detail of one node of a functional taxonomy developed for a state government regulatory agency. The agency organizational structure is based on regulatory programs. Within the program areas are similar (repeated) functions and activities (e.g., permitting, compliance, and enforcement, etc.). When the repeated functions and activities are universalized, the results are a "flatter" taxonomy. *This type of taxonomy is better suited to endure organizational shifts and changes.* In addition, the process of universalizing the functions and activities inherently results in broader and more generic naming conventions. This provides flexibility when adding new record types (transactions) because there will be fewer changes to the hierarchy structure.[38]

One disadvantage of a functional taxonomy is its inability to address case files (or project files). A case file is a collection of records that relate to a particular entity, person, or project. The records in the case file can be generated by multiple activities. For example, at the regulatory agency, enforcement files are maintained that contain records generated by enforcement activities (Notice of Violation, Consent Decree, etc.) and other ancillary, but related activities such as Contracting, Inspections, and Permitting.[39]

A functional taxonomy is better suited to endure organizational changes.

```
Accounting
Procurement
Contracts and Agreements
Licensing and Certification
Technical Assistance
Permitting
Compliance and Enforcement  ←-- Function
•  Inspections                 ←-- Activities
•  Complaints
•  Emergency Response
•  Enforcement
        – Notice of Violation  ←-- Transactions
        – Consent Decree
        – Request for Response Actions
        – Stipulation Agreement
```

Function	Activity
4. Permitting	4.1 Registration
	4.2 Application
	4.3 Public Notice
	4.4 Permit Development & Issuance
	4.5 Termination
5. Compliance and Enforcement	5.1 Inspections
	5.2 Complaints
	5.3 Emergency Response & Preparedness
	5.4 Monitoring Reporting
	5.5 Enforcement Actions

Figure 6.7   State Government Regulatory Agency Functional Taxonomy

To address the case file issue at the regulatory Agency, metadata cross-referencing was used to provide a virtual case-file view of the records collection (see Figure 6.8).

A *hybrid* [taxonomy] is usually the best approach. There are certain business units that usually don't change over time. For example, accounting and human resources activities are fairly constant. Those portions of the taxonomy could be constructed in a business-unit manner even when other areas within the organization use a functional structure (see Figure 6.9).[40]

Faceted taxonomies allow for multiple organizing principles to be applied to information along various dimensions. Facets can contain subjects, departments, business units, processes, tasks, interests, security levels, and other attributes used to describe information. There is never really one single taxonomy, but rather collections of

One disadvantage of a functional taxonomy is its inability to address case files (or project files).

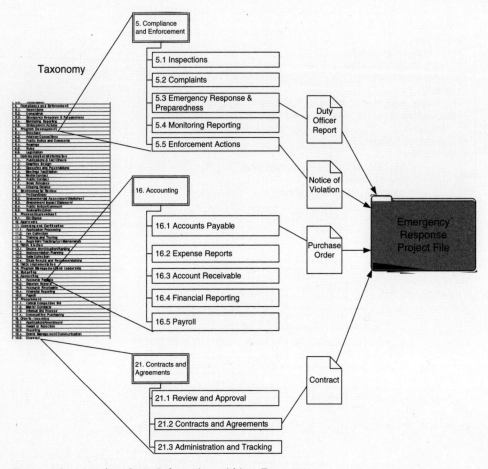

Figure 6.8   Metadata Cross-Referencing within a Taxonomy

taxonomies that describe different aspects of information. In the e-commerce world, facets are used to describe brand, size, color, price, and other context-specific attributes. Records management systems can also be developed with knowledge and process attributes related to the enterprise.[41]

Which Taxonomy Type Should You Use?

Each taxonomy type has its pros and cons as shown in Table 6.1. In most cases, a hybrid approach combining the taxonomy types is the most appropriate.[42]

A hybrid approach to taxonomy design is usually the best.

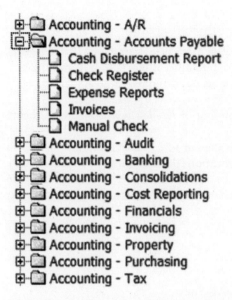

Figure 6.9   Basic Accounting Business-Unit Taxonomy

In choosing a taxonomy type, consider the following:

- Gain an understanding of your organization and how the business units function and interact.
- What are the needs of the users (both internal and external users)? Will you need multiple "views" or methods for records searching and categorization?
- Where will the taxonomy be applied and what are the operating parameters or limitations of those systems (search systems, electronic content, or records management system (ECM/RMS), paper files, shared network drive, website, etc.)?"[43]

Table 6.1   Taxonomy Types: Pros and Cons

Taxonomy Types	Pros	Cons
Subject	Common approach recognizable by most users (library, Yellow Pages, Internet sites)	Requires understanding of terminology or supporting thesaurus
	Many sources of existing and reusable schemes	
Business-unit	Familiar to users (mimics most existing paper-filing systems)	Organizational changes require maintenance of the taxonomy
		Shared documents are difficult to classify
Functional	Endures organizational changes	Difficult to address case files
Faceted	Flexible and context specific	Requires process analysis and understanding of use cases

Taxonomy Project Planning

Developing a corporate taxonomy requires a well thought-out approach that addresses not only how information will be categorized, but, more important, how information units relate to each other and how these will be accessed and retrieved at various points in time.[44]

Development also requires an understanding of *business processes* that are being supported by the taxonomy.[45]

The first step is to define the scope.[46] What is the purpose of the taxonomy? To which systems will the taxonomy be applied? Organizations depend on many different types of information systems to create, receive, store, retrieve, and access records. Here are a few of the different categories of systems where your organization could implement the taxonomy:

- Collaboration Sites
- Document Management
- Electronic Forms Processing
- Enterprise Content Management (ECM) Suites
- Document Imaging
- Records Management
- Web Content Management
- Workflow and Business Process Management (BPM)
- Enterprise Search

Who are the intended users? Internal staff, partner organizations, the public, and so on. When determining the users, consider the following:

- Geographic locations
- Organizational structure
- Creators versus consumers
- Internal versus external
- Business process roles

The taxonomy must address the needs of all of the intended users. These users will likely have different interests, vocabularies, and viewpoints to the document collection.

Leveraging Subject Matter Experts

Developing a taxonomy requires the participation of a group. It is not developed by a single person, with a single point of view. Participants must be identified early in the project. These include stakeholders, **subject matter experts** (SMEs), and testers.

An SME can be a valuable resource in the development of a taxonomy, as they can verify and validate terminology, and provide insights into the business context under analysis.[47]

SMEs must not be relied on completely; a balance must be struck so that user needs are considered and the taxonomy does not become overly complex and filled with jargon. Therefore, spend time with an SME when they are available, sit down in person and interview them, and attempt to grasp an understanding of the domain from their viewpoint, asking them about the needs of the user audience. Then further research user needs by interviewing users and scanning search logs to see which terms and conceptual searches users have been historically looking for. But ultimately, the lens you use to evaluate taxonomy needs must be one that balances the perspectives of users and SMEs, and a taxonomy consultant, if one is available.[48]

Once the participants have been identified, they must be educated. *Most users don't know what a taxonomy is or why they need one.* Hold educational sessions to explain what it is and how the organization intends to use it. It is helpful to have conceptual "mock-ups" of what the taxonomy might look like in one of the targeted systems. The mock-up does not have to be a functioning system, but a visual representation of what the navigation and searching might look like.

It is important to communicate the benefits of participating. Give them the "What's in it for me" rationale. Explain their role in the project and give them an expectation of the time needed to participate. Users need to fit this time commitment into their daily work. Not only do they need to have the directive to participate, but also the support. For example, at a recent consulting engagement for a large organization, employees were required to "charge" their time to certain accounts or projects. Any work performed during nonchargeable time affected their performance evaluations. To remedy this conflict, management set up a project account so that the time spent on the project didn't count as nonchargeable time.

One challenge in leveraging SMEs is that they sometimes lose sight of the goal of the taxonomy and the systems that their taxonomy supports. A SME may look at a purpose-built taxonomy and say "This is not complete, it is missing the following . . ." and then proceed to develop what may be an academically or a theoretically complete taxonomy that is overly complex and granular. They lose sight of the fact that *the purpose of the taxonomy is to support particular functionality, not to be theoretically complete.*[49]

Gather Existing Information Sources

Regardless of the decision of build versus buy or internal development versus external/consultant development, someone from the organization will need to gather existing information sources. Your organization has a wealth of materials that have already been researched, analyzed, and published that can help you in your taxonomy development. Search for materials such as these:

- Strategic plans
- Operating plans
- Organizational charts
- Company history published in books, pamphlets, videos, and so forth
- Budgeting/workforce planning documents

Subject matter experts can be a valuable resource in taxonomy development.

- Time reporting categories in accounting system
- Continuity of operations plans
- File plans
- Retention schedules
- Off-site storage inventory
- Security classification schemes
- Electronically stored information (ESI) data maps
- Business process re-engineering diagrams, flowcharts, and other documentation from improvement efforts
- Quality certification documentation
- Community outreach materials
- Employee/consultant orientation materials

Look for organizing principles that can be reused—file structures, vocabularies, folders, navigation, metadata, term lists, reference data, and so on—from these sources.[50]

Document Inventory

A document inventory is conducted to gather detailed information regarding the documents managed. This information is used to establish the levels of the taxonomy structure. There are various methods to conduct an inventory including questionnaires, physical inspections, interviews, and specialty software used for crawling and analyzing electronic document stores (see Chapter 5, Inventorying E-Records, for more detail).

Although it is advisable to use automated tools to collect indexing and taxonomy data where possible, *the most common inventorying method is to create a questionnaire and follow-up with in-person data gathering.* The questionnaire can be distributed as a spreadsheet, electronic survey, or using specialty software.

The inventory will likely require the effort of more than one staff member per functional area or department. Typically, administrative staff are utilized for a majority of the inventory tasks. However, there must be data gathered from professional/technical staff regarding those documents and records that are not necessarily familiar to administrative staff. It is not unreasonable to expect a resource requirement of 10 to 12 hours per person and a range of one to five people per functional area or department (depending on size) over a period of four to five weeks.

It is important to provide both written and verbal instructions for the appropriate manner in which to conduct the inventory. An initial meeting should be conducted to explain how to complete the document inventory. There should also be provisions for providing assistance for questions that arise during the course of the inventory (via telephone, e-mail, and in person if possible). Follow-up in-person meetings can be used to refine the questionnaire responses.

A document inventory is conducted to gather detailed information regarding the documents managed.

Business Process Analysis

To establish the taxonomy, business processes must be documented and analyzed. (See Chapter 9, ERM Link to Business Process Improvement, for more detail.) There are two basic process analysis methods: top-down and bottom-up. In the top-down method, a high-level analysis of business functions is performed to establish the higher tiers. Detailed analyses are performed on each business process to "fill in" the lower tiers. The detailed analyses are usually conducted in a phased approach and the taxonomy is incrementally updated.

In order to use the bottom-up method, detailed analyses must be performed for all processes in one effort. Using this method ensures that there will be fewer modifications to the taxonomy. However, this is sometimes not feasible for organizations with limited resources. A phased or incremental approach is usually more budget-friendly and places fewer burdens on the organization's resources.

There are many diagramming formats and tools that will provide the details needed for the analysis. The most basic diagramming can be accomplished with a standard tool such as Visio® from Microsoft. There are also more advanced modeling tools that could be used to produce the diagrams that provide the functionality to statistically analyze process changes through simulation and provide information for architecture planning and other process initiatives within the organization.

Any diagramming format will suffice as long as it depicts the flow of data through the processes showing process steps, inputs, and outputs (documents), decision steps, organizational boundaries, and interaction with information systems. The diagrams should depict document movement within as well as between the subject department and other departments or outside entities.

Figure 6.10 uses a swim-lane type diagram. Each horizontal "lane" represents a participant or role. The flow of data and sequence of process steps is shown with lines (the arrows note the direction).

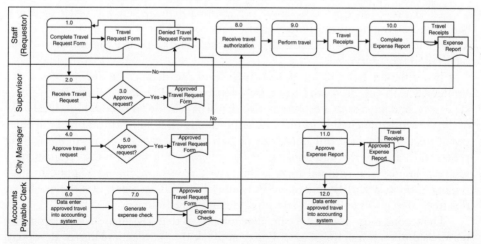

Figure 6.10   Business Process Example—Travel Expense Process
Source: Blackburn Consulting.

> Business processes must be documented and analyzed to develop a taxonomy.

Process steps are shown as boxes.

Decision steps are shown as diamonds.

Documents are depicted as a rectangle with a curved bottom line.

The first step is to review any existing business process documentation (e.g., business plans, procedures manuals, employee training manuals, etc.) in order to gain a better understanding of the functions and processes. This is done in advance of interviews in order to provide a base-level understanding to reduce the amount of time required of the interviewees.

Two different types of interviews (high level and detailed business process) are conducted with key personnel from each department. The initial (high level) interviews are conducted with a representative that will provide an overall high-level view of the department including its mission, responsibilities, and identification of the functional areas. This person will identify those staff that will provide details of the specific processes in each of the functional areas identified. For instance, if the department is Human Resources, functional areas of the department might include: Applicant Processing, Classification, Training, and Personnel File Management. It is expected that this first interview/meeting will last approximately one hour.

The second interviews will be detailed interviews that will focus on daily processes performed in each functional area. For example, if the function is Human Resources Classification, the process may be the creation/management of position descriptions.

It is only necessary to interview one person that represents a particular process—there is little need to interview multiple staff performing the same function. These second interviews will likely last one to two hours each, depending on the complexity of the process.

When there are processes that "connect" (e.g., the output from one process is the input to another), it is useful to conduct group interviews with representatives for each process. This often results in "ah-ha" moments when an employee from one process finally understands why they are sending certain records to another process. It also brings to light **business process improvement** (BPI) opportunities. When employees understand the big picture process, they can identify unnecessary process steps and redundant or obsolete documents that can be eliminated.

One purpose of process analysis is to develop taxonomy facets that can be used to surface information for particular steps in the process. In some cases, process steps can directly inform the types of artifacts that are needed at a particular part of the process and therefore be used to develop content types in knowledge management (KM) use cases. This is related to records management in that KM applications are another lens under which content can be viewed. Process analysis can also help determine the scope of metadata for content. For example, if developing an application to view invoices, if the process includes understanding line item detail, this will dictate a different metadata model than if the process only sought to determine whether invoices over a certain threshold were unpaid. Different processes, different use cases, different metadata.[51]

Construct the Taxonomy

The document inventory and process analysis are used to construct the draft taxonomy. Figure 6.11 is an example from a City Government taxonomy project.

From the business plans we identified "Finance" as a high-level function with the following subfunctions:

- Finance
  - Accounts Payable
  - Accounts Receivable/Billing
  - Asset Management
  - Auditing
  - Bond Management
  - Budget
  - Financial Reporting
  - Grants and Loans
  - Payroll
  - Tax Increment Financing (TIF)
  - Tax Reporting

The document inventory produced a listing that included some finance-related documents. For example, Travel Request Form and Travel Expense Report were listed for many of the departments.

	A	B	C
1	Department	Division	Document Name
2	City Manager		Travel Authorization & Cash Advance Form (Form 103-5A)
3	City Manager		Travel Authorization & Cash Advance Form (Form 103-5A)
4	City Manager		Travel Expense Report (Form 103-5B)
5	Community Development	Community Development	Travel Authorization & Cash Advance Form (Form 103-5A)
6	Community Development	Community Development	Travel Expense Report (Form 103-5B)
7	Community Services	Community Services - Volunteer/Human Services Div	Travel Authorization & Cash Advance Form (Form 103-5A)
8	Community Services	Community Services - Volunteer/Human Services Div	Travel Expense Report (Form 103-5B)

Figure 6.11   Same Document Types Used across Departments
Source: Blackburn Consulting.

The Travel Request Form and Travel Expense Report documents are referenced on the process diagram titled "Travel Expense Process" shown in Figure 6.12.

Based on the process diagrams, we know the activities conducted to produce these two documents fall under an accounts payable process. Therefore, we added a category (activity) under accounts payable for which to classify these documents as shown in Figure 6.13.

What to Do with Items That Do Not Neatly Fit

Not all documents will fit neatly into your taxonomy; there will always need to be an "Other" or "Miscellaneous" term, sort of a "junk drawer" category for items that do not fall into your established taxonomy of terms.[52]

There are several strategies that may be employed to resolve the "other" category:

- **Check for duplication.** Review your thesaurus and question users to see if there are synonyms for the document type.

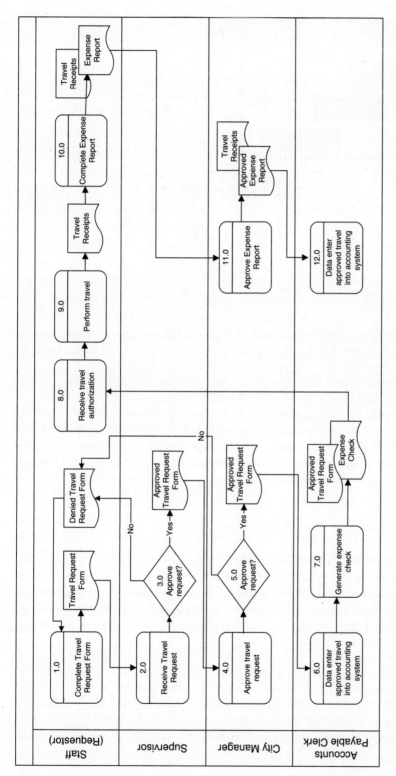

Figure 6.12 Travel Expense Process

103

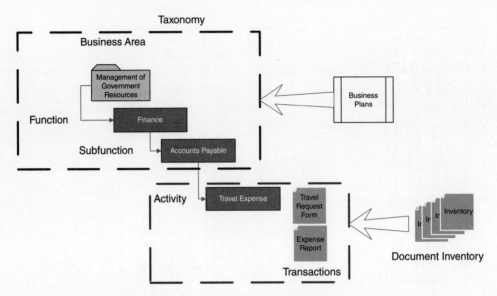

Figure 6.13   Classifying Documents by Activity—Travel Expense

- **Create new categories.** If there is a high enough volume of the document type, perhaps it needs to be a newly named category. For low volumes, perhaps aggregate the items into a "general/broad document name."
- **Frequency of use.** If available, run statistical reports to see how often users have been searching for the items under that document type.[53]
- **Use "not otherwise categorized."** This is a subtle distinction but "other" or "miscellaneous" becomes a dumping ground. Not otherwise categorized lets user consider the fact that there are no categories for this content today, but that may not be the case in the future. This is preferable to "General," "Other," or "Miscellaneous" categories.[54]

Taxonomy Testing: A Necessary Step

Once a new taxonomy is developed, it must be tested and piloted to see if it meets user needs and expectations. To attempt the roll-out of a new taxonomy without testing it first is imprudent, and will end up costing more time and resources in the long run. So budget the time and money for it.[55] Taxonomy testing is where the rubber meets the road; it provides real data to see if the taxonomy design has met user expectations and actually helps them in their work.

User testing provides valuable feedback and allows the taxonomist or taxonomy team to fine-tune the work they have done to more closely align the taxonomy with user needs and business objectives. What may have seemed an obvious term or category may, in fact, be *way off.* This may result from the sheer focus and myopia of the taxonomy team. So getting user feedback is essential.

There are many taxonomy testing tools that can assist in the design effort. Once an initial design is drafted, a "low-tech" approach is to hand-write classification

There's nothing better than getting quantitative feedback to see if you're hitting the mark with users.

categories and document types on post-it notes or index cards. Then bring in a sampling of users and ask them to place the notes or cards in the proper category. The results are tracked and calculated.[56]

Software is available to conduct this card sorting in a more high-tech way, and more sophisticated software to assist in the development and testing effort, and to help to update and maintain the taxonomy.

Regardless of the method used, the taxonomy team or even IG team or task force needs to be the designated arbiter when conflicting opinions arise.

Taxonomy testing is not a one-shot task; with feedback and changes, you progress in iterations closer and closer to meeting user requirements, which may take several rounds of testing and changes.[57]

Taxonomies can be tested in multiple ways. User acceptance throughout the derivation process can be simple conference room pilots or validation, formal usability testing based on use cases, card sorting (open and closed), and tagging processes. Auto-tagging of content with target taxonomies is also an area that requires testing.[58]

Taxonomy Maintenance

After a taxonomy has been implemented, it will need to be updated over time to reflect changes in document management processes as well to increase usability. Therefore, users should have the opportunity to suggest changes, additions, deletions, and so on. *There should be a formal process in place to manage requests for changes.* A person or committee should be assigned the responsibility to determine how and if each request will be facilitated.

There must be guidelines to follow in making changes to the taxonomy. A U.S. state agency organization uses the following guidelines in determining taxonomy changes:

- The new term must have a definition, preferably provided by the proposer of the new term.
- It should be a term someone would recognize even if they have no background within our agency's [or business'] workings; use of industry standard terminology is preferred.
- Terms should be mutually exclusive from other terms.
- Terms that can be derived using a combination of other terms or facilitated with metadata will not be added.
- The value should not be a "temporary" term—it should have some expectation to have a long lifespan.
- We should expect that there would be a significant volume of content that could be assigned the value—otherwise, use of a more general document type and clarification through the metadata on items is preferred: if enough items

> There should be a formal process in place to manage requests for taxonomy changes.

are titled with the new term over time to warrant reconsideration, it will be reconsidered.

- For higher-level values in the hierarchy, the relationship between parents and children (functions and activities) is always "is a kind of . . ." Other relationships are not supported.
- Document type values should not reflect the underlying technology used to capture the content and should not reflect the format of the content directly.

Taxonomy Management Tools for Continued Maintenance

Although your organization may employ an outside consultant to develop a new taxonomy, the ongoing maintenance of a taxonomy is usually going to be the responsibility of your own internal staff members. One of the first issues to arise is that of the choice of taxonomy maintenance and updating tools. Typically, your EDRMS/ERM or ECM system or search engine will *not* include native taxonomy maintenance and management components.[59]

You will need more updating capability than simply adding or deleting standard terms, which requires more sophisticated taxonomy management software.

Taxonomy management systems vary widely in price, indexing and auto-classification capabilities, and other features. They typically will have a focus on a particular area that they are best suited for, and you must map your organization's needs with the strengths of the tool you select.[60]

A good approach is to begin with a lower-cost, less sophisticated tool for taxonomy development and then migrate to the use of more capable tools as your needs change and grow.

Social Tagging and Folksonomies

Social tagging is a method that allows users to manage content with metadata they apply themselves using keywords or metadata tags. Unlike traditional classification, which uses a controlled vocabulary, *social tagging keywords are freely chosen by each individual.*

Folksonomy is the term used for this free-form, social approach to metadata assignment.

> Begin by using low-cost, simple tools for taxonomy development and migrate to more capable ones as your organization's needs grow.

A folksonomy uses free-form words to classify documents. A folksonomy approach is useful for potentially updating your taxonomy structure and improves the user search experience.

Folksonomies are not an ordered classification system; rather, they are a list of keywords input by users that are ranked by popularity.[61]

Taxonomies and folksonomies both have their place. *Folksonomies can be used in concert with taxonomies to nominate key terms for use in the taxonomy*, which contributes toward the updating and maintenance of the taxonomy while making the user experience better by utilizing their own preferred terms.

A combined taxonomy and folksonomy approach may provide for an optional "free-text metadata field" for social tags that might be titled "Subject" or "Comment." Then users could search that free-form, uncontrolled field to narrow document searches. The folksonomy fields will be of most use to a user or departmental area, but if the terms are used frequently enough, they may need to be added to the formal taxonomy's controlled vocabulary to benefit the entire organization.

In sum, taxonomy development, testing, and maintenance is hard work—but it can yield significant and sustained benefits to the organization over the long haul by providing more complete and accurate information when knowledge workers make searches, better IG and control over the organization's documents, records, and information, and a more agile compliance and litigation readiness posture.

CHAPTER SUMMARY: **KEY POINTS**

- 15 to 25 percent of an average workday for knowledge workers is spent searching for information, often due to poor taxonomy design.

- Taxonomies are hierarchical classification structures used to standardize the naming and organization of information using controlled vocabularies for terms.

- Taxonomies speed up the process of retrieving records because end-users can select from subject categories or topics.

- Taxonomies need to be considered from two main perspectives: navigation and classification.

- Poor search results, inconsistent or conflicting file plans, and the inability to locate information on a timely basis are indications that taxonomy work is needed.

- Metadata, which are the characteristics of a document expressed in data fields, must be leveraged in taxonomy design.

- Best practices dictate that taxonomy development includes designing the taxonomy structure and heuristic principles to align with user needs.

(Continued)

(*Continued*)

- There are three basic types of hierarchical taxonomies: subject, business-unit, and functional.

- A *hybrid* approach to taxonomy design is usually the best.

- A subject matter expert (SME) can be a valuable resource in taxonomy development. They should not be relied on too heavily though, or the taxonomy may end up filled with esoteric jargon.

- A document inventory is conducted to gather detailed information regarding the documents managed.

- Business processes must be documented and analyzed to develop a taxonomy.

- User testing is essential and provides valuable feedback and allows the taxonomist or taxonomy team to fine-tune the work.

- Begin by using low-cost, simple tools for taxonomy development and migrate to more capable ones as your organization's needs grow and maintenance is required.

- A folksonomy uses free-form words to classify documents. A folksonomy approach is useful for potentially updating your taxonomy structure and improves the user search experience.

Notes

1. Cadence Group, "Taxonomies: The Backbone of Enterprise Content Management," August 18, 2006, www.cadence-group.com/articles/taxonomy/backbone.htm.
2. Delphi Group, "Taxonomy and Content Classification: Market Milestone Report," 2002, www.delphi-group.com/whitepapers/pdf/WP_2002_TAXONOMY.PDF (accessed April 25, 2012).
3. Ibid.
4. Cadence Group, "Taxonomies: The Backbone of Enterprise Content Management."
5. Daniela Barbosa, "The Taxonomy Folksonomy Cookbook," www.slideshare.net/HeuvelMarketing/taxonomy-folksonomy-cookbook (accessed October 12, 2012).
6. Ibid.
7. Montague Institute Review, "Your Taxonomy Is Your Future," February 2000, www.montague.com/abstracts/future.html.
8. The Free Library, "Creating Order out of Chaos with Taxonomies," 2005, www.thefreelibrary.com/Creating+order+out+of+chaos+with+taxonomies%3A+the+increasing+volume+of...-a0132679071 (accessed April 25, 2012).
9. Susan Cisco and Wanda Jackson, *Information Management Journal*, "Creating Order out of Chaos with Taxonomies" May/June 2005, www.arma.org/bookstore/files/Cisco.pdf.
10. Marcia Morante, "Usability Guidelines for Taxonomy Development," April 2003, www.montague.com/abstracts/usability.html.
11. Seth Earley, e-mail to author, September 10, 2012.
12. Ibid.
13. Cadence Group, "Taxonomies," 3.

14. Dam Coalition, "8 Things You Need to Know about How Taxonomy Can Improve Search," May 16, 2010, http://damcoalition.com/index.php/metadata/story/8_things_you_need_to_know_about_how_taxonomy_can_improve_search/.
15. Ibid.
16. Ibid.
17. Adventures in Records Management, "The Business Classification Scheme," October 15, 2006, http://adventuresinrecordsmanagement.blogspot.com/2006/10/business-classification-scheme.html.
18. Seth Earley, e-mail to author, September 10, 2012.
19. National Archives of Australia, www.naa.gov.au (accessed May 23, 2012).
20. Adventures in Records Management, "The Business Classification Scheme."
21. Ibid.
22. Seth Earley, e-mail to author, September 10, 2012.
23. Cisco and Jackson, "Creating Order out of Chaos with Taxonomies."
24. Seth Earley, e-mail to author, September 10, 2012.
25. www.earley.com/blog/the-popularity-contest-taxonomy-development-in-the-petabyte-era, (accessed April 25, 2012).
26. Ibid.
27. Seth Earley, e-mail to author, September 10, 2012.
28. Heather Hedden, "The Accidental Taxonomist," *Information Today, Inc.* (October 2010), 3.
29. Ibid.
30. Hedden, "The Accidental Taxonomist," 10.
31. Seth Earley, e-mail to author, September 10, 2012.
32. Hedden, "The Accidental Taxonomist," 8.
33. NISO, Project ISO 25964, www.niso.org/workrooms/iso25964 (accessed April 25, 2012).
34. This section is reprinted with permission from Barb Blackburn, "Taxonomy Design Types," www.imergeconsult.com/img/114BB.pdf (accessed October 12, 2012); *e-Doc Magazine*, AIIM International, May/June 2006, 14 and 16.
35. Ibid.
36. Ibid.
37. Ibid.
38. Ibid.
39. Ibid.
40. Ibid.
41. Seth Earley, e-mail to author, September 10, 2012.
42. Blackburn, "Taxonomy Design Types"; Seth Earley, e-mail to author, September 10, 2012 (regarding faceted taxonomies).
43. Blackburn, "Taxonomy Design Types."
44. Lakshmi Stockham and Ganesh Vednere, "Best Practices in Implementing Taxonomy for Enterprise Information Management," August 21, 2008, www.information-management.com/issues/2007_51/10001850-1.html.
45. Seth Earley, e-mail to author, September 10, 2012.
46. Stockham and Vednere, "Best Practices in Implementing Taxonomy."
47. Rebecca Allen, "Subject Matter Experts and Taxonomy Development," September 19, 2008, www.earley.com/blog/subject-matter-experts-and-taxonomy-development.
48. Ibid.
49. Seth Earley, e-mail to author, September 10, 2012.
50. Ibid.
51. Ibid.
52. Ahrenlehnert, "Cleaning up the Other Bucket," September 5, 2008, www.earley.com/blog/cleaning-up-the-other-bucket.
53. Ibid.
54. Seth Earley, e-mail to author, September 10, 2012.
55. Stephanie Lemieux, "The Pain and Gain of Taxonomy User Testing," July 8, 2008, www.earley.com/blog/the-pain-and-gain-of-taxonomy-user-testing.
56. Ibid.
57. Ibid.
58. Seth Earley, e-mail to author, September 10, 2012.
59. Hedden, "Tools for Managing Taxonomies."
60. Ibid.
61. Tom Reamy, "Folksonomy Folktales," *KM World*, September 29, 2009, www.kmworld.com/Articles/Editorial/Feature/Folksonomy-folktales-56210.aspx.

CHAPTER 7

Developing Retention Schedules for E-Records

Robert Smallwood;
edited by Paula Lederman, MLS

With limited resources, today's records manager is faced with an onslaught of increasingly pressing and complex compliance and legal demands. At the core of these demands is the ability of the organization to demonstrate that it has *legally defensible* records management practices that can hold up in court. Organizations can legally destroy records—but will have a greater legal defensibility if the authority to destroy the records is identified on a retention schedule, the retention requirements have been met, the records are slated for **destruction** in the normal course of business, so long as there are no existing legal or financial holds, and all records of the same type are treated consistently and systematically.

The guidance in this chapter applies generally to records in all formats, but also contains specific information for the retention and disposition of electronic records.

The foundation of legally defensible records management practices is a solid **information governance** (IG) underpinning, where policies and processes, supported and enforced by **information technology** (IT), help the organization meet its externally mandated legal requirements and internally mandated IG requirements for handling and controlling information.

A complete, current, and documented records retention program reduces storage and handling costs and improves searchability for records by making records easier and faster to find. *This reduced search time and more complete search capability improves knowledge worker productivity.* It also reduces legal risk by improving the ability to meet compliance demands, while also reducing e-discovery costs and improving the ability to more efficiently respond to discovery requests during litigation. Most large organizations maintain records retention schedules by business unit, department, or functional area. Some organizations, particularly smaller ones, may establish organization-wide IG programs that call for the developing, updating, and improvement of an enterprise or master retention schedule. Developing enterprise-wide records retention schedules requires consultation with stakeholder groups who have valuable input to contribute to the overall development of the IG effort and to specific schedules for retaining record collections, and their planned disposition. Consultation by the records management department, **senior records officer** (SRO), or records team must take place with representatives from the business units that create and own the records as well as with legal, compliance, risk management, information technology (IT), and other relevant stakeholder groups.

A complete, current, and documented records retention program reduces storage and handling costs and improves searchability for records by making records easier and faster to find.

What Is a Records Retention Schedule?

A **records retention schedule** delineates how long a record series is to be retained, and their disposition after their lifecycle is complete (e.g., destruction, transfer, archiving); they also "are lists of records by name or type that authorize the disposition of records."[1] Retention schedules apply to all records regardless of their format or media (e.g., physical or electronic). *Retention schedules are developed for records not individually, but rather, by records series, categories, functions, or systems.* Ideally, they include all of the record series in an organization, although they may be broken down into smaller subset schedules, such as by business unit.

Retention schedules may be maintained separately for electronic records, or they may be included in a combined schedule that includes both e-records and paper, or other physical records.

Corporate records retention schedules *are increasingly being maintained online,* where users and also IT, legal, risk, and records management personnel can view and reference them. Electronic data and documents can easily reference these schedules and initiate a process based on a trigger event so that the life cycle of the electronic document can be automated and managed in a consistent manner. *Retention schedules are a basic tool that allows an organization to prove that it has a legally defensible basis on which to dispose records.*

Retention schedules in large organizations are typically broken down by business function. A **functional retention schedule** groups records series based on business functions, such as financial, legal, product management, or sales. Each function or grouping is also used for classification. Rather than detail every sequence of records, these larger functional groups are less numerous, and are easier for users to understand.

Some organizations keep an enterprise-wide **master retention schedule**, which includes the retention and disposition requirements for records series that cross business unit boundaries. *The master retention schedule contains all records series in the entire enterprise.* An enterprise-wide retention schedule is preferable because it eliminates the possibility that different business units will be following conflicting records retention periods. For example, if one business unit is discarding a group of records after five years, it would not make sense for another business unit to keep the same records for ten years.

Retention schedules are developed by records series, category, function, or system—not for individual records.

Retention schedules are a basic tool that allows an organization to prove that it has a legally defensible basis on which to dispose records.

Benefits of a Retention Schedule

According to the U.S. National Archives and Records Administration, developing and maintaining a records retention schedule provides the following benefits. The retention schedule:[2]

1. Reduces legal risk and legal liability exposure.
2. Supports a legally defensible records management program.
3. Improves IG by enforcing uniformity and standardization.
4. Improves search quality and reduces search time.
5. Provides higher-quality records information to improve decision support for knowledge workers.
6. Prevents inadvertent, malicious, or premature destruction of records.
7. Improves accountability for life-cycle management of records on an enterprise-wide basis.
8. Improves security for confidential records assets.[3]
9. Reduces and minimizes costs for maintaining records.
10. Determines which records have historic value.
11. Saves hardware, utility, and labor costs by deleting records after their life span.
12. Optimizes use of online storage and access resources.

A formal approach to records management has been around since the mid-1900s so a great deal of guidance is available before embarking on developing or updating your records retention program. There are models and guides that can be used to assist in development of records retention schedules for your organization, including the international standard for records management, ISO 15489—Part 1 and 2:2001, "Information and Documentation—Records Management"; the ISO 15489 standard was written to address all kinds of records and additional guidance may be obtained by referencing national standards, such as those in Canada, United Kingdom, Australia, and other countries.[4] Often, in the public sector, retention guidelines are published by an authority such as the office of the national, state, or provincial archivist. Some additional insights may be gleaned from ISO 16175–1:2010, "Information and Documentation—Principles and Functional Requirements for Records in Electronic Office Environments—Part 1: Overview and Statement of Principles," which establishes fundamental principles and functional requirements for software used to create and manage digital records in office environments.[5]

The master retention schedule contains all records series in the entire enterprise.

A records retention schedule is a part of an overall IG program. Due to the fact that a concerted IG program standardizes and enforces uniformity and control, the entire organization benefits in terms of productivity, reduced risk, and improved compliance and e-discovery processes. These overarching goals and benefits should be championed by senior management in words and deeds. This means making the IG effort visible, and providing the proper budget resources in terms of money and employee time to achieve its aims.

General Principles of Retention Scheduling

There are a series of principles common to all retention schedules, as follows:[6]

- The retention schedule must include all records.
- Records scheduling includes all record types, regardless of media or location.[7]
- All legal and regulatory requirements for records must be reflected in the records scheduling process. For public entities, retention scheduling fosters and enables the agency to comply with information requests (e.g., Freedom of Information Act in the United States, Freedom of Information Act 2000 in the United Kingdom, Freedom of Information and Protection of Privacy Act and the Health Information Act in Canada, and Freedom of Information Amendment [Reform] Act 2010 in Australia).
- Records scheduling is a "proactive" planning process, where schedules are set in place and standardized in advance.
- Periodic review of the retention schedule must take place when significant legislation, technology acquisitions, or other changes are being considered; but in any case this should be at least annually, or bi-annually.
- Records scheduling is a continuous process that needs updating and amending, based on legal, technology, or business changes over time.
- Classification and records scheduling are inextricably linked.
- File series with similar characteristics or value should be assigned consistent and appropriate retention periods.
- Records of historical value must be preserved.
- Records retention periods should reflect the business needs of users, the value of the records, and any legal or compliance requirements. The best way to make these determinations are with a team that includes cross-functional representatives from records management, legal, risk, compliance, IT and business unit representatives, headed by an executive sponsor.
- Records management resource use is optimized, and costs are minimized by keeping records a minimum amount of time under a planned and controlled set of processes.
- Records must be retained in a repository (file room, or software system) where the record is protected (e.g., made read-only and monitored with an audit trail) so that the integrity of the record is maintained in a manner that meets all evidence and legal admissibility standards if or when litigation is encountered.
- Senior management must approve of and sign off on the retention schedule and will be legally accountable for compliance with the schedule.

Records retention defines the length of time that records are to be kept and considers legal, regulatory, operational, and historical requirements.[10]

- Senior management must be able to readily review retention schedules, policy documentation, and audit information to insure users are in compliance with the retention schedule.
- Complete documentation of scheduling requirements and activities must take place so that future users and archivists can view and track changes to the retention schedule.[8]

Developing a Records Retention Schedule

A **records retention schedule** *defines the length of time that records are to be kept and considers legal, regulatory, operational, and historical requirements.*[9] The retention schedule also includes direction as to how the length of time is calculated, that is, the event or trigger that starts the retention clock running (e.g., two years from completion of contract). Legal research and opinions are required, along with consultation with owners and users of the records. Users will typically overestimate the time they need to keep records, as they confuse the legal requirements with their own personal wishes. Some hard questioning has to take place, since having these records or copies of records lying around the organization on hard drives, thumb drives, or in file cabinets may create liabilities for the organization.

Disposition means not just destruction but can also mean archiving or transfer and a change in ownership and responsibility for the records. The processes of archiving and preserving are an example where records may be handed over to a historical recordkeeping unit. At that time, the records may be sampled and only selective parts of the group of records may be retained.

Why Are Retention Schedules Needed?

A retention schedule allows for uniformity in the retention and disposition process, regardless of the media or location of the records. Further, it tracks, enforces, and audits the retention and disposition of records, while optimizing the amount of records kept to legal minimums, which saves on capital and labor costs, and reduces liability (by discarding unneeded records that carry legal risk).[11] The ARMA International **Generally Accepted Recordkeeping Principles**® state the critical importance of having a

Disposition means not just destruction but can also mean archiving and a change in ownership and responsibility for the records.

A retention schedule allows for uniformity in the retention and disposition process, regardless of the media or location of the records.

retention schedule (see Chapter 3, Generally Accepted Recordkeeping Principles, for more detail) and provides guidelines for open collaboration in developing one. In the public sector, holding records that have passed their legally required retention period can also have negative ramifications and liabilities in meeting information service requests made during litigation, compliance actions, or, for example, under the U.S. Freedom of Information Act (FOI), or similar acts in other countries. In the private sector, holding records past their legal retention period can mean litigation risk.

Information Included on Retention Schedules

A retention schedule consists of the following components:

- *Title* of the record series.
- *Descriptions* of the records series.
- *Office responsible* for the retention of the record (default is usually the office of origin).
- *Disposal decision*—destroy, transfer to the archives, or, in exceptional circumstances, reconsider at a later (specified) date.
- *Timing of disposal*—a minimum period for which the records should be retained in the office, or in an off-site store before disposal action is undertaken.
- *Event that triggers* the disposal action.
- *Dates on which the schedule was agreed,* signed, or modified.
- *Legal citations or a link to a citation* that reference the retention requirements of that group of records.

A sample of a simple records retention schedule is shown in Figure 7.1.[12]

Steps in Developing a Records Retention Schedule

If you already have existing retention schedules, but are revising and updating them, there may be useful information in those schedules that can serve as a good reference point—but be wary, as they may be out-of-date and may not consider current legal requirements and business needs.

According to the U.S. National Archives, there are at least nine basic steps involved in developing retention schedules:

1. Find out what records you have and how you can describe them based on functions.[13]
2. Find out if any legislation or regulations affect the retention of the records.
3. Find out how long the records are required to be used and their value within the organization.

Records Retention Schedule	ENVIRONMENTAL HEALTH AND SAFETY
December 10, 2013	

Record Type	Responsible Department	Event	Retention Period
Accident / Injury Reports *Includes:* *Accidents* *Diagnosis (Accident or Injury)* *First aid reports* *Injuries* *Medical reviews* *Occupational Health Incident* *Treatment and Progress (Accident or Injury)* *Work related accidents* *Worker health information* *Workers Compensation Claims*	HR	Date of Incident	E+30
Employee Medical Files *Includes:* *Audiology* *Lung Function* *Return to Work Authorization* *Related to:* *Employee Files (Active)*	HR	Termination	E+30
Health and Safety Programs *Includes:* *Health and Safety Committee* *Health and Safety Reports*	Health and Safety		CY+10

Figure 7.1   Sample Records Retention Schedule
Source: IMERGE Consulting, Inc.

4. Create a process for incorporating new record types into the retention schedule.

5. Determine how to calculate the disposition date and the start date to use for the calculation.

6. Determine disposition outcomes for the records when their lifecycle has been completed, including destruction, archiving, or transfer.

7. Set up a process to keep track of dispositions for audit and legal purposes.

8. Set up a process to audit to ensure records are being deleted and/or archived as required.

9. Set up a process to review the retention schedule on a regular basis, at least annually.

What Records Do You Have to Schedule?
Inventory and Classification

Inventory and classification are prerequisites for compiling a retention schedule. Develop an **information map** before starting work, which shows where information is created, where it resides, and the path it takes. What records are created, who uses them, and how is their disposition handled? Questions like these will provide key

An information map is a critical first step in developing a records retention schedule. It shows where information is created, where it resides, and who uses it.

insights in the development of the retention schedule.[14] Confirm that the information map covers all the uses of the records by all parts of the organization, including use for accountability, audit, and reference purposes.

In the absence of a formal information map, at a minimum *you must compile a list of all the different types of records in each business area*. This list should include information about who created them and what they are used for, or record "**provenance**," which parts of the organization have used them subsequently, and for what purpose, its "**usage**," and the actual **content**.

In the absence of any existing documentation or records inventory, you will need to conduct a records inventory or survey to find out what records the business unit (or organization) holds (see Chapter 5, Inventorying E-Records, for more details). There are tools available to scan e-records folders to expedite the inventory process. A retention schedule developed in this way will have a shorter serviceable life than one based on an information map. This is because it will be based on existing structures rather than functions, and will remain usable only as long as the organizational structure remains unchanged.

Once a records inventory or survey is complete, building a records retention schedule begins with grouping or **classification** of records.[15]

This basic classification can be grouped into three areas:

1. Business functions and activities
2. Records series
3. Document types

Business functions are basic business units such as accounting, legal, human resources, and purchasing. (See Chapter 6, Taxonomy Development for E-Records, for details on the process of developing classifications.) It basically answers the question, *What were you doing when you created the record?*

Business activities are the tasks *performed* to accomplish the business function. Several activities may be associated with each function.

A **records series** *is a group or unit of identical or related records that are normally used and filed as a unit* and that can be evaluated as a unit or business function for scheduling purposes.[16]

A **document type** is a term used by many software systems to refer to a grouping of related records. When the records are all created by similar processes, then the

There are tools available to scan e-records folders to expedite the inventory process.

After completing an inventory, developing a retention schedule begins with records classification.

document type is equivalent to the business functions or activities mentioned previously. However, document type often refers to the format of the record (e.g., presentation, meeting minutes). In this case, there is not enough information to determine a retention period because it is ambiguous regarding what type of work was being done when that document was created. Retention schedules require that record series be defined by business function and activity, not by record format or display type.

Rationale for Records Groupings

There are fundamental reasons for grouping records together, which improve information organization and access. These include:

- Grouping by "similar theme" for improved completeness.
- Improving information search speed and completeness.
- Increasing organizational knowledge and memory by providing the "context" within which individual documents were grouped.
- Clearly identifying who the record owner or creator is, and to assign and track responsibility for a group of records.
- Grouping records with the same retention requirements for consistent application of disposition processes to records.

Records Series Identification and Classification

After completing a records inventory (see Chapter 5, Inventorying E-Records) including characterizing, descriptive information about the records such as their contents, use, file size, and projected growth volumes, you will need to interview staff in those target areas you are working with to determine more information about the specific organizational structure, its business functions, services, programs, and plans.[17]

You will find that in the course of business there are several different types of records series; there are **case records**, for instance, which are characterized as having a beginning and an end, but are added to over time. Case records generally have titles that include names, dates, numbers, or places. These titles do not provide insight into the nature of the function of the record series. Examples of case records include personnel files, mortgage loan folders, contract and amendment/addendum records, accident reports, insurance claims, and other records that accumulate and expand over time. Although the contents of case files may be similar, you should break out each type of case record under a unique title.

Subject records (also referred to as **topic** or **function records**) "contain information relating to specific or general topics and that are arranged according to their informational content or by the function/activity/transaction they pertain to."[18] These types of records accumulate information on a particular topic or function to be added to the organization's memory, and make it easier for knowledge workers to find information based on subject matter, topics, or business functions. Records such as those on the progression of relevant laws and statutes, policies, standard operating procedures (SOP), education and training have "long-term reference value" and should be kept until they are no longer relevant or are displaced by more current and relevant records. In a record retention schedule, the trigger event is often defined as "*superseded or obsolete.*" Records of this type that relate to "routine operations of a [project], program or service" do not have as much enduring value and should be scheduled to be kept for a shorter period.

Retention of E-Mail Records

Are e-mail messages records? This has been argued for years. *The short answer is "No," not all e-mail messages constitute a record.* But how do you determine whether certain messages are a business record or not? The general answer is that a record documents a transaction or business-related event that may have legal ramifications or historic value. Most important are business activities that may relate to compliance requirements or those that could possibly come into dispute in litigation. Particular consideration should be given to financial transactions of any type.

Certainly evidence that required governance oversight or compliance activities which have been completed need to be documented and become business records. Also, business transactions, where there is an exchange of money or the equivalent in goods or services, are also business records. Today, these transactions are often documented by a quick e-mail. And, of course, any contracts, (and any progressively developed or edited versions) that are exchanged through e-mail become business records.

Some basic guidelines for determining whether an e-mail message should be considered a business record are:

1. *The e-mail documents a transaction or the progress toward an ultimate transaction where anything of value is exchanged between two or more parties.* All parts or characteristics of the transaction, including who (the parties to it), what, when, how much, and the composition of its components are parts of the transaction. Often seemingly minor parts of a transaction are found buried within an e-mail message with the pace of today's business environment. One example would be a last-minute discount offered by a supplier based on an order being placed or delivery being made within a specified timeframe.

> Not all e-mail messages are records; those that document a business transaction or progress toward it are clearly records and require retention.

> E-mail messages that document business activities, especially those that may be disputed in the future, should be retained as records.

2. *The e-mail documents or provides support of a business activity occurring that pertains to internal corporate governance policies or compliance* to externally mandated regulations.
3. *The e-mail message documents other business activities that may possibly be disputed in the future,* whether it ultimately involves litigation or not (that is to say, most business disputes are actually resolved without litigation, provided proof of your organization's position can be shown). For instance, your supplier may dispute the discount you take that was offered in an e-mail message and, once you forward the e-mail thread to them, they acquiesce.

Managing e-mail business records is challenging, even for technology professionals. According to an AIIM International and ARMA survey, *fully two-thirds of records managers doubt that their IT departments really understand the concept of electronic records life-cycle management.* That is despite the fact that *70 percent of companies rely on IT professionals alone to manage their electronic records.*

Although the significance of e-mail in civil litigation cannot be understated (it is the leading piece of evidence requested at civil trials today), *one-third of IT managers state that they would be incapable of locating and retrieving e-mails that are more than one year old,* according to Osterman Research.[19]

How Long Should You Keep Old E-Mail?

There are different schools of thought on e-mail retention periods and retention schedules. The retention and deletion of your electronic business records may be governed by laws or regulations. *Unless your organization's e-mail and electronically stored information (ESI) records are governed by law or regulations, your organization is free to determine the retention periods and deletion schedules that are most appropriate for your organization.*[20] If your organization's e-mail retention periods are not specified by law or regulation, then consider keeping them for at least as long as you retain paper records. Many software providers provide automated software that allows e-mail messages to be moved to controlled repositories as they are declared as records.

Destruction Retention of E-mail

A **destructive retention program** is an approach to e-mail archiving where e-mail messages are retained for a limited time (say, 90 days), followed by its permanent deletion manually or automatically from the organization network, so long as there is no litigation hold or the e-mail has not been declared a record.

Destruction retention of e-mail is a method whereby e-mail messages are re-tained for a limited period and then destroyed.

E-mail retention periods can vary from 90 days to as long as seven years:

- Osterman Research reports that "nearly one-quarter of companies delete e-mail after 90 days."
- Heavily regulated industries, including energy, technology, communications, and real estate favor archiving for one year or more, according to Fulbright and Jaworski research.
- The most common e-mail retention period has traditionally been five to seven years; however, some organizations are taking a hard line approach and stating that e-mails will be kept for only 90 days or six months, unless it is declared as a record, classified, and identified with a classification/retention category and tagged or moved to a repository where the integrity of the record is protected (i.e., the record cannot be altered and an audit trail on the history of the record's usage is maintained).[21]

Records Appraisal: Value Assessment and Prioritization

Assessing the relative value of records so that they may be prioritized and scheduled for retention and final disposition is the next step after classifying the records series. Values may be structured as "high-medium-low" value, or primary and secondary values (as records will have different uses and values, depending on the user group or business unit). The value of a record series will impact the retention period.[22]

The output of your interviewing and analysis process at the business unit level should explicitly show how long the business units *need* the records (not how long they *want* to keep the records—since often users never want to let them go, "just in case"). If your organization has a senior records officer, or better yet, a corporate archivist, they should be able to provide crucial input in identifying and prioritizing those records with "enduring value."

This value assessment impacts retention periods and the disposition path, (which may be to transfer, archive, or destroy the records). Records that have value must be retained, and those of enduring or historical value must be preserved (see Chapter 17, Long-Term Digital Preservation, for more detail). *The critical task is to document the value of records series in regard to various user groups.* Only then can an appropriate

Assessing the relative value of records is key to determining their retention periods and disposition path.

> Records have different types of value, such as financial, legal, technical, and administrative/operational.

retention period be determined. Bear in mind that records have differing values to differing user groups or business units. Certain records series may be critical to one group, but have only moderate value to others.

When records no longer have any measurable value, they should be destroyed. In the case of e-records, they must be "virtually shredded," leaving no trace of the record—except in cases where metadata must be preserved as a means of maintaining an audit trail of critical data, such as who created a record, when it was created, who authorized a record's destruction, when it was accomplished, and so forth.

Types of Records Values

Records values can be broken out into distinct categories, although some records may fall into more than one category. "Records can have *administrative [operational]*, *financial*, *scientific/technical*, *legal*, *evidential*, or *informational value*. That value can be a *primary* value, which means the records are needed for carrying out the current operations of the organization. These values can also extend for a long time after the records are no longer needed to support the operations of the organization. These records have *secondary* values. A secondary value may also be the value records have to organizations other than the creating [business unit or] agency."[23]

Legal Staff Research and Input Is Essential in Determining Legal Value

Records managers and archivists must conduct their own legislative research to apprise themselves on mandatory retention requirements, and to intelligently discuss these requirements with legal staff, to determine records that have *legal value*. Then further legal and regulatory research must be conducted, and firm legal opinions must be rendered by your legal counsel regarding records retention requirements in accordance with laws and regulations. This is an absolute requirement. Your legal staff or outside legal counsel should provide input as to the legal value of records, to arrive at a consensus on records that have legal value to the organization.

Estimating the Value of Financial Records

Legal and financial records are not mutually exclusive, so there may be some overlap. Any records related to financial transactions and accounting records must be evaluated to determine how long they hold *financial value* for the organization. This will require close consultation with your accounting and financial management staff. Financial records document important functions like cash inputs and outputs and must be retained for audit and tax purposes. These records are critical to enforce accountability.[24] In the process of conducting your retention scheduling research, review the financial records series and consider if they document critical functions, such as revenue collection and expenditures.

Determining Scientific or Technical Value of Records

Records such as research reports, designs, blueprints, computer-aided design/computer-aided manufacturing (CAD/CAM), and the like have *scientific or technical value* for an organization. These types of records have enduring value and typically will command longer retention periods. To conduct your appraisal of these records, consult closely with the technical staff that creates the scientific/technical records, but bear in mind that it is the responsibility of the records manager or senior records officer to ultimately determine the minimum retention period for these records to moderate costs.

Long-Term Archival Records

Inactive records that have historical value or are essential for maintaining corporate memory must be kept the longest. Although they are not needed for present operations, they still have some value to the organization and must be preserved. This process can be complex and technical, when it comes to preserving electronic records (see Chapter 17, Long-Term Digital Preservation, for more detail). If you have a corporate or agency archivist, their input is critical.[25]

Records Having Evidential Value

When records document organizational or operational changes, they document these changes and have *evidential value*. Organizational changes can include the "evolution of powers" or changes in organizational structure, and also changes in policies, procedures, and other organizational functions.[26]

> Records contain evidential values when they show what the organization's responsibilities were and how it carried them out. Records with evidential value show organizational structure, policies that were followed, and the reason these policies were developed. Because these types of records are concerned with policies and procedures, usually records created by the senior management of the organization are of more value than those created by offices lower down in the organizational structure. However, this does depend on the organization, delegation of authority, reporting, and records systems. Records created at the operating level usually are not related to the development of policy, but are usually housekeeping records, routine correspondence, or case files. Case files can be archival records if they possess evidential or informational value.[27]

Records Having Informational Value

Of course, all records contain information, but in this context, records that contain content related to employees, major events, facilities and locations, critical topics, scenarios, and plans, have *informational value*. The value derives from the content itself, not the records creators or originators.[28] Some key factors to consider are the uniqueness of the information, the concentration or density of information, and its useful lifespan.

Assigning Time Periods to Records Values

Some record types, such as vital records (those that the organization must have in order to continue operations—see Chapter 8, Managing Vital E-Records), may need to be kept for extended periods or even indefinitely. Historical records will always need to be retained, but the value of most records declines over time. In working toward building your final detailed retention schedule, a good process to undertake is grossly estimating the retention periods for various records series in years, or even ranges of years by a prioritization analysis that asks questions such as, "What is the likelihood we will need these records series in the future?" and "What would happen if we destroyed and could not recover these records?" or "Is the cost of maintaining these records for longer periods worth the potential benefit?" The answers to questions like these may be stated in rankings (e.g., 1 to 10) or in categories (such as "high-medium-low-very low").[29] Records consistently rated as low/very low are either not required for continuing business purposes or are likely to merit preservation for a short period (e.g., one to two years).[30] This grouping and prioritization process is best done in close consultation with a team that includes records creators/owners, business unit managers, legal and compliance staff, records management staff, archivists, risk management staff, and other stakeholders.

Meeting Legal Limitation Periods

A key consideration in developing retention schedules is researching and determining the minimum time required to keep records that may be demanded in legal actions. "A **limitation period** is the length of time after which a legal action cannot be brought before the courts. Limitation periods are important because they determine the length of time records must be kept to support court action [including subsequent appeal periods]. It is important to be familiar with the purpose, principles, and special circumstances that affect limitation periods and therefore records retention."[31]

Legal Requirements and Compliance Research

Legal requirements trump all others. The retention period for a particular records series must meet minimum retention requirements as mandated by law. Business needs and other considerations are secondary. So, legal research is required before determining retention periods. Legally required retention periods must be researched for each jurisdiction (state, country) in which the business operates, so that it complies with all applicable laws.

In order to locate the regulations and citations relating to retention of records, there are two basic approaches. The first approach is to use a Records Retention Citation Service, which publishes in electronic form all of the retention-related citations. These services are usually bought on a subscription basis, as the citations are updated on an annual or more frequent basis as legislation and regulations change.

Figure 7.2 is an excerpt from a Canadian Records Retention Database product called FILELAW(R).[32] In this case, the Act, Citation, and Retention periods are clearly identified.

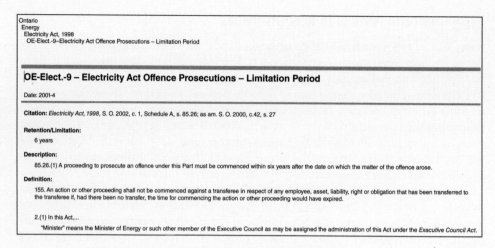

Figure 7.2   Excerpt from Canadian Records Retention Database
Source: Electricity Act, FILELAW database, Ontario: Thomson Publishers, May 2012.

Another approach is to search the laws and regulations directly using online or print resources. Records retention requirements for corporations operating in the United States may be found in the **Code of Federal Regulations (CFR).** "The Code of Federal Regulations (CFR) annual edition is the codification of the general and permanent rules published in the Federal Register by the departments and agencies of the federal government. It is divided into 50 titles that represent broad areas subject to federal regulation. The 50 subject matter titles contain one or more individual volumes, which are updated once each calendar year, on a staggered basis. The annual update cycle is as follows: titles 1 to 16 are revised as of January 1; titles 17 to 27 are revised as of April 1; titles 28 to 41 are revised as of July 1, and titles 42 to 50 are revised as of October 1. Each title is divided into chapters, which usually bear the name of the issuing agency. Each chapter is further subdivided into parts that cover specific regulatory areas. Large parts may be subdivided into subparts. All parts are organized in sections, and most citations to the CFR refer to material at the section level."[33]

There is an up-to-date version that is not yet a part of the official CFR but is updated daily, the **Electronic Code of Federal Regulations (e-CFR).** "It is not an official legal edition of the CFR. The e-CFR is an editorial compilation of CFR material and Federal Register amendments produced by the National Archives and Records Administration's Office of the Federal Register (OFR) and the Government Printing Office."[34] According to the gpoaccess.gov website:

> The Administrative Committee of the Federal Register (ACFR) has authorized the National Archives and Records Administration's (NARA) Office of the Federal Register (OFR) and the Government Printing Office (GPO) to develop and maintain the e-CFR as an informational resource pending ACFR action to grant the e-CFR official legal status.[35] The OFR/GPO partnership is committed to presenting accurate and reliable regulatory information in the e-CFR editorial compilation with the objective of establishing it as an ACFR sanctioned publication in the future. While every effort has been made

to ensure that the e-CFR on GPO Access is accurate, those relying on it for legal research should verify their results against the official editions of the CFR, Federal Register and List of CFR Sections Affected (LSA), all available online at www.gpoaccess.gov. Until the ACFR grants it official status, the e-CFR editorial compilation does not provide legal notice to the public or judicial notice to the courts.

The OFR updates the material in the e-CFR on a daily basis. Generally, the e-CFR is current within two business days. The current update status is displayed at the top of all e-CFR web pages.

Event-Based Retention Scheduling for Disposition of E-Records

Event-based disposition is kicked off with the passage of an event, such as hiring or firing an employee, the end of a project, or the initiation of a lawsuit.

Event-based disposition can have an associated retention schedule, and the clock starts running once the event occurs. The required retention period begins only after the "triggering event" occurs. The length of the retention period may be regulated by law, or it may be determined by IG guidelines set internally by the organization. So, when an employee is terminated, and personnel files are destroyed after (say) five years, then the retention schedule entry would be, "Termination + 5 years."

One other definition of event-based disposition comes from the U.S. e-records standard, DoD 5015.2, which states that a disposition instruction in which a record is eligible for the specified disposition (transfer or destroy) upon or immediately after the specified event occurs. No retention period is applied and there is no fixed waiting period as with "timed" or combination "timed-event" dispositions. Example: "Destroy when no longer needed for current operations."[36]

Some hardware vendors such as IBM and EMC provide solutions that assist in executing event-based disposition with assistance from firmware (fixed instructions on a microchip). The firmware-assisted solution should be considered if your records management or IG team aims to perform a complete and thorough retention solution analysis. These hardware-based solutions can potentially streamline the event-based disposition process.[37]

Triggering events may be record-related, "such as supersession or obsolescence." This is common to a policy statement. For example, if a group of policies are to be destroyed five years after superseded or obsolete, the old policy would be held for five years after the new policy has been created.

Sounds simple. But organizations handle event-based triggers in different ways, in an attempt to meet retention requirements, and which are oftentimes problematic. For instance, the "trigger events" are often not captured electronically and fed directly into the retention scheduling software or records repository to start the clock running, or the event itself is not well-documented in the retention schedule and it is not

Event-based disposition begins with the passage of a triggering event.

consistently being applied and tracked. In other cases, the organization simply does not have the electronic records management (ERM) functionality it needs to manage event-based triggers.

This causes many organizations to simply "over-retain" and keep the records indefinitely, or until disk storage is full, which means that those records are retained for an incorrect—and legally indefensible—time, which is too long or possibly too short, but *always* inconsistent. *And inconsistent means legally indefensible.*

The only prudent and defensible approach is to implement the proper IG policies to manage and control the implementation of event-based disposition.

Prerequisites for Event-Based Disposition

There are three key prerequisite tasks that must be completed before event-based disposition can be implemented:

1. **Clarify trigger events.** Not all of the events that can trigger the beginning of a retention period are as clear as the date an employee is terminated. For instance, "contract completion date" could be the day a vendor finishes work, when they render a final invoice, when the invoice is paid, or some other period such as 30 days following the payment of the final invoice. These definitions, depending on the record series in question, may be regulated by law or governed by IG policies.

   What is needed is an agreement as to what the definition is, so that the retention period will be uniform among the record series in question, providing a defensible policy.

   To gain this agreement on these blurry areas, the records management lead/ manager or team will need to work with the relevant business unit representatives, IT, Compliance, Risk Management, and any other stakeholders.

   The event triggers must be clear and agreed upon so that they may kick off a retention period and disposition process.

   In a number of cases, the answer to these questions will rely on trigger points, such as, "One year after completion," "Four months after the Board of Directors' meeting." *It is important to choose a* ***trigger point*** *that you can implement.* For example, there is no point in saying that records should be kept until an individual dies, if you have no reliable way of knowing whether or not they are alive. Instead, choose a trigger point based on the information you have about the individual; in this case the 100th birthday might be a suitable trigger point.

2. **Automated capture of agreed-on trigger events must be performed and sent to the ERM.** It is easy to know when an employee termination date is from most human resources (HR) management systems or payroll systems, but other types of events are not so easily captured, and may require some customization in order that this information is fed into an ERM. The metadata about the event must be seamlessly entered into the ERM so that it may launch the beginning of the retention period. If systems external to the ERM need to be interfaced, a common locater (e.g., contract number) can link the two.

3. **The ERM systems must have complete retention and disposition capabilities.** In order for the retention to start properly and run to final disposition, this tracking capability must be an inherent feature of the software. (In some cases, organizations may use specialized retention and disposition software that can perform this task minimally without complete ERM functionality, but it falls short of the type of richness that a robust ERM system provides. What is needed is the ability to include the details or retention rules beyond simple date calculations, that is, to store descriptive data or scope notes, and records series code in addition to retention requirements, which are automatically associated with the retention rule, and to have a records hold and release capability. If destruction is the final disposition, then the system must be able to perform a deletion of the record (so long as there is no preservation or legal hold) with no traces that can allow reconstruction of it, and this process must be verifiable.

To accomplish clarity and agreement on event-based triggers requires close consultation and collaboration between records management staff, business units, IT, legal, compliance, risk management, and other stakeholders, as relevant.

Final Disposition and Closure Criteria

After completing the records values analysis, and legislative and legal research, you must determine the closure criteria and final disposition (e.g., destroy, transfer, archive) for each records series. To minimize costs and litigation risk, retention periods should be kept as short as possible while meeting all applicable regulatory, legal, and business requirements.[38]

Retention Periods: Online versus Offline

For e-records, retention periods may be segmented into active and inactive, or online and offline, and offline may be segmented further into on-site and off-site or archival storage.

Going back and combing through records retrieval requests and usage logs may provide helpful insights as to the needs of users for records—but bear in mind these logs may be misleading as users may have (in the past, before a formal IG program was implemented) kept shadow copies of files on their local hard drives or backed up to flash drives or other storage devices.

Closure Dates

A clear closure start date is required to kick off a retention period for any record, whether the retention is scheduled for on- or off-site. Calendar or fiscal year-ends are typical and practical closure dates for subject or topical records. The date used to indicate the start year is usually the date the file closed or the date of last use or update. In a university setting, school year-end may be more logical. Still, a reasoned analysis is required to determine the best closure start date for subject records in your organization.

Case records are different; logically, their closure date is set when a case record is completed, for instance, the date when an employee resigns, retires, or is terminated.

Future dates may be used, such as an employee promotion date, student graduation, or project completion. After consulting those who create and handle the records series you are analyzing, apply good business judgment and common sense when determining closure dates.[39]

Retaining Records Indefinitely

There may be some vital, historical, or other critical records that, in the best interests of the organization, need to be retained permanently. This is rare, and storing records long-term must be scrutinized heavily. If certain electronic records are to be retained indefinitely or permanently, then long-term digital preservation (LTDP) policies and techniques must be used (see Chapter 17, Long-Term Digital Preservation, for more detail).[40]

Retaining Transitory Records

Transitory documents usually do not rise to the level of becoming a record; they are temporary and are useful only in the short-term, such as direct mail or e-mail advertising (brochures, price lists, and the like), draft documents (although not all are transitory, and some may need longer retention periods, such as draft contracts) and work-in-progress, duplicates, external publications (such as magazines, journals, newspapers, etc.), and temporary notices (e.g., company picnic, holiday party, or football pool). You must consider transitory records in your master records retention schedule.

Implementation of the Retention Schedule and Disposal of Records

Automated programs that interpret these retention periods are the best way to ensure that records are disposed of at the correct time, and that an audit trail of the disposition is maintained.

Getting Acceptance and Formal Sign-Off of the Retention Schedule

Upon completion of the records retention schedule, project management best practices dictate that it be signed off by an executive or project sponsor, to indicate it has been completed and there is no more work to be done on that phase of the project. In addition, you may want to gain the sign-off and acceptance by other key stakeholders, such as senior representatives from legal, IT, the board of directors or executive committee, and perhaps audit and information governance. The schedule should be updated when new record types are introduced, and, in any case, at least annually.

Disposition Timing: Records Disposal

It is much easier to time or schedule the disposal of e-records than it is for paper or physical records, but true and complete destruction of all traces of a record cannot be done by hitting a simple "delete" key. There must be a process in place to verify the total destruction of all copies of the record. (See Chapter 17, Long-Term Digital Preservation, for more detail.) Records destruction can occur daily, routinely, or can be scheduled at intervals (i.e., monthly or quarterly).

Automating Retention/Disposal Actions

ERM systems are typically capable of automatically executing a record deletion when a record has reached the end of its lifecycle. Often, these systems have a safety feature that allows an operator who has the authority to review deletions before they are performed.

Disposal Date Changes

To make a retention schedule change, such as extending the life of a record series, IG controls must be in place. So, usually, ERM systems require that a person of higher authority than the system operator make these approvals. Every subsequent delay in destroying the records often requires an escalation in approval period to extend the time that records are kept past the destruction date.

Proving Record Destruction

In some environments, especially in the public sector, a certificate of destruction or other documentation is required to prove that a record and all its copies have been completely deleted (including its metadata—although at times it is beneficial to retain metadata longer than the record itself; see Chapter 16, Metadata Governance, Standards, and Strategies, for more detail). ERM systems can be configured to keep an audit trail and prove that destruction has occurred.

Ongoing Maintenance of the Retention Schedule

Records series are not static; they change, are added to, and are amended. New record functions emerge, based on changes in business, acquisitions, and divestitures. So it is necessary for organizations to review and update—at least annually—their records retention schedule.

In addition, retention requirements change as legislation changes, lawsuits are filed, and the organization refines and improves its IG policies. So development of a records retention schedule is not a one-time project; it requires attention, maintenance, and updating on a regular schedule, and using a controlled change process.

Audit to Manage Compliance with the Retention Schedule

Once your organization establishes records retention schedules for business units, or a master retention schedule, there must be IG policies in place to audit and ensure that policies are being followed. *This is a key requirement of maintaining a legally defensible retention schedule that will hold up to legal challenges.*

CHAPTER SUMMARY: **KEY POINTS**

- A complete, current and documented records retention program reduces storage and handling costs and improves searchability for records by making records easier and faster to find.

- Retention schedules are developed by records series—not for individual records.

- Retention schedules are a basic tool that allows an organization to prove that it has a legally defensible basis on which to dispose records.

- The master retention schedule contains all records series in the entire enterprise.

- Records retention defines the length of time that records are to be kept and considers legal, regulatory, operational, and historical requirements.[41]

- Disposition means not just destruction but can also mean archiving and a change in ownership and responsibility for the records.

- An information map is a critical first step in developing a records retention schedule. It shows where information is created, where it resides, and who uses it.

- After inventorying, developing a retention schedule begins with records classification.

- All e-mail messages are not records; those that document a business transaction, or progress toward it, are clearly records and require retention.

- E-mail messages that document business activities, especially those that may be disputed in the future, should be retained as records.

- Destruction retention of e-mail is a method whereby e-mail messages are retained for a limited period and then destroyed.

- There are tools available to scan e-records folders to expedite the inventorying process.

- Assessing the relative value of records is key to determining their retention periods and disposition path.

- Records have different types of value, such as financial, legal, technical, and administrative/operational.

- Event-based disposition begins with a triggering event.

- Retention schedules, once established, must be maintained and updated to add new records series, as appropriate, and to comply with new or changed legislation and regulatory requirements.

- Auditing to ensure compliance with established retention policies is key to maintaining a legally defensible records retention program.

Notes

1. U.S. Department of Energy, "Records Retention Schedule Definition," https://commons.lbl.gov/display/aro/Records+Retention+Schedule+Definition (accessed July 30, 2012).
2. National Archives, "Frequently Asked Questions about Records Scheduling and Disposition," updated June 6, 2005, www.archives.gov/records-mgmt/faqs/scheduling.html#whysched.
3. Government of Alberta, "Developing Retention and Disposition Schedules," July 2004, www.rimp.gov.ab.ca/publications/pdf/SchedulingGuide.pdf.
4. National Archives, "Frequently Asked Questions about Records Scheduling and Disposition."
5. International Organization for Standardization, "Information and Documentation—Principles and Functional Requirements for Records in Electronic Office Environments—Part 1: Overview and Statement of Principles," ISO 16175-1:2010, www.iso.org/iso/catalogue_detail.htm?csnumber=55790 (accessed July 30, 2012).
6. Government of Alberta, "Developing Retention and Disposition Schedules."
7. National Archives, "Disposition of Federal Records: A Records Management Handbook," 2000, www.archives.gov/records-mgmt/publications/disposition-of-federal-records/chapter-2.html (accessed July 30, 2012).
8. Government of Alberta, "Developing Retention and Disposition Schedules."
9. National Archives, "Frequently Asked Questions about Records Scheduling and Disposition."
10. Ibid.
11. The University of Edinburgh, Records Management Section, July 5, 2012, www.recordsmanagement.ed.ac.uk/InfoStaff/RMstaff/Retention/Retention.htm.
12. Sample provided by IMERGE Consulting, Inc.
13. National Archives, "Frequently Asked Questions about Records Scheduling and Disposition."
14. The University of Edinburgh, Records Management Section.
15. National Archives, "Frequently Asked Questions about Records Scheduling and Disposition."
16. University of Toronto Archives, "Glossary," www.library.utoronto.ca/utarms/info/glossary.html (accessed September 10, 2012).
17. Government of Alberta, "Developing Retention and Disposition Schedules."
18. Ibid.
19. Marty Foltyn, "Getting Up to Speed on FRCP," June 29, 2007, www.enterprisestorageforum.com/continuity/features/article.php/3686491/Getting-Up-To-Speed-On-FRCP.htm.
20. Nancy Flynn, *The E-Policy Handbook* (New York: AMACOM, 2009), 24–25.
21. Ibid.
22. Government of Alberta, "Developing Retention and Disposition Schedules."
23. Ibid.
24. Ibid., 126.
25. Ibid., 127.
26. Ibid., 122–123.
27. Ibid.
28. Ibid.
29. Ibid.
30. The University of Edinburgh, Records Management Section.
31. Government of Alberta, "Developing Retention and Disposition Schedules," 122.
32. Electricity Act, FILELAW database, Ontario: Thomson Publishers, May 2012.
33. The U.S. Government Printing Office (GPO), "Code of Federal Regulations," www.gpo.gov/help/index.html#about_code_of_federal_regulations.htm (accessed April 22, 2012).
34. National Archives and Records Administration, "Electronic Code of Federal Regulations," October 2, 2012, http://ecfr.gpoaccess.gov/cgi/t/text/text-idx?c=ecfr&tpl=%2Findex.tpl.
35. Ibid.
36. Department of Defense, "Design Criteria Standard for Electronic Records Management Software Applications," July 19, 2002, jitc.fhu.disa.mil/cgi/rma/downloads/p50152s2.doc.
37. Craig Rhinehart, IBM, e-mail to author, July 30, 2012.
38. Government of Alberta, "Records and Information Management."
39. Ibid., 125.
40. Ibid., 126.
41. National Archives, "Frequently Asked Questions about Records Scheduling and Disposition."

CHAPTER 8
Managing Vital E-Records

The most critical information assets an organization has are its vital records. Without them, the organization cannot continue to function. Vital e-records must be secured and backed up with the utmost of care and caution, and plans for business resumption must be in place should a major business disruption damage or destroy vital records.

Defining Vital Records

More specifically, **vital records** are *mission-critical records* that are necessary for an organization to continue to operate in the event of disruption or disaster (e.g., fire, flood, hacker attack) and cannot be re-created from any other source. They are the most important records to be protected, and a plan for **disaster recovery** (DR)/**business continuity** (BC) must be developed, tested, and implemented in concert with an organization's disaster planning/emergency response team to safeguard these records. A basic information governance (IG) program must include risk assessments and vital records planning to protect and, if necessary, recover vital records.

According to one public source:

Vital records must be protected from destruction because they offer direct evidence of legal status, ownership, accounts receivable, and the particulars of obligations incurred by government agencies [and businesses]. These records are critical because they contain information required to continue functioning during a disaster, or to reestablish operations after a calamity has ended. Vital records are irreplaceable, and in some instances must be maintained in their original form to be legally admissible as evidence.[1]

Vital records are mission-critical records that are necessary for an organization to continue to operate in the event of a disaster.

135

Vital records include records that maintain and protect the rights of stakeholders[2] and are needed to continue or restart operations in the event of a disaster or other business interruption.[3]

Historically, enterprises have underinvested in security and protections for vital records. Often management seeks to minimize costs by holding off on investing in a DR/BC plan and associated safeguarding tools, such as backup power and communications systems, copies of critical data held off-site, fireproof safes, sprinkler systems, and disaster insurance. Avoiding the cost of protecting vital records can be tempting to cost-conscious, short-sighted managers, especially if an enterprise has never experienced a disaster (and operates under a false sense of security).

As examples, the tragedies of the 9/11 attack in 2001, Hurricane Katrina in 2005, and Superstorm Sandy in 2012 emphasize the importance of DR/BC planning and preparation. *Vital records management is a cost-justifiable strategy because it safeguards critical assets and provides insurance that preserves stakeholder and public trust.*

Managing vital records involves key activities:

- *Inventorying:* Identifying and documenting vital records.
- *Securing:* Protecting them through electronic and physical security.
- *Recovering:* Following a disaster or business interruption, having the capability to quickly obtain access to them (or working copies) and putting them into operation.

IG policies, procedures, and controls, when developed and implemented, provide assurance that business operations can survive a disaster and resume in a timely manner. Failure to plan can destroy the business—*nearly three-quarters of organizations go out of business after having vital records destroyed by a disaster.*

A vital records program is an essential component of a *counter-disaster program,* which aims to minimize the impact of disasters and enable the organization *to execute a business continuity plan* for quick recovery and resumption of operations.[4]

In DR/BC planning, varied considerations need to be given for short versus long business interruptions. Business disruption may be temporary, as in the event of a fire alarm or bomb scare, or long term, such as a disaster caused by a flood, hurricane, tornado, fire, or even a terrorist attack. Different responses need to be fashioned and executed for various scenarios. In each case, the preservation and acquisition (or regeneration) of vital records must be the paramount consideration.

Types of Vital Records

Often, those outside of the records management (RM) community think of vital records in a public sector sense, that is, birth and death certificates, marriage licenses, and other official records. These are a subset of vital records for governments, and it is

> Effective vital records program policies and procedures can protect against continuity disruptions and provide insurance against information damage incurred by disasters.

critical for them to maintain historical records, but *every formal organization—business, nonprofit, or government—has vital records.*

In government, and in most every business, personnel and payroll records are vital records, as employees cannot be paid accurately without them. After Hurricane Katrina, employees of the local New Orleans school district and universities could not be paid correctly once power was restored, since the details of their withholdings and deductions were not available. So the temporary workaround was to run a "plain vanilla" payroll check for employees without accurate deductions and to reconcile them later.

In almost every organization, active contracts are also vital records. In health care, medical records are vital records; pharmaceutical firms cannot operate without their research and drug compound records; in banking and financial services firms, customer information files are vital records; in a university, student academic records are vital records; a law or consulting firm needs its client files to operate; a publisher must have book files; and a manufacturing firm needs current material safety data sheets (MSDS) to continue manufacturing operations safely.

Not all records are vital, in fact; *typically an organization's vital records range from about 1 to 7 percent* (estimates vary) *of total records*, with the majority of organizations' vital records making up between 3 to 5 percent of their total records.

Although each department or business unit will have a tendency to blur the lines between important records and vital records, it is the duty of the vital records team (which may include representatives from records management, information technology [IT], legal, compliance, risk management, and operations), to determine which crucial (and small) subset of important records are, in reality, *vital* records. This is important because the extra investment in IG, auditing procedures, testing, hardware, software, secure filing and storage equipment, backup facilities, and other required components of a vital records program are costly, and in fact, *pay no return unless there is an actual disaster.*

Vital records are not determined by their media or their status (e.g., active or inactive; in use, at rest, or in transit). They can be paper, microfilm, audio/videotape, or electronic records. They can be digital or analog. They are not always permanent or active records, and may not even be original records, but critical copies. They may be only temporarily considered vital, and then their status can change, such as when an organization is in the midst of a significant transaction (e.g., a merger or acquisition). Retention of vital records should be dictated by thoroughly developed IG policies, which must reflect the organization's culture and business goals, and necessarily incorporate any regulatory or legal requirements that a state, province, or federal government imposes.

Impact of Losing Vital Records

The impact of the loss of vital records should not be underestimated. In the event of major disasters, the loss of the building or equipment generally matters less than the loss of vital records; after all, hard capital assets like buildings and equipment can be

Users have a tendency to blur the lines between important records and vital records. Only about 3 to 5 percent of records are vital.

> The majority of organizations that suffer the loss of critical business records
> and software from a disaster go out of business within three years, due partly
> to the inability to recover or regenerate vital records.

replaced through lease, repair, or purchase. *According to one university study, more than 70 percent of organizations go out of business within three years of suffering a fire that caused the loss of business records and software.*[5]

According to United Nations guidelines, key points for managing risks and protecting vital records include the following four:

1. **Small subset.** Your vital records will be small in number—only about 3 to 5 percent of all business records are vital.
2. **Inventory and secure.** Identify and protect them using IG policies, technologies, and physical security measures.
3. **Keep updated.** Remember to exchange older security copies for current versions as necessary. Also, official copies of vital records need to be tested periodically to ensure they are readable and in the most current and prevalent electronic formats.
4. **Test the plan.** Have a plan for accessing the security copies in the event of an emergency—and practice it.[6]

Creating, Implementing, and Maintaining a Vital Records Program

The United Nations describes a vital records program as "a management regimen for vital records that includes preventative and protection measures and procedures, retention requirements and locations, staff and service provider contact details together with documentation."[7]

A vital records program requires IG, which means not only protecting vital records from natural or man-made disasters, but also assuring information confidence and *record integrity*, that is, the accuracy, authenticity, and validity of records. *Vital records, and most especially electronic vital records, are vulnerable to theft, unauthorized alteration, or misuse.* So, for instance, a bank or credit reporting company must protect its vital customer records so that they are not used for identity theft or other fraudulent purposes; a university must protect its student academic records from tampering or alteration; and a law firm must protect its client files from editing, theft, or tampering.

Essential Steps to Implementing a Vital Records Program

A complete vital records program must include all of the following:

- **Sponsorship.** Announcement, planning, and development of the vital records program by senior management.

Senior management sets the tone for vital records program governance and compliance.

- **Policy creation.** Establishment of IG policies for vital records.
- **Inventorying.** Survey, identification, and inventory maintenance of vital records.
- **Assessing risk.** Determination of key threats and potential losses if vital records are lost, damaged, altered, or stolen.
- **Securing.** Evaluation and implementation of appropriate protective, prevention, and recovery measures, including utilization of external services, archiving of safe copies, physical security, and secure cloud computing.
- **Educating.** Training and communicating with employees about vital records issues on an ongoing basis.
- **Auditing.** Ensuring vital records program procedures are being followed.
- **Testing.** Engaging in actual live testing and mock disaster exercises.

U.S. National Archives Approach to Identify Vital Records

The U.S. National Archives has created guidelines that American federal agencies should follow when identifying critical information and creating document inventories:

- Consult with the official responsible for emergency coordination,
- Review agency statutory and regulatory responsibilities and existing emergency plans for insights into the functions and records that may be included in the vital records inventory,
- Review documentation created for the contingency planning and risk assessment phase of emergency preparedness. The offices performing those functions are obvious focuses of an inventory,
- Review current file plans of offices that are responsible for performing critical functions or may be responsible for preserving rights, and,
- Review the agency records manual or records schedule to determine which records series potentially qualify as vital.

Agencies must exercise caution in designating records as vital and in conducting the vital records inventory. A review of the available literature suggests that *from 1 to 7 percent of an agency's records may be vital records.* Only those records series or electronic information systems (or portions of them) *most* critical to emergency operations or the preservation of legal or financial rights should be so designated. Agencies must make difficult and judicious decisions in this regard.

The inventory of vital records should include:

- The name of the office responsible for the records series or electronic information system containing vital information.

- The title of each records series or information system containing vital information.
- Identification of each series or system that contains emergency-operating vital records or vital records relating to rights.
- The medium on which the records are recorded.
- The physical location for off-site storage of copies of the records series or system.
- The frequency with which the records are to be cycled (updated).[8]

Critical Identifiers for Vital Records

All vital records must contain critical identifying information:

- Record series title.
- Rationale for vital record designation, that is, what mission-critical business functions are dependent on these specific records.
- Description of the record series' business role, function, and its medium(s).
- Department responsible for producing and maintaining the vital records.
- Department responsible for protecting and preserving the vital records.
- Protective measures prescribed for safety, preservation, and reproduction.

When identifying which of your records are vital, it may be helpful to divide them into the following categories: (1) vital, (2) important, (3) useful, and (4) nonessential, as shown in Table 8.1, adapted from the vital records policy of the University of Edinburgh in Scotland.[9] Please note that the examples are not exhaustive and will vary from organization to organization.

Table 8.1   Critical Identifiers for Vital Records

1. Vital Records	

Records without which an organization cannot function. These records are essential to the core business of the organization.	Examples:
	1. Records that give evidence of organizational legal status
	
	  ■ Current financial and tax records
	  ■ Records that protect the assets and interests of the organization
	  ■ Current and recent contracts
	  ■ Software source code
	  ■ Research information
	  ■ Records that are subject to a legal retention requirement
	  ■ Minutes of board meetings dealing with major policy issues
	  ■ Historical records, if needed for evidential or other legal purposes
	  ■ Business plan

2. Important Records	
These records are important to the continued operation of the organization.	Examples: 1. Procedures

Table 8.1   (*Continued*)

They can be reproduced or recreated from original sources, but only at considerable time and expense.	2. Training manuals 3. Business timetables 4. Minutes of some meetings 5. Business contact information 6. E-mails with potential legal implications
3. Useful Records	
Loss of these records would cause temporary inconvenience to the organization, but they are replaceable.	Examples 1. Most correspondence 2. Management e-mails 3. Records of historical transactions 4. Marketing plans
4. Nonessential Records	
These records have no value beyond the immediate purpose for which they were created.	Examples: 1. E-mails and materials about one-off events which are now completed 2. Advertisements

Source: Adapted from The University of Edinburgh, "Vital Records version 8," March 22, 2011, www.records management.ed.ac.uk/InfoStaff/RMstaff/VitalRecords/VitalRecords.htm.

Implementing Protective Procedures

Once vital records have been identified, practical steps to preserve and protect them must be taken. A range of events could occur, disrupting your work, and endangering your vital records.[10] These include, but are not limited to:

- **Power surges and outages.** Fluctuations or temporary outages that cause hardware downtime at the desktop, shared network hard drive, or server level.
- **Hardware failures.** Server crash resulting in inability to access e-records for a few hours, or even days.
- **Fire alarm or bomb threat.** Forced evacuation prohibiting building access for a few hours or days.
- **Nonmalicious insider.** Loss or damage through carelessness.
- **Malicious attacks.** Theft or destruction of information assets including vital records.
- **Physical exposure or deterioration.** Excessive humidity, heat, or sunlight, and biological factors (e.g., mold, rats, mice, insects), can deteriorate or destroy physical and electronic vital records.
- **Natural and man-made disasters.** Fire, flood, tornado, hurricane, tsunami, acts of terrorism, and so on can lead to document loss and destruction.

As required by 36 CFR 1236, U.S. governmental agencies must include vital records management procedures in their business continuity plan in the event of disaster or prolonged business interruption.

Under SOX, all business records must be saved for at least five years.

Public corporations are also obligated to protect vital records, under multiple laws and statutes. In the United States, the Sarbanes-Oxley Act of 2002 (SOX) sets regulatory requirements for the disclosure of financial records and statements, accounting practices, and related communications in an attempt to root out fraud. SOX does not specify "*how* a [public or corporate] business should store its records; rather, it defines *which* records are to be stored and for *how long*" (italics added).[11]

The SOX legislation not only impacts financial reporting, it also impacts the records management, compliance, legal, and IT departments—those charged with maintaining the corporation's electronic records. It also affects those who audit public corporations. *The Sarbanes-Oxley Act states that all business records, including e-records, e-mail and other electronic messages, must be saved for "not less than five years."*

The consequences for noncompliance are serious and can include monetary fines, imprisonment of executives, or both. Since SOX was implemented, executives of public corporations have increasingly taken an active role in dictating IG and records management policies, and the records management and compliance functions have gained elevated visibility and importance. Cost-effectively achieving transparency and compliance in records management functions has been a great challenge over the past decade, and it requires new policies, new technologies, and new governance, risk management, and compliance (GRC) tools.

Private corporations are subject to much less scrutiny, so much so that some public enterprises have made the move to turn private. But private corporations are also regulated under the Foreign Corrupt Practices Act (FCPA) of 1977 (amended 1988, 1998), which affects private corporations, limited liability corporations (LLCs), and partnerships. The FCPA was originally intended to prevent the destruction of business records to hide bribery or other crimes. Substantial penalties are imposed for failure to keep proper financial records.

Additional recordkeeping regulations affect specific vertical industries. HIPAA (Healthcare Insurance Portability and Accountability Act) requires application data backup and business continuity plans for electronic data and records kept by health care providers. 45 CFR 164.30 requires healthcare organizations to "protect against any reasonably anticipated threats or hazards to the security and integrity of such information," and business continuity plans are required "to create and maintain retrievable exact copies of electronic protected health information."

The Federal Deposit Insurance Corporation (FDIC) requires banks to have business continuity/disaster recovery plans in place for computing facilities. These plans are reviewed by the Federal Financial Institutions Examination Council (FFIEC).

There are a range of levels of investment that an organization may make in safeguarding its vital records and e-records, from inexpensively storing paper records

E-records are easier to protect than paper or other physical records.

in sturdy cardboard boxes, to portable file cabinets that can be rolled out of an area should the need arise, to fireproof vaults and even costly fire-proofed rooms. The medium and format of the records along with the level and speed of access needed will dictate which choices of protection are suitable. Other factors include budgetary constraints, operating environment, and whether or not a copy exists safely off-site. *The most expensive options should be selected for vital records that cannot be recreated or have lasting historical value.* Choose the highest security alternatives only when absolutely required, such as for classified government operations.

Protective and preventative measures must be undertaken to safeguard your organization's vital e-records. These safeguards must first provide for physical security, using means like control for physical access (e.g., smartcards for file room access, a fireproof safe) and for online access (passwords, access and authentication security measures) and records preservation over the long term.

In general, electronic records are easier to protect from disaster than physical (paper) records, due to their portability and ease of copying for backups. Copying a vital e-record may be as easy as using a few keystrokes to burn it to CD or DVD, or even a flash drive, all of which are fast and inexpensive. *Protecting those e-records from unauthorized copying or use is more difficult than if they were paper records locked in a storage safe.* But it can be accomplished with technologies like encryption and information rights management (IRM), which has the ability to secure an electronic document throughout its lifecycle.

How do you flag records as vital and therefore note their importance, and invoke a set of IG policies that apply to them? It can be as simple as including the word "vital" in the document or folder title, as this will make them easier to search and retrieve—and also it means that their handling must be dictated by IG policies and guidelines that are specific to vital records.

Vital records should not be stored on individual PCs, laptops, or tablets, but rather, on networked servers that make regular backups, and are managed by formal procedures.[12]

Instant Continuous Backup

Organizations may protect themselves by employing software and methods to back up their data and vital records in real time, instantly, on a continuous basis. This can be as basic as disk mirroring (replicating data to two or more disks at once) or using RAID (redundant array of independent disks), which writes all data across an array of disks, with built-in back-up and recovery capabilities. Or, it can be as complex as backing up the data in two or more remote sites over a secure connection such as a virtual private network (VPN), instantaneously. Organizations such as banks and hospitals and critical military units that cannot allow downtime may use this approach to ensure continuity of operations.

> Vital records should be stored in a managed environment on networked servers or central mainframe computers that are backed-up up regularly—not on individual PCs, laptops, or tablets.

Off-site Continuity Options

An organization may make arrangements to switch its computing operations over to an alternate, backup site for complete redundancy and for backup operations in the event of a business disruption. This may be accomplished through a remote unit of the same organization, a sister organization, or a third-party data center. *There are three basic types of backup sites: hot sites, warm sites, and cold sites.*

A **hot site** is one that has identical or nearly identical hardware and operating system configurations, and copies of application software, and receives live, real-time backup data from business operations. In the event of a business interruption, the IT and electronic vital records operations can be switched over automatically, providing uninterrupted service. *This is the most expensive option.* It may be offered by corporate data centers, service bureaus, hardware manufacturers, and specialized disaster recovery service organizations.

A **warm site** may have all (or mostly all) identical hardware and operating systems, such as a hot site does, and software licenses for the same applications, and needs only to have data loaded to resume normal operations. Internal IT staff may have to retrieve magnetic tapes, optical disks, or other storage media containing the most recent backup data, and some data may be lost if the backup is not real-time and continuous.

A **cold site** is simply an empty computer facility or data center that is ready with air-conditioning, raised floors, telecommunication lines, and electric power. Backup hardware and software will have to be purchased and shipped in quickly to resume operations. Arrangements can be made with suppliers for rapid delivery in the event of a disaster. *A cold site is the least expensive option, but will take the longest for the organization to get running again.* The site may be shared among multiple business units, or even organizations, to spread the cost.

Cloud Computing Offers a New Option

A relatively new option, another tool in the toolkit of a vital records program, is the use of secure cloud computing (see Chapter 12, Managing E-Records in the Cloud, for more details) for storing vital records off-site and out of the reach of a local or regional disaster. Cloud computing has various levels of functionality, from basic infrastructure to fully functioning applications, and in its fundamental software-as-a-service (SaaS) offering–a sort of metered information utility that allows modulated access to software applications—it is using the Internet or a more secure VPN and remote servers to store or process electronic files, documents, software application programs, e-mail, and other potential vital records. Some organizations use cloud computing to process e-mail, store large or critical files, or to operate key information management software applications and it provides an option for records managers and emergency response teams.

Cloud computing is relatively new and immature but, with proper security, may be a good option for storing third or fourth copies of vital records, or backups of backup copies that can be accessed quickly in the event of a disaster or business interruption.

> Storage in the cloud may be a good option for a third or fourth copy of vital e–records.

Auditing the Vital Records Program

Regular, periodic audits, some conducted by an internal audit team and some by a trusted third party, will ensure that IG policies and legal compliance requirements are being met. Audits can take a sampling or subset of vital records and follow them through the entire vital records program process to see that each critical step is taken. The vital records program audit may be coordinated with, or a component of, an overall governance audit, compliance audit, or even an accounting audit, to reduce costs and duplication of effort while providing a complete view of the organization's IG and compliance status.

Some of the questions that must be answered are included in this checklist, based on recommendations from the U.S. National Archives:

1. Has the agency [or business unit] prepared and disseminated written information to appropriate agency staff, describing the vital records program, including the responsibilities of various agency officials?

2. Has the agency [or business unit] assigned an official responsibility for managing the vital records program and coordinating it with other appropriate officials?

3. Have liaison officers been delegated responsibility for implementing the program in the agency's [or business unit] field offices?

4. Has the agency [or business unit] identified its vital records, i.e., its emergency operating records and records needed to protect legal and financial rights?

5. Does the agency [or business unit] make copies of the vital records for offsite storage?

6. Does the agency [or business unit] store duplicates at a remote location not subject to the same fire or other risks (such as high-risk geographic areas prone to flooding or earthquakes) present in storage areas where original records are kept?

7. Are agency [or business unit] personnel trained in their vital records responsibilities?

8. Does the agency [or business unit] conduct a periodic review of its vital records plan and update it to ensure that it is current, complete, and usable in case of emergency?

9. If special records (such as electronic information systems or microform records) are designated as vital records, have provisions been made for access to the equipment needed to use the records in the event of an emergency?[13]

Creating a checklist that is specific to your organization can begin with these questions and then be revised and expanded appropriately until it is complete. Planning and testing are key elements of any program to recover business operations in the event of a disruption and to secure vital records in the event of a disaster.

Additional Resources

ARMA International published an American National Standard on managing vital records programs, which is a useful resource. It is entitled, "ANSI/ARMA 5–2010, Vital Records Programs: Identifying, Managing, and Recovering Business-Critical Records." Go to ARMA.org for additional information and pricing.

CHAPTER SUMMARY: **KEY POINTS**

- Vital records are mission-critical records that are necessary for an organization to continue to operate.

- Effective vital records program policies and procedures can protect against continuity disruptions and provide insurance against information damage incurred by disasters.

- Typically only about 3 to 5 percent of an organization's total records are vital records.

- The majority of organizations that suffer the loss of critical business records and software from a disaster go out of business within three years, due mostly to the inability to recover or regenerate vital records.

- A vital records program is a management regimen for vital records that includes preventative and protection measures and procedures, retention requirements and locations, and staff and service provider contact details, as well as with documentation.

- Vital records should be stored in a managed environment on networked servers or central mainframe computers that are backed-up up regularly— not on individual PCs, laptops, or tablets.

- Managing vital records involves: (1) identifying and documenting vital records; (2) protecting them through electronic and physical security; and (3) recovering them quickly and putting them into operation after a business interruption or disaster.

- An organization may make arrangements to switch its computing operations over to an alternate backup site. There are three basic types of backup sites: hot sites, warm sites, and cold sites.

- A hot site is the most expensive option, but provides the fastest recovery.

- Cloud computing offers new options for backing up and restoring vital e-records in the event of a disaster or business interruption, but it should not be the first choice due to the immaturity of the technology and potential risks.

- Regular, periodic audits, some internal and some by a trusted third party, will ensure that IG policies and legal compliance requirements are being met in a vital records program.

Notes

1. State of Delaware, "Vital Records Management," January 5, 2010, http://archives.delaware.gov/govsvcs/records_policies/vital%20records%20management.shtml.
2. The University of Edinburgh, "Vital Records," March 22, 2011, www.recordsmanagement.ed.ac.uk/InfoStaff/RMstaff/VitalRecords/VitalRecords.htm.
3. NSW Government, "State Records," www.records.nsw.gov.au/recordkeeping/dirks-manual/doing-a-dirks-project/manage-your-vital-records (accessed December 21, 2011).
4. Ibid.
5. The University of Edinburgh, "Vital Records."
6. United Nations, Archives and Records Management, "Section 15—Managing Risks and Protecting Vital Records," http://archives.un.org/unarms/en/unrecordsmgmt/unrecordsresources/managingrisksandprotectingvitalrecords.htm#main (accessed December 21, 2011).
7. Ibid.
8. The U.S. National Archives and Records Administration, "Vital Records and Records Disaster Mitigation and Recovery: An Instructional Guide," 1999, www.archives.gov/records-mgmt/vital-records/#Vital (accessed December 21, 2011).
9. The University of Edinburgh, "Vital Records."
10. Ibid.
11. SearchCIO.com, "Sarbanes-Oxley Act (SOX)" (accessed December 5, 2012), http://searchcio.techtarget.com/definition/Sarbanes-Oxley-Act.
12. The University of Edinburgh, "Vital Records."
13. The U.S. National Archives and Records Administration, "Vital Records and Records Disaster Mitigation and Recovery."

CHAPTER 9

ERM Link to Business Process Improvement

Stephen Goodfellow, CRM

A **"business process** is the end-to-end coordinated set of collaborative and transactional work activities carried out by both automated systems and people to produce a desired result or achieve a goal."[1] While this is just one of many possible definitions of a business process, often many may simply think of a *business process* as "what we do as part of our normal job." Certain work-related tasks have to be done in order to meet a stated goal or objective given by a supervisor or senior level executive.

When trying to improve the management of electronic records or implementing an **electronic records management** (ERM) system, business processes will need to be redesigned. Since electronic records, whether an e-mail, spreadsheet, presentation, scanned image or other electronic file, are ingrained into the daily activities of knowledge workers, business processes associated with better managed e-records also benefit. So, in order to understand how to improve the management of electronic records, one must understand how electronic records are used within a process. That is where **business process improvement** (BPI) analysis skills are required.

The previous scenario could lead to asking the question, Which came first, the chicken or the egg? Do we improve the overall business process and see how that affects the e-records or do we focus on the records and see how the business process improves? The answer depends on your specific business goals, but in most cases, *efforts to streamline and improve a business process must be addressed prior to changing how records are managed* or before implementing an ERM system.

Improving Processes, Improving Quality

A century ago, process improvement in business was focused on the manufacturing floor. Factory owners' desires to produce products faster and at a lower cost drove them to seek new, more efficient ways to streamline manufacturing processes. "How can we produce *widgets* faster and cheaper?" was the most-asked question posed by factory owners at the time.

A business process is a coordinated set of collaborative and transactional work activities carried out by systems and people to produce a desired result.

> Generally, efforts to streamline and improve a business process must be addressed prior to changing how records are managed or before implementing an ERM system.

In the aftermath of World War II, the word *quality* became the focal point for a number of organizations and would help to shape process improvement efforts for decades. Raising the quality of the outcome from a process, as well as the process itself, would help businesses become more efficient in addition to helping separate them from their competition.

In the postwar years, W. Edward Deming's name became synonymous with process improvement and quality. Along with Joseph Juran, Deming became a leading figure in the Total Quality Management (TQM) business philosophy movement. *In a TQM effort, all members of an organization participate in improving processes, products, services, and the culture in which they work.*

As a cornerstone in implementing TQM, Deming created his 14 points—key principles to be adopted by management for transforming businesses through increasing quality and productivity.[2] His belief was that if these 14 points were adopted and acted upon, management intended to stay in business.

While TQM was popular during the 1960s and 1970s, it is no longer a popular term in business today. "Total Quality Management" has often been replaced with *quality assurance or quality management in context of process improvement.*

Six Sigma

Inspired by the TQM movement and born from efforts within Motorola in the late 1970s, **Six Sigma** became the face of the quality movement through the 1980s and 1990s. Popularized by GE and its famous CEO Jack Welch, as well as many other organizations, *Six Sigma is a highly structured approach for eliminating defects in any process*, whether from manufacturing or transactional processes. It can be applied to a product or a service-oriented process in any organization.

From GE's website: "Six Sigma is a highly disciplined process that helps us focus on developing and delivering near-perfect products and services." Sigma is defined as "a statistical term that measures how far a given process deviates from perfection." The goal of the Six Sigma is to systematically measure and eliminate defects in a process, aiming for a level of less than 3.4 defects per million instances or "opportunities."

Six Sigma became popular because it focuses strongly on a balance of:[3]

- **A focus on the customer.** From the outset of Six Sigma, Motorola focused on the importance of customer satisfaction in product development and service delivery. The original six steps included three key points:

    1. Identify your product or service.
    2. Identify the customer(s) for your product or service; determine what they consider important.

3. Identify your needs to provide the product/service so that it satisfies the customer.[4]

- **A value proposition of decreasing the costs of nonquality.** The Six Sigma approach seek projects in a Pareto (a/k/a "the 80-20 rule") fashion that are expected to recover returns from $100,000 to more than $1 million. After the first year or so of GE's breakeven Six Sigma efforts, the payback accelerated. The company recovered $750 million in 1998 and approximately $1.5 billion in 1999—with billions of potential recovery since then.[5]

- **A focus on process improvement and process design or redesign as the means of addressing nonquality.** Define-measure-analyze-improve-control (DMAIC) packages the measurement processes with process improvement or design/redesign and control. It does not even consider measurement for measurement's sake. Nor does DMAIC discuss scrap and rework as a means of "improvement." It is centered around improving, controlling, and performing processes to approach Six Sigma–level quality, based on what customers care about.

- **Active involvement of top management who understand and champion the value proposition and the imperatives of quality principles and processes to accomplish the value proposition.** The story of GE illustrates the importance of top management and its ability to transform even the largest of organizations. When Jack Welch saw the value of Six Sigma, he quickly became its champion, urging "his top lieutenants to become 'passionate lunatics' about Six Sigma." He has described GE's commitment to Six Sigma as "unbalanced."[6] The Motorola and GE experiences illustrate that even large organizations can make dramatic and radical culture changes if they want to.

- **A rigorous set of processes and techniques to measure, improve and control the quality of the product, service or information based on what is important to the customer.** The processes of measurement and techniques for improvement are not new to Six Sigma. According to one of the Six Sigma experts at Motorola, Motorola did not invent these techniques. Indeed, they are basically the same best practices that were developed by quality pioneers such as Shewhart (PDCA—plan-do-check-act—process improvement cycle) and Ishikawa (fishbone and cause-and-effect diagrams).

- **Six Sigma improvement projects are sponsored, led, and coached by personnel who are certified in the Six Sigma techniques as "master black belts," "black belts," or "green belts," depending on the size and complexity of the projects.** These are levels of competence or required skill sets, using the ranking system in karate and other martial arts as a metric.

While a slew of organizations have professed the value of Six Sigma, over the years, there has also been those less enthralled with the side effects. In a *BusinessWeek* article, former CEO James McNerney's introduction of Six Sigma at 3M saw immediate benefits for the company's stock price and operating performance, but there was a long-term effect that stifled creativity. *With the primary goals of improving quality, saving time and money, there was less focus on creativity.* Creativity is the heart of research and development (R&D) and innovation, especially at an innovation-rich company such as 3M.[7]

> Processes cannot change without considering the "people factor"; business process improvements require a change management effort to train and convince workers of the business benefits of the new process.

Learning from the Failures of the Past

There are numerous examples that can be presented of the "in" terminology or the acronym flavor of the day, especially in technology. When it came to process improvement in the 1990s, the term *process reengineering* was in vogue.

Michael Hammer and James Champy's book *Reengineering the Corporation* created a whirlwind of interest in organizations of all sizes.[8] Re-engineering business processes became the focal point of CEOs, COOs, and CIOs and others in many organizations. You either had an active reengineering project, or several, in the works or you were considered stagnant or "old school."

But what many organizations realized after countless man-hours and dollars were spent, is that they forgot something along the way—*people*.

Processes cannot change without affecting people—and many people resist or do not like change. In some cases, workers can go out of their way to subvert or otherwise avoid changing the way they do their work or adopting a new practice or system put forth by the organization. The resistance to the new process can be due to many reasons, from a lack of comfort in the new process, not understanding the reasons for the change, or not seeing how the change provides any benefit to the individual affected by the change. Therefore, **change management** principles need to be applied in advance to educate and "sell" employees on the benefits that the new processes will bring to the organization.

Managers fearing the risk of upsetting one of their most valuable employees, or maybe even an outright revolt among staff members, may allow variations in how a new process or practice is followed to ease tensions or avoid conflict altogether. *As these variations or modifications to a newly designed practice are allowed, they tend to expand and further dilute the intended goals.* Now other workers, however slightly, may have to adapt their work practices to allow for the variations on how their coworkers feed into a process or share the electronic records they create. This downward spiral accelerates to further minimize the intended benefits of the new business process—or it may lead to abandoning the change altogether.

What early reengineering or process improvement initiatives failed to address was *managing change* and the resulting impact on the people involved or affected by the processes.

Workers may resist change due to fear of potential layoffs (i.e., if a process is streamlined, then fewer workers may be needed to do the work). Managers may resist change due to fear of losing control of their domain or elimination of their domain in entirety. Others may resist change if the organization has tried to implement changes in the same process previously and saw limited benefits or an outright failure to meet that project's objective.

> Most re-engineering efforts forget about *people*.

Understanding and addressing "change" upfront before any discussions, interviews, announcements, or other discovery work is performed *must* be considered in any business process improvement project.

Typical Components When Improving a Business Process

While TQM, Six Sigma, and reengineering are just a few of the popular methodologies used over the years to improve processes, countless variations and offshoots of these methods are offered by vendors and consulting organizations around the world. Numerous process improvement methodologies exist, but they often include many of the same basic principles:

- Understanding the organization's strategic goals and business objectives, and then aligning them with the underlying processes performed.
- Having a general knowledge of inefficient processes needing improvement.
- Determining the stakeholders of the targeted process both within and outside the organization.
- Documenting or flowcharting the current process(es).
- Verifying the information collected.
- Designing a new process and leveraging technology when appropriate.
- Testing or piloting the new process.
- Refining and expanding the new process implementation.
- Managing the new process.

Figure 9.1 graphically depicts the steps in process improvement, which begin with discovery and investigation, using interviews and process-mapping tools, and continues through from analysis to refinement and management—and then continues through that cycle of steps again.

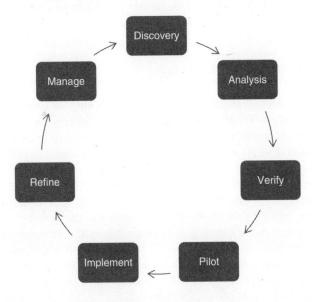

Figure 9.1   Iterative Steps for Business Process Improvement

> Business process improvement when combined with ERM not only stream-lines processes, but also improves access to information and greater awareness of what else exists.

Changing a business process requires active stakeholder involvement, support, and vision, in the early stages of a project and right through to the completion and beyond. Leveraging the knowledge of **subject matter experts** (SMEs), along with creativity and **project management** (PM) are critical components of any process change.

Business Process and E-Records Link

When examining a business process used by knowledge workers, electronic records are typically involved somewhere within the process. Records can be feeding into a process; used within and during a process; be part of the output of a process; and/or recording how a process was performed. Any change to a record, volume, format, storage repository, or manner in which a user would access those records, affects a process. Sometimes the change is minor, other times it may completely alter a process or how an individual interacts with the process.

So separation of electronic records and how they are managed cannot be done without an examination of the business processes they are a part of.

Business process improvement, when combined with ERM, not only streamlines processes, but also improves *access* to information and greater *awareness* of what information may exist. Greater efficiencies are realized in elimination of unnecessary steps (labor savings), reduced errors, and less worker frustration when they cannot find the information they need to do their job. In addition, **information governance** (IG) controls are more easily tracked, verified, and audited.

Documenting Business Processes

A business process, or subprocess, must have a beginning ("What triggers the start of a process?"), a middle ("What steps occur during the process?"), and an end ("What conditions signal the completion of a process?"). In order to fully understand what occurs within a process flow—and the e-records associated with the process—each step within the existing process must be documented.

Business processes typically have many more steps than are initially thought of, particularly when discussing exceptions to a process. This is why any BPI initiative must include documenting the existing processes *before any redesign* is attempted.

How often have you, or someone else you know, stated something similar to "My boss has no idea what it takes to do this job!" No matter how well someone thinks they know a process, not until that process is documented and the results shared with others involved with the process to get their additional input, will the intricate details and nuances associated with that process be fully known.

Two of the most commonly utilized techniques for documenting processes are (1) developing a process narrative; and (2) creating a flowchart of the targeted process.

When these documented processes are shared with other knowledge workers involved with the targeted business process, comments are often heard, such as:

- "I had no idea you had to do all that!"
- "Did you know that so-and-so also has that information?"
- "Why do you do that?" (Answer: "Because we have always done it that way!")

While there are various approaches to documenting existing business processes, *two of the most commonly utilized techniques include developing a process narrative and creating a flowchart of the targeted process*, as described later within this chapter.

First Steps in Documenting a Process: Information Gathering

Before beginning any face-to-face interviews or in-depth discussions to learn more about a particular process, one of the first steps should be to identify any SME or a small groups of individuals most familiar with a given business process. Additionally, any previously assembled documentation (e.g., organization charts, policies and procedures, audits, retention schedules, etc.) should be gathered and reviewed to assist in familiarizing oneself with the department, process, and organization. Reviewing existing documentation provides the interviewer with a running start and minimizes the need to ask questions when the answers are already documented. This can also be used as a way to verify areas described in the documentation for their accuracy and relevance to the current environment.

Performing a high-level walkthrough with the department manager, supervisor, or SME provides additional insight and context for the ensuing process related discussions. Whether actually walking through the office that performs the process or conducting a tabletop walkthrough (e.g., sitting around a conference table discussing the process steps), physically seeing the environment in which the process is performed *must be done* at some point during the documenting process.

During the physical walkthrough, one can see *where* the primary steps within a process occur, where the general *document types used and volumes* are stored, the *tools used*, the *people involved, and their working conditions*. All of which helps provide a more complete picture to further assist in documenting processes and sub processes accurately.

Depending on the complexity of the process and the number of individuals needed to be interviewed, a series of sit-down meetings with the designated SMEs occurs. Discussing the primary steps occurring within a process is typically done in a series of reiterative passes; first identifying the major steps along the process and then further reviewing and breaking down the process into the subprocesses that occur as a part of the primary process. The key is to approach the *discovery* discussion in small, discrete phases, peeling the layers back to uncover more details as needed.

Creating a process narrative often becomes a reiterative process where more detail is added as more information is gathered and shared during interviews.

Creating a Process Narrative

Documenting a process involves the capturing and sharing of critical project steps and related information as they occur. This allows interested parties to share this information, leading to informed decisions. Creating a process narrative often becomes a collaborate event where a high level process is described and the results are shared among other knowledge workers. More detail is then added as additional information and exceptions to a process are noted during the interviews and review sessions.

During an interview, the SMEs describe, step-by-step, the process for completing the targeted business process. Each step of the process including any comments (both positive and negative) is written down by the interviewer as the SME describes it.

Since the tools to develop a process narrative usually depend on word-processing software, the entry point for acquiring tools to assist in developing a narrative is low. Narratives can provide a lot of detail, but because process narratives are usually linear in nature, they require more time for the reader of the narrative to get even a general understanding of the complete process. Descriptions of mildly complicated processes will stretch into several pages for the reader to go through. Another challenge with the narrative approach is the difficulty in expressing multiple exceptions to a process or when multiple outcomes result depending on the input received into a process. The skillfulness and writing style of the narrative's author becomes critical to the presentation of the issues at hand.

When trying to document a process, especially when the SME is excitable or otherwise enthusiastic about their job, the challenge becomes taking detailed notes at the pace that the information is being expressed by the SME. *Think of trying to drink from a fire hose!* Since the SME knows their job and the specific work processes involved, the information just gushes out. The information outflow has to be matched with the note-taking skills of the interviewer. *That is why having two interviewers present is preferred: one interviewer primarily asks questions while the other one takes notes.*

While it may seem like recording all conversations would provide the most detail and avoid missing key points when scribing your notes, audio recordings often make the interviewee nervous. No one wants their words to come back to haunt them later, especially in a tenuous job market. Employees may be less likely to share information knowing you are recording the session and their comments. The key is to put the interviewee at ease so that the information flows in an unfiltered manner, and then to try to restate what your understanding is so that you gain clarification and agreement along the way.

The interviewer can gain the interviewee's willing participation with phrases like: "I am basically here to try to make your job easier for you," and "The organization is

> Flowcharting graphically depicts process steps and decision points in order of occurrence within a business process.

trying to remove the daily headaches from your job." This may assist in creating a freer flowing atmosphere in which to gather information about a process.

A process narrative allows for additional descriptors to be included in the text that may not otherwise be included. Descriptions of work environments (low lighting, tight workspaces, lack of storage area, noise levels, etc.) and the quality of the tools utilized (PCs with older operating systems and applications, manual forms, office equipment, etc.) and available space (working and document filing areas) are best conveyed using a process narrative.

Creating a process narrative helps articulate the steps needed to perform a process and can facilitate the development of a flowchart describing the process.

Flowcharting

Flowcharting a process is another method used for documenting a process in a more visual manner than a process narrative. Flowcharting makes it easier to grasp the process flow at a high level, conceptually. Process steps and decision points are graphically depicted in their order of occurrence, connected by arrows indicating the process flow. While various software applications are available to facilitate the creation of a flowchart, Microsoft Visio is a popular tool used by many organizations.

To assist in visually segmenting various subprocesses within a primary business process, a common approach is to use a *swim-lane*. Simply put, a swim-lane is a visual element that can be used to separate subprocesses or responsibilities associated with a task. Whether using simple lines or a shaded section of a flowchart, the use of swim-lanes will present a visual segmentation between selective processes or actions.

For example, in visually presenting the entire procurement process within a company, swim-lanes can divide the various functional components into logical groups (or individual lanes) such as:

- Requesting the purchase of an item and the associated approval process.
- Developing a requirements definition and a Request for Proposal (RFP).
- Purchase order creation and issuance to the selected vendor.
- Receiving the purchased item.
- Invoice processing and accounts payable (paying for the item).

Swim-lanes can also be used to separate functions occurring in different departments. Such as in a "new hire" process, Human Resources will process the initial paperwork, but send information to Payroll (so the newly hired employee can be paid) or to the IT department (to set up a new computer) or to other functional groups within the organization. Each lane covers the activities each department is responsible for when there is a new employee hired (see Figure 9.2).

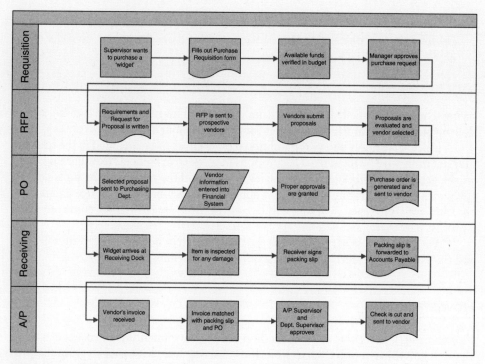

Figure 9.2   Simple Procurement Process Workflow Showing Swim-Lanes

Process Analysis

After performing the various interviews and collecting all associated data and documents involved with the target processes, as well as developing process narratives and flowcharts, *the real fun begins.* This is where knowledge leveraged from multiple disciplines (e.g., business operations, legal, IT, library science, records management, human resources, training, and more) can be combined with *creativity* for an innovative approach to accomplishing the goals for the organization. The use of brainstorming techniques and leveraging internal and external resources such as consultants can provide the unbiased view and utilize the pool of knowledge from each individual's experiences.

The efficiency of a process or the time needed to complete a process is directly affected by any *bottlenecks* in a process flow. *A bottleneck is the step within a process that slows the entire process down or causes other subprocesses to be delayed until the work gets through the bottleneck.* Identifying the bottlenecks thus becomes an essential part of the analysis process.

When reviewing a documented process, especially using visual tools such as a flowchart, often areas where redundant steps occur can be more easily identified. This can be an area where duplicate data entry or redundant information capture (such as identification or demographic information on similar hardcopy forms) is typically found.

Identifying bottlenecks, redundant processes, and opportunities to capture and reuse data to eliminate unnecessary steps are just a few of the primary objectives when

> Workflow software moves and routes files and folders through a series of work steps in an automated way.

analyzing a documented process in a BPI effort. Additional follow-up interviews and having "what if" discussions with SMEs and senior management can further uncover opportunities to streamline processes.

Workflow

Implementing an ERM system with workflow capabilities can automate typically manual processes as well as provide monitoring capabilities of the process for compliance and further enhancements as needed. *Workflow software routes files and folders through a series of work steps in an automated way and exchanges information between an ERM system and other applications used within an organization.*

Workflow can manage a series of tasks within an organization, department, or functional group, thereby streamlining a process and reducing mundane and repetitive work. As a result, knowledge workers are freed up to focus on more important tasks.

For example, an accounts payable process can leverage workflow software within an ERM system to speed up the overall A/P process and provide immediate identification of exactly *where in the process* an invoice payment is. After an invoice is received, the process to approve the payment and actually cut a check for the vendor is a common process in which to apply workflow automation. At each step in the workflow, an individual or group is presented with a specific task. Once the task is completed, the next individual or group in the process is notified and presented with the information needed to complete the task they are responsible for. If tasks are not completed in a timely manner or by predetermined parameters, then notifications, reminders, and rerouting of tasks to help load-balance the workflow can be performed.

Customer service or clerical staff within the Accounts Payable department can quickly answer incoming questions about the status of a payment without having to interrupt or hunt down an answer from other staff members.

The flowchart in Figure 9.3 outlines a typical Account Payable workflow process.

Workflow systems cannot only automate processes, but through the use of capabilities within ERM systems and electronic forms, can replace paper forms. For example, in Figure 9.3, a separate voucher form required to authorized payment can be replaced with an e-form and e-signature authorizing payment.

Figure 9.4 is an example of the same Accounts Payable process *after* a BPI analysis and re-design of the process was conducted, which resulted in leveraging an ERM system.

Workflow software can also include modeling capabilities for organizations to apply their own *what if* scenarios to a given task. For example, if a manager wants to know how a 25 percent increase in monthly sales orders would affect his or her department,

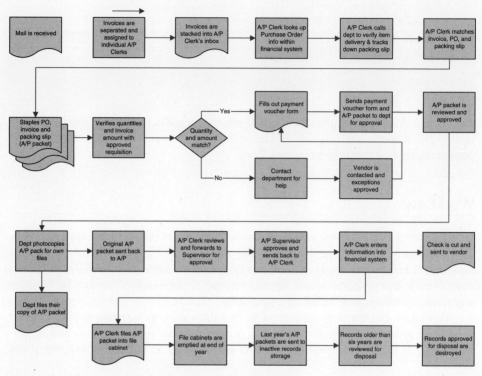

Figure 9.3 Typical Accounts Payable Process—Before BPI

workflow software can model and analyze this scenario and present the outcome to the manager, who then can take the appropriate steps as needed. Modeling can also be used to further refine and streamline processes (i.e., test a proposed process) without actually implementing the changes or affecting the people involved and the work in process.

Typically, workflow systems can be implemented with no programming skills involved, utilizing graphical interfaces and drag-and-drop features that can be built upon basic templates that are often included in software for common business processes, such as accounts payable, expense claim processing, new employee hire processing, and more.

Workflow can also validate information against existing data sources as well as receive data from and feed data to other software applications and repositories.

E-Records Are Very Personal to People

Often, the electronic files that organizations are trying to manage, and the processes they are a part of, are created by individuals. Those word-processing files, spreadsheets, presentations, e-mails, and the like were created on someone's PC, tablet, or other mobile device and then used to feed into or are a result of a business process. These separate files may be created by individuals or groups of individuals in a collaborative environment. As

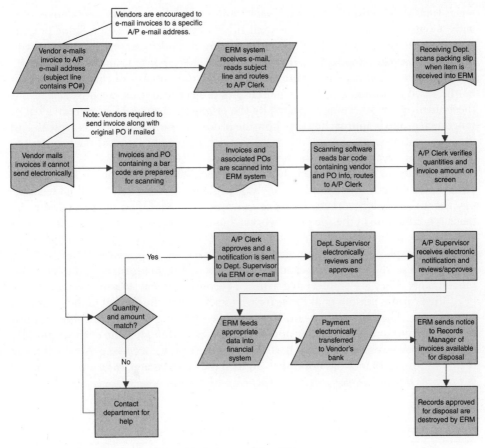

Figure 9.4   Typical Accounts Payable Process—After BPI

such, these *personal* creations can be looked upon by their authors much like a painting created by an artist or a book written by an author. They become personal creations that the author *believes* they have an ownership stake in. Even though these files may be the property of the organization, personal pride clouds the perception of the author (as well as the policies set by the organization)—correctly or incorrectly.

So when trying to manage electronic records or changing a business process, these *changes* cannot be done in a vacuum. Changing a process such as how and where these individual creations are stored, how they are managed and accessed, can be *personal*. When emotions become involved, standard business logic can go out the door.

Change Management

Many "process-oriented" consultants will present a glossy brochure or give a presentation to their prospective customers on how their methodology is better than the competition. These pitches often contain numerous flow diagrams with boxes using terms such as "Discovery, Analysis, Verify, Pilot, Refine, Implement," and then ending with "Continuous Improvement" or some other overused terminology. Some precede these process-flow diagrams with clichés relating to understanding or aligning with the business's goals, hoping to gain a warm and fuzzy response from the audience.

But what is missing from these pitches is how the initiator of change, whether it be the hired consultants or the organization's project leader or executive, *approaches* those involved or otherwise impacted by the proposed change. How an individual or functional group is approached (i.e., how the process improvement idea is presented to the organization as whole) will directly affect the degree of success of the project—or even if the project gets out of the starting gates.

Resistance to change, especially involving technology components, is often perceived to be directly related to someone's age. Younger workers tend to adopt technology faster than older workers. But is this always the case? Often the perceived resistance is not because of the age of the worker, but has more to do with having a comfort level with a current process. For example, if a younger worker was using an application on their smartphone or tablet for one or two years and was happy with its functionality and ease of use, they may resist changing to a new mobile platform even if it has more functionality. They are comfortable with the current platform, so why change?

Often various reasons could arise for why staying with the current mobile platform is important, whether valid or not. Workers start thinking of every possible scenario that "could" occur as a reason for not switching—even though some of those possible scenarios have never occurred or have little chance of ever occurring. Maybe the *real* reason for the resistance has nothing to do with the business app, *but more to do with the fact that the new mobile platform is incompatible with their personal music or video library!*

Communicate, Communicate, Communicate

It has been said many times and proven through many tests and surveys that people need to see a message about five times before it really registers and evokes a response. Marketers have used this general statistic to explain why frequency is needed in advertising, that is, one ad just won't do it; an ad has to be run over and over again. So humans, especially when confronted with today's massive amounts of information, need to have a message announced and reinforced before it sinks in. Yet, too often organizations send out a brief e-mail blast to employees announcing a new process improvement initiative (sometimes even after the project was started). With the flood of other information pouring into inboxes and through other communication vehicles, the message is often lost, ignored, or received with an attitude of "Here we go again with another improvement project."

More thought has to be given ot the entire communication campaign as well as each individual message delivered by senior and mid-level management to ensure consistent communication as well as thinking about how each message will be "received" by staff.

> Often the perceived resistance is not because of the age of the worker, but has more to do with having a comfort level with a current process.

The information grapevine or water cooler conversations enable employees to find out more, and sooner, than management often believes.

Communication must occur early on—maybe even before a project is formalized—to assist in the change management effort. The information grapevine or water-cooler conversations are the fastest means of communication in any organization. Staff members find out more information and sooner than management often believes. While messages delivered through the grapevine travel wider and faster, they can also carry more weight in "believability" than management thinks. If the grapevine says something is going to happen—whether true or not—no matter what the formal communications says, it becomes too late. Management then is fighting an uphill battle of *believability*—even before a project gets going.

Therefore *communicate early, often, and consistently* to head off the grapevine before false or misleading information derails your process improvement efforts.

Find the Source; Avoid the Cycle

Before changing anything, it is important to clearly understand how things work *today*. Documenting the steps in a targeted process is paramount to discovering not only the "bumps" in the current process, but also other requirements (known and unknown) and even other unknown opportunities for improvement. Mapping out these existing processes is a standard component of most successful BPI initiatives. Using a third party such as an outside consultant will usually provide a more unbiased approach and will uncover details that insiders normally skip over (since they already know a process or *think* they know how someone else does their work).

After performing the needed discovery work and mapping out processes, many times there are "ah ha" moments in which the realization occurs that the same information is handled more than once, but in different formats. For example, an employee fills out one or more forms that contain information on themselves, whether as part of a newly hired employee process or a change in their information (e.g., marriage, payroll deductions, benefit changes, etc.). After completing these forms, they are forwarded to various other staff members to complete the tasks needed. So, in the case of a new employee, forms may be copied and sent from Human Resources to Payroll (to enter into the financial system), to Facilities (to get a desk assigned and phone hooked up), to IT (for setting up their computer with the appropriate application and security rights needed), and then to their new supervisor, who creates their own "file" on the new hire.

Along the way, information is photocopied and manually entered into various information systems and repositories used by separate functional groups within the organization. Often as information is entered (as this becomes electronic), it is later printed and forwarded to other entities due to application incompatibilities and thus stored in various information silos. When stepping back and taking a look at the entire process, the information flow from manual data entry, to electronic data, to paper, to electronic format, and back to paper for duplicated data entry is seen in many organizations. Most managers would be stunned at how often similar cycles—from paper to electronic to paper and then back into electronic format—occur.

Somewhere along the process, one functional group or manager, let's say the Human Resources VP, gets frustrated with the volume of paper and wants to transfer data to electronic records. This group may then investigate an ERM solution for their department, and begin scanning their files and storing them along with the electronic records they create (e.g., e-mails, evaluations, announcements, memos, etc.). So, in this example, an ERM evaluation and implementation project is begun for HR which results in scanning documents containing information that HR or other departments have in an electronic format to begin with.

The goal is to follow the trail to the source and then determine where and how information can be captured *once*—and repurposed—in a practical manner. Balancing the efforts needed to accomplish the desired result with the perceived benefits to the organization and each functional group must occur. If the effort or cost to capture the information outweighs the benefits, then senior management must make the appropriate decision.

Efforts to focus on finding the original source of information and then capturing that information *one time* will provide benefits in overall organization efficiency and greater employee job satisfaction. The result is not only a streamlined process, but leads to fewer records needing to be "managed." Lessening the duplication of information also leads to lower storage costs—both electronic and physical storage.

Avoid Scope-creep: Defining "The Project" and Its Scope

A key in any project is defining the scope and avoiding "scope-creep." *Scope-creep occurs when it is thought that additional benefits will be gained by widening the reach of a project as more and more opportunities are uncovered.* While some of these additions may be small and easy to accomplish, other *perceived* low-hanging fruit adds to the time needed to complete the BPI initiative and/or the amount of individuals affected by the changes. The result can lead to timeframes not being met and budgets being busted—all of which can be seen as an unfavorable showdown on a project and could bring *an abrupt ending to a project. So, do not succumb to the temptations of scope-creep (i.e., unplanned expansion of the project); garner an early success, keep the project on schedule, and keep moving forward.*

So how does one avoid scope-creep and keep a project focused while uncovering additional opportunities for improvement? After documenting an existing process flow and discovering the sources of information and the various formats of the information, close examination of the demarcation points to create a more manageable project have to occur. For example, scanning one form from a particular department into an ERM repository may be easier than getting the staff from that department to move to electronic forms or than providing them access to the ERM solution at this time. So one option could be to scan these forms into the ERM today and then in a future project examine the other department's internal processes and their potential transfer to electronic forms when resources allow.

Implementing a change in business processes on a smaller scale, such as a pilot project involving only a handful of individuals is a preferred approach. Having a smaller-scale pilot project will impact a smaller number of workers and will not disrupt the rest of the

> Implementing a change in business processes on a smaller scale, such as a pilot project involving only a handful of individuals is a preferred approach.

organization. These pilot projects can then be refined as needed before a more wide-spread change is implemented affecting a larger number of workers.

A smaller, more limited in scope project allows definitive timelines to be set and met, thereby demonstrating a show of success by meeting project deadlines. Building on this success allows expansion of the pilot or otherwise smaller-scale project into a more wide-reaching effort later on. No matter what, having senior management support and their involvement *must* be attained for any project to truly succeed. Having management send out an initial e-mail announcing a project (thereby showing support for the project), only to never be heard from again—except to criticize the results of the project—is not an example of senior management support. Earlier in this chapter there is discussion of the importance of consistent and clear communications throughout a project. This must occur in conjunction with *consistent communication from senior-level executives, too.*

Changing Processes Gets Personal

While, on the surface, moving from hardcopy to electronic records appears to be a goal of many organizations, changing *how* records can be managed typically cannot be done without changing or affecting business processes. Understanding how workers *do their work* (e.g., their piece of a specific business process) and how the e-records they create, use, access, and share interact with the processes cannot be done in isolation. *Improving the management of electronic records must involve BPI.* But remember, it gets "personal" when you are changing how a worker handles their own e-records.

CHAPTER SUMMARY: **KEY POINTS**

- A business process is a sequence of work activities carried out by both automated systems and people to produce a desired result within an organization.

- Generally, efforts to streamline and improve a business process must be addressed prior to changing how records are managed or before implementing an ERM system.

- Processes cannot change without considering the "people factor"; business process improvements require a change management effort to train and convince workers of the business benefits of the new process.

(Continued)

(Continued)

- Most early re-engineering efforts forgot about *people*.

- Improving the management of electronic records requires examining the business processes they are a part of.

- Change management, especially preparing the individuals involved for a change, is paramount in the success of your project.

- Business process improvement (BPI), when combined with ERM, not only streamlines processes, but also improves access to information and greater awareness of what else exists.

- Communicate frequently and consistently during the BPI initiative.

- Two of the most commonly utilized techniques for documenting processes are (1) developing a process narrative and (2) creating a flowchart of the targeted process.

- Creating a process narrative often becomes an iterative process where more detail is added as more information is gathered and shared during interviews. Process narratives can get drawn out and depend on the writing skills of the interviewer.

- Flowcharting graphically depicts process steps and decision points in order of occurrence within a business process for visual inspection.

- Workflow software moves and routes files and folders through a series of work steps in an automated way.

- Often the perceived resistance is not because of the age of the worker, but more a matter of the employee being comfortable with a current process.

- Proper project definition and avoiding scope-creep must be kept in mind.

- Improving the management of electronic records must involve BPI.

- Implementing a change in business processes on a smaller scale, such as a pilot project involving only a handful of individuals, is a preferred approach.

- It gets "personal" when you are changing how a worker handles their own e-records.

Notes

1. Peter Fingar and Joe Bellini, *The Real-Time Enterprise: Competing on Time with the Revolutionary Business S-Ex Machine* (Tampa, FL: Meghan Kiffer Press, 2004).
2. W. Edwards Deming, *Out of the Crisis* (Cambridge, MA: MIT Press, 2000), Chapter 2, 22–28.
3. Larry English, "Six Sigma and Total Information Quality Management," *Information Management*, July 18, 2008, www.information-management.com/issues/20041001/1011016-1.html.
4. "Utilizing the Six Steps to Six Sigma," Motorola University, 1992, as cited in C. Sengstock, Jr., *Quality in the Communications Process* (Chicago: Motorola University Press, 1997), 11.
5. Peter Pande, Robert Neuman, and Roland Cavanagh, *The Six Sigma Way: How GE, Motorola, and Other Top Companies Are Honing Their Performance* (New York: McGraw-Hill, 2000), 5.
6. Ibid., 4.
7. Brian Hindo, "At 3M, a Struggle between Efficiency and Creativity," *BusinessWeek*, June 6, 2007.
8. Michael Hammer and James Champy, *Reengineering the Corporation* (New York: HarperBusiness, 1993).

CHAPTER 10

Workflow and Business Process Management Software

Jon Pyke and Robert Smallwood

The processes deployed in all organizations define the culture of that entity, they are what differentiate it from other seemingly similar entities—they define the corporate backbone and are, quite simply, "the way things get done around here." Needless to say then, they are pretty important and need to be managed and exploited just like any other corporate asset. Therefore, to maximize the true efficiencies that are gained in implementing an **electronic records management** (ERM) program, improvements in redesigned business processes must be supported by information technology (IT) that automates and speeds processing, reduces errors and manual intervention, and improves auditability. (For more information on how to redesign and improve business processes, see Chapter 9.)

This much-needed technology can be defined under the banner of **process-enabled technology**. Process-enabled technology is often divided into two categories: **workflow automation** or **business process management**. The two technologies have a significant amount in common. Indeed it is fair to say that a good deal of the technology that underpins business process management concepts has its roots in the late 1980s and early 1990s and stems from the early efforts of the workflow community. The need to automate and manage processes is not new. Business software has long supported major business processes. What *has* changed is the realization that business managers need to understand and improve those processes. Getting a handle on the myriad processes that exist in all organizations is the easiest way to become a more competitive, adaptable, and responsive organization, while managing costs. Using process-based software is the key to achieving that.

Workflow software and **business process management systems** (BPMS) software are designed to improve business process efficiency by routing files and folders at electronic speeds, and they are capable of eliminating bottlenecks and work-step redundancies.

Despite the fact that the two types of software are often lumped together as being essentially the same (even in leading texts), *there are key distinctions*.

BPMS is often referred to as "workflow on steroids," but it is much more than that—it provides a complete and integrated operations platform upon which many other technologies can be deployed—and this is an even more important capability when technologies such as the cloud come into play. So *BPMS provides a much more robust and complex set of functions to support the automation and optimization of business processes, including more extensive modeling of the full end-to-end process rather than the self-contained departmental flow maps associated with workflow.*

Also, BPMS (often) includes process simulation and analytics. (There is an open question as to whether simulation is best tested by a tool included in a BPM suite, or by a third-party simulation tool, since those included in the BPMS may be biased or skewed in their results).

Workflow Software

As noted in Chapter 9, *workflow software routes files and folders through a series of work-steps in an automated way.* Stated differently, workflow "is a simple automation tool for directing documents and tasks to the responsible users in a business process for further actions."[1]

A basic example where workflow is used is scanning letters in a mailroom, indexing them and routing them to the intended recipients. The organization is then able to insert the letters into folders (e.g., a customer correspondence file) and move them through the organization electronically.

Or think of an electronic folder moving a mortgage loan application and supporting documentation through the approval process, or an auto insurance claim folder that is routed for verification and approval/denial.

Workflow also enables the exchange of information between an ERM system and other applications used within an organization, so in the loan folder application, the software could retrieve and capture additional bank account details and insert them to complete or update the folder or, in the case of the insurance claim, a previous history of claims could be routed to the folder for review.

In more detail, basic workflow software characteristics are:

- **Fixed sequencing.** Using predefined business rules that are application-specific to sequence tasks; that is, the workflow routes and conditional routes are diagrammed, programmed, and set, based on a business process analysis that aims to streamline the process.
- **Limited integration with external systems**. That is, typically only allowing the exchange or updating of documents and data.
- **Limited content analysis reporting capability.** That is, capturing and analyzing business-process-cycle data and work-step statistics.
- **Nonadaptive.** Performing routing over a fixed process flow, rather than having the ability to adapt or use alternate paths, based on conditional data. Although workflow does perform some basic splits or changes in routes based on "if yes, then X" or "if no, then Y" types of decision points, and it can even split work folders to route parts of their contents to different users, for actions or decisions, and later unite (or perform a *rendezvous*) the complete folder. Yet these capabilities are rudimentary, compared to BPMS capabilities.[2]

> Workflow software routes files and folders through a series of work-steps in an automated way.

Workflow is typically implemented to automate routine operations at the departmental level.[3] Rarely is pure workflow utilized across an entire enterprise, unless it is quite small. It is largely a tactical IT deployment, helping to gain efficiencies but not radically transforming a business. A good example is the first type of application that was automated using workflow, which was developed in the late 1980s and used in matching purchase orders with invoices and processing them for payment in the accounts payable department. Digital images were routed to clerical staff so that data could be input into the accounting system and the business was able to pay invoices in a timely manner and take full advantage of small discounts (typically about 2 percent) offered to pay the invoices within 10, 15, or 30 days. This provided a real economic savings and improved cash flow and the bottom line, but did not wholly transform the business.

There are different types of workflow software: Some control and coordinate human tasks, and others route and manage documents, scanned images, and records (unstructured and semistructured content).[4] The latter type of workflow falls within the scope of this book.

Few "pure-play" workflow software providers exist anymore (most include document management and some embed workflow into their applications), although newer workflow vendors have emerged that complement MS SharePoint deployments.

Business Process Management Suites

BPMS software is much more sophisticated in its design and capabilities, and could be called a superset of workflow, although that is an oversimplification.

BPMS software offers five main capabilities:[5]

1. Puts existing and new application software under the direct control of business managers.
2. Makes it easier to improve existing business processes and create new ones.
3. Enables the automation of processes across the entire organization, and beyond it.
4. Gives managers "real-time" information on the performance of processes.
5. Allows organizations to take full advantage of new computing services.

The result is an improved ability to respond to or anticipate changing business demands. Also, the organization saves money whenever it changes computerized working methods—usually an expensive and protracted rigmarole. As a bonus, the organization becomes better positioned to exploit future business and computing opportunities, including **business process outsourcing** (BPO) and web services.

In the previous example of a loan application being processed, BPMS software can retrieve and capture data from external sources, such as credit bureaus and real estate listing services, and then, according to whatever threshold levels are set, make

Workflow is often seen implemented in departments to automate routine operations.

> BPM software is more than a sophisticated superset of workflow and includes adaptive capabilities.

a decision based on established business rules written into its business rules engine to route the application to the proper parties for analysis or digital signatures for approval. (Although true BPMS software has more robust capabilities and features and can perform much more sophisticated and complex tasks.)

Or, in the case of an auto insurance claim, a BPMS is capable of capturing a police incident report, an underwriter's report, and a car dealer repair estimate and making intelligent decisions for routing and processing, based on established business rules. These are very basic examples to show that BPMS software is much more capable than workflow software.

In more detail, distinguishing characteristics of BPMS are:[6]

- *Modeling* of defined business process (often including simulation) in a virtual environment to optimize them for effectiveness and efficiency. This is done using graphical icons in a diagram to represent processes.
- *Coordination* of work-steps and tasks among users.
- *Integration* and the ability to import and share data among disparate applications, using a dashboard or central interface.
- *Capture* of information from external sources to use as input into business processes.
- *Adaptability* and the capability to adjust and find better routes and work-steps, or to seek additional data, based on conditional data and feedback received.

According to Gartner, Inc., *the ideal BPMS implements 10 technologies, of which workflow is only one.* Some of the technologies included in BPMS software that are not included in workflow are modeling, simulation and optimization, content management, collaboration, system connectivity, **business activity monitoring** (BAM), business rules engine, and more (although the distinctions can overlap and become blurred, depending on the vendor offering).[7]

But there is much more to this than the automation of a process.[8] The automation does not let you predict what may happen in the future. It doesn't help with contingency or capacity planning: It just supports the process. This is needed, but any competitive advantage the technology provides will, by definition, be short-lived. What do we mean by this? Well, let's look at how this works. In 2003, Nicholas Carr wrote a controversial article in *Harvard Business Review* (followed the next year by his book) in which he argued that it is a mistake to assume that as IT's potency and ubiquity

> BPMS software typically includes modeling, simulation, capture of information from external sources, and the ability to adapt routes based on business rules and conditional data that is analyzed.

have increased, so too has its strategic value.[9] This ruffled the feathers of IT titans at major companies like Microsoft and HP. What makes a resource truly strategic, Carr argued—what gives it the capacity to be the basis for a sustained competitive advantage—is not ubiquity but *scarcity*. Competitive advantage can only be gained over rivals by having or doing something that they cannot have or do. By now, the core functions of IT—data storage, data processing, and data transport—have become available and affordable to all, and this is especially so since the advent of cloud collaboration technologies.

Carr's article spawned a "may-bug"[10] industry of counterargument and rebuke—books were written, behemoths were angered. So we will not enter the fray except to ask, What if Carr is right? What if buying more IT simply keeps you in the game of acquiring yet more IT? What this suggests is that if an organization is only going to maintain a "me, too" position by spending vast sums on IT infrastructure, then they need to look at what it is that will give them a business edge and apply technology to that aspect to gain a competitive advantage. The obvious candidate is process—the way you do things—the backbone of your organization's operations.

Applying IT to process technology is going to give your organization that competitive advantage: It will show a return on the investment—it will keep you in front—and that is where the value will come from. That is what the so-called "Process Revolution" is all about.

But we must now recognize that BPM technology has become mainstream; one effect of this widespread adoption is that there will be less differentiation of large-scale BPM engines. They will all:

- Be very scalable.
- Support key standards.
- Have good integration capabilities.
- Be infrastructure products.

So where do the benefits come from? The key area will be simulation and statistics—or **enterprise process analytics**.

Organizations are beginning to realize that *although they can implement BPM without analytics capabilities, they do not have a complete end-to end solution.* As stated earlier, their BPM system does not help their strategic planning nor enable them to accurately develop contingency plans for opportunistic and threatening scenarios. They do not have real insight into their processes or the outcomes they produce, let alone an automated way of addressing them.

Analytics give business managers and executives the ability to track and measure operations performance based on real-time feedback of their processes. This gives them real insight into how the organization is operating. Once good and accurate analytics are in place, end users can make informed decisions because they are presented with issues that need to be addressed, as well as with the context and factual data so they can take the right action. They have the ability to "drill down" into a process or performance anomaly and to look at the information from different dimensions, giving them greater understanding of the "information behind the information." Forecasting is made possible through ongoing statistical data capture, and reporting functions ensure that real-time and predictive information is available.

> Enterprise process analytics provide powerful tools for managers, all the way up to the level of CEO, to better understand their operational environments and gain insights on how and where to make improvements.

The powerful combination of real-time process analytics and Business Operations Management means that users can:[11]

- Adjust processes to changing business dynamics.
- Move from managing business processes to managing business process life-cycles.
- Tie together business objectives, strategic planning, process modeling, work-flow, application/content management, and analytics so that they interact and create business synergy.
- Develop feedback loops for change management and incremental optimization of business processes.
- Eliminate gaps between strategy and business objectives.
- Ensure workflow and processes support key business objectives.
- Gain the control of operations to manage process lifecycles from end-to-end.

By implementing BPM, an organization's business units will have the capability to build and execute processes that are designed with customers in mind, while delivering better quality, faster, and at lower costs. Organizations can retain and advance a competitive advantage by being able to execute processes that deliver the business strategy. The CEO does not care about systems integration or the concepts of "straight-through processing," however valid that may be. *But the CEO does care about monitoring how the business is performing, being able to react to changes in the market, handling exceptions quickly and effectively, and having a complete view of the organization.*

The CIO has the task of making sure the needs of the CEO are fully met quickly, effectively, and with zero disruption to the business. Systems implemented in today's rapidly changing technology world must show fast **return on investment** (ROI) and bring benefits to the bottom line, without having to discard what is viable and operational.

Providing technology that enables users to define the business process in clear understandable notation is an important aspect of the technology, but it is only part of the solution. Being able to execute that process, facilitate simple integration with legacy systems and commercially available packages, and monitor/manage how those processes are executing, are also vital components. Furthermore, BPM as defined here, enables the CIO to implement new applications quickly and tie together the front office applications and the back office systems. This reduces maintenance costs, time to deploy, and makes the IT function far more responsive to business needs.

The success of all this depends on how managers introduce and use this technology. *Business process management is as much about organizational design, human communication, employees' insights, and mutual consideration as it is about technology.* It is not just a matter of optimizing communication between computer programs.

Moving forward, we need to look at the changing way we use technology, in particular the cloud and social networking. These two aspects alone are likely to have a profound effect on the business processes we use and manage. The new world business order demands flexibility—we have to deal with the unexpected. This is not just about using a set of tools to deal with every anticipated business outcome or rule; we are talking about the management of true interaction that takes place between individuals and groups that cannot be predicted or encapsulated beforehand. This is because business processes and social interactions now exist at two levels: the predictable (the systems) and the un-predictable (the people). It is at the process level where the systems and humans collide—that is where "the rubber meets the road," so to speak (see Figure 10.1).

Understanding that business processes exist at two levels (the silicon [computer] and the carbon [human]) takes us a long way toward understanding how we solve this problem. The key point is to recognize that the unpredictable actions of the human components are not ad-hoc processes, nor are they exception handling. This is all about the unstructured interactions between people—in particular, knowledge workers. These unstructured and unpredictable interactions can, and do, take place all the time—and they are only going to increase! The advent of social computing, hosted and cloud applications, and so on are already having, and will continue to have, a profound effect on the way we manage and do business.

Process-based technology that understands the needs of people and supports the inherent "spontaneity" of the human mind is the next logical step, and we might be tempted to name this potential paradigm shift, "social BPM (SBPM)."

SBPM falls into two main categories, which will probably merge over time, and the first vendors to recognize that potential will have a great advantage. At the simplest level there is case management, and at a second level, we have *human interaction management*. There are few, if any, BPM products on the market today that will be able to meet this seismic shift in requirements—certainly those that rely on aging technologies such as business process execution language (BPEL) and service-oriented architecture will not; what's more, any that have been in the market for longer than five years will likely need to make radical architectural changes or rewrite their systems from the ground up to meet the coming changes.

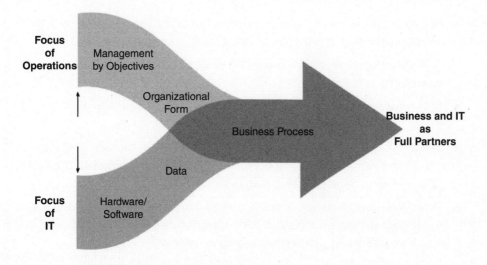

Figure 10.1   Where Systems and People Collide

> BPM is as much about organizational design, human communication, employees' insights, and mutual consideration as it is about technology.

The future for BPM technology is bright—arguably it has the potential to provide the biggest return on investment of any information technology deployed to date.

The basic technologies that formed the foundation for BPMS software began with workflow and have been around since the early 1990s, but the uptick in sales and implementations did not occur until almost 20 years later. Growth estimates for the BPMS software are optimistic through 2017 and beyond.

Workflow software provides support for redesigned business processes in an ERM implementation, and substantial improvements in efficiency can be gained; but BPMS software, along with proper process redesign and **business process improvement** (BPI) efforts, *can yield significant improvements in efficiency and effectiveness, providing a real competitive advantage and great gains in productivity that can truly transform a business.*

Without an accompanying significant BPI effort, supported by BPMS software, an ERM implementation is merely an electronic filing cabinet, and the ERM program will never reach its full potential.

CHAPTER SUMMARY: **KEY POINTS**

- Workflow and business process management suite (BPMS) software both automate work-steps and route files and folders at electronic speeds.

- Workflow and BPMS software are often seen as the same, although there are key differences. Workflow is just one of potentially 10 key technologies that a BPMS may employ.

- Workflow software routes files and folders through a series of work steps in an automated way. It provides statistical feedback on process cycle times.

- Workflow is often seen implemented in departments to automate routine operations.

- BPM software is more than a sophisticated superset of workflow and includes adaptive capabilities.

- BPMS software typically includes modeling, simulation, capture of information from external sources and the ability to adapt routes based on business rules and conditional data that is analyzed.

- Enterprise process analytics provide powerful tools for managers all the way to the CEO to better understand their operational environment and gain insights on how and where to make improvements.

(Continued)

(*Continued*)

- BPMS can transform a business and provide a real competitive advantage.
- To gain the true benefits of an ERM implementation, it must be implemented alongside significant (and continual) improvements in business processes.

Notes

1. "BPM versus Workflow," www.bpmvsworkflow.com/bpm-vs-workflow.html (accessed July 10, 2012).
2. Ibid.
3. Anatoly Belychook, *BPM Blog*, "Difference between BPM and Workflow: Not Just Technologies," April 28, 2010, http://mainthing.ru/item/204.
4. Janelle Hill, "Do You Understand the Difference between Workflow and BPM?" *Gartner Blog*, April 22, 2010, http://blogs.gartner.com/janelle-hill/2010/04/22/do-you-understand-the-difference-between-workflow-and-bpm.
5. John O'Connell, Jon Pyke, and Roger Whitehead, *Mastering Your Organization's Processes* (New York: Cambridge University Press, 2006), 14.
6. Ibid.
7. Hill, "Do You Understand the Difference between Workflow and BPM?"
8. Jon Pyke, "The Value of Business Process Management," White Paper presented at AIIM Conference, 2003.
9. Nicholas G. Carr, "IT Doesn't Matter," *Harvard Business Review*, May 1, 2003.
10. Driven purely by the instinct for self-preservation and thankfully short-lived.
11. Jon Pyke, "BPM vs. Workflow," Staffware Plc White Paper, 2001.

PART THREE
Information Delivery Platforms: Managing E-Records

CHAPTER 11

Managing E-Mail and IM Records*

E-mail is the most common business software application and the backbone of business communications today. Employees utilize it all day, including during their personal time. Social media use has skyrocketed in recent years, and has actually surpassed e-mail for personal use, but the fact remains that in business, knowledge workers rely on e-mail for almost all communications, *including those of a sensitive nature.*

A 2011 survey of 2,400 corporate e-mail users worldwide found that nearly two-thirds stated that e-mail was their favorite form of business communication, surpassing not only social media, but also telephone and in-person contact.[1]

These e-mail communications may contain discoverable information in litigation, and a percentage of them will be declared as formal business records. E-mail often contains records, such as financial spreadsheets and reports, product price lists, marketing plans, competitive analyses, safety data, recruitment and salary details, progressing contract negotiations, and other information that may be considered as constituting a business record.

E-mail systems can be hacked, monitored, and compromised and cause far-reaching damage to a victimized organization. The damage may occur slowly, and go undetected, while information assets—and business value—are eroded.

In mid-2011, it was reported that the "hacktivist" group AntiSec claimed responsibility for hacking a U.S. government contractor, Booz Allen Hamilton, and publically exposing 90,000 military e-mail addresses and passwords from the contractor by posting them online. It was the second attack on a government defense contractor in a single week.[2]

Booz Allen employees "maintain high government security clearances" while working with the defense sector, yet AntiSec penetrated the communications systems with relative ease and noted it "basically had no security measures in place."[3]

AntiSec was able to go even further, by running its own rogue application to steal software source code and to search and find access credentials to steal data from other servers, which the group said would help it to infiltrate other federal contractors and agencies. It even stated it might pass the security information on to other hackers.

---

* Reprinted with permission from John Wiley & Sons, Inc.

The attack didn't stop there. Later that week, another federal defense and FBI contractor, IRC Federal, was hacked, databases were invaded, the website was modified, and information from internal e-mail messages was posted online.[4]

Employees Regularly Expose Organizations to E-Mail Risk

A 2011 global e-mail survey, commissioned by a leading hosted e-mail services provider, found that nearly 80 percent of all employees send work e-mail to and from their personal accounts, and 20 percent do so regularly, which means that critical information assets are exposed to uncontrolled security risks.[5]

"Awareness of the security risks this behavior poses does not act as a deterrent" (italics added). Over 70 percent of people questioned recognize that there is an additional risk in sending work documents outside the corporate e-mail environment, but almost half of "these same respondents feel it is acceptable to send work emails and documents to personal email accounts anyway." According to the survey, the reasons for using personal e-mail accounts for work purposes range from working on documents remotely (71 percent), to sending files that are too big for the company mailbox (21 percent), taking documents with them when they leave a company (18 percent), and those who simply don't want to carry a laptop home (9 percent).[6] The top two frustrations users had with work e-mail were restrictions on mailbox size, which has a negative impact on e-mail management, and the inability to send large attachments. This second issue often forces workers to use a personal account to send and receive necessary files. If size limits are imposed on mailboxes and attachments, companies must provide a secure alternative to file storage and transfer. Otherwise, employees are pushed into risking corporate information assets via personal e-mail. This scenario not only complicates things for e-mail administrators, but it also has serious legal and regulatory implications. Clearly, as stated by Paul Mah, "email retention and archival becomes an impossible task when emails are routed in a haphazard manner via personal accounts."[7]

This means that security, privacy, and records management issues must be addressed by first creating information governance (IG) policies to control and manage the use of e-mail. These policies can utilize the e-mail system's included security features and also employ additional monitoring and security technologies where needed.

The e-mail survey also found an overall lack of clear e-mail policies and weak communication of existing guidelines. Nearly half of the respondents stated that either their company had no e-mail policy or that they were unaware of one. Among those aware of a corporate e-mail policy, 4 in 10 think it could be communicated better. Among companies that have a policy, most (88 percent) deal with the appropriate use of e-mail as a business tool, but less than one-third (30 percent) address e-mail retention from a security standpoint.

Generally, employees are aware that sending work documents outside of their corporate network is unsafe, and yet they continue to do so. It is abundantly clear that *e-mail policies have to be updated and upgraded to accommodate and manage the increasingly sophisticated and computer-savvy generation* of users who are able to find ways to work around corporate e-mail restrictions. (These users have been dubbed *Generation Gmail*.) In addition, new e-mail monitoring and security technologies need to be deployed to counter this risky practice, which exposes information assets to prying eyes or malicious attacks, and puts a legally defensible records management policy at risk.

E-Mail Polices Should Be Realistic and Technology Agnostic

E-mail policies must not be too restrictive. It may be tempting to include catch-all policies that attempt to tamp down user behavior, but such efforts cannot succeed.[8] An important step is consulting with stakeholders to understand their usage patterns and needs, and then going through a series of drafts of the policy, allowing for input. It may be determined that some exceptions and changes in technologies need to be factored in, and that some additional technology is needed to accommodate users while keeping information assets safer and meeting records management, compliance and legal demands. Specifics of these policies and tools should be progressively tightened down on a regular basis as the process moves forward.

These new IG guidelines and policies need to refer to technology in a generic sense—a "technology-neutral" sense—rather than specifying proprietary software programs or features.[9] That is to say, they should be written so that they are *not* in need of revision as soon as new email technologies are deployed, or there is a change in software provider.

Developing organization-wide IG policies is time-consuming and expensive; they are a defensive measure that does not produce revenue, so managers, pressed for performance, often relegate policy-making to the low-priority list. Certainly, it is a tedious, difficult task, so organizations should aim to develop policies that are flexible enough to stand the test of time. But it is also necessary to establish a review process to periodically revise policies to accommodate changes in the business environment, the law, and technology.

Here is an example of a technology-agnostic policy directive:

> All confidential information must be encrypted before being transmitted over the Internet.

This statement does not specify the technology to be used, or the mode of transmission. The policy is neutral enough to cover not only e-mail and instant messaging (IM), but also social media, cloud computing, mobile computing, and other means of communication. The policy also does not specify the method or brand of the encryption technology, so the organization can select the best method and technology available in the future without adapting the policy.[10]

E-Record Retention: Fundamentally a Legal Issue

Considering the massive volume of e-mail exchanged in business today, most e-mail messages do not rise to the level of being formal business records. But many of them do, and are subject to IG, regulatory compliance, and legal requirements for maintaining and producing business records. And any email can be requested in the e-discovery process of litigation.

Although often lumped in with other information technology (IT) concerns, the retention of e-mail and other e-records is ultimately a legal issue. Other departments, including records management and business units, should certainly have input, and should work to assist the legal team to record retention challenges and archiving solutions. But e-mail and e-record retention is "fundamentally a *legal* issue," particularly for public or highly regulated companies. According to Nancy Flynn of the ePolicy

> Managing e-records is primarily a legal issue, especially for public and heavily regulated companies.

Institute, "It is essential for the organization's legal department to take the lead in determining *precisely* which types of email messages will be preserved, *exactly* how and where data will be stored, and *specifically when*—if ever—electronically stored information [ESI] will be deleted."[11]

Since they are often shot out in the heat of battle, e-mail messages can be evidence of a smoking gun in lawsuits and investigations, and are the most requested type of evidence in civil litigation today. The content and timing of e-mail messages can provide exonerating information, too.

In January 2010, a U.S. House of Representatives committee probing bailout deals subpoenaed the Federal Reserve Bank of New York for e-mail and other correspondence from Treasury Secretary Timothy Geithner (former president of the New York Federal Reserve Bank) and other officials. The House Oversight and Government Reform Committee was in the process of examining New York Fed decisions that funneled billions of dollars to big banks, including Goldman Sachs Group and Morgan Stanley.[12]

This is just one example of how crucial e-mail messages can be in legal investigations, and how they play an important role in reconstructing events and motives for legal purposes.

Preserve E-Mail Integrity and Admissibility with Automatic Archiving

Most users are not aware that e-mail contents and characteristics can be changed—" and rendered legally invalid"—by anyone with malicious motives, including those who are essentially "covering their tracks." Not only can the content be edited, but metadata that includes information like the time, date, and total number of characters in the message can also be changed retroactively.[13]

To offset this risk and ensure that **spoliation** does not occur, that is, the loss of proven authenticity of an e-mail, *all messages, both inbound and outbound should be captured and archived automatically, and in real-time*. This preserves legal validity and forensic compliance. Additionally, e-mail should be indexed to facilitate the searching process, and all messages should be secured in a single location, with appropriate backup measures. With these immediate and secure preservation measures, e-mail records can be assured to be authentic and reliable.

E-Mail Archiving Rationale: Compliance, Legal, and Business Reasons

There are good reasons to archive e-mail and retain it according to a specific retention schedule that follows your organization's IG policies. Having a handle on managing voluminous e-mail archives translates to being able to effectively and rapidly search and retrieve exactly the right messages, which can provide a significant legal advantage.

It gives your legal team more and better information, and more time to figure out how to leverage it in legal strategy sessions. This means the odds are tipped in your organization's favor in the inevitable litigation arena. Your legal opponent may be driven to settle a weak claim when confronted with indisputable e-mail evidence, and, in fact, "email often produces supportive evidence that may help 'save the day' by providing valuable legal proof" of innocence.[14] This may stop frivolous lawsuits in their tracks. Further, reliable e-mail evidence—and bear in mind that e-mail is the most common type of information requested in civil lawsuits today—can also curtail lengthy and expensive lawsuits, and prevail. And if your company is public, Sarbanes-Oxley (SOX) regulations require the archiving of e-mail.

Don't Confuse E-Mail Archiving with Backup

All backups are not created equal. *There is a big difference between traditional system backups and specialized e-mail archiving software.*

Backups are huge dumps to mass storage, where the data is stored sequentially, and not compressed or indexed.[15] So it is impossible to search except by date, and even that would mean combing through troves of raw, nonindexed data.

The CEO may not be aware of it, but without true e-mail archiving, system administrators could spend long nights loading old tapes and churning out volumes of data, and legal teams will bill hourly for manual searches through troves of data. This compromises your enterprise's legal position, and not only increases raw costs, but also leads to less capable and informed legal representation. According to one study, fully one-third of IT managers state they would have difficulty producing an e-mail that is more than one year old. *"A backup system is no substitute for automatic archiving technology"* (italics added).[16]

No Personal Archiving in the Workplace

Employees are naturally going to want to back up their most important files, just as they probably do at home. But for an overall IG records mangagement program to be effective, personal archiving at work must be prohibited. This underground archiving results in hidden shadow files and is time-consuming and risky. According to Flynn, *"Self-managed email can result in the deletion of electronic records, alteration of email evidence, time-consuming searches for back-up tapes, and failure to comply with legal discovery demands"* (italics added). Also, users may compromise formal electronic records, or they may work from unofficial records, which, therefore by definition might be inaccurate or out-of-date, posing compliance and legal ramifications.[17]

Are All E-Mails Records?

This has been argued for years. *The short answer is no, not every e-mail message constitutes a record.* But how do you determine whether a message is a business record or not? The general answer is that a record documents a transaction or business-related event that may have legal ramifications or historic value. Most important are e-mails that document business activities that may relate to compliance requirements or those that could possibly come into dispute in litigation. Particular consideration should be given to financial transactions of any type.

Certainly evidence that required governance oversight or compliance activities that have been completed needs to be documented and becomes a business record. Also, business transactions, where there is an exchange of money or the equivalent in goods or services, are also business records. Today, these transactions may be documented by a quick e-mail. And, of course, any contracts (and any progressively developed or edited versions thereof) that are exchanged through e-mail become business records.

Three basic guidelines for determining whether an e-mail message should be considered a business record are:

1. The e-mail documents a transaction or the progress toward an ultimate transaction where anything of value is exchanged between two or more parties. All parts or characteristics of the transaction, including who (the parties to it), what, when, how much, and the composition of its components are parts of the transaction. Often seemingly minor parts of a transaction are found buried within an e-mail message with the pace of today's business environment. One example would be a last-minute discount offered by a supplier based on an order being placed or delivery being made within a specified timeframe.
2. The e-mail documents or provides support of business activity that pertains to internal corporate governance policies or compliance to externally mandated regulations.
3. *The e-mail documents other business activities that could possibly be disputed in the future*, whether it ultimately involves litigation or not (that is to say, most business disputes are actually resolved without litigation, provided proof of your organization's position can be shown). For instance, your supplier may dispute the amount of a discount, but once you forward the e-mail thread to them, they acquiesce.[18]

Destructive Retention of E-Mail

Destructive retention is an approach to e-mail archiving where e-mail messages are retained for a limited time (e.g., 90 days or six months), "followed by its permanent deletion manually or automatically, from the company's network"[19]—if it is not declared a business record, in accordance with IG and records management policies. Implementing this as a policy may shield the enterprise from retaining potentially libelous or litigious e-mail that is not a formal business record (e.g., off-color jokes or other personnel violations).

For heavily regulated industries, such as health care, energy, and financial services, organizations may need to archive e-mail for longer periods of time.

Instant Messaging

Instant messaging (IM) use in enterprises has proliferated—despite the fact that frequently proper policies, controls, and security measures are not in place to prevent e-document and data loss, or to manage IM records. There are a variety of threats to IM use that enterprises must defend against to keep their information assets secure and manage their records in a legally defensible way.

The first basic IM systems had real-time text capabilities for routing messages to users logged on to the same mainframe computer, which came into use in the mid-1960s. Early chat systems, like AOL Instant Messenger, have been in use since the late 1980s, but true IM systems that included buddy list features appeared on the scene in the mid-1990s, followed by the release of Yahoo! and Microsoft IM systems. The use of these personal IM products in the workplace has created new security risks and records management challenges.[20]

There are also more secure enterprise instant messaging (EIM) products that can be formally deployed. Leading EIM installed systems include IBM Lotus Sametime, Microsoft Office Communications Server, Cisco Unified Presence, and Jabber XCP. In the financial sector, Bloomberg Messaging and Reuters Messaging are leading platforms.

By the year 2000 it was estimated that nearly 250 million people worldwide were making use of IM,[21] and today estimates are that more than 2 billion people use IM, with the addition of hundreds of millions of users in China.

As with many technologies, IM became popular first for personal use, then crept into the workplace—and exploded. IM is seen as a quicker and more efficient way to communicate short messages than engaging in a telephone conversation or going through rounds of sending and receiving endless e-mail messages. *The problem with IM is that many organizations are blind to the fact that their employees are going to use it one way or another*, sometimes for short personal conversations outside the organization, and if left unchecked, it exposes the organization to a myriad of risks and gives hackers another way to compromise confidential information assets, and a percentage of these IM messages are actually business records and they must be captured and preserved, while assuring their integrity and reliability for legal purposes.

Best Practices for Business IM Use

Employing best practices for enterprise IM use can help mitigate its security risks while helping to capitalize on the business agility and velocity benefits IM can provide. Best practices must be built in to IG policies governing the use of IM, although "the specifics of these best practices must be tailored for each organization's unique needs."[22]

A methodology for forming IM-specific IG policies and implementing more secure use of IM must begin with surveying and documenting the proliferation of IM use in the organization. It should also discover how and why users are relying on IM—perhaps there is a shortcoming with their available IT tools and IM is a work-around.

Typically, executives will deny there is much use of IM, and that if it is being used, its impact is not worth worrying about. Also, getting users to come clean about their IM use may be difficult, since this may involve personal conversations and violations of

Documenting IM use in the organization is the first step in building IG policies to govern its use. Those policies must be tailored to the organization and its IM use.

corporate policy. A survey is a good place to start, but more sophisticated network monitoring tools need to be used to factually discover what IM systems are actually in use.

Once this usage discovery process has concluded, and the use of IM is mapped out, the IG team or steering committee must create or update policies to decide which IM systems it will allow to be used, how, when, and by whom; what restrictions or safeguards must be imposed; and guidelines as to appropriate use and content must be formulated. As a part of an overall IG effort, Quest Software determined that a successful IM policy will:

- **Clearly and explicitly explain the organization's instant messaging objectives.** Users should know why the organization permits IM and how it is expected to be used.
- **Define expectations of privacy.** Users should be made aware that the organization has the right to monitor and log all IM sessions for corporate compliance, safety, and security reasons.
- **Detail acceptable and unacceptable uses.** An exhaustive list of permitted and forbidden activities may not be necessary, but specific examples are helpful in establishing a framework of IM behaviors for users.
- **Detail content and contact restrictions (if any).** Most organizations will want to limit the amount of idle IM chat that may occur with family, friends, and other nonbusiness related contacts. There may also be additional issues related to information confidentiality and privacy. Some businesses may choose to block the distribution of certain types of information via live IM chat session or file transfer.
- **Define consequences for violations of the policy.** Users should be advised of the consequences of policy violations. Generally these should be aligned with the company's personnel and acceptable use policies.[23]

The use of a standard disclaimer, to be inserted into all users' IM sessions, can remind employees of appropriate IM use and that all chat sessions are being monitored and archived, and can be used in court or compliance hearings.

The next major step is to work with the IT staff to find the best and most appropriate email and IM real-time monitoring and capture tools, given the computing environment. Alternatives must be researched, selected, and deployed. In this research and selection process, it is best to start with at least an informal survey of enterprises within the same industry to attempt to learn what has worked best for them. Then a records management policy and methodology must be established, and the appropriate software deployed to support records capture and preservation efforts.

The key to any compliance effort or legal action will be ensuring that IM records are true and authentic, so the exact, unaltered archiving of IM messages along with associated metadata *must* be implemented in real time. This is the only way to preserve business records that may be needed in the future. But also, a policy for deleting IM messages after a period of time, so long as they are not declared business records, must be formulated.

Records of IM use must be captured in real time and preserved to ensure they are reliable and accurate.

IG requires that these policies and practices not be static, but rather, they must be regularly revisited and updated to reflect changes in user behavior, technology and legal requirements, and also to address any shortcoming or failure of the IG policies or technologies deployed.

Technology to Monitor IM

Today, it has been estimated that as much as 80 percent of all IM used by corporate employees comes from free IM providers like Yahoo!, MSN, or AOL. These programs are also *the least secure*. Messages using these IM platforms can fly around the Internet unprotected. So any monitoring technology implemented must have the capability to apply and enforce established IM use policies by constantly monitoring Internet traffic to discover IM conversations. Traffic containing certain key words can be monitored or blocked, and chat sessions between forbidden users (e.g., those who are party to a lawsuit) can be stopped before they start. But this all necessarily starts with IG and policy formulation.

Tips for Safer IM

Organizations should assume that IM is being used, whether they have sanctioned it or not. And that may not be a bad thing—employees may have found a reasonable business use for which IM is expedient and effective. So management should not rush to ban its use in a knee-jerk reaction. Here are some tips for safer use of corporate IM:

- Just as e-mail attachments and embedded links are suspect and can contain malicious executable files, beware of IM attachments, too. The same rules governing e-mail use apply to IM, in that employees should never open attachments from people they do not know. Even if they do know them, with phishing and social-engineering scams, these attachments should first be scanned for malware using anti-virus tools.
- Do not divulge any more personal information than is necessary. This comes into play even when creating screen names—so the naming convention for IM screen names must be standardized for the enterprise. Microsoft advises, "Your screen name should not provide or allude to personal information. For example, use a nickname such as SoccerFan instead of BaltimoreJenny."[24]
- Keep IM screen names private; treat them as another information asset that needs to be protected to reduce unwanted IM requests, phishing, or spam (actually *spim*, in IM parlance).
- Prohibit transmission of confidential corporate information. It is fine to set up a meeting with auditors, but do not attach and route the latest financial report through unsecured IM.
- Restrict IM contacts to known business colleagues. If personal contacts are allowed for emergencies, limit personal use for everyday communication. In other words, do not get into a long personal IM conversation with a spouse or teenager while at work. Remember, these conversations are going to be monitored and archived.

- Use caution when displaying default messages when you are unavailable or away. Details such as where an employee is going to have lunch or where their child is being picked up from school may expose the organization to liability if a hacker takes the information and uses it for criminal purposes. This can mean that employees may be unknowingly putting themselves in harm's way by giving out too much personal information.
- Ensure that IM policies are being enforced by utilizing IM monitoring and filtering tools, and by archiving messages in real time for a future verifiable record, should it be needed.
- Conduct an IM usage policy review at least annually; more often in the early stages of policy development.

Email and IM use are a part of the business operating environment today; proper IG measures must be in place and enforced to capture accurate and reliable records, and to delete the vast majority that are not business records, as soon as is legally feasible to eliminate any lingering liabilities, and operate in a more cost-efficient fashion.

CHAPTER SUMMARY: **KEY POINTS**

- Nearly 80 percent of all employees send work e-mail messages to and from their personal e-mail accounts, which exposes critical information assets to uncontrolled security risks.

- Meeting e-mail retention and archival requirements becomes an impossible task when e-mail messages are routed in a haphazard manner via personal accounts.

- In developing e-mail policies, an important step is consulting with stakeholders.

- E-mail policies must not be too restrictive or tied to a specific technology. They should be flexible enough to accommodate changes in technology and should be reviewed and updated regularly.

- Not all e-mail messages constitute a business record.

- Not all e-mail rises to the level of admissible legal evidence. Certain conditions must be met to prove reliability and integrity of the records.

- Automatic archiving protects the integrity of e-mail for legal purposes.

- Instant messaging (IM) use in business and the public sector has become widespread, despite the fact that often few controls or security measures are in place.

- Typically as much as 80 percent of all IM use in corporations today is over a free public network, which heightens security concerns.

- IM monitoring and management technology provides the crucial components that enable the organization to fully implement best practices for managing records of business IM.

(*Continued*)

(Continued)

- Enterprise IM (EIM) systems provide a greater level of security than IM from free services like Yahoo! and MSN.

- Regular analysis and modification (if necessary) of business IM policies and practices will help organizations leverage the maximum benefit from the technology.

- Records of IM use must be captured in real time and preserved to ensure they are reliable and accurate.

Notes

1. "Research Finds That Restrictive Email Policies Are Creating Hidden Security Risks for Businesses," *BusinessWire*, March 9, 2011, www.businesswire.com/news/home/20110309005960/en/Research-Finds-Restrictive-Email-Policies-Creating-Hidden.
2. Elizabeth Montalbano, "AntiSec Hacks Booz Allen, Posts Confidential Military Email," *InformationWeek*, July 12, 2011, www.informationweek.com/news/security/attacks/231001418?cid=nl_IW_daily_2011-07-12_html.
3. Ibid.
4. Mathew J. Schwartz, "AntiSec Hacks FBI Contractor," *InformationWeek*, July 11, 2011, www.informationweek.com/news/security/attacks/231001326.
5. "Research Finds That Restrictive Email Policies Are Creating Hidden Security Risks for Businesses."
6. Ibid.
7. Paul Mah, "How to Reduce the Email Security Risks to Your Business," *The EmailAdmin*, March 10, 2011, www.theemailadmin.com/2011/03/how-to-reduce-the-email-security-risks-to-your-business.
8. Blair Kahn, *Information Nation: Seven Keys to Information Management Compliance* (Silver Spring, MD: AIIM International, 2004), 98–99.
9. Ibid, 95–96.
10. Ibid.
11. Nancy Flynn, *The E-Policy Handbook: Rules and Best Practices to Safely Manage Your Company's E-Mail, Blogs, Social Networking, and Other Electronic Communication Tools* (New York: AMACOM, 2009), 20.
12. Hugh Son and Andrew Frye, "Geithner's E-Mails, Phone Logs Subpoenaed by House (update3)," January 13, 2010, www.bloomberg.com/apps/news?pid=newsarchive&sid=aGzbhrSxFlXw,.
13. Flynn, *The E-Policy Handbook*, 37.
14. Blake Lyons, *Email Archiving and the Law*, bllaw.co.uk, March 27, 2007; and Nancy Flynn, *The E-Policy Handbook*, 40–41.
15. Nancy Flynn and Randolph Kahn, *Email Rules, A Business Guide to Managing Policies, Security, and Legal Issues for E-Mail and Digital Communication* (New York: AMACOM, 2003), 81–82.
16. Flynn, *The E-Policy Handbook*, 41.
17. Ibid., 43.
18. Robert F. Smallwood, *Taming the Email Tiger: Email Management for Compliance, Governance, & Litigation Readiness* (New Orleans: Bacchus Business Books, 2008).
19. Flynn, *The E-Policy Handbook*, 25.
20. Quest Software, Inc., "Best Practices in Instant Messaging Management," October 2008, http://media.govtech.net/Digital_Communities/Quest%20Software/Best_Practices_in_Instant_Messaging_Management.pdf, 5.
21. Ibid.
22. Quest Software, "Best Practices in Instant Messaging Management."
23. Ibid.
24. M. Adeel Ansari, "10 Tips for Safer IM Instant Messaging," July 6, 2008, http://adeelansari.wordpress.com/tag/safer-im-instant-messaging.

CHAPTER 12

Managing E-Records in the Cloud*

Cloud computing represents one of the most significant paradigm shifts in information technology (IT) in history. Sure, it is similar in concept to sharing an application-hosting provider, which has been around for a half-century and was common in highly regulated vertical industries, such as banks and health-care institutions. But it has evolved into a computing resource that is very different, with advances in IT architecture, improved hardware speeds, and lower storage costs as the computer industry continues to advance.

The "big idea" behind cloud computing is that it provides economies of scale by spreading costs across many client organizations by pooling computing resources and matching client computing needs to consumption, in a flexible, (nearly) real-time way. Cloud computing can be considered as a sort of utility that is vastly scalable and can be readily modulated, like the temperature control on a heater, or air conditioner. This approach has great potential, promising on-demand computing power, off-site backups, heavy security, and "innovations we cannot yet imagine."[1] It is a new animal for compliance, risk, and records managers, and policies specific to cloud use must be developed, enforced, and refined regularly to ensure information governance (IG) policy guidelines are met, and accurate business records are captured and preserved.

When executives hear of the potential cost savings and elimination of capital outlays associated with cloud computing, their ears perk up. Users are glad to have some autonomy and independence from their information technology (IT) department, and IT departments are enthused to have instant resources at their disposal and to shed some of the responsibilities for infrastructure so they can focus on applications. Most of all, they are enthused by the agility offered by the on-demand provisioning of computing and the ability to align IT with business strategies more nimbly and readily.

But for all the hoopla and excitement, *there are also grave concerns about security risks and loss of direct IT control*, while managers and IT leaders who are customers of cloud computing services still hold ultimate responsibility for IT performance for which they are held accountable.

There are also critical **records management** (RM) issues to consider, in that most cloud applications do not offer RM functionality, and there are metadata management and custody issues that must be addressed, in order that a legally defensible RM policy can be created and supported.

---

* Reprinted with permission from John Wiley & Sons, Inc.

193

Organizations need to understand the security risks of cloud computing, and they must have IG policies and controls in place for leveraging cloud technology to manage electronic documents and records. An investigation and analysis of how the cloud services provider(s) will deliver RM capability is crucial to supporting RM and related functions, such as archiving and e-discovery, and meeting IG policy requirements.

Defining Cloud Computing

The definition of **cloud computing** is, rather, well, *cloudy*, if you will. The flurry of developments in cloud computing make it difficult for managers and policymakers to define it clearly and succinctly, and to evaluate available options. There are many misconceptions and vagaries surrounding cloud computing. Some misconceptions and questions include:

- "That hosting thing is like SaaS."
- "Cloud, SaaS, all the same, we don't own anything."
- "OnDemand is Cloud Computing."
- "ASP, Hosting, SaaS seems all the same."
- "It all costs the same so what does it matter to me?"
- "Why should I care if it's multitenant or not?"
- "What's this private cloud versus public cloud?"[2]

Cloud computing is a shared resource that provides dynamic access to computing services that may range from raw computing power, to basic infrastructure, to fully operational and supported applications. It is a set of newer information technologies that provides for on-demand, modulated, shared use of computing services remotely. This is accomplished by telecommunications via the Internet or a virtual private network (VPN, which provides more security). It eliminates (or minimizes) the need to purchase server hardware and deploy IT infrastructure to support computing resources and gives users access to applications, data, and storage within their own business unit environments or networks.[3] Perhaps the best feature of all is that services can be turned on or off, increased or decreased, depending on user needs.

There are a range of interpretations and definitions, some of which are not completely accurate. Some merely define it as renting storage space or applications on a host organization's servers; others center definitions around web-based applications like social media and hosted application services.

Someone has to be the official referee, especially in the public sector. The National Institute of Standards and Technology (NIST) is the official federal arbiter of definitions, standards, and guidelines for cloud computing. NIST defines cloud computing as:

a model for enabling convenient, on-demand network access to a shared pool of configurable computing resources (e.g., networks, servers, storage,

Cloud computing encompasses any subscription-based or pay-per-use service that, in real time over the Internet, extends IT's existing capabilities.[4]

> Cloud computing enables convenient, on-demand network access to a shared pool of configurable computing resources that can be rapidly provisioned.

applications, and services) that can be rapidly provisioned and released with minimal management effort or service provider interaction.[5]

Given the changing nature of IT, especially for newer developments, NIST has stated that the definition of cloud computing "is evolving." If looking for the latest official definition, one should consult the most current definition available from NIST's website at www.nist.gov (and other resources).

Key Characteristics of Cloud Computing

NIST also identifies five essential characteristics of cloud computing:

1. *On-demand self-service.* A [computing] consumer can unilaterally provision computing capabilities, such as server time and network storage, as needed automatically without requiring human interaction with each service's provider.

2. *Broad network access.* Capabilities are available over the network and accessed through standard mechanisms that promote use by heterogeneous thin or thick client platforms (e.g., mobile phones, laptops, and PDAs).

3. *Resource pooling.* The [hosting] provider's computing resources are pooled to serve multiple consumers using a multi-tenant model, with different physical and virtual resources dynamically assigned and reassigned according to consumer demand. There is a sense of location independence in that the customer generally has no control or knowledge over the exact location of the provided resources but may be able to specify location at a higher level of abstraction (e.g., country, state, or datacenter). Examples of resources include storage, processing, memory, network bandwidth, and virtual machines.

4. *Rapid elasticity.* Capabilities can be rapidly and elastically provisioned, in some cases automatically, to quickly scale out and rapidly released to quickly scale in. To the consumer, the capabilities available for provisioning often appear to be unlimited and can be purchased in any quantity at any time.

5. *Measured service.* Cloud systems automatically control and optimize resource use by leveraging a metering capability at some level of abstraction appropriate to the type of service (e.g., storage, processing, bandwidth, and active user accounts). Resource usage can be monitored, controlled, and reported providing transparency for both the provider and consumer of the utilized service.[6]

Among metatrends, "Cloud computing is the hardest one to argue with in the long term."[8]

What Cloud Computing Really Means

It's fast. It's cheap. It's efficient. Yes, cloud computing is all the rage. NIST has offered its official definition, but "the problem is that (as with Web 2.0) everyone seems to have a different definition."[7]

The phrase "the cloud" has entered the mainstream—it is promoted on prime-time TV—but its meaning and description are in flux: that is, if you ask 10 different people to define it, you will likely get 10 different answers. According to Eric Knorr and Galen Gruman in *InfoWorld*, it's really just "a metaphor for the Internet" but when you throw in "computing" alongside it, "the meaning gets bigger and fuzzier." Cloud computing provides "a way to increase capacity [e.g., computing power, network connections, storage] or add capabilities dynamically on the fly without investing in new infrastructure, training new personnel, or licensing new software. Cloud computing encompasses any subscription-based or pay-per-use service that, in (near) real time over the Internet, extends IT's existing capabilities."[9]

The use of **service-oriented architecture** (SOA)—which separates infrastructure, applications, and data into layers—permeates enterprise applications, and the idea of loosely coupled services running on an agile, scalable infrastructure may eventually "make every enterprise a node in the cloud." That is the direction the trend is headed. "*It's a long-running trend with a far-out horizon. But among big metatrends, cloud computing is the hardest one to argue with in the long term*" (italics added).[11]

Cloud Deployment Models

Depending upon user needs and other considerations, cloud computing services are typically deployed using one of the following four models, as defined by NIST:

1. *Private cloud.* This is dedicated to and operated by a single enterprise. This is a particularly prudent approach when privacy and security are key issues, such as in the health care and financial services industries, and also for sensitive government or military applications and data. A private cloud may be managed by the organization or a third party and may exist on-premise or off-premise.
2. *Community cloud.* Think co-ops, nonprofit organizations, and nongovernmental organizations (NGOs). In this deployment, the cloud infrastructure

The idea of loosely coupled services running on an agile, scalable infrastructure should eventually "make every enterprise a node in the cloud."[10]

There are four basic cloud-computing models: private, public, community, and hybrid (which is a combined approach).

is *shared by several organizations* and supports a specific community that has shared concerns (e.g., mission, security requirements, policy, and compliance considerations). It may be managed by the organizations or a third party and may exist on-premise or off-premise.

3. *Public cloud.* Open to the public, this cloud can be maintained by a user group, or even a fan club. In this case, "the cloud infrastructure is made available to the general public or a large industry group and is owned by an organization selling cloud services."

4. *Hybrid cloud.* This utilizes a combined approach, using parts of the aforementioned deployment models: private, community, and/or public. The cloud infrastructure is a "*composition of two or more clouds,* (private, community, or public) that remain unique entities but are bound together by standardized or proprietary technology that enables data and application portability (e.g., cloud bursting for load-balancing between clouds)" (italics added).[12]

Greatest Security Threats to Cloud Computing

Cloud computing comes with serious security risks—some of which have not yet been uncovered—but the business benefits largely outweigh the security threats for the vast majority of enterprises, so long as they are planned for, and preventive action is taken. In planning and information governance policy development, these risks must be borne in mind and dealt with through controls and counter measures. Controls must be tested and audited, although the actual enforcement must be carried out by management. The following are key cloud computing security threats, with specific examples, and remedial fix measures that can be taken. The majority of this information is courtesy of the Cloud Security Alliance.

Document and Data Breaches

Many times damage to e-documents and data is malicious, while other times damage is unintentional. *Lack of training and awareness, for example, can cause an information user to accidentally compromise sensitive data.* Organizations must have proactive IG policies that combat either type of breach. The loss of data, documents, and records is always a threat and can occur whether cloud computing is utilized or not.

Cloud computing carries serious security risks—some of which have not yet been uncovered.

When officially declared business records are deleted or altered without a backup of the original record or content, they may be lost forever. A record can also be lost by unlinking it from its indexes, deleting its identifying metadata, or losing its encoding key, which may render it unrecoverable. Another way data/document loss can occur is by storing it on unreliable media.[13] And as with any architecture—not just cloud computing—unauthorized parties must be prevented from hacking into the system and gaining access to sensitive data. In general, providers of cloud services have more resources at their disposal than their individual clients typically have.

But the threat of data compromise inherently increases when using cloud computing, due to "the number of and interactions between risks and challenges which are either unique to cloud, or more dangerous because of the architectural or operational characteristics of the cloud environment."[14]

Examples

- Lack of **document lifecycle security** (DLS) technologies, such as data loss prevention (DLP) and information rights management (IRM) technologies.
- Insufficient **authentication, authorization, and audit** (AAA) controls to govern login access.
- Ineffective encryption and software keys, including lost keys or inconsistent encryption.
- Basic operational failures, such as server or disk drive crashes.
- Security challenges related to persistent data or ineffective disposal methods.
- Inability to verify disposal at the end of a business record's lifecycle.
- Risk of association with any larger failures of the cloud provider.
- Jurisdiction and political issues that may arise due to the fact that the cloud provider likely resides outside of the geographic region of the client.
- Data center reliability, backup, and disaster recovery/business continuity issues.

The Fix

- IG policies and controls to protect the most sensitive documents and data.
- DLS implementation where needed to protect documents from creation to their final disposition.
- More robust and secure application programming interface (API) access control.
- Strong **e-mail and e-document encryption** to protect sensitive data at rest, in use, and in transit.
- IG policies for data and document security during the software application design phase, as well as testing and auditing the controls for those policies during live operation.
- Strong encryption generation, as well as secure storage, management, and document destruction practices.

Lack of training on cloud use can lead to users compromising sensitive data.

- Contractual agreement by cloud service providers to completely delete data before storage media are reused by other clients.
- Agreement by cloud provider to follow standard operating procedures for data backup, archiving, and retention.

The Enemy Within: Insider Threats

Since the advent of the WikiLeaks scandal and the slew of other examples in the corporate world, the threat of the malicious insider is well known. *"This threat is amplified for consumers of cloud services by the convergence of IT services and customers under a single management domain, combined with a general lack of transparency into provider process and procedure"* (italics added).[15] For example, question a cloud provider on its security procedures—for not only the applications and services, but also for their employees: How are they screened? Are background checks performed? How is physical access to the building and data center granted and monitored? What are its remedial procedures for noncompliance?

When these security, privacy, and support issues are not fully investigated, it creates an opportunity for hackers, industrial spies, and even "nation-state sponsored intrusion. The level of access granted could enable such an adversary to harvest confidential data or gain complete control over the cloud services with little or no risk of detection."[16]

Examples

- An internal company employee steals information to give or sell to a competitor.
- A cloud provider's employee steals information to give or sell to one of your company's competitors.
- Inadequate screening processes (by your company or a cloud provider) can result in the hiring of people with criminal records, granting them access to sensitive information.
- A cloud provider's employee allows unauthorized access to data that your company believes is secure in the cloud. The physical cloud storage facility lacks security, so anyone can enter the building and access information.

The Fix

- IG policies and controls to secure information assets.
- Implementation of data loss prevention (DLP) and IRM technologies and related technology sets at all stages of DLS.
- Assessment of suppliers' practices and complete supply chain.
- Screening and hiring requirements (e.g., background checks) as part of contract with cloud provider.

It is prudent to investigate the security and personnel screening processes of a potential cloud provider.

- Transparent policies regarding information security, data management, compliance, and reporting, as approved by the client.
- Clear delineation of the process for notifying the client of a security breach or data loss.[17]

Hacking and Rogue Intrusions

Although cloud computing providers, as a rule, invest heavily in security, they can also be the target of attacks, and those attacks can affect many client enterprises. Providers of cloud infrastructure service (e.g., network management, computing power, databases, storage) offer their customers the illusion of unlimited infrastructure expansion in the form of computing, network resources, and storage capacity. This is often coupled with a very easy sign-up process, free trials (even for anonymous users), and simple activation with a credit card. This is a boon to hackers who can assume multiple identities.[18] Using these anonymous accounts to their advantage, hackers and spammers can engage in criminal operations while remaining elusive.

Examples

- Cloud services providers have often unknowingly hosted malicious code, including Trojan horses, keystroke loggers, bot applications, and other programs that facilitate data theft. Recent examples include the Zeus botnet and InfoStealer.
- Malware can masquerade as downloads for Microsoft Office, Adobe PDFs, or other innocuous files.
- Botnets can infect a cloud provider to gain access to a wide range of data, while leveraging the cloud provider's control capabilities.
- Spam is a perennial problem—each new countermeasure is met with new ways to sneak spam through filters to phish for sensitive data.

The Fix

- IG policies and monitoring controls must require tighter initial registration and thorough user verification processes.
- IG policies and technologies to combat credit card fraud.
- Total network monitoring, including deep content inspection.
- Requirement that the cloud provider regularly monitor public blacklists to check for exploitation.

Insecure Points of Cloud Connection

An **application programming interface** (API) is a way of standardizing the connection between two software applications. They are essentially standard hooks that an

> Easy sign-up procedures for cloud services mean that hackers can easily assume multiple identities and carry out malicious attacks.

APIs must be thoroughly tested to ensure they are secure and abide by policy.

application uses to connect to another software application—in this case, the cloud. System actions like provisioning, management, orchestration, and monitoring are all performed using these API interfaces.

It comes down to this: A chain is only as strong as its weakest link, so *APIs must be more thoroughly tested to ensure that all connections abide by established policy*. This will thwart hackers seeking workarounds for ill intent, as well as valid users who have made a mistake. It is possible for third parties to piggyback value-added services on APIs, resulting in a layered interface that is more vulnerable to security breaches.

Examples
- Weak APIs provide opportunities for data compromise.
- Anonymous logins and reusable passwords can undermine the security of an entire cloud community.
- Unencrypted transmission or storage and unencrypted verification allow successful man-in-the-middle data theft.
- Rigid basic access controls or false authorizations pose a threat.
- Poor management, monitoring, and recording of cloud logins and activity make it difficult to detect malicious behavior.
- Dependency on unregulated API interfaces, especially third-party add-ons can allow critical information to be stolen as necessary connections are made.

The Fix
- An understanding of the security model of cloud provider APIs and interfaces, including any third-party or organization-created dependencies.
- Utilization of multiple logon authentication steps and strong access controls.
- Encryption of sensitive data during transmission.
- Understanding how the API impacts associated cloud usage.

Issues with Multitenancy and Technology Sharing

The foundations of many cloud services providers were not developed to support multiple tenants on a single piece of hardware, or to isolate each tenant on its own system. Basic cloud infrastructure is designed to leverage scale through the sharing of components. Despite this, many component manufacturers have not caught up, and their products have not been designed to function in a multitenant system. Surely, newer architectures will evolve to address this issue.

In the meantime, virtual computing is often used, allowing for multiple instances of an operating system (and applications) to be walled off from others that are running on the same computer. Essentially, each instance of the operating system (OS) runs independently as if it were the only one on the computer. A "virtualization hypervisor mediates access between guest operating systems and the physical compute resources" (like CPU processing power). Yet flaws have been found in these hypervisors "that have enabled guest operating systems to gain inappropriate levels of control or influence on the underlying platform"—and therefore indirectly impact the other guest operating systems running on the machine. To combat this, "security enforcement and monitoring" of all shared computing resources must be employed. Solid partitions between the guest operating systems—known as compartmentalization—should be employed to ensure that one client's activities do not interfere with others running on the same cloud provider. Customers should *never* have access to any other tenant's "actual or residual data, network traffic," or other proprietary data.[19]

Examples

- Joanna Rutkowska's Blue Pill root technique, which describes how an unauthorized user could intercept data by using virtual hardware called a hypervisor. The Blue Pill would be undetectable as long as the host system was functioning properly. Rutkowska also developed a Red Pill, which could detect a Blue Pill hypervisor, allowing the owner to eliminate it.
- Kostya Kortchinksy's CloudBurst is another example of hypervisor exploitation.

The Fix

- Security IG that leverages best practices for installation, configuration, monitoring, testing, and auditing of cloud computing resources.
- Requirements for monitoring the computing environment for any rogue intrusions or misuse of cloud resources.
- Control and verify access. Promote a more secure two-factor authentication procedure.
- Enforceable service-level agreements (SLAs) for patching software bugs, addressing data breaches, and fixing vulnerabilities.
- An IG policy that requires regular audits and evaluations to detect weaknesses in cloud security and configuration.[20]

Hacking, Hijacking, and Unauthorized Access

Hacking into accounts to assume the identity of a victim has been happening almost since personal e-mail existed. It can be as simple as stealing passwords with a keystroke logger. Attack methods such as social engineering (e.g., phishing), fraud by identity theft, and exploitation of software vulnerabilities are still effective at compromising systems. Most people recycle a few passwords and reuse them for multiple accounts, so once one is breached, criminals can gain access to additional accounts, including client databases and sensitive documents. If login credentials are compromised, a hacker can monitor nearly everything your organization is doing: A less passive hacker might alter or destroy sensitive documents, create false information, or replace your links with

Cloud providers use virtualization heavily and hypervisors may allow intrusions.

fraudulent ones that direct users to sites harboring malware or phishing scams. Once they have control, it can look like *your organization* is the origin of the malicious downloads or information capture. From here, the attackers can assume the good name and reputation of an organization to further their attacks.

Examples

- Examples are widespread in the general population; however, no clear instances of this occurring with cloud services providers are known (as this book goes to press).

The Fix

- IG policies should clearly state that users and providers should never reveal their account information to anyone.
- An IG policy should require more secure two-factor authentication techniques to verify login identity, where possible.
- Require your cloud services provider to actively monitor and log all activity in order to quickly identify users engaging in fraudulent actions or those that otherwise fail to comply with the client's IG policy.
- Understand, analyze, and evaluate the cloud provider's contract, especially regarding security protocols. Negotiate improved terms in SLAs to improve or enhance security and privacy.[21]

Who Are Your Neighbors?

The primary selling point of cloud computing is that enterprises are freed up to focus on their core business, rather than being focused on providing IT services. Modulating computer hardware and software resources without making capital expenditures is another key advantage. Both of these business benefits allow companies to invest more heavily in line-of-business activities and focus on their core products, services, and operations. The security risks must be weighed against the financial and operational advantages—and projected estimates for costs are often understated, which throws off the entire cost-justification analysis. Further complicating things is the fact that cloud deployments are often enthusiastically driven by overzealous cost-cutters who focus inordinately on potential benefits, and do not factor in risk and security issues.

An analysis of an organization's exposure to risk *must* include checking on software versions and revision levels, overall security design, and general IG practices. This includes updating software, tools, and policy, as needed.

Knowing your neighbors—those who are sharing the same infrastructure with you—is also important and, as we all know, good fences make good neighbors. If the cloud services provider will not or cannot be forthcoming about who else is sharing their infrastructure services with your organization and this becomes a significant issue, then you may want to insert contract language that forbids any direct competitor

It is important to know what other clients are being hosted with your cloud services provider, as they may represent a threat. Moving to a private cloud architecture is a solution.

from sharing your servers, although these types of terms are always difficult to verify and enforce, so moving to a private cloud architecture may be the best option.

Examples

- Amazon's Elastic Compute Cloud (EC2) service was utilized by the Internal Revenue Service (IRS). When the IRS asked Amazon for a certification and accreditation (C&A) report, Amazon declined. Note: The C&A process was developed to help ensure compliance with NIST standards and mandated by the Office of Management and Budget, which oversees Federal Information Security Management Act of 2002 (FISMA) compliance.
- Heartland, a payment processing corporation, suffered a data breach in 2008. Hackers stole account details for over 100 million credit and debit cards. This data was stored on Heartland's network, which the hackers broke into using information (pertaining to employees, corporate structure, company networks, and related systems) it had stolen in the weeks leading up to the major breach.

The Fix

- An IG policy that requires full disclosure of activity and usage logs, and related information. Audit the policy for compliance.
- Investigate the architecture of your cloud services provider (e.g., version levels, network operating systems, firewalls, etc.).
- Robust and vigilant supervision, logs, and reporting of all system activity, particularly that requesting expansive and detailed reports on the handling of sensitive information.[22]

Additional RM and Privacy Threats and Concerns

- Inability (of the cloud services provider) to manage records *at the file level.*
- Inability to closely *follow the user's retention schedule* and produce audited certificates of destruction at the end of a records' lifecycle.
- Inability to *enforce legal holds* when litigation is pending or anticipated.
- *Poor response time*—inability to deliver files quickly and in line with user expectations.
- Storage of personally identifiable information (PII) on servers in Europe or other locales that *prohibit or restrict the release of PII back to the United States* (or home country of the cloud services client organization).[23]

IG Guidelines: Managing Documents and Records in the Cloud

The following guidelines have been established by the National Archives and Records Administration (NARA) for creating standards and policies for managing an organization's e-documents records that are created, used, or stored in cloud computing environments:

1. Include the Chief Records Management Officer and/or lead RM staff in the planning, development, deployment, and use of cloud computing solutions.

2. Define which copy of records will be declared as the organization's record copy and manage these in accordance with information governance policies and regulations (e.g., for federal agencies, 36 CFR Part 1222). Remember, the value of records in the cloud may be greater than the value of any other set because of indexing or other reasons. In such instances, this added value may require designation of the copies as records.

3. Include instructions for determining if records in a cloud environment are covered under an existing records retention schedule.

4. Include instructions on how all records will be captured, managed, retained, made available to authorized users, and retention periods applied.

5. Include instructions on conducting a records analysis, developing and submitting records retention schedules to an organization's central records department for unscheduled records in a cloud environment. These instructions should include scheduling system documentation, metadata, and related records.

6. Include instructions to periodically test transfers of records to other environments, including departmental servers, to ensure the records remain portable.

7. Include instructions on how data will be migrated to new formats, operating systems, etc., so that records are readable throughout their entire life cycles. Include in your migration planning provisions for transferring permanent records in the cloud to central records.

8. Resolve portability and accessibility issues through good records management policies and other data governance practices. Data governance typically addresses interoperability of computing systems, portability of data (able to move from one system to another), and information security and access. However, such policies by themselves will not address an organization's compliance and information governance demands and requirements.[24]

Managing E-Docs and Records in the Cloud: A Practical Approach

The risks and security vulnerabilities of cloud computing have been reviewed in this chapter—so much so that perhaps some readers are thinking, "Is it really worth it?" The answer is a *qualified* yes—it can be, based on your organization's business needs and computing resource capabilities.

Formal business records are the most valuable documents in an organization. For recordkeeping purposes, records held within the cloud are subject to a higher risk of loss and inaccessibility, which can cause the organization to be noncompliant, lose in litigation, be fined, and experience other negative results. So what is the solution to managing these critical records?[25]

Sometimes people overthink and overcomplicate things. Perhaps the solution is a simple approach: Research and define organizational business requirements and then, "*only allow those documents and records into the cloud that need to be shared across collaborative teams that do not require significant time for retention or are at low risk for litigation*" (italics added).[26]

What is a *significant* retention time period? As a practical matter, anything that needs to be retained for over two years probably should not be put into the cloud. Your organization will have to conduct its own business-specific analysis and develop IG policies for records management in the cloud that are best suited, and most appropriate. A thorough records inventory, retention schedule, and risk analysis in relation to business requirements should be conducted, which includes examining security and compliance concerns such as privacy, in addition to high-risk litigation issues.[27]

Another possible approach for utilizing cloud services for managing records is to *maintain hard copies of records held in the cloud.* If the information suddenly disappears, then the hard copy is available as a backup. *But that may be even more problematic*—you have to determine which copy is the *official* record, as well as analyze and identify which hard copies to keep, how to keep the paper and electronic copies synchronized, how and where to store paper copies, what file organization system to use, how to document it, and how and when hard copy records can be accessed. The other thorny issue is that printing out all electronic records is contrary to what most RM experts advise, and eco-conscious organizations will especially want to avoid this. All organizations have been moving toward the paperless office, becoming more sustainable, and reducing their carbon footprint.[28]

Long-Term Content Migration Issues

Let's say it's a go. Your organization is moving to the cloud. Before moving headlong into storing your documents and records with a cloud services provider, some long-term thinking is called for. Consider what might happen in the future when cloud technologies improve and mature, and perhaps a better alternative for cloud services becomes clear. Or what if your provider goes out of business or is bought up by a conglomerate? Now, how do you get your terabytes of content moved over to a new cloud service, or back in-house?

Most cloud services, such as Box.com (as of this printing), have no mass migration capability. If you are going to migrate, say, 500,000 files, you will not be able to do it programmatically and will have to work with the vendor. They may, for example, ask you to dump the file to magnetic tape and send them and the cloud services provider will migrate the files for you. But that is time consuming and there are metadata preservation issues to investigate. So the caution may be that migrations are difficult and original metadata may not come through correctly, or be verifiably preserved for legal purposes.[29]

Take a practical approach and limit cloud use to documents that do not have long retention periods and carry a low litigation risk.

Most cloud services providers do not have mass content migration or records management capabilities.

Cloud Services Lack Basic Records Management Capabilities

Typical cloud collaboration **software as a service** (SaaS) applications, such as Box and Dropbox, do not provide any records management (RM) capability (as of this printing). Also, SaaS applications like SalesForce do not have any RM capabilities—even Google Docs does not have RM capabilities (as of this printing). There are some third-party providers that have emerged and provide RM functionality.

So, if you are operating in a regulated industry or have other legal issues such as heavy litigation loads and e-discovery requirements, your organization should likely not be storing documents in any SaaS cloud applications without further investigating how to meet your RM needs.[30]

CHAPTER SUMMARY: **KEY POINTS**

- Organizations are rapidly moving applications and storage to the cloud. Cloud computing allows users to access and use shared data and computing services via the Internet or a VPN.

- Organizations need to understand cloud computing's security risks and formulate IG policies and controls before deploying.

- Five key characteristics of cloud computing are: (1) on-demand self-service, (2) broad network access, (3) resource pooling, (4) rapid elasticity, and (5) measured service.

- Cloud computing services are typically deployed using one of four models: (1) private cloud, (2) public cloud, (3) community cloud, and (4) hybrid cloud.

- Utilizing cloud computing carries significant security risks, which can be offset by establishing IG policies and preventive measures so that the business benefits of agility and reduced cost may be exploited.

- Cloud application services may have weaknesses related to supporting RM functions, such as the inability to manage records at the file level; the inability to closely follow the user's RM retention schedule, and the inability to enforce legal holds when litigation is pending or anticipated.

(Continued)

(*Continued*)

- Cloud applications may lack the capability to implement records disposition schedules and to prove that every instance of a record was destroyed after its final disposition, so that defensible disposition practices can be argued in court.

- Carefully determine which types of documents should be stored in the cloud. The most likely candidates are those that are unlikely to pose a litigation risk, do not have long retention requirements (less than two years), and are shared for collaborative projects.

- Migration of content to or from a cloud services provider must be examined closely to determine if metadata is also kept intact, and can be legally proven to be. Also, most cloud providers do not offer records management features.

Notes

1. Cloud Security Alliance, "Top Threats to Cloud Computing V1.0," March 2010, https://cloudsecurityalliance.org/topthreats/csathreats.v1.0.pdf, 6.
2. R. "Ray" Wang, "Tuesday's Tip: Understanding the Many Flavors of Cloud Computing and SaaS," March 22, 2010, http://blog.softwareinsider.org/2010/03/22/tuesdays-tip-understanding-the-many-flavors-of-cloud-computing-and-saas.
3. "NARA Bulletin 2010-05," September 8, 2010, www.archives.gov/records-mgmt/bulletins/2010/2010-05.html.
4. Eric Knorr and Galen Gruman, "What Cloud Computing Really Means," *InfoWorld*, July 2010, www.infoworld.com/d/cloud-computing/what-cloud-computing-really-means-031.
5. NIST Definition of Cloud Computing, Version 15, 10-07-2009, nist.gov (accessed March 30, 2012).
6. Ibid.
7. Knorr and Gruman, "What Cloud Computing Really Means."
8. Ibid.
9. Ibid.
10. Ibid.
11. Ibid.
12. All definitions are from NIST Definition of Cloud Computing, Version 15, 10-07-2009 (accessed August 15, 2011).
13. Cloud Security Alliance, "Top Threats to Cloud Computing V1.0."
14. Ibid.
15. Ibid.
16. Ibid.
17. Ibid.
18. Ibid.
19. Ibid.
20. Ibid.
21. Ibid.
22. Ibid.
23. Gordon E. J. Hoke, CRM, e-mail to author, June 10, 2012.
24. "NARA Bulletin 2010-05," September 8, 2010, www.archives.gov/records-mgmt/bulletins/2010/2010-05.html.

25. Rhizome Digital, "Records Management and the Cloud," March 9, 2010, http://rhizomedigital
    .wordpress.com/2010/03/09/records-management-the-cloud.
26. Ibid.
27. Ibid.
28. Ibid.
29. Bud Porter-Roth, e-mail to author, May 16, 2012.
30. Ibid.

CHAPTER 13

Managing Social Media Business Records*

S ocial media use has skyrocketed over the past several years. Organizations are using social media and Web 2.0 platforms like blogs, podcasts, and wikis to connect people to corporate and government organizations, and to share information. In the government sector, agencies are able to directly provide information to the public, and can solicit responses on planned projects or policy changes in new, more collaborative, and personal ways.[1] These new social media platforms are creating content that must be managed, monitored, and archived, and, in fact, some of the content supports key marketing or strategic business processes and may be classified as business records. *Often social media content is not managed by information governance (IG) policies and monitored with controls that ensure protection of critical information assets and preservation of business records.*

Types of Social Media in Web 2.0

The term *Web 2.0* was coined to characterize the move from static websites on the Internet that passively provided information to consumers to more participative, interactive, collaborative, and user-oriented websites and web applications that allow for input, discussion, and sharing. Users actually can add content, increasing the value of the website or service. Examples may be blogs or podcasts (usually audio) where readers can post comments or pose questions; wikis that hyperlink to related information to create a knowledge base that shows interrelationships and that allow users to add content; and RSS (really simple syndication) feeds that provide a stream of fresh content to the user or consumer.

Web 2.0 does not literally mean a new revision level of the web, but rather, a newer approach that software developers have taken to allow consumers of web content to participate, collaborate, and add content. These development efforts reflect consumer needs and preferences that surfaced as a result of increased use of the web for daily information and communications.

Social media sites like LinkedIn, Twitter, and Facebook encourage social networking online by allowing users to create their own close network of business associates or friends—essentially a hand-picked audience—and to post their own content in the

---

* Reprinted with permission from John Wiley & Sons, Inc.

form of comments, links, photos, videos, and so forth. Others in their social network may view, forward, share, organize, and comment on this content.[2]

Web 2.0 and social media platforms began as outward-facing, public web services that could link users from around the world. Subsequently, businesses discovered that social media technology could also be leveraged for internal use, such as by creating a directory and network of subject matter experts (SMEs) that users can search for special projects, or by sending out short microblog messages to keep their workforce informed. These internal social networks may be extended to include other stakeholders, like suppliers and customers, in a controlled environment. A number of platform and software options exist for enterprise social media development and use.

According to the U.S. National Archives and Records Administration (NARA):

Social media platforms can be grouped into the categories below. Some specific platforms may fit into more than one category depending on how the platform is used:

Web Publishing: Platforms used to create, publish, and reuse content.

- Microblogging (Twitter, Plurk)
- Blogs (WordPress, Blogger)
- Wikis (Wikispaces, PBWiki)
- Mashups (Google Maps, popurls)

Social Networking: Platforms used to provide interactions and collaboration among users.

- Social Networking tools (Facebook, LinkedIn)
- Social Bookmarks (Delicious, Digg)
- Virtual Worlds (Second Life, OpenSim)
- Crowdsourcing/Social Voting (IdeaScale, Chaordix)

File Sharing/Storage: Platforms used to share files and host content storage.

- Photo Libraries (Flickr, Picasa)
- Video Sharing (YouTube, Vimeo)
- Storage (Google Docs, Drop.io)
- Content Management (SharePoint, Drupal)

Agencies [and businesses] use a variety of software tools and platforms. The examples given above are not meant to be an exhaustive list.[3]

Additional Social Media Categories

Breaking out the categories of social media further, we can see the wide range of social media applications that continue to develop in the marketplace. These categories will continue to expand and fluctuate as the market matures, and the companies will expand, merge, be acquired, or die off:

- **Content curation** (Buzzfeed, Flipboard, Skygrid, Storify, Summify)
- **Social ad networks** (Oneriot, Lifestreet, Media6degrees, Rockyou)
- **Social analytics** (Awe.sm, Bluefin, Omniture, Mixpanel, Webtrends)
- **Social business software** (Lithium, Jive, Pluck, Mzinga, Telligent, Ingage, Leverage Software, Huddle, Cubetree, Yammer, Socialcast, Igloo, Socialtext, Watchtoo, Acquia, Maxie)[4]
- **Social brand engagement** (Socialvibe, Mylikes, Adly, Sharethrough)
- **Social commerce platforms** (Payvment, Moontoast, Shop Tab, Dotbox, Storenvy, VendorShop)
- **Social community platforms** (Ning, Mixxt, Grou.ps, Groupsite)
- **Social data** (GNIP, DataSift, Rapleaf)
- **Social intelligence software** (Alterian, Attensify, Backtype, Netbase, Postrank, Synthesio, Trendrr, Trackur, Visible)
- **Social marketing management** (Shoutlet, Syncapse, Context Optional, Vitrue, Involver)
- **Social promotion platforms** (Offerpop, Seesmic, Strutta, Votigo, Fanzila, Zuberance, Extole, Social AppsHQ, Social Amp)
- **Social publishing platforms** (Hootsuite, Spredfast, Hearsay, Awareness, Mutual Mind, Sprout Social, Flowtown, Socialware)
- **Social referral** (500Friends, Curebit, Socialfeet, Turnto)
- **Social search and browsing** (Aardvark, StumbleUpon, Topsy, Wink)
- **Social scoring** (Klout, EmpireAvenue, PeerIndex)[5]

There are certainly additional categories, and the categories will continue to expand. Also, social media companies do not always fit neatly into one category.

Social Media in the Enterprise

Consumer-facing social networks manage and interact with the subnetworks of millions of public users. Implementing tight security on these types of mass networks would likely slow response time, inhibit the user experience, and may not provide a sufficient level of security to warrant its investment.

In the business world, Facebook-like social networking software is offered for private, closed networks with a finite number of users. In this computing environment, implementing security is more manageable and practical. Some services are cloud-based, others operate internally behind the enterprise firewall, and some operate either way or in conjunction as a hybrid architecture. In addition, usage statistics that reflect trends, adoption rates, and areas of content interest can be provided to help feed the metrics needed to chart out the progress and effectiveness of the enterprise social network.[6]

> Implementing security is more manageable and practical with enterprise social networking software.

Enterprise social networking is being adopted by business and public sector entities at a rapid rate. With the entry of Generation Gmail into the workforce, many of these initiatives take on an experimental, "cool" image, although it is crucial to establish social media business objectives, to define time-limited metrics, and to measure progress. But there does need to be some leeway, as calculating return on investment (ROI) for enterprise social networks is very new, and all the benefits have not been discovered or defined. Certainly the network load and required bandwidth for e-mail and attachments will decrease; instead of a 25MB PowerPoint file being sent back and forth among 10 co-workers, it can sit in a common workspace for collaboration.

Another intangible benefit is the competitive value in being a market leader or industry innovator. Engaging in online conversations with customers and other stakeholders is one sign of a progressive-thinking organization. This can attract and retain prospective employees.

Key Ways Social Media Is Different from E-Mail and Instant Messaging

Social media offers some of the same functionality as other messaging and collaboration systems like e-mail and instant messaging (IM), yet its architecture and underlying assumptions are quite different.

When implementing enterprise versions of social media applications, a company may exert more control over the computing and networking environment through in-house implementation rather than outsourcing. When the use of consumer-oriented social media applications like Facebook and Twitter springs up in the organization, application servers are outside the enterprise and cannot be controlled. This creates IG and records management challenges, and poses legal risks.[7]

Obviously, social media is new, so standards, design, and architecture are in flux, whereas e-mail has been stable and established for 15–20 years or more. E-mail is a mature technology set, meaning it is unlikely to change much. There are standard e-mail communications protocols and the technology's use is pervasive and constant. So when e-mail IG policies are formed, there is less updating and fine-tuning required. With social media, new features are being added, standards do not exist, privacy settings change overnight, and the legalese in terms of service agreements continues to change to include these new features and settings.

E-mail, IM, and social media all are ways to share content and collaborate, but social media also features user interaction abilities, such as "Like" on Facebook or "retweet" (copying and posting a tweet) on Twitter, which brings attention to the content in the user's network and can be construed as an endorsement or rejection of content, based on user opinions expressed and associated with the content.[8]

Further confounding the organization's ability to control the social media environment is the fact that the sites are ever-changing and dynamic, with comments and

Social media differs greatly from e-mail use. There are important ramifications in these distinctions.

opinions being published in real time. This is not true with e-mail and IM systems, which are more stable and static.

Biggest Risks of Social Media

Social media is the Wild West of collaboration and communication. Vulnerabilities are still being exposed, and rules are still being established. Users are still often unsure of exactly who can see what they have posted. They may believe that they have posted a comment only for the eyes of a friend or colleague, not realizing it may have been posted publicly. "One of the biggest risks that social networking poses to organizations is that *employees may be exposing information that's not meant for public consumption*, especially in highly regulated environments like banking and healthcare, in industries that rely heavily on proprietary research and development, or even in the military" (italics added).[9]

According to Chris Nerney of *Network World*, two of the greatest security threats in social media are:

1. **Lack of a social media policy**. Many organizations are just now discovering that social media has popped up in the pockets of their organization. They may believe that their e-mail and communications policy will pretty much cover social media use, and it is not worth the time and expense to update IG policies to include social media.

   This invites complexities, vagaries, and potential disaster. A simple comment could invite litigation; "Our new project is almost ready, but I'm not sure about the widget assembly." It's out there. There is a record of it. Instant potential liability in 140 characters or less.

   Social media can add value to an organization's efforts to reach out to customers and other stakeholders, but this must be weighed carefully with its risks.

   The objectives of a social media initiative must be spelled out and metrics must be in place to measure progress. But more than that, *who can utilize social media on behalf of the company and what they can state needs to be established with clarity in IG policy*. If not, employees are essentially flying blindly without controls, and they are more likely to put the enterprise at risk.[10]

   More than policy is needed. If your organization is going to embark on a social media program, it needs an executive sponsor to champion and drive the program, communicating policy to key leaders. You will also need to conduct training—on a consistent basis. *Training is key, since social media is a moving target.*

2. **Employees—the accidental insider threat.** This may be in part due to lack of social media policy, or monitoring and enforcement. Sometimes an employee intends to do harm to an organization, but *most times* they do not realize the negative impact of their behavior in posting to social media sites. People might use social media to vent about a bad day at work, but the underlying message can damage the company's reputation and alienate coworkers and clients. Other times, a post that is seemingly unrelated to work can backfire and take a toll on business. We're all human and sometimes emotion gets the

best of us, before we have rationally thought out the consequences. And that is especially true in the new world of social media, where it may be unclear exactly who can see a comment.

The dangers of social media are quite different than an isolated, off-color, or offensive verbal comment in the workplace, or even one errant e-mail. With social media it is possible that the whole world will be able to see a comment meant only for a limited and controlled audience. For example, consider Ketchum PR Vice President James Andrews, who in 2009 "fired off an infamous tweet trashing the city of Memphis, hometown of a little Ketchum client called FedEx, the day before he was to make a presentation to more than 150 FedEx employees (on digital media, no less!)." FedEx employees complained to Ketchum and their own executives, pointing out that while they suffered from salary reductions, money was being spent on Ketchum, which had been clearly disrespectful of FedEx. Andrews was forced to make a "very public and humiliating apology."[11]

This story shows that high-level executives must be just as careful as lower-level employees. Andrews was not only a corporate vice president, but also a PR, communications, and social media expert, well-versed in the firm's policies and mission. He also had no ill intent. Knowing this, *consider what a rogue employee intent on damaging the company might do.* Such impact could be much worse. For instance, what if the CEO's assistant were to release details of strategic plans, litigation, or ethics investigations to the public? The impact could be quite costly.

Legal Risks of Social Media Posts

With over 140 million users and an estimated 330 million tweets (140-character posts) per day in 2012 to the microblogging site Twitter,[12] a number that continues to increase, surely some employees in your organization are utilizing it. As of the first quarter of 2012, 161 million professionals in over 200 countries and territories were members of the LinkedIn network, and it continues to grow, with students and recent college graduates being the fastest-growing segment. Approximately 39 percent of members are in the United States.[13]

The casual use of public comments can easily create liability for a company. *With no IG policy, guidelines, monitoring, or governance, legal risks of using social media increase significantly. This is an avoidable risk.*

While many people are posting birthday wishes and pictures of what they had for dinner, others may be venting about specific companies and individuals within those companies. There's a difference between, "I can't stand Wall Street," and "Goldman is run by Satan, and his name is John Smith. We're going to sue his butt off." Instant liability.

Two of the biggest threats of social media use for organizations include lack of a social media policy and liabilities from employee use.

> With no IG policy, guidelines, monitoring, or governance, legal risks of using social media increase significantly. This is an avoidable risk.

Now, the specifics of where and how an employee posted or tweeted a message may be the difference in whether a lawsuit against your company is successful. If a personal LinkedIn or Twitter account is used, but it was posted after hours using a PC from home, the company *may* be off the hook. But if it was done using a company computer, or network, or from a company-authorized account, a defense will be difficult. Questions about the policy for posting will be the first to be asked by opposing counsel. One thing is true, "Much of this remains unsettled ground."[14]

Just when compliance and records managers thought they had nailed down information governance for e-mail, IM, and electronic records—social media came on the scene creating new, dynamic challenges. "Tweets are no different from letters, e-mail, or text messages—they can be damaging and discoverable, which is especially problematic for companies that are required to preserve electronic records, such as the securities industry and federal contractors. Yet another compliance headache is born."[15]

Blogs are simply web logs, a sort of online journal, if you will, that is focused on a particular topic. Blog readers can become followers and receive notices when new content is posted, as well as add their own comments, although comments may be moderated or restricted. It seems confounding, but with the explosion in the use of blogs, there have been actual incidents where employees have "disclosed trade secrets and insider trading information on their blogs. Blogs have also led to wrongful termination and harassment suits."[16]

So the liability and potential for leakage or erosion of information assets isn't just theoretical, it is *real*.

To safeguard the enterprise that sanctions and supports blog use, *IG policies must be clear and real-time archiving of blog posts should be implemented.* Remember, these can be business records that are subject to legal holds, and authenticity and accuracy are crucial in supporting a legal case. So a true and original copy must be archived, and, this may, in fact, be a legal or regulatory requirement, depending on the industry.

If content-posting guidelines are not clear, then the informal nature of social media posts can be potentially damaging to an organization. The usual fact-checking and vetting that is done for traditional press releases and advertising is not done so social media posts are typically unscreened and unfiltered, which poses problems when IG policies are not clear and fully enforced.[17] Beyond that, the consequences of violating policy should be severe and clearly stated in policies, a message that should be reinforced consistently over time.

Tools to Archive Social Media

New approaches to archiving social media are emerging. Launched in March 2012, Jolicloud Me "takes a filesystem approach to social media, so we can sort and search through the Facebook, Flickr, Instagram, Picasa, and Twitter content that we've previously interacted with or shared."[18] The service "slurps" (extracts) content from social media sites you use and makes it available for viewing through any mainstream Internet browser (and soon, on smartphones). As users perform social media functions like sharing, "liking," and "favoriting" content on their various social media services, the content is automatically saved to their Jolicloud account, which can later be sorted and searched.

Jolicloud primarily assists in archiving and organizing files, but also allows for sharing of previously shared content through its own social layer. It has commonalities with other "personal social web memory" products such as Facebook Timeline, Memolane, and TimeHop. If you prefer not to utilize cloud technology, or it has not been approved by your organization, an alternative to Jolicloud is a product called SocialFolders.[19] And there are more alternatives emerging.

Since Facebook and Twitter did not initially provide archiving tools themselves, some other third-party applications have popped up to perform the task. These may not provide a legally defensible audit trail in court, so choosing between the tools requires a critical analysis, and may require additional technology layers. Other alternatives, such as real-time content archiving tools and even in-house developed customizations, would also have to be considered.

TwInbox is a free MS Outlook plug-in that archives Twitter postings, and TweetTake is a utility that archives followers and tweet posts, and is also free of charge. TwInbox allows users to install a (Twitter) menu option to send tweets directly from Outlook; these tweets are archived into a standard Outlook folder. It can even be configured to capture those tweets that a user sends outside of Outlook, so that everything is stored in one folder.

TweetTake does not require a software download, and the archive can be stored as a zip file, and then imported into a spreadsheet like Excel. By the time this book goes to press there will be even more options, and the existing ones will have changed and (hopefully) improved.

So, if your organization uses Twitter and social media archiving is required by law, regulations, or your internal IG policies, a good place to start your research is with software like TwInbox, if you operate in a Microsoft Office environment, and also evaluate TweetTake, among any new entrants, or other options your organization may have.[20]

For archiving Facebook posts, there are several options. In 2012, Facebook released the capability for users to download and archive their own content under their account settings. Also, there are free plug-ins for Mozilla's Firefox browser. One comes directly from Mozilla, which archives everything but fan pages into a zip file. Another is a Firefox plug-in called ArchiveFacebook. Other tools, including SocialSafe, PageFreezer, and Wayback Machine, charge a small fee. All of these options and any new ones need to be evaluated when selecting an archiving solution for Facebook that meets your organization's requirements.

For archiving LinkedIn posts and information, SocialSafe, PageFreezer, and Wayback Machine can be used, and other tools will surface.

There are also options to create PDF documents out of social media posts, with PDF995 and PrimoPDF.[21] Nuance Software also provides PDFCreate.

There are more archiving tools being developed as the social media market matures. Bear in mind that third-party developed tools always carry some risk that tools directly from the software or service provider do not.

IG Considerations for Social Media

In her report, "How Federal Agencies Can Effectively Manage Records Created Using Social Media Tools," Dr. Patricia Franks addressed building an IG framework for social media. An IG model provides the overarching policies, guidelines, and boundaries for social media initiatives.[22]

An IG framework for social media should incorporate social media policy, controls, and operational guidelines, and spell out consequences for violations. Best practices for social media are evolving and still being established, and they should also include vertical market considerations that are industry-specific. A cross-section of functional groups within the enterprise should provide input into the policy-making process. At the very minimum, marketing, finance, information technology (IT), legal, human resources, and records management must be consulted, and business units should be represented. Clear roles and responsibilities must be spelled out, and controls establishing acceptable use—essentially what is allowed and what is not—and even writing style, logo format, branding, and other marketing considerations should be weighed. The enterprise's image and brand are at risk and prudent steps must be taken to protect this valuable, intangible asset. And most important, all legal and regulatory considerations must be folded into the new IG policy governing the use of social media.[23]

Key Social Media Policy Guidelines

Your social media policy development process can begin by examining the published policies of major organizations, especially those in your industry, or closely related industries. *But social media policies must be hand-crafted and customized for each organization.*

A prudent and properly crafted social media policy:

- Outlines the types of negative impact on the company's brand and reputation that unscreened, poorly considered posts may have.[24]
- Draws clear distinctions between business and personal use of social media, and whether personal access is allowed during work hours.
- Underscores the fact that employees should not have any expectation of privacy when using social media for corporate purposes, just as in using other forms of communications such as e-mail, IM, and voicemail, which may be monitored.
- Clearly state what is proper and allowed on the organization's behalf, and what is forbidden in social media posts or using organization resources.
- Instruct employees to always avoid engaging in company-confidential or even controversial discussions.

An IG framework for social media should incorporate social media policy, controls, and operational guidelines, and spell out consequences for violations.

> U.S. corporations must archive social media records under Rule 34 of the FRCP.

- Strictly forbid the use of profanity, and use a professional business tone, albeit more informal than in other corporate communications.
- Strictly forbid any statements that could be construed as defamatory, discriminative, or inflammatory.
- Outline clear punishments and negative actions that will occur to enforce social media policy.
- Authorize specifically who can speak on the organization's behalf—and who cannot (by role/responsibility).
- Draw clear rules on the use of the company name and logo.[25]

Records Management Considerations for Social Media

Legal requirements and demands trump all others when making decisions about capturing and preserving social media records. Social media is no different from other forms of **electronically stored information** (ESI) in that it is potentially discoverable during litigation.[26] If an organization employs social media and makes a conscious decision *not* to archive all or some portion of that data, they need to be able to point to a specific (perhaps state or provincial) law that allows it, in order to maintain a legally defensible policy.

U.S. corporations that utilize social media are compelled to preserve those records, including metadata and associated link content, according to Rule 34 of the **Federal Rules of Civil Procedure** (FRCP), which states that opposing parties in litigation may request, "any designated documents or ESI—including writings, drawings, graphs, charts, photographs, sound recordings, images, and other data or data compilations—stored in any medium from which information can be obtained either directly or, if necessary, after translation by the responding party into a usable form. . ."[27] This echoes a key principle of *The Sedona Principles*, a leading records management and legal retention think tank. Also, another part of the FRCP, Rule 26, requires that any and all information that might be discoverable or "potentially responsive" must be preserved and produced if requested by the opposing party. So it is clear that there is a legal duty to preserve social media records.

From a records management perspective, it is critical to consider that social media posts are more than the post itself; for legal or compliance purposes, they include metadata and also include hyperlinks to external content—*and that external content in its native format*—which must also be preserved in a sort of "snapshot" fashion, preferably in real-time. That external content may be a PDF document, a PowerPoint presentation, website content, or even a video on YouTube, which would require that video archiving, along with associated metadata, is in place.[28]

Social media policy will be unique to each particular organization.

To truly capture the necessary content required by law, records and compliance managers must understand how software programs communicate with each other. They use "open hooks" with available specifications to connect to each other, which are called an **application programming interface** (API). The best way to preserve the web-based data of social media applications is to use the APIs that social media providers offer (at the time of this printing).[29] Further innovations making capturing these records easier will surely develop over time. Connecting an **electronic records management** (ERM) application to a social media API will allow for full capture of all relevant data needed for archiving.

The ideal method from a records management standpoint is to capture all potentially discoverable social media data *in real-time*, to be able to prove authenticity and fight claims of records **spoliation,** which is corruption or adulteration of the evidence.[30]

Robust search capabilities are perhaps the most crucial component of a social media ERM or archiving solution. It is fine to preserve the records perfectly, but if you cannot easily *find and produce* the information, compliance and e-discovery efforts will fall short and may cost the organization dearly.

Social media policy will be unique to each particular organization. It is fine to start with a social media policy example or template, but it must be tailored to the needs of the organization for it to be effective and legally defensible.[31]

Records Retention Guidelines

Here are some basic records retention guidelines:

- **Make records threshold determinations.** Examine the content to see if it in fact constitutes a record *by your own organization's definition of a record,* which should be contained in your IG policies. This records determination process likely will also require consultation with your legal counsel. If the social media site has not been maintained, or it was used for a specific project that has been completed, then its content may not require retention of records.[32]
- **Use existing retention schedules if they apply.** If your organization already has retention policies for, say, e-mail, then any e-mail sent by social media should adhere to that same scheduling guideline, unless there is some legal reason to change it.
- **Apply basic content management principles.** Meaning focus on capturing all related content for social media posts that may be required in legal discovery to maintain the completeness, authenticity, and integrity of the records.
- **Risk avoidance in content creation.** Instruct and reinforce the message to employees participating in corporate social media that content on the web stays

there indefinitely, and that it carries potential legal risks. In addition, attempting to completely destroy the content at the end of its retention period is nearly impossible once it is posted on the web.[33]

Content Control Models

There are several basic ways to manage social media content, ranging from tightly controlling it through one single, accountable person (such as has been implemented at the U.S. Department of Defense), to delegating control to the business unit level, all the way to letting the social media participants post their thoughts unmoderated and unfettered to encourage spontaneity and enthusiastic use of the tool. The approach your organization takes will depend on the specified business objectives you have for utilizing social media.[34]

Emerging Best Practices for Managing Social Media Records

Best practices for managing social media business records are still evolving, and will continue to develop as records and information (RIM) practitioners gain more experience with social media records. Here are some emerging best practices:

- **Cross-functional communications.** A social media team of representatives from various departments, such as IT, social media, legal, compliance, records management, and other stakeholders is formed and communication and collaboration is encouraged and supported.
- **Consultation in policy development.** Extending beyond the social media team, input and advice from multiple stakeholder groups is essential for creating IG policies that cover social media records management.
- **Clear roles and responsibilities.** The cross-functional social media team must lay out clear expectations and responsibilities, and draw lines of accountability so that stakeholders understand what is expected of them.
- **Content management principles.** Management of social media content should fall under an **enterprise content management** (ECM) software implementation, which can capture and track content, including associated metadata and external content, and manage that social media content through its lifecycle.[35]
- **Control the content.** Clear guidelines and monitoring mechanisms must be in place to control and manage content *before* it gets published on the web, if there is any potential legal risk at all.
- **Capture content in real-time.** By implementing a real-time content capture solution, organizations will begin their control and management of the content at the soonest point, and can more easily prove it is authentic and reliable from a legal perspective.
- **Champion search capabilities.** After capture and preservation of records, search capabilities are the single most important feature that the technology must provide.
- **Train, train, train.** Social media is a new and immature technology that changes rapidly. Users must be trained and that training must be updated and reinforced on a regular basis so that employees are clear on guidelines, understand the technology, and understand the business objectives for its use.

CHAPTER SUMMARY: **KEY POINTS**

- Organizations are increasingly using social media and Web 2.0 platforms to connect people to companies and government.

- Social media use presents unique challenges because of key differences with other electronic communications systems, such as e-mail and IM.

- Two of the biggest risks that social networking poses to organizations are (1) not having a social media policy; and (2) employees may be—intentionally or not—exposing information that is not meant for public consumption.

- Enterprise social networking software has many of the features of consumer social applications such as Facebook, but with more oversight and control, and they come with analytics features to measure adoption and use.

- Various software tools have become available in recent years for archiving social media posts and followers for records management purposes.

- An IG framework provides the overarching policies, guidelines, and boundaries for social media initiatives, so that they may be controlled, monitored, and archived.

- Social media posts are more than the post itself; they include metadata and also include hyperlinks to external content—and that external content must be preserved in its native format to meet legal standards.

- Robust search capabilities are the most crucial component of a social media ERM or archiving solution.

- Social media policy will be unique to each particular organization.

- Best practices for managing social media business records are still evolving, but include forming cross-functional social media teams with clear responsibilities, encouraging communication, and capturing complete content in real time.

Notes

1. The U.S. National Archives and Records Administration, "NARA Bulletin 2011-02," October 20, 2010, www.archives.gov/records-mgmt/bulletins/2011/2011-02.html.
2. Ibid.
3. Ibid.
4. Terry Kawaja, Luma Partners, http://static5.businessinsider.com/image/4fb5077becad045f47000003-960/buddy-media-social-marketing.jpg (accessed May 21, 2012).
5. Ibid.
6. Andrew Conry-Murray, "Can Enterprise Social Networking Pay Off?" March 21, 2009, www.internetevolution.com/document.asp?doc_id=173854.
7. Patricia C. Franks, "How Federal Agencies Can Effectively Manage Records Created Using New Social Media Tools," IBM Center for The Business of Government, San Jose State University, 2010,

www.actgov.org/sigcom/SIGs/SIGs/CTSIG/Documents/Best%20Practices%20in%20Collaborative%20
Technology%20Retention%20Policies/All%20Related%20Studies/IBM-How%20Federal%20
Agencies%20Can%20Effectively%20Manage%20Records.pdf, 20–21 (accessed March 30, 2012).

8. Ibid.

9. Paul McDougall, "Social Networking Here to Stay Despite Security Risks," *Information Week*, May 12, 2011, www.informationweek.com/news/security/privacy/229500138.

10. Chris Nerney, "5 Top Social Media Security Threats," *Network World*, May 31, 2011, www.network-world.com/news/2011/053111-social-media-security.html.

11. Ibid.

12. Mary Long, All Twitter, "#Twitter4Brands Shares Some Statistics to Consider," May 21, 2012, www.mediabistro.com/alltwitter/twitter-statistics-2_b22862.

13. LinkedIn, "About Us," http://press.linkedin.com/about (accessed May 23, 2012).

14. Sharon Nelson, John Simek, and Jason Foltin, "Capturing Quicksilver: Records Management for Blogs, Twittering and Social Networks," Sensei Enterprises, 2009, www.senseient.com/storage/articles/Capturing_Quicksilver.pdf.

15. Ibid.

16. Ibid.

17. Sharon Nelson and John Simek, "Mitigating Legal Risks of Using Social Media," *Information Management*, HT9, September/October 2011.

18. Liz Gannes, "Saving the Social Web for Later Use: Jolicloud Organizes Everything You've Shared, Liked, and Favorited," March 19, 2012, http://allthingsd.com/20120319/saving-the-social-web-for-later-use-jolicloud-organizes-everything-youve-shared-liked-and-favorited.

19. Ibid.

20. Andy Opsahl, "Backing Up Twitter and Facebook Posts Challenges Governments," Government Technology, January 20, 2010, www.govtech.com/policy-management/Backing-Up-Twitter-and-Facebook-Posts.html?utm_source=related&utm_medium=direct&utm_campaign=Backing-Up-Twitter-and-Facebook-Posts.

21. Ibid.

22. Franks, "How Federal Agencies Can Effectively Manage Records Created Using New Social Media Tools."

23. Ibid.

24. Nelson and Simek, "Mitigating Legal Risks of Using Social Media," HT11.

25. Ibid.

26. Rakesh Madhava, "10 Things to Know about Preserving Social Media," *Information Management* (September/October 2011), 34–35.

27. Ibid.

28. Ibid.

29. Ibid.

30. Madhava, "10 Things to Know about Preserving Social Media," 37.

31. Ibid., 36–37.

32. New York State Archives, "Records Advisory: Preliminary Guidance on Social Media," May 24, 2010, www.archives.nysed.gov/a/records/mr_social_media.shtml.

33. Ibid.

34. Ibid.

35. Ibid.

CHAPTER 14

SharePoint Governance for E-Records and Documents

Monica Crocker, CRM, PMP; edited by Robert Smallwood

Microsoft's SharePoint server product has been a "game changer" for the content and records management market. At a basic level, it is a content repository, but it can be leveraged into much more than that. If properly implemented, SharePoint can eliminate duplication of content, automate business processes, create a common lexicon for categorizing content, provide a social media platform, give users access to current and historical documents, dramatically reduce network traffic loads (by cutting the number of e-mails with attachments) and stop the growth of shared drives.

That goes a long way toward helping organizations manage their documents and records. But it is not so simple to accomplish.

For SharePoint deployments, as with most things in life, "An ounce of prevention is worth a pound of cure." Since every SharePoint environment includes e-records, organizations can avoid a lot of headaches and future **information governance** (IG) risks if they invest time and deliberation in *planning* how they will deploy SharePoint. These plans should be based on the business objectives for SharePoint and include making all the necessary policy decisions *before* rolling out the solution to users.

SharePoint itself is a tool; it is not a panacea for poor document management processes or file plans, and it will not suddenly fix document sharing collaboration problems or **records management** (RM) problems. "Like any records management solution, SharePoint alone will not solve your needs unless it is used to support clearly defined processes."[1] Therefore, IG policy development and business process analysis are necessary in the planning process.

SharePoint is often expected to perform RM, help control document sprawl, and address e-discovery requests and legal holds. But sometimes, instead of solving records and document management problems, they become worse, as users:

- Do not understand which SharePoint content (documents, discussions, announcements, lists) should be managed as a record.
- Are not clear on when to declare a document a business record (and either make everything a record or nothing a record as a result).
- Simply replicate their existing file share folder structure, creating a new set of disorganized documents on SharePoint.
- Do not know how to attach metadata to content to make it "findable" in the long term.
- Do not understand how to apply appropriate security restrictions to content.

And if users decide that SharePoint is actually making their work more difficult instead of easing the burden, they will begin to revert back to old, established (disorganized) ways of managing their information. In other words, they may continue to keep duplicate documents on their C-drives, go back to their familiar shared drives, and keep sharing information by attaching documents to e-mails.

A good SharePoint governance model supports **Generally Accepted Recordkeeping Principles**® ("GAR Principles"). The **governance model** should make it clear *where and how users should both store and find content*. A well-governed SharePoint environment provides enough consistency in how content is categorized to support sorting and filtering of search results so that users can quickly narrow results to the specific records or documents they need.[2]

But keep in mind, a SharePoint governance model *needs to be tailored to your organization*. It will not work if it does not fit with your culture and resources.

There is no such thing as one set of SharePoint governance best practices that every organization can adopt. Rather, developing a SharePoint governance model involves a series of questions you need to answer in the context of your organization's constraints and goals, and validated against a broad sample of use cases for the system.

Process Change, People Change

As with any initiative that requires behavior change or additional effort, you will encounter resistance. The nature of the resistance will depend on the culture of your organization and the personalities of the individuals involved. Some of the objections you should be prepared to counter are the premise that "nothing in SharePoint is a record" or that the very nature of SharePoint dictates that it should just be turned on and allowed to spread virally. Another is that "Users won't follow those procedures" or "Governance is too much of a burden to the user."

Too many organizations deploy SharePoint without putting the necessary *effort into planning how this technology tool will be governed. The result is similar to what is often found with e-mail or network shared drives*—scattered documents and files with no organization or governing policies. Only the situation is worse, because SharePoint has more types of content and quickly collects an even greater volume of content. Therefore, in an ungoverned SharePoint environment, you have:

- *Content chaos*—because there is no way to identify who owns specific content, no context for content, and no consistent organization or hierarchy to content.
- *Orphaned content*—which results when the individual who understood the context of the content leaves the organization or when the site or library is no longer used.
- *Redundant content*—if no one knows *who* should put *what* on SharePoint, multiple users may upload the same new document to a dozen different locations and users have no way to identify the "authentic" version of a piece of content when multiples are found.

> As with any initiative that requires behavior change or additional effort, you will encounter resistance.

Lack of governance can significantly diminish the business value and increase the risk of your SharePoint deployment.

- *Unfindable content*—which results when everyone decides for themselves how to secure a given piece of content and if and how to tag it with metadata. Then no one can find anything outside the sphere of the content they control or know if they have "found everything" in a search.
- *Noncompliant retention*—the organization cannot apply any records retention periods to content if there is no means to determine which records series applies to specific content.[3]
- *E-discovery risk*—Ungoverned content limits the means to narrow the list of potentially responsive information, requiring the organization to review and produce *a lot* of content in response to an e-discovery request.
- *Inappropriate use*—Lack of governance means the organization is at risk from individuals or teams deciding to use SharePoint in a way that may not be appropriate or legally defensible.

In sum, *lack of governance can significantly diminish the business value and increase the risk of your SharePoint deployment*.

However, if you have already started your SharePoint project or need to start before you feel your governance model is complete, don't give up. Late is better than never and gradual definition of governance is better than none at all.

Where to Begin the Planning Process

As with any well-managed project, *the first step in a SharePoint deployment is to draft a project charter that defines the scope, budget, timeline and business objectives for your Share-Point environment.*[4]

The next step is to draft a **project schedule** that includes *copious* amounts of time for the up-front planning effort necessary to create the SharePoint governance model. Make sure to get the project sponsor to sign off on this timeline so that they understand you are going to take some time to think through key issues prior to deployment and why that is critical for your organization.

Then, assemble your governance team. Make sure it includes someone who understands the organization's culture and the business objectives for SharePoint (such as a business analyst), someone who understands the technical aspects of SharePoint (like a system administrator) and someone who understands the compliance aspects of SharePoint (such as a compliance officer or records manager). And, most importantly, make sure your governance team has the necessary authority level to dictate the governance approach.

Critical to success in SharePoint deployments is consulting with users about their processes and needs.

Governance decisions can be very controversial and require documentation.

This SharePoint governance model planning process necessarily involves consulting with users about their collaboration, business process, document usage and information storage needs. Otherwise, users will start creating and storing documents without knowing what rules to follow, or why the rules exist, and they will find their own workarounds to satisfy their unique records and information management (RIM) business requirements. For instance, if you restrict file size requirements too much, the users will store them somewhere—perhaps unsecured in the cloud. If you do not allow certain file types, and the users need them, they will find a place to store them. And soon you will have all sorts of variations of folder and file systems and scattered documents and records which results in the aforementioned, "content chaos" scenario.

There are also regulatory and compliance factors that must be incorporated into SharePoint governance decisions for most organizations. Therefore, the process must include RIM staff for guidance on crucial records management issues, and legal staff for legal and compliance requirements.

This is more than a mess. It is a costly mess, because the organization is not achieving the maximum business benefit from SharePoint. Further, economically and efficiently retrieving e-documents and records during e-discovery for legal proceedings will be fraught with search and retrieval challenges.

Finally, create a formal SharePoint governance model "document." Do not rely on meeting notes or design documents to reflect the decisions made during governance discussions. *Governance decisions can be very controversial, so the governance model selected needs to be explicitly stated and officially "approved" by the appropriate stakeholders.*

Begin at a High Level

Start from a high level, with strategy and corporate governance issues. *Develop a problem statement in your project charter so that you know what you are trying to accomplish,* and then develop measureable, time-constrained business objectives so progress and success toward milestones can be measured. Next, be sure to align these objectives with your organization's overall vision statement or strategic plan. Aligning the technology with business considerations is key to a successful SharePoint deployment.

In order to identify specific business objectives for SharePoint, you may find it useful to conduct some focus group sessions with thought leaders from across the organization. The following are some examples of questions you might ask:

- How do you find information owned by your unit?
- How do you share information within your team?

First, develop a problem statement and formulate business objectives for the SharePoint deployment. Then, align those objectives with your overall strategic plan.

- How do you find information owned by other units?
- How do you share information with other teams?
- How do you find expertise to assemble a project team?
- How do you find expertise to perform a single task?
- How do you exchange information with external business partners?
- What processes are particularly painful?
- How comfortable would you be sharing information with others in your unit? With others outside your unit?
- How would you like to connect with others in your organization?

Themes in survey responses that might apply to your organization are:

- It is difficult to find information without prior knowledge of its existence and location.
- It is difficult to find a personnel resource with specific expertise (a **subject matter expert**, or SME).
- It is difficult to determine whether or not a given piece of content is the current version.
- The organization relies heavily on e-mail to create, share, and manage information and, therefore, the effort spent managing e-mail is burdensome.
- Most document creation processes included review and approval steps among multiple users.
- Users are struggling to find a way to communicate outside their immediate work group, but they have strong motivation to do so.
- It takes too long to onboard a new employee.
- Users want solutions that provide seamless access for remote workers.[5]

Understanding the organization's current information management challenges allowed the SharePoint Governance Team to identify business objectives for SharePoint and ensure that each individual governance decision supports accomplishment of the business objectives without compromising compliance with records management policy.

Once business objectives are formed, use them to define the **Guiding Principles** for the SharePoint governance model. It is prudent to lay out the guiding principles early in the governance document since they provide a framework for everything that follows. Questions that can help shape the guiding principles are:

- **Required or optional.** Is this governance model a "mandated" approach or just "recommendations?" This must be clear to users and enforcement actions against violations must be taken if governance is mandated.
- **Appropriate use.** What are the rules for SharePoint usage? For instance, you could declare that SharePoint is for business content only so that users know it is not OK to run their fantasy football league on a SharePoint site.
- **Content access policy.** Clarify your organization's philosophy about access to content; is it open to everyone by default, or is it strictly secured and available "on a need to know" basis only? As a compromise, sites could be open to all by default, with secured content as an exception.
- **Accountability.** Who is accountable for content and managing governance at a site level?

- **Level of control.** Clarify how tightly SharePoint will be managed. This might range from rigid control, where a typical user can only publish content that has gone through a review process, or "semicontrolled," which permits some "superusers" to create libraries and lists, or very loosely controlled, where site owners in the business are given complete site collections to manage according to their needs.
- **Content ownership.** Since users come and go and site administrators are very often administrative staff with little authority, content ownership must be clearly defined (e.g., the responsibility of the manager or director of a business unit).

In keeping with the Generally Accepted Recordkeeping Principles® (see Chapter 3 on this topic for more detail) principle of *Compliance* (adhering to laws and regulations, as well as the organization's internal policies), each of these guiding principles should be linked to any appropriate organizational policy or applicable law. In addition, they should be linked to the business objectives for SharePoint. For instance, a guiding principle could be:

Using SharePoint (in a way that follows good governance) should be as easy for users as their current information management processes.

This sets a standard that the technical team has to follow and eliminates concerns that the governance model may be too burdensome for users.[6]

Establish Scope

After business objectives are formed and sharpened, and Guiding Principles are established, make sure to next determine the *scope* of the SharePoint deployment—just where are the boundaries of content types you are going to manage? Any governance model will likely cover sites and pages and documents. But will it also include specific types of content such as calendar items, announcements, discussions, and lists? Which specific documents will be governed in SharePoint? How will documents be managed in the different stages of their lifecycle? How will your organization address e-discovery requirements? Which document and content types are *not* governed in SharePoint? For instance, some organizations govern down to the "X" level (three levels deep in the site structure, for instance), but not below.

These are the types of questions you should be asking, not only from an IG perspective, but also to optimize future system performance of SharePoint. Better processes and fewer documents means faster performance when you are in the heat of the business battle.

Your governance model needs to address the following two issues related to scope:

- The *first* is to describe the scope of SharePoint as a technology solution. In terms of the scope of SharePoint itself, document whether it is purely for internal use or whether it also includes external access, whether MySites are deployed, and which existing systems it was designed to replace, if applicable. Add any other information you can about what is included when you refer to "the SharePoint solution" in your organization.

- The *second* is to define the scope of the governance model. In your description of the scope of the governance model, you should enumerate if governance applies to all types of sites, all types of content, all users or some subset of those; and who has the authority to change the scope of SharePoint governance.[7]

Exactly *what* content will be stored and managed in SharePoint? And, of that, which content or documents rise to the level of being records?

The selection criteria for storing content in SharePoint must be clear to all users and administrators of the system. They need to know not only what file sizes are allowed, but also what file formats are permitted—or prohibited—as well as size limits for lists, libraries, and the entire site itself.

Records Management Policy Considerations

In order to address the Generally Accepted Recordkeeping Principle® of *Retention and Disposition*, you must determine how your organization's Records Management policies relate to SharePoint. Microsoft has structured SharePoint so that every piece of content is a "content type." In addition, the tool allows you to configure records management policies/actions at various levels in the system; you can set them at a site collection level, a site level, a library or list level or all the way down to the specific item level. Every particular instance of every content type could have a retention schedule associated with it, but that might be a lot of overhead for very little payback. *What do you manage and what don't you?* Examples of things you might *not* manage are workflow configurations, views, searches, and page templates. Examples of things you probably want to manage are documents and lists.

Your Records Management policy section should answer the following questions:

- Which items in SharePoint are managed as records?
- Who decides what gets managed?
- At what point in the content's SharePoint existence is a records management action taken?

Any existing retention schedules must be translated into defensible disposition policies within your SharePoint environment. Finally, specific processes for managing records must be established.

At some point in the SharePoint governance model document, you also need to address if and how you going to use Document IDs and how major and minor versions of content are used and retained. The Records Management policy section is a good place for those items.[8]

Roles and Responsibilities

Clear roles and their associated responsibilities for contributing to, maintaining, and utilizing the content in SharePoint must be established. By spelling out "who is responsible for what" you are able to document that your SharePoint environment meets the GAR Principles' key principle of *Accountability*.[9]

Questions to ask with regard to definition of roles and responsibilities include the following:

- Who is the executive sponsor for the solution?
- Who owns the system?
- Who is the sponsor/steward for a specific site or site collection?
- Who owns the content in the site?
- Who is responsible for completing the initial deployment of a site or collection?
- Who is responsible for day-to-day administration of the site?
- Who defines and sets up content types? Columns? Term store values?
- Who is responsible for controlling access to a site? For making changes as users' roles change or they are terminated?
- Who will train users initially? On an ongoing basis?
- Who will contribute content?
- Who will be allowed to view and/or edit content?

Some examples of possible SharePoint roles within a given organization are:

- Executive sponsor
- Content owner or "steward" for a site or site collection
- Site owner
- Site member
- Site contributor
- Site visitor
- System administrator
- Site collection administrator
- Business analyst
- Training, education and user support
- Information architect/taxonomist
- Information governance representative (records manager?)

The Roles and Responsibilities section of the SharePoint governance model will need to describe how users can request a site and how they get support for their sites, including the support escalation process. For this purpose, a **service level agreement** (SLA) that outlines the basic support levels, timeframes, problem escalation processes, cost allocations, and other issues related to service is useful. Wherever possible, create an SLA and refer to it so that users have clear expectations regarding how long it will take them to get a new site or get support for an existing site.

Establish Processes

Guiding principles provide the "what" of Governance and Roles and Responsibilities define the "who." The governance model, or a separate set of procedures referenced by the governance model, also needs to describe the "how" of governance. Most important, it should detail the process of creating SharePoint sites. Also critical, the model must include a process for decommissioning sites. Further, as the ownership of the site may change in the future, the process of transferring site ownership must be established and standardized. In addition, more specific processes, such as those for migrating content into SharePoint must be created. If a business record is created, you need a process to manage it accordingly, whether that is by sending it to a central records repository to complete its lifecycle or managing it in the library where it originated. When Legal Holds are required, standard processes must be established to produce records requested during e-discovery. A demonstrated ability to produce trustworthy records—*records* that can be proven to be authentic and unaltered—is an absolute requirement. All these processes must be designed to be as efficient and low-cost as possible.

Training Plan

Incorporating training into your SharePoint governance model supports all aspects of the GAR Principles, but especially *Integrity*, because a well-defined training model shows that your organization gave users the rules about SharePoint usage and the necessary tools to comply with those rules.[10]

The training section of your SharePoint governance model should break down the overall training strategy; whether that is to train everyone, just train site owners or just refer users to training resources. This section should explain the process for obtaining training. It should also describe or include a reference to a detailed training plan. The training plan describes the ways training will be delivered and how training content will be created. It should include a level of detail sufficient to identify the different types of training (site owner training, content custodian training, user training, basic training, advanced training, and so on). As you define the training plan, remember that any given individual may fill more than one role; they might be an owner on one site, a contributor on another and a reader on many. So the training plan should allow them to get all the training they need, without having to endure the same training modules multiple times.

An important Training consideration is that SharePoint is a popular technology right now and individuals with SharePoint skills are a hot commodity in the marketplace. Therefore, in order to eliminate any "single points of failure" in your SharePoint roles, make sure to cross train every role to ensure you have more than one person that can perform any given function.

Communications Plan

Your communication plan for SharePoint governance needs to take into account that you are asking people to change the fundamental way in which they manage much of

> Your training plan needs to consider any given individual may fill more than one role on different SharePoint sites.

Your communication plan needs to consider that you are asking people to change the fundamental way they access and manage documents.

the core information they use to do their work. So your communication plan needs to clearly state that the proposed SharePoint governance model:

- Is *good* for the organization.
- Makes it easier for team members to manage and find the information they need to do their jobs.

An understanding of the SharePoint governance model should make it clear to users what the organization intends to do with SharePoint. It should also be very clear what they are expected to do and the training they will receive so that they can work well in the SharePoint environment. Every SharePoint role should be able to review the communications regarding governance and understand how, exactly, it will impact them.[11]

CHAPTER SUMMARY: **KEY POINTS**

- Lack of governance can significantly diminish the business value and increase the risk of your SharePoint deployment.
- Your SharePoint governance model needs to be tailored to your organization.
- As with any initiative that requires behavior or attitude change, you will encounter resistance when implementing information governance within SharePoint.
- Critical to success in most SharePoint deployments is an understanding of the business objectives for the solution and how those map to the organization's strategic plan.
- Your communication plan needs to consider that you are asking people to change the fundamental way they access and manage documents and records.

Notes

1. Don Lueders, "It's All about the Processes," June 18, 2009, http://sharepointrecordsmanagement .com/2009/06/18/its-all-about-the-processes.
2. Monica Crocker, e-mail to author, April 30, 2012.
3. Ibid.
4. Monica Crocker, e-mail to author, April 30, 2012.
5. Monica Crocker, telephone interview with author, April 30, 2012.
6. Monica Crocker, e-mail to author, April 30, 2012.
7. Ibid.
8. Ibid.
9. Ibid.
10. Monica Crocker, e-mail to author, April 30, 2012.
11. Ibid.

PART FOUR

Technical Issues

CHAPTER 15

International
E-Records Standards

Standards can be meaningful and relevant, providing guidance for managers to consider; and specific **records management** (RM) and **electronic records management** (ERM) standards are useful tools for system selection decision-makers, records managers, software developers, and implementers of software applications and computer systems.

But they do not always have their intended effect. There are standards that are formally established and completely ignored. And there are standards that emerge through popular use although they are not formalized by any standards-setting body. So adhering to a standard does not, in itself, guarantee any kind of safe harbor or compatibility with future systems or standards. It depends on *which* standard you select, *how* it arose, and *what* its characteristics and requirements may be.

There are two general types of standards: de jure and de facto. De jure ("the law") standards are those published by recognized standards-setting bodies, such as the International Organization for Standardization (ISO), American National Standards Institute (ANSI), National Institute of Standards and Technology (NIST), British Standards Institution (BSI), Standards Council of Canada (SCC), and Standards Australia. Standards promulgated by authorities such as these have the formal status of standards.

De facto ("the fact") standards are not formal standards but are regarded by many as if they were. They may arise through popular use (e.g., Windows at the business desktop in the 2000–2010 decade), or may be published by other bodies, such as the U.S. National Archives and Records Administration (NARA) or Department of Defense (DoD), for the U.S. military sector. They may also be published by formal standards-setting bodies without having the formal status of a "standard" (such as some "Technical Reports" like ISO-TR 13028 published by ISO).[1]

Standards in records management, whether de jure or de facto, address one of two completely different things. Some address principles or details of records management; others address requirements for records management *systems*. The former is a more mature area based on principles of physical records management that have long been established; the latter pertains to the evolving field of ERM. Certainly there is overlap, as "records management is records management," regardless of media. But there are new records management and technology issues and techniques that are specific only to the electronic environment.

In December 1995, Australia became the *first country in the world* to develop a standard on records management with AS 4390–1996, followed closely by Canada,

> Standards can be formal de jure ("the law") standards or de facto ("the fact") that arise from popularization or are provided by bodies without standards-setting status.

which established Records/Document/Information Management (RDIM): Integrated Document Management System for the Government of Canada in 1996.[2]

Standards in the ERM space are relatively new and developing. *At this time, there is no established, accepted, and testable international standard for ERM systems worldwide,* although guidance from ISO has been established in the form of published standards, and de facto standards exist.

A number of attempts have been made at establishing standards internationally and in different regions and countries; some have survived and some have been ignored or have been supplanted by new standards and fallen by the wayside. Mostly, standards for e-records in specific countries are utilized in those countries and have gained little support elsewhere, perhaps with the exception of the U.S. Department of Defense (DoD) standard for electronic records systems, DoD 5015.2 STD, and to a lesser extent the UK's Public Records Office (PRO) Requirements of 2002. The PRO Requirements have proved influential in several countries, acting as a basis for some national standards. In 2003 PRO became The National Archives (TNA).

All ERM software vendors of any significance in the United States (and most worldwide) adhere to DoD 5015.2, which includes a testing and certification regime conducted and monitored by the Joint Interoperability Test Command (JITC), a military arm. DoD 5015.2 is the most basic requirement that buyers narrow selection lists by initially (although at this writing, it is scheduled for updating in 2012, it was last done in 2007), yet most buyers and records and information management (RIM) professionals have never read it and cannot describe what it requires.

The exception to major ERM vendors supporting the U.S. standard is Microsoft's SharePoint 2010/2013, which does not conform to the standard at the time of the printing of this book (it did initially with SharePoint 2007, but this lapsed), but rather, provides a platform and relies on third-party software development partners to achieve adherence to the standard.

Various standards bodies monitor, develop, and approve standards. ISO develops and publishes international standards that serve as guidance or models, rather than those with specific requirements for testing regimes. ISO standards also influence and help develop national standards, such as ANSI and NIST in the United States and BSI in the United Kingdom.[3]

ANSI "oversees the creation, promulgation and use of thousands of norms and guidelines that directly impact businesses in nearly every sector . . . [and] is also actively engaged in accrediting programs that assess conformance to standards—including

> There is no established, accepted, and testable international standard for ERM systems worldwide.

> International standards represent a consensus that helps to streamline and improve software development efforts and encourage interoperability.

globally recognized cross-sector programs such as the ISO 9000 (quality) and ISO 14000 (environmental) management systems."[4]

The Information Technology Laboratory (ITL) at the National Institute of Standards and Technology (NIST) "develops tests, test methods, reference data, proof of concept implementations and technical analysis to advance the development and productive use of information technology. ITL's responsibilities include developing technical, physical, administrative, and management standards and guidelines for cost effective security and privacy of sensitive unclassified information in Federal computer systems."[5]

BSI publishes standards, makes recommendations, and provides other guidance. BSI is "[a] global business services organization providing standards-based solutions in more than 150 countries."[6]

Benefits of Standards

Some benefits of developing and promoting standards are:

- *Quality assurance support*—if a product is certified to meet a standard you can be confident of a certain level of quality.
- *Interoperability support*—some standards are detailed and mature enough to allow for system interoperability between different vendor platforms.
- *Implementation frameworks and certification checklists*—these help to provide guides for projects and programs to help ensure all necessary steps are taken.
- *Cost reduction*—due to supporting uniformity of systems—users have lower maintenance requirements, and training and support costs when systems are more uniform.
- *International consensus*—standards can represent "best practice" recommendations based on global experiences.[7]

Some *downside* considerations are:

- *Possible decreased flexibility*—in development or implementation—standards can, at times, act as a constraint when they are tied to older technologies or methods, which can reduce innovation.
- *"Standards confusion"*—from competing and overlapping standards; for instance, an ISO standard may be theory-based and use different terminology, whereas regional or national standards are more specific, applicable and understandable than broad international ones.
- *Real-world shortcomings due to theoretical basis*—standards often are guides based on theory, rather than practice.
- *Changing and updating requires cost and maintenance*—there are costs to developing, maintaining and publishing standards.[8]

> Too many standards can confuse buyers and fall short of real-world needs.

Major International Standards

ISO 15489–1:2001 is the international standard for **records management** (RM). It identifies the elements of RM and provides a framework and high-level overview of RM core principles. Records management is defined as "[the] field of management responsible for the efficient and systematic control of the creation, receipt, maintenance, use and disposition of records, including the processes for capturing and maintaining evidence of and information about business activities and transactions in the form of records."[9]

The second part of the standard, ISO 15489–2:2001, contains the technical specifications and a methodology for implementing the standard, originally based on early standards work in Australia ("**Design and Implementation of Recordkeeping Systems—DIRKS**." Note: Although still actively used in Australian states, DIRKS has not been recommended for use by Australian national agencies by the National Archives of Australia since 2007, and has been removed from its website.)[10]

The ISO 15489 standard makes little mention of electronic records, being written to address all kinds of records; nonetheless was widely viewed as the definitive framework of what "records management" means.

In 2008, the International Council on Archives (ICA) formed a multinational team of experts to develop, "Principles and Functional Requirements for Records in Electronic Office Environments," commonly referred to as ICA-Req.[11] The project was cosponsored by the Australasian Digital Recordkeeping Initiative (ADRI), which was undertaken by the Council of Australasian Archives and Records Authorities (CAARA), which "comprises the heads of the government archives authorities of the Commonwealth of Australia, New Zealand, and each of the Australian States and Territories."[12] The National Archives of Australia is responsible for providing a training and guidance manual to assist in implementing the principles, which was presented at the 2012 International Congress on Archives Congress in Brisbane, Australia.

In Module 1 of ICA-Req, principles are presented in a high-level overview; Module 2 contains specifications for Electronic Document and Records Management Systems (EDRMS) that are "globally harmonized;" and Module 3 contains a requirements set "and implementation advice for managing records in business systems.[13] Module 3 recognizes that digital recordkeeping does not have to be limited to the EDRMS (central repository) paradigm—the insight that has now been picked up by MoReq2010 [the European standard released in 2011]."[14]

In early 2011, the ICA-Req standard was adopted as ISO 16175, parts 1–3. The standard may be purchased at www.ISO.org, and additional information on the Australian initiative may be found here: www.adri.gov.au/.

ISO 16175 is guidance, and not a standard that can be tested and certified against. This is the criticism by advocates of testable, certifiable standards like U.S. DoD 5015.2 and the European standard, "Modular Requirements for Records Systems," or MoReq2010.

In 2011, the ICA-Req standard was adopted as ISO 16175. It does not contain a testing regime for certification.

In November 2011, ISO issued new standards for ERM, the first two in the ISO 30300 series, which are based on a *managerial* point of view and targeted at a management-level audience, rather than for records managers or technical staff:

- **ISO 30300:2011** "Information and Documentation—Management Systems for Records—Fundamentals and Vocabulary"
- **ISO 30301:2011** "Information and Documentation—Management Systems for Records—Requirements"

The standards apply to "**management systems for records**" (MSR), (a term that, to the point of the time of this printing, has not been typically used to refer to ERM or records management application [RMA] software in the United States or Europe, and is not commonly found in ERM research or literature).

The ISO 30300 series is a systematic approach to the creation and management of records that is "*aligned with organizational objectives and strategies.*[15]

ISO 30300 MSR—'Fundamentals and Vocabulary' explains the rationale behind the creation of an MSR, the guiding principles for its successful implementation, and provides the terminology that ensures that it is compatible with other management systems standards.

ISO 30301 MSR—'Requirements' specifies the requirements necessary to develop a records policy. It also sets objectives and targets for an organization to implement systemic improvements. This is achieved through designing records processes and systems, estimating the appropriate allocation of resources, and establishing benchmarks to monitor, measure, and evaluate outcomes. These steps help to ensure that corrective action can be taken and continuous improvements are built into the system in order to support an organization in achieving its mandate, mission, strategy, and goals."[16]

Some additional ISO standards relevant to RM and ERM are discussed in the following paragraphs."

ISO 22310:2006 "Information and Documentation—Guidelines for Standards Drafters for Stating Records Management Requirements in Standards" "allows the appropriate incorporation of records requirements, according to ISO 15489–1, ISO/TR 15489–2 and 23081–1, which are applicable to all standards that require the creation and retention of records, into other standards. It also highlights the different elements that need to be considered as components of a comprehensive records management framework."[17]

The ISO 30300 series of e-records standards are written for a managerial audience and encourage ERM that is aligned to organizational objectives.

ISO 23081–1:2006 "Information and Documentation—Records Management Processes—Metadata for Records—Part 1: Principles" "covers the principles that underpin and govern records management metadata. These principles apply through time to:

- Records and their metadata.
- All processes that affect them.
- Any system in which they reside.
- Any organization that is responsible for their management."[18]

ISO/TS 23081–2:2009 "Information and Documentation—Managing Metadata for Records—Part 2: Conceptual and Implementation Issues" "establishes a framework for defining metadata elements consistent with the principles and implementation considerations outlined in ISO 23081–1:2006. The purpose of this framework is to:

1. Enable standardized description of records and critical contextual entities for records,
2. Provide common understanding of fixed points of aggregation to enable interoperability of records, and information relevant to records, between organizational systems, and
3. Enable reuse and standardization of metadata for managing records over time, space and across applications."[19]

"It further identifies some of the critical decision points that need to be addressed and documented to enable implementation of metadata for managing records. It aims to:

- Identify the issues that need to be addressed in implementing metadata for managing records,
- Identify and explain the various options for addressing the issues, and
- Identify various paths for making decisions and choosing options in implementing metadata for managing records."[20]

ISO 23081–3:2011 "Information and Documentation—Records Management Processes—Metadata Records" "provides guidance on conducting a self-assessment on records metadata in relation to the creation, capture and control of records.
The self-assessment helps to:

1. Identify the current state of metadata capture and management in or across organizations;
2. Identify priorities of what to work on and when;
3. Identify key requirements from ISO 23081–1:2006 and ISO 23081–2:2009;
4. Evaluate progress in the development of a metadata framework for the implementation of specific systems and projects;
5. Evaluate system and project readiness (move to the next phase in a system or project) when including records metadata functionality in a system. A records metadata readiness evaluation is provided for key steps from project inception through to the implementation/maintenance phase."[21]

ISO/TR 26122:2008, "Information and Documentation—Work Process Analysis for Records" "provides guidance on work process analysis from the perspective of the creation, capture and control of records.

"It identifies two types of analyses, namely:[22]

1. Functional analysis (decomposition of functions into processes), and
2. Sequential analysis (investigation of the flow of transactions)."

"Each analysis entails a preliminary review of context (i.e., mandate and regulatory environment) appropriate for the analysis. The components of the analysis can be undertaken in various combinations and in a different order from that described here, depending on the nature of the task, the scale of the project, and the purpose of the analysis. Guidance provided in the form of lists of questions/matters to be considered under each element of the analysis is also included."[23]

ISO 10244:2010 "Document Management—Business Process Base Lining and Analysis" "specifies the detailed information associated with the activities organizations perform when documenting existing work or business processes (business process base lining), defining the level of information required to be gathered, methods of documenting the work or business processes, and the procedures used when evaluating or analyzing the work or business processes."[24]

In the standard, tools are offered to zero in and focus on the "relevant aspects" of business processes and a standardized way of documenting the processes to allow for more detailed analyses and to facilitate the identification of enabling technologies that can be leveraged to improve them.

ISO 13008:2012 "Information and Documentation—Digital Records Conversion and Migration Process" (supersedes ANSI/ARMA 16–2007, "The Digital Records Conversion Process") provides guidance on the organizational and business framework for conversion and migration to the electronic environment, and an understanding of recordkeeping requirements in that process.[25] It "specifies the planning issues, requirements and procedures for the conversion and/or migration of digital records (which includes digital objects plus metadata) in order to preserve the authenticity, reliability, integrity, and usability of such records as evidence of business transactions.[26] These digital records can be active or residing in a repository." The procedures do not comprehensively cover (1) backup systems, (2) preservation of digital records, (3) functionality of trusted digital repositories, or (4) the process of converting analogue formats to digital formats and vice versa.

ISO/TR 13028:2010 "Information and Documentation—Implementation Guidelines for Digitization of Records" "establishes guidelines for creating and maintaining records in digital format only, where the original paper, or other nondigital source record, has been copied by digitizing; establishes best practice guidelines for digitization to ensure the trustworthiness and reliability of records and enable consideration of disposal of the nondigital source records; establishes best practice guidelines for the trustworthiness of the digitized records which may impact on the legal admissibility and evidential weight of such records; establishes best practice guidelines for the accessibility of digitized records for as long as they are required; specifies strategies to assist in creating digitized records fit for long-term retention; and establishes best practice guidelines for the management of non-digital source records following digitization."[27]

ISO/TR 13028 "is applicable for use in the design and conduct of responsible digitization by all organizations undertaking digitization, either business process digitization or back capture digitization projects for records management purposes, as outlined in ISO 15489–1:2001 and ISO/TR 15801:2009.

"ISO/TR 13028 is not applicable to: capture and management of born-digital records; technical specifications for the digital capture of records; procedures for making decisions about records' eventual disposition; technical specifications for the long-term preservation of digital records; or digitization of existing archival holdings for preservation purposes."[28]

ISO/TR 15801:2009 "Document Management—Information Stored Electronically—Recommendations for Trustworthiness and Reliability" "describes the implementation and operation of document management systems that can be considered to store electronic information in a trustworthy and reliable manner.[29]

"ISO/TR 15801 is for use by any organization that uses a document management system to store authentic, reliable and usable/readable electronic information over time. Such systems incorporate policies, procedures, technology and audit requirements that ensure that the integrity of the electronic information is maintained during storage.

"ISO/TR 15801 does not cover processes used to evaluate whether information can be considered to be authentic prior to it being stored or imported into the system. However, it can be used to demonstrate that, once the information is stored, output from the system will be a true and accurate reproduction of the original."[30]

ISO 18923:2000 "Imaging Materials—Polyester Base Magnetic Tape—Storage Practices" "provides recommendations concerning the storage conditions, storage facilities, enclosures, and inspection for recorded polyester base magnetic tapes in roll form. It covers analog and digital tape and includes tape made for audio, video, instrumentation, and computer use."[31] This International Standard applies to medium- and long-term magnetic tape storage (not work-in-progress or daily use) and applies to records stored on magnetic tape as master tapes (for archival storage). Not following the guidelines set forth in the standard can cause shortened life expectancy of the media.

ISO 19005–1:2005 "Document Management—Electronic Document File Format for Long-Term Preservation—Part 1: Use of PDF 1.4 (PDF/A-1)" "specifies how to use the portable document format (PDF) 1.4 for long-term preservation of electronic documents. It is applicable to documents containing combinations of character, raster and vector data."[32]

ISO 14721:2003 "Space Data and Information Transfer Systems—Open Archival Information Systems—Reference Model (OAIS)" is applicable to **long-term digital preservation** (LTDP).[33] (Please see Chapter 17, Long-Term Digital Preservation, by experts Charles Dollar and Lori Ashley for more detail). ISO 14271 "specifies a reference model for an open archival information system (OAIS). The purpose of ISO 14721 is to establish a system for archiving information, both digitalized and physical, with an organizational scheme composed of people who accept the responsibility to preserve information and make it available to a designated community."[34] The fragility of digital storage media combined with ongoing and sometimes rapid changes in computer software and hardware poses a fundamental challenge to ensuring access to trustworthy and reliable digital content over time. Eventually, every digital repository committed to long-term preservation of digital content must have a strategy to mitigate computer technology obsolescence. Toward this end the Consultative Committee for Space Data Systems (CCSDS) developed an **open archival information system** ("OAIS") reference model to support formal standards for the long-term preservation of space science data and information assets. OAIS was not designed as an implementation model.

OAIS is the "lingua franca" of digital preservation as the international digital preservation community has embraced it as the framework for viable and technologically sustainable digital preservation repositories. *An LTDP strategy that is OAIS-compliant offers the best means available today for preserving the digital heritage of all organizations, private and public.*[35]

ISO TR 18492 (2005) "Long-Term Preservation of Electronic Document Based Information" provides practical methodological guidance for the long-term preservation and retrieval of authentic electronic document-based information, when the retention period exceeds the expected life of the technology (hardware and software) used to create and maintain the information assets. ISO 18492 takes note of the role of ISO 15489 but does not cover processes for the capture, classification, and disposition of authentic electronic document-based information. (Again, see Chapter 17 on LTDP for more detail.)

ISO 16363:2012 "Space Data and Information Transfer Systems—Audit and Certification of Trustworthy Digital Repositories" "defines a recommended practice for assessing the trustworthiness of digital repositories. It is applicable to the entire range of digital repositories."[36] It is an audit and certification standard organized into three broad categories: Organization Infrastructure, Digital Object Management, and Technical Infrastructure and Security Risk Management. *ISO 16363 represents the "gold standard" of audit and certification for trustworthy digital repositories.*[37]

ISO/IEC 27002: 2005 "Information Technology—Security Techniques—Code of Practice for Information Security" "comprises ISO/IEC 17799:2005 and ISO/IEC 17799:2005/Cor.1:2007. Its technical content is identical to that of ISO/IEC 17799:2005. ISO/IEC 17799:2005/Cor.1:2007 changes the reference number of the standard from 17799 to 27002."[38]

"ISO/IEC 27002 establishes guidelines and general principles for initiating, implementing, maintaining, and improving information security management in an organization. The objectives outlined provide general guidance on the commonly accepted goals of information security management. ISO/IEC 27002 contains best practices of control objectives and controls in the following areas of information security management:

- Security policy
- Organization of information security
- Asset management
- Human resources security
- Physical and environmental security
- Communications and operations management
- Access control
- Information systems acquisition, development and maintenance
- Information security incident management
- Business continuity management
- Compliance

"The control objectives and controls in ISO/IEC 27002 are intended to be implemented to meet the requirements identified by a risk assessment. ISO/IEC 27002 is intended as a common basis and practical guideline for developing organizational security standards and effective security management practices, and to help build confidence in inter-organizational activities."[39]

ISO 8601:2004 "Data Elements and Interchange Formats—Information Interchange—Representation of Dates and Times" may seem obscure relative to ERM, but it is referred to in the U.S. DoD 5015.2 specification, MoReq2010 and other standards. It "is applicable whenever representation of dates in the Gregorian calendar, times in the 24-hour timekeeping system, time intervals and recurring time intervals or of the formats of these representations are included in information interchange. It includes:

- Calendar dates expressed in terms of calendar year, calendar month and calendar day of the month
- Ordinal dates expressed in terms of calendar year and calendar day of the year;
- Week dates expressed in terms of calendar year, calendar week number and calendar day of the week
- Local time based upon the 24-hour timekeeping system
- Coordinated Universal Time of day
- Local time and the difference from Coordinated Universal Time
- Combination of date and time of day
- Time intervals
- Recurring time intervals

"ISO 8601:2004 does not cover dates and times where words are used in the representation and dates and times where characters are not used in the representation.

"ISO 8601:2004 does not assign any particular meaning or interpretation to any data element that uses representations in accordance with ISO 8601:2004. Such meaning will be determined by the context of the application."[40]

ISO/TR 22957: 2009 "Document Management—Analysis, Selection and Implementation of Electronic Document Management Systems (EDMS)" provides guidance on the steps involved in the analysis, selection, and implementation of EDMS technologies.[41]

Additional Guidance from ANSI, ARMA, AIIM, NIST, BSI

ANSI/ARMA 19–2012 "Policy Design for Managing Electronic Messages"—This American National Standard sets forth the requirements for a policy guiding the management of electronic messages as records throughout their life cycle—from creation to final disposition. It extends to text-based electronic messages or communications, including e-mail (and related attachments/metadata), instant messaging, and text messaging, but it does not include requirements for video messaging, voicemail/audio-based messaging applications, and other electronic messaging platforms within the context of social media. It is for use by records and information management practitioners and educators, and it may be of interest to archivists, consultants, IT professionals, and individuals employed in a legal setting."[42]

ANSI/ARMA 5–2010 "Vital Records Programs: Identifying, Managing, and Recovering Business-Critical Records"—provides guidance for establishing vital records management programs to identify, assess, and protect vital records, and to estimate the impact on the organization in the event of their destruction or loss.[43]

ANSI/ARMA 18–2011 "Implications of Web-Based, Collaborative Technologies in Records Management"—provides guidance for policymaking and processes in the use of web portals, wikis, blogs, mash-ups and related collaborative team technologies, including best practice recommendations.[44]

ANSI/AIIM TR31–2004 "Legal Acceptance of Records Produced by Information Technology Systems"—"This report is a 2004 composite of material published in 1992–1994 as ANSI/AIIM TR31–1992, ANSI/AIIM TR31–1993, and ANSI/AIIM TR31–1994 (Part III).[45] Those reports dealt with the admissibility in USA federal and state courts of printouts of document and data records that are stored digitally. The reports gave performance guidelines and a self-assessment checklist to help ensure the admissibility and trustworthiness of the printouts. In combining the material the portions dealing with problems in state laws at that time and advocating changes to the laws were dropped, while the portions dealing with fundamental legal principles and expectations were consolidated. The three-part organization was retained. Part I gives an overview of evidence law. Part II presents a performance guideline for the legal acceptance of records produced by IT systems. Part III offers a self-assessment for accomplishment of the performance guideline. Although the report is oriented heavily towards information recorded initially on paper and then entered into an IT system, much of the material applies also to system environments that are entirely digital."[46]

NIST SP 500–252 "Care and Handling of CDs and DVDs—A Guide for Librarians and Archivists"—provides guidance on how to handle and care for CDs and DVDs to maximize their lifespan and reduce deterioration or errors due to environmental factors and physical handling.[47]

The following is their short "Quick Reference Guide" for the handling and care of CDs and DVDs.[48]

Quick Reference Guide for Care and Handling

Do:

1. Handle discs by the outer edge or the center hole.
2. Use a non-solvent-based felt-tip permanent marker to mark the label side of the disc.
3. Keep dirt or other foreign matter from the disc.
4. Store discs upright (book style) in plastic cases specified for CDs and DVDs.
5. Return discs to storage cases immediately after use.
6. Leave discs in their packaging (or cases) to minimize the effects of environmental changes.
7. Open a recordable disc package only when you are ready to record data on that disc.

8. Store discs in a cool, dry, dark environment in which the air is clean.

9. Remove dirt, foreign material, fingerprints, smudges, and liquids by wiping with a clean cotton fabric in a straight line from the center of the disc toward the outer edge.

10. Use CD/DVD-cleaning detergent, isopropyl alcohol, or methanol to remove stubborn dirt or material.

11. Check the disc surface before recording.

Do not:
1. Touch the surface of the disc.
2. Bend the disc.
3. Use adhesive labels.
4. Store discs horizontally for a long time (years).
5. Open a recordable optical disc package if you are not ready to record.
6. Expose discs to extreme heat or high humidity.
7. Expose discs to extremely rapid temperature or humidity changes.
8. Expose recordable discs to prolonged sunlight or other sources of ultraviolet light.
9. Write or mark in the data area of the disc (the area the laser "reads").
10. Clean by wiping in a direction going around the disc.

For CDs especially do not:
1. Scratch the label side of the disc.
2. Use a pen, pencil, or fine-tip marker to write on the disc.
3. Write on the disc with markers that contain solvents.
4. Try to peel off or reposition a label.

General recommendations for long-term storage conditions:
For archiving recordable (R) discs, it is recommended to use discs that have a gold metal reflective layer. Archival Storage Facility—Recommendation for storing CDs and DVDs together.

Media Temperature Relative Humidity (RH)
CD, DVD Less than 20°C (68°F) 20% to 50% RH

Greater than 4°C (39°F)

A temperature of 18°C and 40% RH would be considered suitable for long-term storage. A lower temperature and RH is recommended for extended-term storage.

NIST SP 800–88 "Guidelines for Media Sanitization"—provides guidance for proper transfer, reuse, or disposal of media to maintain quality and reduce the likelihood of security breaches from recovering and hacking data on used discs or errors caused by media degradation.[49]

"These [CD and DVD] media may require special disposition in order to mitigate the risk of unauthorized disclosure of information and to ensure its confidentiality. . . . With the use of increasingly sophisticated encryption, an attacker wishing to gain access to an organization's sensitive information is forced to look outside the system itself for that information. *One avenue of attack is the recovery of supposedly deleted data from media.* These residual data may allow unauthorized individuals to reconstruct data and thereby gain access to sensitive information. Sanitization can be used to thwart this attack by ensuring that deleted data cannot be easily recovered.

"When storage media are transferred, become obsolete, or are no longer usable or required by an information system, it is important to ensure that residual magnetic, optical, electrical, or other representation of data that has been deleted is not easily recoverable. **Sanitization** refers to the general process of removing data from storage media, such that there is reasonable assurance that the data may not be easily retrieved and reconstructed" [italics added].[50] **BS 10008:2008** "Evidential weight and legal admissibility of electronic information" addresses issues relating to the authenticity and integrity of records. **BIP 0008-1:2008** "Evidential Weight and Legal Admissibility of Information Stored Electronically" is a code of practice for the implementation of BS 10008.[51]

Major National and Regional ERM Standards

United States E-Records Standard

The U.S. Department of Defense 5015.2 *Design Criteria Standard for Electronic Records Management Software Applications*, standard was established in 1997 and is endorsed by the leading archival authority, the U.S. National Archives and Records Administration (NARA). There is a testing regime that certifies software vendors that is administered by JITC. JITC "builds test case procedures, writes detailed and summary final reports on 5015.2-certified products, and performs on-site inspection of software."[52] The DoD standard was built for the defense sector, and logically "reflects its government and archives roots."

Since its endorsement by NARA, the standard has been the key requirement for ERM system vendors to meet, not only in U.S. public sector bids, but also in the commercial sector.

In 1993, the U.S. Department of Defense formed a task force to examine and redesign its records management processes. The need for keeping records that could be held up as complete, authentic and with reliable integrity arose out of the many claims of Gulf War Syndrome by soldiers who fought in Operation Desert Storm in 1991. During Congressional investigations it became clear that critical records had been lost, damaged, or destroyed and the need for new, improved, and documented RM processes was clear, and Congress ordered the DoD to embark on the effort.[53]

The task force that included representatives from NARA, the Army, Air Force, and Army Research Laboratory published the "Functional Baseline Requirements and Data Elements for Records Management Application Software" two years later, in

The U.S. DoD 5015.2-STD has been the most influential worldwide since it was first introduced in 1997. It best suits military applications.

> The DoD 5015.2-STD testing regime does not measure ease-of-use or system performance factors like retrieval speed, scalability, or integration.

1995. The report was the basis for functional specification requirements and data elements for an ERM system (a/k/a RMA).[54]

The Defense Information Systems Agency (DISA) then created testable design specifications and, two years later, at JITC, published "DoD 5015.2-STD, Design Criteria Standard for Electronic Records Management Software Applications." It should be noted that *the testing does not measure system performance issues such as speed of search and retrieval, scalability to handling large volumes of records, ease of use and training, integration of modules or other critical issues in software evaluation.* It merely tests whether required feature sets *can* function in a way that conforms to the specification.

In the United States, DoD 5015.2-STD provided market clarity and helped the ERM industry to progress, and this progress and visibility of e-records management also had the effect of broadening and raising the level of responsibility for managing records. Along with increased regulation and legal demands, records management has become the concern of higher and higher management levels of organizations. The U.S. standard also established the fact, certainly in the public sector, that e-records could be kept as complete, authentic, and with reliable integrity. *Prior to the standard being established, electronic documents in the U.S. Defense sector had to be printed and managed as paper records,* e-messages could not be stored in their native format, ERM software was weak and inconsistent functionally, and records managers were the only ones who could declare, manage, and control records. Also, managing records created by voice mail, instant messaging (IM), and web content was not possible as no established practices or standards were in place.[55]

The 5015.2 standard has since been updated and expanded, in 2002 and 2007, to include requirements for metadata, e-signatures and Privacy and Freedom of Information Act requirements, and, as previously stated, was scheduled for update by 2013—although it has slipped.

Canadian Standards and Legal Considerations for Electronic Records Management*

The National Standards of Canada for electronic records management are: (1) *Electronic Records as Documentary Evidence* CAN/CGSB-72.34–2005 ("72.34"), published in December 2005; and, (2) *Microfilm and Electronic Images as Documentary Evidence* CAN/CGSB-72.11–93, first published in 1979 and updated to 2000 ("72.11").[56] 72.34 incorporates all that 72.11 deals with and is therefore the more important of the two. Because of its age, 72.11 should not be relied upon for its "legal" content. However, 72.11 has remained the industry standard for "imaging" procedures—converting original paper records to electronic storage. The Canada Revenue Agency has adopted these standards as applicable to records concerning taxation.[57]

72.34 deals with these topics: (1) management authorization and accountability; (2) documentation of procedures used to manage records; (3) "reliability testing" of

---

*This section was contributed by Ken Chasse JD, LLM, a records management attorney and consultant, and member of the Law Society of Upper Canada (Ontario) and of the Law Society of British Columbia, Canada.

The 5015.2 U.S. DoD standard has been updated to include specifications such as those for e-signatures and FOI requirements.

electronic records according to existing legal rules; (4) the procedures manual and the chief records officer; (5) readiness to produce (the "prime directive"); (6) records recorded and stored in accordance with "the usual and ordinary course of business" and "system integrity," being key phrases from the Evidence Acts in Canada; (7) retention and disposal of electronic records; (8) backup and records system recovery; and, (9) security and protection. From these standards practitioners have derived many specific tests for auditing, establishing, and revising electronic records management systems.[58]

The "prime directive" of these standards states: "An organization shall always be prepared to produce its records as evidence."[59] *The duty to establish the "prime directive" falls upon senior management:*[60]

"5.4.3 Senior management, the organization's own internal law-making authority, proclaims throughout the organization the integrity of the organization's records system (and, therefore, the integrity of its electronic records) by establishing and declaring:

a. the system's role in the usual and ordinary course of business;
b. the circumstances under which its records are made; and
c. its prime directive for all RMS [records management system] purposes, i.e., an organization shall always be prepared to produce its records as evidence. This dominant principle applies to all of the organization's business records, including electronic, optical, original paper source records, microfilm, and other records of equivalent form and content."

Being the "dominant principle" of an organization's electronic records management system, the duty to maintain compliance with the "prime directive" should fall upon its senior management.

Legal Considerations

Because an electronic record is completely dependent upon its ERM system for everything, compliance with these National Standards and their "prime directive" should be part of the determination of the "admissibility" (acceptability) of evidence and of electronic discovery in court proceedings (litigation) and in regulatory tribunal proceedings.[61]

There are 14 legal jurisdictions in Canada: 10 provinces, 3 territories, and the federal jurisdiction of the Government of Canada. Each has an Evidence Act (the Civil Code in the province of Quebec[62]), which applies to legal proceedings within its legislative jurisdiction. For example, criminal law and patents and copyrights are within federal legislative jurisdiction, and most civil litigation comes within provincial legislative jurisdiction.[63]

The admissibility of records as evidence is determined under the "business record" provisions of the Evidence Acts.[64] They require proof that a record was made "in the usual and ordinary course of business," and of "the circumstances of the making of the record."

In addition, to obtain admissibility for electronic records, most of the Evidence Acts contain electronic record provisions, which state that an electronic record is admissible as evidence on proof of the "integrity of the electronic record system in which the data was recorded or stored."[65] This is the "system integrity" test for the admissibility of electronic records. The word "integrity" has yet to be defined by the courts.[66]

However, by way of sections such as the following, the electronic record provisions of the Evidence Acts make reference to the use of standards such as the National Standards of Canada:

> For the purpose of determining under any rule of law whether an electronic record is admissible, evidence may be presented in respect of any standard, procedure, usage or practice on how electronic records are to be recorded or stored, having regard to the type of business or endeavour that used, recorded, or stored the electronic record and the nature and purpose of the electronic record.[67]

Integration of Law and Records Information Management

There are six areas of law and records and information management (RIM) applicable to paper and electronic records:

1. The laws of evidence applicable to electronic and paper records[68]
2. The National standards of Canada concerning electronic records[69]
3. The records requirements of government agencies, such as the Canada Revenue Agency[70]
4. The electronic commerce legislation[71]
5. The privacy laws[72]
6. The guidelines for electronic discovery in legal proceedings[73]

These six areas are closely interrelated and are based upon very similar concepts. They all make demands of records systems and of the chief records officer or others responsible for records. *Therefore, a failure to satisfy the records management needs of any one of them will likely mean a failure to satisfy all of them.* Agencies that manage these areas of law look to the decisions of the courts to determine the requirements for acceptable records.

Each of these areas of law affects records and information management, just as they are affected by the laws governing the use of records as evidence in legal proceedings—the laws of evidence. These relationships make mandatory, compliance with the "prime directive" provided by the national standards, which states: "an organization shall always be prepared to produce its records as evidence."[74]

Electronic discovery is the most rapidly developing area concerning the use of electronic records in legal proceedings, and the need for ERM standards. The need to access and review many thousands of records has resulted in many reported court decisions that analyze the cost, complexity, and "proportionality" (reasonableness) of demands for the disclosure and discovery of electronic records. Guidelines as to "proportionality" have been devised.[75] They refer to there being "Compliance with a reasonable records management policy."[76] ERM policies should not be merely "reasonable"; they must be compliant with established standards of records management.[77] And the realization that the adequacy and fairness of electronic discovery is dependent upon the quality of

Electronic discovery is the most rapidly developing area concerning the use of electronic records in legal proceedings, and the need for ERM standards.

ERM will make demands for proof of compliance with recognized standards of ERM a common procedure in electronic discovery proceedings. That will create a need for a simple and efficient procedure for certifying such compliance by experts in ERM. Compliance with the "prime directive" of the National Standards of Canada is essential for the adequacy, cost-efficiency, and fairness of electronic discovery.[78]

Further ERM Considerations

Organizations have records in several formats, including paper, microfilm, and in electronic format. Various divisions of an organization could have some or all five of the following types of records—each of the five having different legal rules for determining its admissibility (acceptability) and "weight" (probative value, credibility) as evidence in legal proceedings:

1. Original paper records
2. Electronic records (i.e., they are created or stored electronically)
3. Microfilmed or imaged (scanned) records
4. "Relied upon printouts" of electronic records within the meaning of the Evidence Acts and comparable provisions of the Civil Code of Quebec[79]
5. Records created through EDI (electronic data interchange)

The standard to be applied in determining the acceptability of one's records for any of the previous purposes is that applied by the law governing the use of records as evidence in legal proceedings. The greatest difference lies in the requirements for paper and electronic records. A paper record can exist apart from its records system; an electronic record cannot. Therefore their management must be different and so must the standards applicable to each be different. Therefore the laws of evidence applicable to each should be different or applied differently.

Even if an organization is rarely involved in legal proceedings, its records systems will be subject to audit, and to formal demands for records from government and other agencies. The standards to be applied by such audits and demands are those applied in legal proceedings (i.e., the tests used by the courts to determine what are acceptable electronic and paper records). In Canada, they depend upon four key legal phrases applicable to electronic records (except for the province of Quebec):

1. "The integrity of the electronic records system."
2. "Relied upon printouts" of electronic records.
3. "The usual and ordinary course of business."
4. "The circumstances of the making of the record."[80]

The first two phrases are found in the "electronic record" provisions of the federal and provincial Evidence Acts. The second two are found in the "business record" provisions. The first two are alternative ways of satisfying the electronic record provisions.

But the second two are cumulative (i.e., one must be prepared to satisfy both of them). Therefore the first, third, and fourth must be satisfied for records that are: (a) recorded or stored in an electronic record system; and also, (b) "business" records (which includes government records). Proof of the "integrity of the electronic records system" as being in accordance with the national standard 72.34, should satisfy the other two provisions as well. However, because the courts have not yet dealt with this issue, there is no certainty that this is so. Given the all-encompassing definition of "business" used in the Evidence Acts, and the prevalence of electronic records management, it is best to consider all records as being subject to these legal tests.

But the previous key phrases in the Evidence Acts are not defined by those Acts. Therefore they also provide that for the purpose of determining under any rule of law whether an electronic record is admissible as evidence in legal proceedings, evidence may be presented in respect of any standard, procedure, usage, or practice concerning the manner in which electronic records are to be recorded or stored.[81] The words "any rule of law" should enable the application of the national standards 72.34 and 72.11 to the business record as well as the electronic record provisions of the Evidence Acts.

Those legal tests, and the national standards created to facilitate their application, are meant to be applied as much in business and government activities as in legal proceedings. Records and information management systems should therefore be designed, initiated, and maintained in accordance with that law and those standards. Such compliance is necessary in order to meet the requirements of the six areas of law and records and information management listed earlier.[82]

U.K. and European Standards

In the United Kingdom, The National Archives (TNA) (formerly the Public Record Office, or PRO) "has published two sets of functional requirements to promote the development of the electronic records management software market (1999 and 2002)." It ran a program to evaluate products against the 2002 requirements.[83] Initially these requirements were established in collaboration with the central government, and they later were utilized by the public sector in general, and also in other nations. The National Archives 2002 requirements remain somewhat relevant, although no additional development has been underway for years. It is clear that the second version of Model Requirements for Management of Electronic Records, MoReq2, largely supplanted the UK standard, and subsequently the newer MoReq2010 may further supplant the UK standard.

MoReq2010s predecessor, MoReq2, was released in 2008. It had significant influence in Europe, and to a degree, globally (it was translated into more than a dozen languages, and was used as the basis for other standards, such as Brazil's), although it was a guidance and *not* a de jure standard— reportedly only one certification of software was completed—which is one reason why MoReq2010 was developed. It includes a testing regime (testing of the MoReq2 standard existed, but was quite limited) that some contend is not as rigid and transparent as its predecessor.[84]

MoReq2010, "unbundles" some of the core requirements in MoReq2, and sets out functional requirements in modules. The approach seeks to permit the later creation of e-records software standards in various vertical industries such as defense, health care, financial services, and legal services.

> The European MoReq2010 standard differs from previous versions of MoReq in that it provides for testing and certification.

MoReq2010 is available free—all 525 pages of it (by comparison, the U.S. DoD 5015.2 standard is less than 120 pages long). For more information on MoReq2010, visit www.moreq2010.eu. The entire specification may be downloaded at: http://moreq2010.eu/pdf/moreq2010_vol1_v1_1_en.pdf.

The European Commission was actively involved in the establishment of the DLM Forum, which promulgated MoReq. DLM was originally chosen as it is the acronym for "machine-readable data" in French (*données lisibles par machine*); but in 2002 the DLM Forum decided that its name should instead refer to "Document Lifecyle Management." The DLM Forum is based on the June 1994 conclusions of the European Council (94/C 235/03) regarding increased cooperation in the field of archives. In close cooperation with representatives from the member states, it organized the first DLM Forum in 1996.[85]

The need for a comprehensive specification of requirements for electronic records management was first articulated by the DLM Forum in 1996, as one of the 10 action points arising from its meeting. Subsequently, the European Commission Enterprise DG's Interchange of Data between Administrations (IDA) programme commissioned the development of this model specification. The resulting specification, "Model Requirements for the Management of Electronic Records" (MoReq) was published in 2002.[86] This was followed by a major "update and extension" (MoReq2) in 2008.[87]

MoReq2010

In November 2010, the DLM Forum, a European Commission supported body, announced the availability of the final draft of the MoReq2010 specification for electronic records management systems (ERMS), following extensive public consultation. The final specification was published in mid-2011.[88]

The DLM Forum explains that "With the growing demand for [electronic] records management, across a broad spectrum of commercial, not-for-profit, and government organizations, MoReq2010 provides the first practical specification against which all organizations can take control of their corporate information. IT software and services vendors are also able to have their products tested and certified that they meet the MoReq2010 specification."[89]

MoReq2010 supersedes its predecessor MoReq2 and has the continued support and backing of the European Commission.

MoReq2010 Going Forward

MoReq2010 has the following five characteristics:

1. It applies to both the public and private sector, in that it makes provisions for future vertical market requirements such as for banking, oil and gas, and pharmaceuticals, and also provides a template for compliance requirements to be added by regulatory bodies.

2. Is multilingual—"available in a multiplicity of languages with guidance for local national requirements."
3. Is testable and certifiable—includes a (developing) network of compliance testing suppliers of both corporate and application requirements.
4. Provides training—through a (developing) roll-out of approved centers for MoReq2010 education.
5. Is supported and endorsed by the European Commission (as was MoReq2, and MoReq).

In December, 2011, "The DLM Forum held their tri-annual conference in Brussels. . . . The conference brought together archivists and records managers from across Europe. The DLM forum had earlier in the year [2011] published the MoReq2010 electronic records management system specification, and there was much talk of the specification at the conference."[90]

The first sets of test scripts for certification on the new standard were released by the DLM forum. The release of test scripts is a critical juncture in the launch of a new standard—it makes testing against the standard possible for the first time, and software suppliers can see how their product will be evaluated, and they can make development decisions on making needed modifications to conform to the standard.[91]

The future of MoReq2010 is unknown, and the number of vendor suppliers that go down the path of testing and certification is unknown at this time; the acceptance of a standard in the vendor community is key to its success. How MoReq2010-compliant products might re-shape the direction of ERM software depends on not only vendor acceptance, but also user demands, that is, if major public sector contracts call for MoReq2010-compliant products, vendors seeking these contracts must comply. But it is very early in the game, and only time will tell. Some experts believe "that MoReq2010 will lead to a very heterogeneous set of products, ranging from products that simply manage records held in one type of application (products that simply manage records held in SharePoint, products that simply manage records held in an e-mail system) to products that can manage records held in any application that the organisation uses. This is in contrast to the previous generation of electronic records management specifications (from DoD 5015.2 to MoReq2) that led to a very homogenous set of products—namely those products dubbed 'electronic records management systems' (EDRMS)."[92]

To this point, "*the most influential electronic records management specification in the world is the US DoD 5015.2*" (italics added). That specification is looking increasingly jaded and outdated. It was last revised in 2007, and the latest version does not reflect the changed nature of the digital landscape in organisations since the rise of both social computing and of SharePoint."[93] And, as Marc Fresko, primary author of MoReq2, observed, "It [DoD5015.2-STD] was, in fact, designed to meet U.S. military requirements, so its applicability in other vertical and geographic markets is not evident."[94]

MoReq 2010 applies to the public and private sector, and makes provisions for vertical market applications.

How MoReq2010 Differs from Previous Standards

"MoReq2010 *has been written to encourage different models of records management system to emerge.* It does this by adopting a modular structure.[95] Reflecting this, its title stands for "Modular Requirements . . ." whereas its predecessors were "Model Requirements . . ." There are a set of core MoReq2010 requirements that all vendors seeking certification must meet, but there are also modules that vendors may optionally test against. Vendors utilizing traditional (repository-based) ERM approaches will certainly seek certification, but also some subset of those—or new vendors entirely—"submit systems for testing that meet a completely different model, for example:

- Systems that end-users do not interact with directly, but instead capture and store records that users had created in other systems.
- Systems that do not store records, but instead govern and protect records held in other systems.
- Line of business systems or single purpose applications that are not intended to be a general records system but which have the ability to manage the records that they capture.
- Systems that can fulfill two or more of those roles—for example a system that could be deployed as a traditional EDRM that some end-users would interact with directly, but which also possessed the capability to manage records held in other content repositories."[96]

MoReq 2010 Takes a New Direction[97]

MoReq 2010 is a break not only with the previous two versions of MoReq issued by the European Union (MoReq and MoReq 2) but also with the UK's TNA 2002 standard and the U.S. DoD 5015.2 standard."

According to James Lappin in the United Kingdom, MoReq 2010 "abandons three big aspirations that all those previous specifications shared." It changes the approach, by:

- **Moving to "aggregations" versus a traditional file approach.** "This is a major break with the vocabulary of the hard copy era. In a MoReq2 compliant system a 'file' was limited to two levels of hierarchy beneath it (file/sub-file/ parts). In a MoReq2010 compliant system an aggregation can have any number of levels of hierarchy. The MoReq2010 'aggregation' has a different relationship to a business classification/fileplan than a MoReq2 'file'. The MoReq2 file sat at the very bottom of the business classification/fileplan. *An aggregation can be a multilevel hierarchy in its own right, so it can sit separate from the business classification,* whose role is not so much to act as the only means of navigating around the records system, but more to apply retention rules to records."
- **Abandoning the single business classification scheme (BCS) or "corporate file plan" approach.** "In Moreq2010 compliant systems there is the

> MoReq 2010 has been written to allow new models for ERM to emerge, versus the traditional back-end, central repository approach.

MoReq2010 introduces the concept of "aggregations" versus a traditional file structure.

possibility of having several classifications, any number of which can be used to apply retention rules to records. If a record is classified against more than one classification then one of them should be nominated as the 'primary classification' for that record. The primary classification is the one that the record inherits its retention rule from."

- **Allowing for new ERM models vs. the static architecture of previous systems created for all vertical market application needs.** "MoReq2010 has been written so that the core module contains only requirements that are common to all or most organisations. If a sector has specific requirements they are able to write a separate MoReq2010 module to capture those needs. Vendors that wished to target that sector could add that functionality to their system and ask for it to be tested and certified against that module." The primary author of MoReq2010, Jon Garde, "argues that the MoReq2010 will be more sustainable over time than previous specifications, as new needs can be incorporated into new modules without having to republish the whole specification. *Marc Fresko [has given] gave the counter argument that the structure of MoReq2010 will be more complex for records managers in organisations to work with, because they are going to have to decide which modules are important enough for their organisation to insist upon.*"[98] (italics added).

In addition, MoReq2010 is written in highly technical language that makes it challenging for many records managers to read and understand, in contrast with MoReq2 and other specifications that are accessible to non-IT professionals. *This combined with its vastly increased length and complexity mean that its adoption and future acceptance remain unsure.*[99]

Australian ERM and Records Management Standards

Australia has adopted all three parts of ISO 16175 as its e-records management standard.[100] (For more detail on this standard, see its coverage earlier in this chapter, and go to ISO.org.)

Australia has long led the introduction of highly automated electronic document management systems and records management standards. Following the approval and release of the AS 4390 standard in 1996, the international records management community began work on the development of an International standard. This work used AS 4390–1996 Records Management as its starting point.

Development of Australian Records Standards

In 2002 Standards Australia published a new Australian Standard on records management, AS ISO 15489, based on the ISO 15489 international records management standard. It differs only in its preface verbiage.[101] AS ISO 15489 carries through all these main components of AS 4390, but internationalizes the concepts and brings them up to date. The standards thereby codify Australian best practice but are also progressive in their recommendations.

Additional Relevant Australian Standards

The **Australian Government Recordkeeping Metadata Standard Version 2.0** provides guidance on metadata elements and sub-elements for records management. It is a baseline tool that "describes information about records and the context in which they are captured and used in Australian government agencies." This standard is intended to help Australian agencies, "meet business, accountability and archival requirements in a systematic and consistent way by maintaining reliable, meaningful and accessible records." The standard is written in two parts, the first describing its purpose and features and the second outlining the specific metadata elements and subelements.[102]

The **Australian Government Locator Service**, AGLS, is published as AS 5044–2010, the metadata standard to help find and exchange information online. It updates the 2002 version, and includes changes made by the Dublin Core Metadata Initiative (DCMI). (For more information on metadata and metadata standards, see Chapter 16 on Metadata). Its major changes and improvements are:

> Revising terminology, property descriptions and recommended formatting to remain consistent with the Dublin Core Metadata Initiative (DCMI)

- Assigning free standing descriptive labels to metadata terms
- A clear distinction between Vocabulary Encoding Schemes and Syntax Encoding Schemes
- Including a DCMI property not previously in the AGLS standard (conformsTo)
- Including four new DCMI properties (accessRights, dateCopyrighted, rightsHolder and license)
- Introducing two new AGL properties (dateLicensed and protectiveMarking)
- Introducing three additional sets of terms (Agent Metadata Terms, Availability Metadata Terms, and Administrative Metadata Terms)
- Deprecation of one element refinement from the previous standard (DC.coverage.postcode)
- Changes to the obligation status of some properties
- Including a new obligation status "Recommended"
- Updating references to the most recent versions of Request for Comment (RFC) standards and ISO standards
- Examples in eXtensible Hypertext Markup Language (XHTML)
- Expanding the AGLS Audience Vocabulary Encoding Scheme[103]

Another standard, **AS 5090:2003 "Work Process Analysis for Recordkeeping,"** complements AS ISO 15489, and provides guidance on understanding business processes and workflow, so that recordkeeping requirements may be determined.[104]

Other National Standards

Other countries have also developed or adopted their own standards for ERM/EDRMS systems and/or archiving digital records. Among them are Brazil, Finland, Germany, New Zealand, and Norway.

Brazil

e-ARQ Brasil (v1.1), the Brazilian standard, was updated in late 2009. The standard is "Modelo de Requisitos para Sistemas Informatizados de Gestão Arquivística de Documentos, v1.1," which was published by the National Council of Archives of Brazil.[105]

Finland

Published in 2008, SÄHKE2, is the Finnish national standard for electronic records management. It is made up of SÄHKE2 regulation; Attachment 1- Creation of metadata; Attachment 2—Metadata model; XML schema for transfer files; Guide about transferring records to National Archives Service.

Germany

DOMEA 2.0 Requirements Catalogue was the German national standard, adopted in 2009;[106] it was officially terminated at the end of 2011. Replacing it is a new concept without certification, which is called OKeVA "Organisationskonzept elektronische Verwaltungsarbeit," issued by the German Ministry of the Interior.[107]

New Zealand

In 2010, Archives New Zealand published a "discretionary best practice" standard, Digital Recordkeeping Standard (DRS), which replaced the Electronic Recordkeeping Systems Standard (ERKSS) "in accordance with the Public Records Act 2005."[108] Similar to Australia's approach, DRS is the ICA standard, *Principles and Functional Requirements for Records in Electronic Office Environments (ICA-Req), which became* ISO 16175, with an added Section One to explain how the standard fits within other New Zealand recordkeeping guidelines and standards.

Norway

NOARK 5 was adopted in 2009. Noark is a Norwegian abbreviation for *Norsk arkivstandard*, or "Norwegian Archive Standard." Noark was developed as a specification of requirements for electronic recordkeeping systems used in public administration in 1984 and quickly became established as the de facto standard.[109]

Where to Find More Information on ERM Standards

Guidance on standards and the management of electronic records can be found at www.iso.org, and from leading trade associations for records managers, such as the Association of Records Managers and Administrators (www.ARMA.org), the Information and Records Management Society (www.irms.org.uk/), and the Records and Information Management Professionals Australasia (known as the RIM Professionals Australasia at www.rimpa.com.au).

Information can also be found on the many websites of national, provincial, and state archives, such as the NARA (www.archives.gov), The National Archives (TNA) in the U.K. (www.nationalarchives.gov.uk), and the National Archives of Australia

Guidance on standards can be found at ISO.org, from trade associations such as ARMA.org and IRMS.org.uk, and from national archives websites.

(www.naa.gov.au/), or from certain vertical market industry groups, such as the American Health Information Managers Association (at AHIMA.org), which is the leading U.S. trade association for healthcare records managers. Supplemental European information can be found at www.moreq2010.eu. Additional e-records standards information is available at AIIM.org.

CHAPTER SUMMARY: **KEY POINTS**

- International standards represent a consensus that helps to streamline and improve software development efforts and encourage interoperability.

- Too many standards can confuse buyers and fall short of real-world needs.

- ISO develops and publishes international standards that serve as guidance or models, rather than those with specific requirements for testing regimes.

- In early 2011, the International Council on Archives ERM standard (ICA-Req) was adopted as ISO 16175. It is guidance and does not include a testing regime or certification.

- The ISO 30300 series of e-records standards are written for a managerial audience and encourages ERM that is aligned to organizational objectives.

- The U.S. DoD 5015.2-STD has been the most influential worldwide since it was first introduced in 1997. It best suits military applications.

- The 5015.2 standard has been updated to include specifications such as those for e-signatures and FOI requirements.

- The Canadian Electronic Commerce Strategy encourages the use of electronic records in e-commerce.

- The primary Canadian ERM standard is: National Standards of Canada *Electronic Records as Documentary Evidence* CAN/CGSB-72.34–2005.

- Europe's MoReq2010 applies to the public and private sector, and makes provision for the later development of extensions to address vertical market applications.

(Continued)

(Continued)

- MoReq2010 has been written to allow new models for ERM to emerge, versus the traditional back-end, central repository approach.

- MoReq2010 introduces the concept of "aggregations" versus a traditional file structure.

- Australia was an early leader in defining recordkeeping standards.

- Australia and New Zealand have adopted national versions of ISO 16175.

- Guidance on standards can be found at ISO.org, from trade associations like ARMA.org and IRMS.org.uk, rimpa.com.au, and from national archives websites.

Notes

1. E-mail to author from Marc Fresko, May 13, 2012.
2. MoReq, 2009, http://moreq2.eu/other-specifications (accessed July 12, 2012).
3. Hans Hofman, "The Use of Standards and Models," in *Managing Electronic Records, ed. Julie McLeod and Catherine Hare (London: Facet Publishing, 2005)*, 19.
4. ANSI, "About ANSI Overview," www.ansi.org/about_ansi/overview/overview.aspx?menuid=1 (accessed May 3, 2012).
5. National Institute of Standards and Technology, "Guidelines for Media Sanitation: Recommendations of the National Institute of Standards and Technology," NIST Special Publication 800-88, September 2006, http://csrc.nist.gov/publications/nistpubs/800-88/NISTSP800-88_with-errata.pdf.
6. BSI, "About BSI Group," www.bsigroup.com/en/About-BSI/ (accessed July 12, 2012).
7. Hofman, "The Use of Standards and Models," 20–21.
8. Ibid.
9. International Organization for Standardization, "ISO 15489-1:2001 Information and Documentation—Records Management. Part 1: General" (Geneva: ISO, 2001), section 3.16.
10. National Archives of Australia, www.naa.gov.au/records-management/publications/DIRKS-manual.aspx (accessed October 15, 2012).
11. International Council on Archives, "ICA-Req: Principles and Functional Requirements for Records in Electronic Office Environments: Guidelines and Training Material," November 29, 2011, www.ica.org/11696/activities-and-projects/icareq-principles-and-functional-requirements-for-records-in-electronic-office environments-guidelines-and-training-material.html.
12. Council of Australasian Archives and Records Authorities (CAARA), www.caara.org.au (accessed May 3, 2012).
13. Adrian Cunningham, blog post comment, May 11, 2011, http://thinkingrecords.co.uk/2011/05/06/how-moreq-2010-differs-from-previous-electronic-records-management-erm-system-specifications.
14. Ibid.
15. "Relationship between The ISO 30300 Series of Standards and Other Products of ISO/TC 46/SC 11: Records processes and controls," White paper, by ISO TC46/SC11—Archives/records management, March 2012, www.iso30300.es/wp-content/uploads/2012/03/ISOTC46SC11_White_paper_relationship_30300_technical_standards12032012v6.pdf.
16 Ibid.
17. ISO 22310:2006, "Information and Documentation—Guidelines for Standards Drafters for Stating Records Management Requirements in Standards," www.iso.org/iso/iso_catalogue/catalogue_tc/catalogue_detail.htm?csnumber=40899 (accessed May 5, 2012).
18. International Organization for Standardization, "ISO 23081-1:2006 Information and Documentation—Records Management Processes—Metadata for Records—Part 1: Principles," www.iso.org/iso/iso_catalogue/catalogue_tc/catalogue_detail.htm?csnumber=40832 (accessed May 5, 2012).

19. International Organization for Standardization, "ISO 23081-2:2009 Information and Documentation—Managing Metadata for Records—Part 2: Conceptual and Implementation Issues," www.iso.org/iso/iso_catalogue/catalogue_tc/catalogue_detail.htm?csnumber=50863 (accessed May 5, 2012).
20. Ibid.
21. International Organization for Standardization, "ISO/TR 23081-3:2011 Information and Documentation—Managing Metadata for Records—Part 3: Self-Assessment Method," www.iso.org/iso/iso_catalogue/catalogue_tc/catalogue_detail.htm?csnumber=57121 (accessed May 5, 2012).
22. International Organization for Standardization, "ISO/TR 26122:2008 Information and Documentation—Work Process Analysis for Records," www.iso.org/iso/iso_catalogue/catalogue_tc/catalogue_detail.htm?csnumber=43391 (accessed May 5, 2012).
23. Ibid.
24. International Organization for Standardization, "ISO 10244:2010 Document Management—Business Process Baselining and Analysis," www.iso.org/iso/catalogue_detail.htm?csnumber=45935 (accessed July 23, 2012).
25. Virginia A. Jones, "Standards for Establishing Records and Information Management Programs," *Information Management*, July/August, 2012, http://content.arma.org/IMM/July-August2012/rimfundamentalsstandardsforestablishing.aspx.
26. Swedish Standards Institute, "Information and Documentation—Digital Records Conversion and Migration Process (ISO 13008:2012, IDT)," www.sis.se/en/standard/std-86731 (accessed July 23, 2012).
27. "Relationship between The ISO 30300 Series of Standards and Other Products of ISO/TC 46/SC 11."
28. International Organization for Standardization, "ISO/TR 13028:2010 Information and Documentation—Implementation Guidelines for Digitization of Records," www.iso.org/iso/iso_catalogue/catalogue_tc/catalogue_detail.htm?csnumber=52391 (accessed May 5, 2012).
29. International Organization for Standardization, "ISO/TR 15801:2009 Document Management—Information Stored Electronically—Recommendations for Trustworthiness and Reliability," www.iso.org/iso/home/store/catalogue_tc/catalogue_detail.htm?csnumber=50499 (accessed July 23, 2012).
30. Ibid.
31. American National Standards Institute (ANSI), ISO 18923:2000, "Imaging Materials—Polyester-Base Magnetic Tape—Storage Practices," http://webstore.ansi.org/RecordDetail.aspx?sku=ISO+18923:2000 (accessed July 23, 2012).
32. International Organization for Standardization, "ISO 19005-1:2005 Document Management—Electronic Document File Format for Long-Term Preservation—Part 1: Use of PDF 1.4 (PDF/A-1)," www.iso.org/iso/catalogue_detail?csnumber=38920 (accessed July 23, 2012).
33. International Organization for Standardization, "ISO 14721:2003 Space Data and Information Transfer Systems Open Archival Information System—Reference Model," www.iso.org/iso/catalogue_detail.htm?csnumber=24683 (accessed May 21, 2012).
34. Ibid.
35. Charles Dollar and Lori Ashley, Chapter 17 of this book.
36. International Organization for Standardization, "ISO 16363:2012 Space Data and Information Transfer Systems—Audit and Certification of Trustworthy Digital Repositories," www.iso.org/iso/iso_catalogue/catalogue_tc/catalogue_detail.htm?csnumber=56510 (accessed July 23, 2012).
37. Charles Dollar and Lori Ashley, Chapter 17 of this book.
38. International Organization for Standardization, "ISO/IEC 27002:2005 Information Technology—Security Techniques—Code of Practice for Information Security Management," www.iso.org/iso/catalogue_detail?csnumber=50297 (accessed July 23, 2012).
39. Ibid.
40. International Organization for Standardization, "ISO 8601:2004 Data Elements and Interchange Formats—Information Interchange—Representation of Dates and Times," www.iso.org/iso/home/store/catalogue_ics/catalogue_detail_ics.htm?ics1=01&ics2=140&ics3=30&csnumber=40874 (accessed October 15, 2012).
41. International Organization for Standardization, "ISO/TR 26122:2008 Information and Documentation—Work Process Analysis for Records," www.iso.org/iso/home/store/catalogue_tc/catalogue_detail.htm?csnumber=43391 (accessed July 23, 2012).
42. American National Standards Institute (ANSI), ANSI/ARMA 19-2012, "Policy Design for Managing Electronic Messages," http://webstore.ansi.org/RecordDetail.aspx?sku=ANSI%2FARMA+19-2012 (accessed July 23, 2012).
43. Jones, "Standards for Establishing Records and Information Management Programs.
44. Ibid.
45. Techstreet, ANSI/AIIM TR31-2004, "Legal Acceptance of Records Produced by Information Technology Systems," Association for Information and Image Management Staff, AIIM International—The

Enterprise Content Management Association, December 26, 2004, www.techstreet.com/cgi-bin/detail?doc_no=aiim|tr31_2004;product_id=1221185.

46. Ibid.

47. Information Access Division (IAD), Digital Media Group (DMG), updated January 3, 2008, www.itl.nist.gov/iad/894.05/publications.html.

48. NIST, "Quick Reference Guide for Care and Handling," www.itl.nist.gov/iad/894.05/papers/onepage.pdf (accessed July 23, 2012).

49. Richard Kissel, Matthew Scholl, Steven Skolochenko, and Xing Li, "Guidelines for Media Sanitization: Recommendations of the National Institute of Standards and Technology," NIST Special Publication 800-88, September 2006, http://csrc.nist.gov/publications/nistpubs/800-88/NISTSP800-88_with-errata.pdf.

50. Ibid.

51. Accessed at http://www.nas.gov.uk/recordKeeping/ERGuidance/Standards.asp on February 12, 2013.

52. Julie Gable, *Information Management Journal*, November 1, 2002, www.thefreelibrary.com/Everything+you+wanted+to+know+about+DoD+5015.2:+the+standard+is+not+a...-a095630076.

53. JITC, "DoD 5015.2-STD—What's the Big Deal?," http://jitc.fhu.disa.mil/cgi/rma/dod50152bigdeal.aspx (accessed May 5, 2012).

54. Ibid.

55. Ibid.

56. These standards were developed by the CGSB (Canadian General Standards Board), which is a standards-writing agency within Public Works and Government Services Canada (a department of the federal government). It is accredited by the Standards Council of Canada as a standards development agency. The Council must certify that standards have been developed by the required procedures before it will designate them as being National Standards of Canada. *72.34* incorporates by reference as "normative references": (1) many of the standards of the International Organization for Standardization (ISO) in Geneva, Switzerland. ("ISO," derived from the Greek word *isos* (equal) so as to provide a common acronym for all languages); and (2) several of the standards of the Canadian Standards Association (CSA). The "Normative references" section of 72.34 (p. 2) states that these "referenced documents are indispensable for the application of this document." 72.11 cites (p. 2, "Applicable Publications") several standards of the American National Standards Institute/Association for Information and Image Management (ANSI/AIIM) as publications "applicable to this standard." The process by which the National Standards of Canada are created and maintained is described within the standards themselves (reverse side of the front cover), and on the CGSB's website (see, "Standards Development"), from which website these standards may be obtained; www.ongc-cgsb.gc.ca.

57. The Canada Revenue Agency (CRA) informs the public of its policies and procedures by means, among others, of its *Information Circulars* (IC's), and *GST/HST Memoranda*. (GST: goods and services tax; HST: harmonized sales tax, *i.e.*, the harmonization of federal and provincial sales taxes into one retail sales tax.) In particular, see: *IC05-1*, dated June 2010, entitled, *Electronic Record Keeping*, paragraphs 24, 26 and 28. Note that use of the National Standard cited in paragraph 26, *Microfilm and Electronic Images as Documentary Evidence* CAN/CGSB-72.11-93 is mandatory for, "Imaging and microfilm (including microfiche) reproductions of books of original entry and source documents . . ." Paragraph 24 recommends the use of the newer national standard, *Electronic Records as Documentary Evidence* CAN/CGSB-72.34-2005, "To ensure the reliability, integrity and authenticity of electronic records." However, if this newer standard is given the same treatment by CRA as the older standard, it will be made mandatory as well. And similar statements appear in the GST Memoranda, *Computerized Records* 500-1-2, *Books and Records* 500-1. IC05-1. *Electronic Record Keeping*, concludes with the note, "Most Canada Revenue Agency publications are available on the CRA website www.cra.gc.ca under the heading 'Forms and Publications.'"

58. There are more than 200 specific compliance tests that can be applied to determine if the principles of 72.34 are being complied with. The analysts—a combined team of records management and legal expertise—analyze: (1) the nature of the business involved; (2) the uses and value of its records for its various functions; (3) the likelihood and risk of the various types of its records being the subject of legal proceedings, or of their being challenged by some regulating authority; and (4) the consequences of the unavailability of acceptable records—for example, the consequences of its records not being accepted in legal proceedings. Similarly, in regard to the older National Standard of Canada, 72.11, there is a comparable series of more than 50 tests that can be applied to determine the state of compliance with its principles.

59. *Electronic Records as Documentary Evidence* CAN/CGSB-72.34-2005 ("72.34"), clause 5.4.3 c) at p. 17; and *Microfilm and Electronic Images as Documentary Evidence* CAN/CGSB-72.11-93 ("72.11"), paragraph 4.1.2 at p. 2, *supra* note 49.

60. Ibid., 72.34, Clause 5.4.3.
61. "Admissibility" refers to the procedure by which a presiding judge determines if a record or other proffered evidence is acceptable as evidence according the rules of evidence. "Electronic discovery" is the compulsory exchange of relevant records by the parties to legal proceedings prior to trial." As to the admissibility of records as evidence see: Ken Chasse, "The Admissibility of Electronic Business Records" (2010), 8 Canadian Journal of Law and Technology 105; and Ken Chasse, "Electronic Records for Evidence and Disclosure and Discovery" (2011) 57 The Criminal Law Quarterly 284. For the electronic discovery of records see: Ken Chasse, "Electronic Discovery—*Sedona Canada* is Inadequate on Records Management—Here's *Sedona Canada* in Amended Form," *Canadian Journal of Law and Technology* 9 (2011): 135; and Ken Chasse, "Electronic Discovery in the Criminal Court System," *Canadian Criminal Law Review* 14 (2010): 111. See also note 18 *infra*, and accompanying text.
62. For the province of Quebec, comparable provisions are contained in Articles 2831-2842, 2859-2862, 2869-2874 of Book 7 "Evidence" of the Civil Code of Quebec, S.Q. 1991, c. C-64, to be read in conjunction with, An Act to Establish a Legal Framework for Information Technology, R.S.Q. 2001, c. C-1.1, ss. 2, 5-8, and 68.
63. For the legislative jurisdiction of the federal and provincial governments in Canada, see The Constitution Act, 1867 (U.K.) 30 & 31 Victoria, c. 3, s. 91 (federal), and s. 92 (provincial), www.canlii.org/en/ca/laws/stat/30—31-vict-c-3/latest/30—31-vict-c-3.html.
64. The two provinces of Alberta and Newfoundland and Labrador do not have business record provisions in their Evidence Acts. Therefore "admissibility" would be determined in those jurisdictions by way of the court decisions that define the applicable common law rules; such decisions as, *Ares v. Venner* [1970] S.C.R. 608, 14 D.L.R. (3d) 4 (S.C.C.), and decisions that have applied it.
65. See for example, the Canada Evidence Act, R.S.C. 1985, c. C-5, ss. 31.1-31.8; Alberta Evidence Act, R.S.A. 2000, c. A-18, ss. 41.1-41.8; (Ontario) Evidence Act, R.S.O. 1990, c. E.23, s. 34.1; and the (Nova Scotia) Evidence Act, R.S.N.S. 1989, c. 154, ss. 23A-23G. The Evidence Acts of the two provinces of British Columbia and Newfoundland and Labrador do not contain electronic record provisions. However, because an electronic record is no better than the quality of the record system in which it is recorded or stored, its "integrity" (reliability, credibility) will have to be determined under the other provincial laws that determine the admissibility of records as evidence.
66. The electronic record provisions have been in the Evidence Acts in Canada since 2000. They have been applied to admit electronic records into evidence, but they have not yet received any detailed analysis by the courts.
67. This is the wording used in, for example, s. 41.6 of the Alberta Evidence Act, s. 34.1(8) of the (Ontario) Evidence Act; and s. 23F of the (Nova Scotia) Evidence Act, *supra* note 10. Section 31.5 of the Canada Evidence Act, *supra* note 58, uses the same wording, the only significant difference being that the word "document" is used instead of "record." For the province of Quebec, see sections 12 and 68 of, An Act to Establish a Legal Framework for Information Technology, R.S.Q., chapter C-1.1.
68. *Supra* notes 54 to 59 and accompanying texts.
69. *Supra* notes 49 and 52 and accompanying texts.
70. *Supra* note 50 and accompanying text.
71. All 14 jurisdictions of Canada have electronic commerce legislation except for the Northwest Territories. See for example, the Personal Information Protection and Electronic Documents Act, S.C. 2000, c. 5, Parts 2 and 3; Ontario's Electronic Commerce Act, 2000, S.O. 2000, c. 17; and British Columbia's Electronic Transactions Act, R.B.C. 20001, c. 10. The concept of "system integrity" in the Evidence Acts (*supra* note 58 and accompanying text), is also found in the electronic commerce legislation. See for example, s. 8 of the Ontario Electronic Commerce Act, 2000, under the heading, "Legal Requirement re Original Documents."
72. For example, Part 1, "Personal Information Protection," of the federal Personal Information Protection and Electronic Documents Act (PIPEDA), S.C. 2000, c. 5, which applies within provincial legislative jurisdiction as well as federal, until a province enacts its own personal information protection Act (a PIPA), which displaces it in the provincial sphere. British Columbia, Alberta, and Quebec are the only provinces that have done so.
73. The dominant guideline for electronic discovery in Canada is *The Sedona Canada Principles—Addressing Electronic Discovery*; online: The Sedona Conference, Canada, January 2008, www.thesedonaconference.com/content/miscFiles/canada_pincpls_FINAL_108.pdf   or   www.thesedonaconference.org/dltForm?did=canada_pincpls_FINAL_108.pdf. See also the E-Discovery Canada website, hosted by LexUM (at the University of Montreal), online: www.lexum.umontreal.ca and the law journal articles concerning electronic discovery cited in note 54 *supra*.
74. *Supra* notes 52 and 53 and accompanying texts.

75. See *The Sedona Canada Commentary on Proportionality in Electronic Disclosure & Discovery*, available from The Sedona Conference, Working Group 7 series, October 2010; online: www.thesedonaconference .org/dltForm?did=Canadian_Proportianality.pdf. See also: *The Sedona Canada Commentary on Practical Approaches for Cost Containment—Best Practices for Managing the Preservation, Collection, Processing, Review & Analysis of Electronically Stored Information*, April 2011, available from the Sedona Conference, Working Group 7 series; online: www.thesedonaconference.org/dltForm?did=cost_containment.pdf.
76. See "Comment 11.e. Reasonable Records Management Policies," at p. 38 of *The Sedona Canada Principles—Addressing Electronic Discovery*, *supra* note 66.
77. See the discussion of this principle in the law journal articles concerning electronic discovery cited in note 54 *supra*.
78. The "prime directive," *supra* note 52 and 53 and accompanying texts.
79. The "relied-upon printout" is one that is relied upon for the accuracy of its content, quite apart from the quality of the electronic records system from which the printout comes. For example, a printout of a contract might be relied upon to settle the rights and obligations of the contracting parties without regard to the ability of the electronic records system from which such printout comes to satisfy the "system integrity" test of the Evidence Acts, which test would otherwise be applicable. See for example: s. 31.2(2) of the Canada Evidence Act, R.S.C. 1985, c. C-5; s. 34.1(6) of the (Ontario) Evidence Act, R.S.O. 1990, c. E.23; and s. 41.4(3) of the Alberta Evidence Act, R.S.A. 2000, c. A-18.
80. For Quebec, see the legislation cited in note 55, *supra*. Note that "business" includes all types of commercial and institutional activity.
81. See the text accompanying note 60 *supra*.
82. See the text accompanying notes 61 to 66 *supra*.
83. "Giving Value: Funding Priorities for UK Archives 2005–2010," a key new report launched by the National Council on Archives (NCA) in November 2005, www.nationalarchives.gov.uk/documents/ standards_guidance.pdf (accessed October 15, 2012).
84. Ulrich Kampffmeyer, Project-Consult, e-mail to author, August 2, 2012.
85. MoReq, www.moreq2.eu (accessed May 5, 2012).
86. Downloadable (in English and in numerous translations) from www.cornwell.co.uk/edrm/moreq.asp, published in paper form as ISBN 92-894-1290-9 by the Office for Official Publications of the European Communities, Luxembourg.
87. Downloadable (in English and in numerous translations) from http://dlmforum.eu/index .php?option=com_jotloader&view=categories&cid=10_f56391a0c9ea9456bf24e80b514f5dda&Itemid =145&lang=en, published in paper form as ISBN 978-92-09772-0 by the Office for Official Publications of the European Communities, Luxembourg.
88. DLM Forum Foundation, *MoReq2010®: Modular Requirements for Records Systems—Volume 1: Core Services & Plug-in Modules*, 2011, http://moreq2010.eu/ (accessed May 7, 2012); published in paper form as ISBN 978-92-79-18519-9 by the Publications Office of the European Communities, Luxembourg.
89. DLM Forum, "Information Governance across Europe," www.dlmforum.eu (accessed December 14, 2010).
90. James Lappin, "MoReq2010 Update," *Thinking Records blog*, January 5, 2012, http://thinkingrecords .co.uk/2012/01/05/moreq2010-update.
91. Ibid.
92. Ibid.
93. Ibid.
94. Marc Fresko telephone interview with author, April 23, 2012.
95. James Lappin, "How MoReq 2010 Differs from Previous Electronic Records Management (ERM) System Specifications," *Thinking Records blog*, May 6, 2011, http://thinkingrecords.co.uk/2011/05/06/ how-moreq-2010-differs-from-previous-electronic-records-management-erm-system-specifications/.
96. Ibid.
97. Ibid.
98. Ibid.
99. E-mail to author from Marc Fresko, May 13, 2012.
100. National Archives of Australia, "Australian and International Standards," 2012, www.naa.gov.au/ records-management/strategic-information/standards/ASISOstandards.aspx (accessed July 16, 2012).
101. E-mail to author from Marc Fresko, May 13, 2012.
102. National Archives of Australia, "Australian Government Recordkeeping Metadata Standard," 2012, www.naa.gov.au/records-management/publications/agrk-metadata-standard.aspx (accessed July 16, 2012).
103. Ibid.

104. National Archives of Australia, "Australian and International Standards," 2012, www.naa.gov.au/re-cords-management/strategic-information/standards/ASISOstandards.aspx (accessed July 16, 2012).
105. MoReq, "Other Specifications," 2009, www.moreq2.eu/other-specifications/categories/6_6055e8015559f394b183125350784ef2 (accessed July 16, 2012).
106. d.velop, "Top-Bewertung: DOMEA 2.0 Zertifikat für die d.velop AG," www.d-velop.de/de/news/information/Seiten/DOMEA20Zertifikatf%C3%BCrdiedvelopAG.aspx (accessed July 16, 2012).
107. Ulrich Kampffmeyer, Project-Consult, e-mail to author, August 2, 2012.
108. Archives New Zealand, "Digital Recordkeeping Standard," August 2010, http://archives.govt.nz/advice/continuum-resource-kit/continuum-publications-html/s5-digital-recordkeeping-standard.
109. MoReq, "Other Specifications."

CHAPTER 16

Metadata Governance, Standards, and Strategies

*M*etadata can be a scary term to a lot of people. It just *sounds* complicated. And it can get complicated. It is often defined as "data about data," which is true but somewhat confusing, and this does not provide enough information for most people to understand.

"Meta" derives from the Greek word that means "alongside, with, after, next." Metadata can be defined as "structured data about other data."[1]

In **electronic records management** (ERM), metadata identifies a record and its contents. *ERM metadata describes a record's characteristics so that it may be classified more easily and completely.* Metadata fields, or *terms*, for e-records can be as basic as identifying the name of the document, the creator or originating department, the subject, the date it was created, the document type, the length of the document, its security classification, and its file type.

Creating standardized metadata terms is part of an information governance (IG) effort that enables faster, more complete, and more accurate searches and retrieval of records. This is important not only in everyday business operations, but also, for example, when searching through potentially millions of records during the discovery phase of litigation.

Good metadata management also assists in the maintenance of corporate memory, and improving accountability in business operations.[2]

Using a standardized format and controlled vocabulary provides a "precise and comprehensible description of content, location, and value."[3] *Using a controlled vocabulary means your organization has standardized a set of terms used for metadata elements describing records.* This "ensures consistency across a collection" and helps with optimizing search and retrieval functions and records research, as well as meeting e-discovery requests, compliance demands, and other legal and regulatory requirements. Your organization may, for instance, decide to use the standardized Library of Congress Subject Headings as standard terms for the "subject" metadata field.[4]

Metadata also describes a record's relationships with other documents and records, and what actions may have been taken on the record over time. This helps to track its history and development.

The role of metadata in managing records is multifaceted; it helps to:

- Identify the records, record creators and users, and the areas within which they are utilized.

Metadata terms or fields describe a record's characteristics so that it may be classified, managed, and found more easily.

- Determine the relationships between records and the knowledge workers who use them, and the relationships between the records and the business processes they are supporting.
- Assist in managing and preserving the content and structure of the record.
- Support IG efforts that outline who has access to records, and the context (when and where) in which access to the records is granted.
- Provide an audit trail to document changes to or actions upon the record and its metadata.
- Support the finding and understanding of records and their relationships.[5]

In addition, good metadata management provides additional business benefits including increased management control over records, improved records authenticity and security, and reusability of metadata.[6]

Often, organizations will establish mandatory metadata terms that must accompany a record, and some optional ones that may help in identifying and finding it. *A record is more complete with more metadata terms included, which also facilitates search and retrieval of records.*[7] This is particularly the case when knowledge workers are not quite sure which records they are searching for, and therefore enter some vague or conceptual search terms. So, the more detail that is in the metadata fields, the more likely the end user is to find the records they need to complete their work. This provides a measurable productivity benefit to the organization, although it is difficult to quantify. Certainly, search times will decrease upon implementation of a standardized metadata program, and improved work output and decisions will also follow.

Standardizing the metadata terms, definitions, and classifications for documents and records is done by developing and enforcing IG policy. This standardization effort gives users confidence that the records they are looking for are, in fact, the complete and current set they need to work with. And it provides the basis for a *legally defensible* records management program that will hold up in court.

A metadata governance program must be an ongoing effort that keeps metadata up-to-date and accurate. Often, once a metadata project is complete, attention to it wanes and maintenance tasks are not executed and soon the accuracy and completeness of searches for documents and records deteriorates. So metadata maintenance is an ongoing process and it must be formalized into a program that is periodically checked, tested, and audited.

Metadata terms can be as basic as the name of the document, the creator, the subject, the date it was created, the document type, the length of the document, its security classification, and its file type.

A metadata governance and management program must be ongoing.

Types of Metadata

There are several types or categories of metadata, including:

Descriptive metadata. Metadata that describes the intellectual content of a resource and is used for the indexing, discovery, and identification of a digital resource.

Administrative metadata. Metadata that includes management information about the digital resource, such as ownership and rights management.

Structural metadata. Metadata that is used to display and navigate digital resources and describes relationships between multiple digital files, such as page order in a digitized book.

Technical metadata. Metadata that describes the features of the digital file, such as resolution, pixel dimension, and hardware. The information is critical for migration and long-term sustainability of the digital resource.

Preservation metadata. Metadata that specifically captures information that helps facilitate management and access to digital files over time. This inherently includes descriptive, administrative, structural, and technical metadata elements that focus on the provenance, authenticity, preservation activity, technical environment, and rights management of an object.[8]

Core Metadata Issues

Some key considerations and questions that need to be answered for effective implementation of a metadata governance program are:

- **Who is the audience?** Which users will be using the metadata in their daily operations? What is their skill level? Which metadata terms/fields are most important to them? What has been their approach to working with documents and records in the past and how can it be streamlined or improved? What terms are important to management? How can the metadata schema be designed to accommodate the primary audience and other secondary audiences? Answers to these questions will come only with close consultation with these key stakeholders.[9]

The main types of metadata are: descriptive, administrative, structural, technical, and preservation metadata.

- **Who else can help?** That is, which other stakeholders can help build a consensus on the best metadata strategy and approach? What other records creators, users, custodians, auditors, and legal counsel personnel can be added to the team to design a metadata approach that maximizes its value to the organization? Are there subject matter experts (SMEs)? What standards and best practices can be applied across functional boundaries to improve the ability of various groups to collaborate and leverage the metadata?
- **How can metadata governance be implemented and maintained?** Creating IG guidelines and rules for metadata assignment, input, and upkeep are a critical step—but how will the program continue to be updated to maintain its value to the organization? What business processes and audit checks should be in place? How will the quality of the metadata be monitored and controlled? Who is accountable?
- **What will the user training program look like?** How will users be trained initially, and how will continued education and reinforcement be communicated? Will there be periodic meetings of the IG or metadata team to discuss issues and concerns? What is the process for adding or amending metadata terms as the business progresses and changes? These questions must be answered and a documented plan must be in place.
- **What will the communications plan be?** Management time and resources are also needed to continue the practice of informing and updating users, and encouraging compliance with internal metadata standards and policies. Users need to know on a consistent basis why metadata is important and the value that good metadata management can bring to the organization.[10]

International Metadata Standards and Guidance

Metadata is what gives an e-record its record status, or, in other words, electronic records metadata is what makes an electronic file a record. There are a number of established international standards for metadata structure, and additional guidance on strategy and implementation has been provided by standards groups such as ISO and ANSI/NISO, and other bodies, such as the Dublin Core Metadata Initiative (DCMI).

ISO 15489 Records Management Definitions and Relevance

The international records management standard ISO 15489 states that "a record should correctly reflect what was communicated or decided or what action was taken. It should be able to support the needs of the business to which it relates and be used for accountability purposes" and its metadata definition is "data describing context, content, and structure of records and their management through time."[11]

A key difference between a document and a record is that a record is fixed, whereas a document can continue to be edited. Preventing records from being edited can be partly accomplished by indicating their formal record status in a metadata field, among other controls.

Proving that a record is, in fact, authentic and reliable, necessarily includes proving that its metadata has remained intact and unaltered through the entire chain of custody of the record.

Proving that a record is authentic and reliable includes proving that its metadata has remained intact and unaltered through the record's entire chain of custody.

ISO Technical Specification 23081–1: 2006 Information and Documentation—Records Management Processes—Metadata for Records—Part 1: Principles

ISO 23081–1 "covers the principles that underpin and govern records management metadata. These principles apply through time to:

- Records and their metadata;
- all processes that affect them;
- any system in which they reside;
- any organization that is responsible for their management."[12]

The ISO 23081–1 standard provides guidance for metadata management within the "framework" of ISO 15489, and addresses the relevance and roles that metadata plays in records management intensive business processes. There are *no mandatory* metadata terms set, as these will differ by organization and by location and governing national and state/provincial laws.[13] The standard lists 10 purposes or benefits of using metadata in records management, which can help build the argument for convincing users and managers of the importance of good metadata governance, and its resultant benefits.

Dublin Core Metadata Initiative

The DCMI produced a basic or core set of metadata terms that have served as the basis for many public and private sector metadata governance initiatives. Initial work in workshops filled with experts from around the world took place in 1995 in Dublin, Ohio (*not* Ireland). From these working groups the idea of a set of "core metadata" or essential metadata elements with generic descriptions arose.[14] "The fifteen-element 'Dublin Core' achieved wide dissemination as part of the Open Archives Initiative Protocol for Metadata Harvesting (OAI-PMH) and has been ratified as IETF RFC 5013, ANSI/NISO Standard Z39.85–2007, and ISO Standard 15836:2009."

Dublin Core has as its goals:[15]

Simplicity of creation and maintenance

The Dublin Core element set has been kept as small and simple as possible to allow a nonspecialist to create simple descriptive records for information

ISO 23081 defines needed metadata for records, and provides guidance for metadata management within the "framework" of ISO 15489.

> Goals of the Dublin Core Metadata Initiative are simplicity, commonly understood semantics, international scope, and extensibility.

resources easily and inexpensively, while providing for effective retrieval of those resources in the networked environment.

Commonly understood semantics

Discovery of information across the vast commons of the Internet is hindered by differences in terminology and descriptive practices from one field of knowledge to the next. The Dublin Core can help the "digital tourist"—a nonspecialist searcher—find his or her way by supporting a common set of elements, the semantics of which are universally understood and supported. For example, scientists concerned with locating articles by a particular author, and art scholars interested in works by a particular artist, can agree on the importance of a "creator" element. Such convergence on a common, if slightly more generic, element set increases the visibility and accessibility of all resources, both within a given discipline and beyond.

International scope

The Dublin Core Element Set was originally developed in English, but versions are being created in many other languages, including Finnish, Norwegian, Thai, Japanese, French, Portuguese, German, Greek, Indonesian, and Spanish. The DCMI Localization and Internationalization Special Interest Group is coordinating efforts to link these versions in a distributed registry.

Although the technical challenges of internationalization on the World Wide Web have not been directly addressed by the Dublin Core development community, the involvement of representatives from virtually every continent has ensured that the development of the standard considers the multilingual and multicultural nature of the electronic information universe.

Extensibility

While balancing the needs for simplicity in describing digital resources with the need for precise retrieval, Dublin Core developers have recognized the importance of providing a mechanism for extending the DC element set for additional resource discovery needs. It is expected that other communities of metadata experts will create and administer additional metadata sets, specialized to the needs of their communities. Metadata elements from these sets could be used in conjunction with Dublin Core metadata to meet the need for interoperability. The DCMI Usage Board is presently working on a model for accomplishing this in the context of "application profiles."

"The fifteen element 'Dublin Core' described in this standard is part of a larger set of metadata vocabularies and technical specifications maintained by the Dublin

Core Metadata Initiative (DCMI). The full set of vocabularies, DCMI Metadata Terms [DCMI-TERMS], also includes sets of resource classes (including the DCMI Type Vocabulary [DCMI-TYPE]), vocabulary encoding schemes, and syntax encoding schemes. The terms in DCMI vocabularies are intended to be used in combination with terms from other, compatible vocabularies in the context of application profiles and on the basis of the DCMI Abstract Model [DCAM]."[16]

Global Information Locator Service

Global Information Locator Service *(GILS) is ISO 23950, the international standard for information searching* over networked (client/server) computers, which is a simplified version of structured query language (SQL). ISO 23950 is a federated search protocol that equates to the U.S. standard ANSI/NISO Z39.50. The U.S. Library of Congress is the official maintenance agency for both standards, "which are technically identical (though with minor editorial differences)."[17]

ISO 23950 grew out of the library science community, although it is widely used, particularly in the public sector.[18] The use of GILS has tapered off as other metadata standards, at the international, national, industry level, and agency level have been established.[19]

"It [GILS] specifies procedures and formats for a client to search a database provided by a server, retrieve database records, and perform related information retrieval functions." While it does not specify a format, information retrieval can be accomplished through full-text search, although it "also supports large, complex information collections." The standard specifies how searches are made and how results are returned.

GILS helps people find information, especially in large, complex environments, such as across multiple government agencies. It is used in over 40 U.S. states and a number of countries, including Argentina, Australia, Brazil, Canada, France, Germany, Hong Kong, India, Spain, Sweden, Switzerland, United Kingdom, and many others.[20]

National Metadata Standards

National governments have set forth metadata standards for use within their countries. Below is a review of available metadata standards for the United States, Canada, United Kingdom, and Australia.

United States

In the United States, the DoD 5015.2 standard specifies basic required metadata, but not format, so that 5015.2-compliant ERM systems from differing vendors may not be able to easily share and search metadata across servers. Vendors have an interest in keeping a customer's e-records locked into their proprietary metadata format, making a move away from the vendor more costly and difficult.

ISO 23950 (GILS) is the international standard for information searching over networked computers.

Multiple federal government agencies, such as the Food and Drug Administration, have established metadata standards to facilitate the search and exchange of e-records. Also, many states have established metadata standards for records; Minnesota was an early pioneer in establishing the Minnesota Recordkeeping Metadata Standard (Minnesota Office of Enterprise Technology standard IRM 20), which was established in 2003.[21] It uses 20 elements, requiring 10, and is based on Dublin Core and also other Minnesota-specific metadata guidelines.

Canada

A standard approach to metadata structure has been put forth by the Canadian government for use within and between the Government of Canada (GC) in agencies and institutions, titled, "The **Government of Canada Records Management Metadata Standard** (GC RMMS)." The effort to standardize and streamline metadata structures is aimed at making information easier to find, and thus yielding more complete searches of records, regardless of where they are in their lifecycle. This ultimately is intended to improve decision-making within the GC.[22]

"Metadata identified in the GC RMMS helps institutions to meet their legislative, regulatory, policy, and compliance requirements. It supports the implementation of the GC's Management of Government Information Policy (MGI Policy), the purpose of which is to 'ensure that information under the control of the Government of Canada is managed effectively and efficiently throughout its life cycle.'"

GC RMMS is aimed at doing what all proper metadata governance efforts should do: standardizing the metadata terms within the overall organization, which improves access and findability across large records collections. Further, it helps to support archiving and record preservation efforts by Library and Archives Canada to help ensure that records contain the proper metadata to facilitate "continued access and retrieval."

"The Government of Canada Records Management Application Profile (GC RMAP) is a companion document to the Government of Canada Records Management Metadata Standard (GC RMMS). The latter defines the semantics of each element while the former provides business rules for the use of each element and the relationships among elements. The GC RMAP encompasses the core set of elements necessary to ensure the authenticity, reliability, integrity and usability of records as espoused by ISO International Standard 15489–1 and ISO Technical Specification 23081–1."[23]

United Kingdom

In the United Kingdom, the metadata standard for the public sector is the e-Government Metadata Standard (eGMS), which mandates the following metadata terms:[24]

1. *Accessibility*—Indicates the resource's availability and usability to specific groups.
2. *Addressee*—The person (or persons) to whom the resource was addressed.

Metadata terms in the GC Records Management Metadata Standard helps Canadian institutions meet their legislative, regulatory, policy, and compliance requirements.

3. *Aggregation*—The resource's level or position in a hierarchy.
4. *Audience*—A category of user for whom the resource is intended.
5. *Contributor*—An entity responsible for making contributions to the content of the resource.
6. *Coverage*—The extent or scope of the content of the resource.
7. *Creator*—An entity primarily responsible for making the content of the resource.
8. *Date*—A date associated with an event in the life cycle of the resource.
9. *Definition*—An account of the content of the resource.
10. *Digital signature*—the presence of a digital signature to verify the identity of any persons taking action on the record.
11. *Disposal*—The retention and disposal instructions for the resource.
12. *Format*—The physical or digital manifestation of the resource.
13. *Identifier*—An unambiguous reference to the resource within a given context.
14. *Language*—A language of the intellectual content of the resource.
15. *Location*—The physical location of the resource.
16. *Mandate*—Legislative or other mandate under which the resource was produced.
17. *Preservation*—Information to support the long-term preservation of a resource.
18. *Publisher*—An entity responsible for making the resource available.
19. *Relation*—A reference to a related resource.
20. *Rights*—Information about rights held in and over the resource.
21. *Source*—A reference to a resource from which the present resource is derived.
22. *Status*—The position or state of the resource.
23. *Subject*—A topic of the content of the resource.
24. *Title*—A name given to the resource.
25. *Type*—The nature or genre of the content of the resource.[25]

Australia

Australia has adopted and mandated the use of the Australian Government Locator Service (AGLS) Metadata Standard. It is intended to help "improve the visibility and accessibility" of records, web services, and linked or interfaced business applications.[26] AGLS is the **AS 5044:2010** standard, as issued by Standards Australia.

Work on the metadata standard began in December 1997. It was originally released in 1998 and has since then gone through several revisions and updates.

"The AGLS Metadata Standard is an application profile (a set of metadata properties, policies and guidelines defined for a particular application or implementation) of Dublin Core metadata. Dublin Core metadata aims to facilitate description of a wide range of networked resources. The DCMES used a minimal set of properties, the semantics (meanings) of which were established through consensus by an international, cross-disciplinary group of professionals from librarianship, archives, computer science, text encoding, the museum community, and other related fields of scholarship."[27]

The Australian AGLS Metadata Standard leverages Dublin Core metadata terms.

"The 2010 revision supersedes AS 5044–2002 AGLS Metadata Element Set and is renamed the AGLS Metadata Standard. This revised version takes into account changes introduced by the Dublin Core Metadata Initiative (DCMI) in January 2008. It also makes technical changes to support linked data and Semantic Web projects, recognising that the internet is no longer just a medium for publishing human-readable documents."[28]

Metadata Strategies

The best approach to strategically and effectively managing metadata for your organization is going to depend on many factors, such as legal requirements, organizational needs, infrastructure, business objectives, resources, and even corporate culture. Consultation with stakeholders will help uncover issues and with research and collaboration, you can arrive at an understanding of how to leverage and maintain your metadata to meet information needs and business objectives.

Legally, in most jurisdictions, e-records can only be considered authentic and reliable if their accompanying metadata provides not only the needed identifying information, but also provides an audit trail that can attest to its proper management through an entire chain of custody.[29] But often metadata efforts in organizations fall short and the results are only known much later down the line, when adverse consequences are suffered.

A metadata strategy can start off being as fundamental as increasing the quality and frequency of training for staff to ensure the proper terms are being captured.

There are seven critical steps that must be taken to develop an effective metadata strategy:[30]

1. **Consult with stakeholders to understand business processes, needs, and requirements.** Front-line knowledge workers will have specific metadata needs but also managers and others using the e-records down the line will have additional needs that must be addressed upon creation of the record. Legal requirements trump all others. So if there is a metadata term that needs to be added for e-discovery purposes that can save time and money in the event of litigation, it should be weighed carefully.

A metadata strategy can be as fundamental as increasing the quality and frequency of training to ensure the proper terms are being captured.

2. **Understand business applications in use or anticipated to be implemented.** Investigating your ERM system, business process management suite (BPMS), and functional area business applications will provide answers to technical and data capture/input needs. Some research of the documentation in your business application software manuals will help you to learn what metadata is captured or used by the systems, and what their data dictionaries and data models look like.

3. **Survey relevant standards.** There are various national, state, and provincial metadata standards, especially pertaining to public sector organizations. There may also be vertical industry standards, or industry guidelines that you need to identify. And there are a variety of international standards and guidance that may be useful in helping to craft your metadata strategy.

4. **Build in ERM functionality.** As basic as this sounds, it is often overlooked. Your metadata or IG team must consider records retention requirements, end-of-cycle disposition, and other records management functions that must be supported by metadata terms. For instance, if retention of a record is known to be required for the long term, is there a term/field in the metadata that indicates that long-term digital preservation (LTDP) practices must be employed through its lifecycle?

5. **Determine from whom and where metadata will originate.** That is, where will the metadata derive from? It can be automatically captured by many systems—this will help reduce input errors—but also it can be input by individuals working on the records. In addition, some systems can generate needed metadata by using system rules (e.g., linear or sequential numbering), derived from recordkeeping tools or classification schemes, or inherited from business systems, time/data stamps, system clocks, or login credentials.

6. **Decide where the metadata will be stored.** Will it be in a central records repository? In department business applications? In a database? Bear in mind who the primary audience and users are for the metadata, and keep their priorities and business needs in mind when making a determination as to where metadata should be stored and maintained.

7. **Develop IG policies and rules to govern metadata generation and assignment.** Policies must be in place to identify who is responsible and accountable for capturing metadata and how this policy will be enforced and audited. Metadata values can be derived from a variety of sources, including access controls (as a part of data governance), file plans, or business classification schemes (BCS), disposal authorities and thesauri. The goal should be to make records easier to find and use by enforcing the standardization of metadata in a way that best suits the organization.[31]

Using these steps and guidelines, and in collaboration with your key stakeholders—especially your records management lead and legal counsel—you can design a proper metadata strategy that meets your organization's needs. However, controls and checkpoints need to be in place to ensure that a formal program is established and that e-records metadata is constantly and consistently updated and maintained, and that new or merging metadata elements are considered as the organization progresses.

CHAPTER SUMMARY: **KEY POINTS**

- Metadata terms or fields describe a record's characteristics so that it may be classified, managed, and found more easily.

- Good metadata management also assists in the maintenance of corporate memory.

- Metadata terms can be as basic as the name of the document, the creator, the subject, the date it was created, the document type, the length of the document, its security classification, and its file type.

- Using a controlled vocabulary means your organization has standardized a set of terms used for metadata elements describing records.

- Metadata not only defines a record but also describes a record's relationships with other documents and records, and what actions may have been taken on the record over time.

- A metadata governance and management program must be ongoing.

- Proving that a record is authentic and reliable includes proving that its metadata has remained intact and unaltered through the record's entire chain of custody.

- The main types of metadata are: descriptive, administrative, structural, technical, and preservation metadata.

- Goals of the Dublin Core Metadata Initiative are simplicity, commonly understood semantics, international scope, and extensibility.

- ISO 23081 defines needed metadata for records, and provides guidance for metadata management within the "framework" of ISO 15489.

- ISO 23950 (GILS) is the international standard for information searching over networked computers. It was widely deployed in government agencies worldwide, although its use has waned.

- A metadata strategy can be as fundamental as increasing the quality and frequency of training to ensure the proper terms are being captured.

- Consultation with stakeholders to understand how they use records in their business processes is an essential step in developing a metadata policy for records in any organization.

- It is essential to survey metadata standards, to understand the metadata requirements of e-records-centered business processes, and understand its origins and storage needs in order to craft a viable e-records metadata strategy.

Notes

1. National Archives of Australia, "AGLS Metadata Standard, Part 2—Usage Guide," Version 2.0, July 2010, www.naa.gov.au/Images/AGLS%20Metadata%20Standard%20Part%202%20%20Usage%20Guide_tcm16-47011.pdf.
2. Kate Cumming, "Metadata Matters," in *Managing Electronic Records*, ed. Julie McLeod and Catherine Hare (London: Facet Publishing, 2005), 34.
3. Minnesota State Archives, "Electronic Records Management Guidelines," March 12, 2012, www.mnhs.org/preserve/records/electronicrecords/ermetadata.html.
4. Ibid.
5. Cumming, "Metadata Matters," 35.
6. Ibid.
7. "Understanding Metadata," NISO, ww.niso.org/publications/press/UnderstandingMetadata.pdf (accessed October 15, 2012).
8. Minnesota State Archives, "Electronic Records Management Guidelines."
9. Ibid.
10. Ibid.
11. The National Archives, "Requirements for Electronic Records Management Systems," 2002, www.nationalarchives.gov.uk/documents/metadatafinal.pdf (accessed June 21, 2012).
12. International Organization for Standardization, "ISO 23081-1:2006 Information and Documentation—Records Management Processes—Metadata for Records—Part 1: Principles," www.iso.org/iso/iso_catalogue/catalogue_tc/catalogue_detail.htm?csnumber=40832 (accessed June 26, 2012).
13. Carl Weise, "ISO 23081-1: 2006, Metadata for Records, Part 1: Principles," January 27, 2012, www.aiim.org/community/blogs/expert/ISO-23081-1-2006-Metadata-for-records-Part-1-principles
14. Dublin Core Metadata Initiative, http://dublincore.org/metadata-basics (accessed June 26, 2012).
15. Diane Hillman, Dublin Core Metadata Initiative, User Guide, November 7, 2005, http://dublincore.org/documents/usageguide.
16. Dublin Core Metadata Initiative, "Dublin Core Metadata Element Set," Version 1.1, June 14, 2012, http://dublincore.org/documents/dces.
17. Library of Congress, International Standard Maintenance Agency, www.loc.gov/z3950/agency/ (accessed July 7, 2012).
18. National Information Standards Organization (NISO), "ANSI/NISO Z39.50- 2003 (R2009) Information Retrieval: Application Service Definition & Protocol Specification," www.niso.org/apps/group_public/project/details.php?project_id=49 (accessed July 7, 2012).
19. Jenn Riley, "Glossary of Metadata Standards," 2009–2010, www.dlib.indiana.edu/~jenlrile/metadata-map/seeingstandards_glossary_pamphlet.pdf (accessed July 9, 2012).
20. Global Information Locator Service (GILS), "Initiatives," www.gils.net/initiatives.html (accessed July 7, 2012).
21. Minnesota State Archives, "Minnesota Recordkeeping Metadata Standard (IRM 20)," April 24, 2009, www.mnhs.org/preserve/records/metadatastandard.html.
22. Government of Canada, Policy on Information Management, April 1, 2012, www.tbs-sct.gc.ca/pubs_pol/ciopubs/TB_GIH/mgih-grdg_e.asp.
23. Ibid.
24. ESD Standards, E-GMS e-Government Metadata Standard, www.esd.org.uk/standards/egms (accessed June 26, 2012).
25. Ibid.
26. National Archives of Australia, "AGLS Metadata Standard, Part 2—Usage Guide," Version 2.0, July 2010, www.naa.gov.au/Images/AGLS%20Metadata%20Standard%20Part%202%20%20Usage%20Guide_tcm16-47011.pdf.
27. National Archives of Australia, "AGLS Metadata Standard, Part 1—Reference Description," July 2010, www.naa.gov.au/Images/AGLS%20Metadata%20Standard%20Part%201%20Reference%20Description_tcm16-47010.pdf.
28. Ibid.
29. Cumming, "Metadata Matters," 37.
30. Ibid., 38.
31. Ibid., 43–45.

CHAPTER 17

Long-Term Digital Preservation

Charles M. Dollar and Lori J. Ashley

Every organization—public, private, or not-for-profit—now has electronic records and digital content that it wants to access and retain for periods in excess of 10 years. This may be due to regulatory or legal reasons, a desire to preserve organizational memory and history, or may be driven entirely by operational reasons. But *long-term continuity of digital information does not happen by accident*—it takes information governance (IG), planning, sustainable resources, and a keen awareness of the information technology (IT) and file formats in use by the organization, as well as evolving standards and computing trends.

Defining Long-Term Digital Preservation

Information is universally recognized as a key asset that is essential to organizational success. Digital information, which relies on complex computing platforms and networks, is created, received, and used daily to deliver services to citizens, consumers, customers, businesses, and government agencies. Organizations face tremendous challenges in the twenty-first century to manage, preserve, and provide access to electronic records for as long as they are needed.

Digital preservation is defined as: long-term, error-free storage of digital information, with means for retrieval and interpretation, for the entire time span the information is required to be retained. *Digital preservation applies to content that is born digital as well as content that is converted to digital form.*

Some digital information assets must be preserved permanently as part of an organization's documentary heritage. Dedicated repositories for historical and cultural memory such as libraries, archives, and museums need to move forward to put in place trustworthy digital repositories that can match the security, environmental controls, and wealth of descriptive metadata that these institutions have created for analog assets (such as books and paper records). Digital challenges associated with records management affect all sectors of society—academic, government, private and not for profit enterprises—and ultimately all citizens of all developed nations.

The term *preservation* implies permanence, but it has been found that electronic records, data, and information that is retained for only 5 to 10 years is likely to face challenges related to storage media failure and computer hardware/software

285

Digital preservation is defined as: long-term, error-free storage of digital information, with means for retrieval and interpretation, for the entire time span that the information is required to be retained.

obsolescence. A useful point of reference for the definition of *long term* comes from the ISO 14721 standard, which defines long-term as: "long enough to be concerned with the impacts of changing technologies, including support for new media and data formats, or with a changing user community. Long term may extend indefinitely."[1]

Long-term records are common in many different sectors including government, health care, energy, utilities, engineering and architecture, construction, and manufacturing. During the course of routine business, thousands or millions of electronic records are generated in a wide variety of information systems. Most records are useful for only a short period of time (up to seven years), *but some may need to be retained for long periods or permanently.* For those records, organizations must plan for and allocate resources for preservation efforts to ensure that the data remains accessible, usable, understandable, and trustworthy over time.

In addition, *there may be the requirement to retain the metadata associated with records even longer than the records themselves.*[2] A record may have been destroyed according to its scheduled disposition at the end of its lifecycle, but the organization may still need its metadata to identify the record, its lifecycle dates, and the authority or person who authorized its destruction.

Key Factors in Long-Term Digital Preservation

Some electronic records must be preserved, protected, and monitored over long periods of time to ensure they remain authentic, complete, and unaltered and available into the future. Planning for the proper care of these records is a component of an overall records management program and should be integrated into the organization's IG policies and technology portfolio, as well as its privacy and security protocols.

Enterprise strategies for sustainable and trustworthy digital preservation repositories have to take into account several prevailing and compound conditions: the complexity of electronic records, decentralization of the computing environment, obsolescence and aging of storage media, massive volumes of electronic records, and software and hardware dependencies.

Capabilities for properly ensuring access to authentic electronic records over time, in addition to the challenges of technological obsolescence, are a sophisticated combination of policies, strategies, processes, specialized resources, and adoption of standards.

Most records are useful for only a short period of time, but some may need to be retained for long periods or permanently.

The challenges of managing electronic records significantly increased with the trend of decentralization of the computing environment. In the centralized environment of a mainframe computer, prevalent from the 1960s to 1980s, but also in use today, it can be relatively easy to identify, assess, and manage electronic records. This is not the case in the decentralized environment of specialized business applications and office automation systems, where each user creates electronic objects that may constitute a formal record and thus will have to be preserved under IG polices that address record retention and disposition rules, processes, and accountability.

Electronic records have evolved from simple text-based word processing files or reports to include complex "mixed media" digital objects that may contain embedded images (still and animated), drawings, sounds, hyperlinks, or spreadsheets with computational formulas. Some portions of electronic records, such as the content of dynamic web pages, are created "on demand" from databases and exist only for the duration of the viewing session. Other digital objects, such as electronic mail, may contain multiple attachments, and they may be threaded (i.e., related e-mail messages linked in send-reply chains). These records cannot be converted to paper or text formats for preservation without the loss of context, functionality, and metadata.

Electronic records are being created at rates that pose significant threats to our ability to organize, control, and make them accessible for as long as they are needed. This includes documents that are digitally scanned or imaged from a variety of formats to be stored as electronic records.

Electronic records are stored as representations of bits—1s and 0s—and therefore depend upon software applications and hardware networks for the entire period of retention, whether it is 3 days, 3 years, or 30 years or longer. As information technologies become obsolete and are replaced by new generations, the capability of a specific software application to read the representations of 1s and 0s and render them into human understandable form will degrade to the point that the records are neither readable not understandable. As a practical matter this means that the readability and understandability of the records can never be recovered, and there can be serious legal consequences.

Storage media are affected by the dual problems of obsolescence and decay. They are fragile, have limited shelf life, and become obsolete in a matter of a few years. *Mitigating media obsolescence is critical to long-term digital preservation* because the bit streams of 1s and 0s that comprise electronic records must be kept "alive" through periodic transfer to new storage media.

Electronic records are being created at rates that pose significant threats to our ability to organize, control, and make them accessible for as long as they are needed.

In addition to these current conditions associated with technology and records management, organizations face tremendous internal **change management** challenges with regard to reallocation of resources, business process improvements, collaboration and coordination between business areas, accountability, and the dynamic integration of evolving recordkeeping requirements. Building and sustaining the capability to manage digital information over long periods of time is a shared responsibility of all stakeholders.

Threats to Preserving Records

There are a number of known threats that may degrade or destroy electronic records and data:[3]

- **Failure of storage media.** Storage media is inherently vulnerable to errors and malfunction including disk crashes. Solid-state drives (SSD) largely address these concerns as there are no moving parts and data can be stored without needing electrical power.
- **Failure of computer systems.** Computer hardware has moving parts and circuits that deteriorate and fail over time, at an average rate called mean time between failure (MTBF). Some failures are complete and irrecoverable, and some are minor and can be fixed with no loss of data. Computer software is prone to bugs and malware that can compromise the safekeeping of data.
- **Systems and network communications failures.** A small number of network communications is likely to contain errors or misreads, especially undetected checksum errors, which may impact the authenticity of a record. Network errors can occur from changes or redirection of URLs, and any communication over a network is subject to intrusions, errors, and hackers.
- **Component obsolescence.** As hardware, software, and media age, they become obsolete over time, due to the continued innovation and advances by the computer industry. Sometimes obsolescence is due to outdated component parts, changes in software routines, or changes in the hardware to read removable media.
- **Human error.** People make mistakes, and they can make mistakes in selecting, classifying, storing, or handling archived records. Some of these errors may be detected and can be remedied; some go unnoticed or cannot be fixed.
- **Natural disaster.** Hurricane Katrina is the clearest U.S. example of how a natural disaster can interrupt business operations and destroy business records, although in some instances, damaged records were able to be recovered. Floods, fires, earthquakes, and other natural disasters can completely destroy or cause media or computer hardware/software failures.
- **Attacks.** Archived electronic records are subject to external attacks from malware such as viruses and worms, so preserved records must be scanned for malware and kept separate from external threats. Preserved records can also be subject to theft or damage from insiders, such as the theft of historical radio recordings by a National Archives and Records Administration (NARA) employee, which was reported in 2012. Proper monitoring and auditing procedures must be in place to detect and avoid these types of attacks.

> Threats to LTDP of records can be internal or external, from natural disasters, computer or storage failures, and even the financial viability of an organization.

- **Financial shortfall.** It is expensive to preserve and maintain digital records. Power, cooling and heating systems, personnel costs, and other preservation-associated costs must be budgeted and funded.
- **Business viability.** If an organization has financial or legal difficulties, or suffers a catastrophic disaster, it may not survive, placing the preserved records at risk. Part of the planning process is to include consideration of successor organization alternatives, should the originating organization go out of business.

The impact upon the preserved records can be gauged by determining what percentage of the data has been lost and cannot be recovered or, for the data that can be recovered, what the impact or delay to users may be.

It should be noted that the threats noted above can be interrelated and more than one type of threat may impact records at a time. For instance, in the event of a natural disaster, operators are more likely to make mistakes; and computer hardware failures can create new software failures.[4]

Digital Preservation Standards

The digital preservation community recognizes that open-standard technology-neutral standards play a key role in ensuring that digital records are usable, understandable, and reliable for as far into the future as may be required.

There are two broad categories of digital preservation standards. The first category involves systems infrastructure capabilities and services that support a trustworthy repository. The second category relates to open-standard technology-neutral file formats.

Digital preservation infrastructure capabilities and services that support trustworthy digital repositories include the international standard **ISO 14721:2003 Space Data and Information Transfer Systems—Open Archival Information Systems—Reference Model** (OAIS), which is a key standard applicable to long term preservation.[5]

The fragility of digital storage media in concert with ongoing and sometimes rapid changes in computer software and hardware pose a fundamental challenge to ensuring access to trustworthy and reliable digital content over time. Eventually, every digital repository committed to long-term preservation of digital content must have a strategy to mitigate computer technology obsolescence. Toward this end the Consultative Committee for Space Data Systems (CCSDS) developed an **open archival information system** ("OAIS") reference model to support formal standards for the long-term preservation of space science data and information assets. OAIS was not designed as an implementation model.

The OAIS reference model defines an archival information system as an archive consisting of an organization of people and systems that has accepted the responsibility to preserve information and make it available and understandable for a Designated Community (i.e., potential users or consumers), who should be able to understand the information. Thus, the context of an OAIS-compliant digital repository includes producers who originate the information to be preserved in the repository, consumers who retrieve the information, and a management/organization that hosts and administers the digital assets being preserved.

OAIS encapsulates digital objects into information packages. Each information package includes the digital object content (a sequence of bits) and representation information that enables rendering of an object into human usable information along with **preservation description information** (PDI) such as provenance, context, and fixity.

The OAIS information model employs three types of information packages: A **Submission Information Package** (SIP), an **Archival Information Package** (AIP), and a **Dissemination Information Package** (DIP). An OAIS-compliant digital repository preserves AIPs and any PDI associated with them. A Submission Information Package encompasses digital content that a Producer has organized for submission to the OAIS. After the completion of quality assurance and normalization procedures, an Archival Information Package is created, which as noted previously is the focus of preservation activity. Subsequently, a Dissemination Package is created that consists of an AIP or information extracted from an AIP that is customized to the requirements of the Designated Community of users and consumers.

The core of OAIS is a functional model that consists of six entities:

1. **Ingest** processes the formal incorporation (in archival terms, *accession*) of submitted information (i.e., a SIP) into the digital repository. It acknowledges the transfer, conducts quality assurance, extracts metadata from the SIP, generates the appropriate AIP, and populates PDI and extracted metadata into the AIP.
2. **Archival Storage** encompasses all of the activities associated with storage of AIPs. They include receipt of AIPs, transferring AIPs to the appropriate storage location, replacing media as necessary, transforming AIPs to new file formats as necessary, conducting quality assurance tests, supporting backups and business continuity procedures, and providing copies of AIPs to the Access Entity.
3. **Data Management** manages the storage of description and system information, generates reports, and tracks use of storage media.
4. **Administration** encompasses a host of technical and human processes that include audit, policy-making, strategy, and Provider and Customer service, among other management and business functions. OAIS Administration connects with all of the other OAIS functions.
5. **Preservation Planning** does not execute any preservation activities. Rather, it supports a Technology Watch program for sustainable standards, file formats, and software for digital preservation, monitoring changes in the access needs of the Designated Community, and recommending updated digital preservation strategies and activities.
6. **Access** receives queries from the Designated Community, passes them to Archival Storage, and makes them available as DIPs to the Designated Community.

Figure 17.1 displays the relationships between these six functional entities.[6]

In Archival Storage the OAIS reference model articulates a migration strategy based on four primary types of AIP migration that are ordered by an increasing risk of potential information loss: Refreshment, Replication, Repackage, and Transformation:[7]

1. **Migration Refreshment** occurs when one or more AIPs are copied exactly to the same type of storage media with no alterations occurring in the Packaging Information, the Content Information, the Preservation Description Information (PDI), or the AIP location and access Archival Storage mapping infrastructure.

2. **Migration Replication** occurs when one or more AIPs are copied exactly to the same or new storage media with no alterations occurring in the Packaging Information, the Content Information, and the Preservation Description Information (PDI). However, there is a change in the AIP location and access Archival Storage mapping infrastructure.

3. **Migration Repackage** occurs when one or more AIPS are copied exactly to new storage media with no alterations in the Content Information and the Preservation Description Information (PDI). However, there are changes in the Packaging Information and the AIP location and to the access to the Archival Storage mapping infrastructure.

4. **Migration Transformation** occurs when changes in bit streams result when a new content encoding procedure replaces the current one (e.g., Unicode representation of A through Z replaces the ASCII representation of A through Z), a new file format replaces an existing one, or a new software application is required to access and render the AIP content.

OAIS is the "lingua franca" of digital preservation as the international digital preservation community has embraced it as the framework for viable and technologically sustainable digital preservation repositories. *A LTDP strategy that is OAIS-compliant offers the best means available today for preserving the digital heritage of all organizations, private and public.*

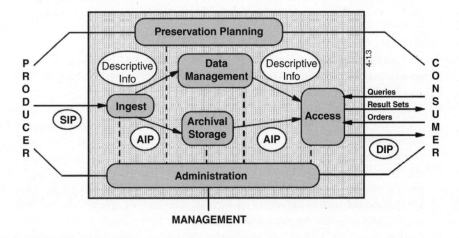

Figure 17.1 Open Archival Information System Reference Model

An OAIS-compliant LTDP strategy is the best way to preserve an organization's digital heritage.

ISO TR 18492 (2005), Long-Term Preservation of Electronic Document-Based Information

ISO 18492 provides practical methodological guidance for the long-term preservation and retrieval of authentic electronic document-based information, when the retention period exceeds the expected life of the technology (hardware and software) used to create and maintain the information assets. It emphasizes both the role of open-standard technology-neutral standards in supporting long-term access and the engagement of information technology specialists, document managers, records managers, and archivists in a collaborative environment to promote and sustain a viable digital preservation program.

ISO 18492 takes note of the role of the international records management standard ISO 15489 but does not cover processes for the capture, classification, and disposition of authentic electronic document-based information. Ensuring the usability and trustworthiness of electronic document-based information for as long as necessary in the face of limited media durability and technology obsolescence requires a robust and comprehensive digital preservation strategy. ISO 18492 describes such a strategy that includes media renewal, software independence, migration, open-standard technology-neutral formats, authenticity protection, and security:

- **Media renewal.** ISO 18492 defines media renewal as a base line requirement for digital preservation because it is the only known way to keep bit streams of electronic-document-based information alive. It specifies the conditions under which copying and reformatting of storage media and storage devices should occur.
- **Open-standard technology-neutral formats.** The fundamental premise of ISO 18492 is that open-standard technology-neutral formats are at the core of a viable and technologically sustainable digital preservation strategy because they help mitigate software obsolescence. ISO 18492 recommends the use of several standard formats, including: eXtensible Markup Language (XML), Portable Document Format/Archival (PDF/A), tagged image file format (TIFF), and Joint Photographic Experts Group (JPEG).
- **Migrating electronic content.** ISO 18492 recommends two ways of migrating electronic content to new technologies. The first relies upon backwardly compatible new open-standard technology-neutral formats that are displacing existing ones. Generally, this is a straightforward process and typically can be executed with minimal human intervention. The second involves writing computer code that exports the electronic content to a new target application or open-standard technology-neutral format. This can be a very labor-intensive activity and requires rigorous quality control.
- **Authenticity.** ISO 18492 recommends the use of hash digest algorithms to validate the integrity of electronic content after execution of media renewal

ISO 18492 provides practical methodological guidance for the long-term preservation of e-documents, when the retention period exceeds the expected life of the technology that created it.

activities that do not alter underlying bit streams of electronic content. In instances where bit streams are altered as a result of format conversion, comprehensive preservation metadata should be captured that documents the process.

- **Security.** ISO 18492 recommends protecting the security of electronic records by creating a firewall between electronic content in a repository and external users. In addition, procedures should be in place to maintain backup/disaster recovery capability, including at least one off-site storage location.

ISO 16363 (2012)—Space Data and Information Transfer Systems—Audit and Certification of Trustworthy Digital Repositories

ISO 14721 (OAIS) acknowledged that an audit and certification standard was needed that incorporated the functional specifications for Records Producers, Records Users, Ingest of digital content into a trusted repository, Archival Storage of this content, and Digital Preserving Planning and Administration. *ISO 16363 is this audit and certification standard.* Its use enables independent audits and certification of trustworthy digital repositories and thereby promotes public trust in digital repositories that claim they are trustworthy. To date only a handful of ISO 16363 test audits have been undertaken so additional time will be required to determine how widely adopted the standard becomes.

ISO 16363 is organized into three broad categories: Organization Infrastructure, Digital Object Management, and Technical Infrastructure and Security Risk Management. Each category is decomposed into a series of primary elements or components, some of which may be more appropriate for digital libraries than for public records digital repositories. In some instances there are secondary elements or components. There is an explanatory discussion of each element accompanied by "empirical metrics" relevant to that element. The "empirical metrics" typically include high-level examples of how conformance can be demonstrated. Hence, they are subjective high-level conformance metrics rather than explicit performance metrics.

Organizational Infrastructure[8] consists of the following primary elements:

- *A Mission Statement* that reflects a commitment to the preservation of, long term retention of, management of, and access to digital information.

ISO 16363 is an audit and certification standard organized into three broad categories: Organization Infrastructure, Digital Object Management, and Technical Infrastructure and Security Risk Management.

- *Preservation Strategic Plan* that defines the approach the repository will take in the long-term support of its mission.
- *Collection Policy* or other document that specifies the types of information it will preserve, retain, manage, and provide access to.
- *Identification and establishment of the duties identified* and establishment of the duties and roles that are required to perform along with a staff with adequate skills and experience to fulfill these duties.
- *Dissemination of the definitions* of its Designated Community and associated knowledge base(s).
- *Preservation Policies* that ensure that the Preservation Strategic Plan will be met.
- *Documentation* of the history of changes to operations, procedures, software, and hardware.
- A *commitment to transparency and accountability* in all actions supporting the operation and management of the repository that affect the preservation of digital content over time.
- *Dissemination* as appropriate of the definition, collection, and tracking of information integrity measurements.
- *Commitment to a regular schedule of self-assessment* and external certification.
- *Short- and long-term business planning* processes in place to sustain the repository over time.
- *Deposit agreements* for digital materials transferred to the custody of the organization.
- *Written policies* that specify when the preservation responsibility for contents of each set of submitted data objects occurs.
- *Intellectual property (IP) ownership rights* policies and procedures.

Digital Object Management,[9]*which is the core of the standard*, comprises the following primary elements:

- Methods and factors used to determine the different types of information for which an organization accepts preservation responsibility.
- An understanding of digital collections sufficient to carry out the preservation necessary for as long as required.
- Specifications that enable recognition and parsing of Submission Information Packages (SIP).
- An Ingest procedure that verifies each SIP for completion and correctness.
- An Ingest procedure that validates successful ingest of each SIP.
- Definitions for each AIP or class of AIPS used that are adequate for parsing and suitable for long-term preservation requirements.
- Descriptions of how AIPs are constructed from SIPs, including extraction of metadata.
- Documentation of the final disposition of SIPs, including those not Ingested.
- A convention that generates unique, persistent identifiers of all AIPs.
- Reliable linking services that support the location of each uniquely identified object, regardless of its physical location.
- Tools and resources that support authoritative Representation Information for all of the digital objects in the repository, including file type.

- Documented processes for acquiring and creating Preservation Description Information (PDI).
- Understandable Content Information for the Designated Community at the time of creation of the AIPs.
- Verification of the completeness and correctness of AIPs at the point of their creation.
- Contemporaneous capture of documentation of actions and administration processes that are relevant to AIP creation.
- Documented digital preservation strategy(ies).
- Mechanisms for monitoring the digital preservation environment.
- Documented evidence of the effectiveness of digital preservation activities.
- Specifications for storage of AIPs down to the bit level.
- Preservation of the Content Information of AIPs.
- Monitoring the integrity of AIPs.
- Documentation that preservation actions associated with AIPs complied with the specifications for those actions.
- Specification of minimum information requirements that enable the Designated Community to discover and identify material of interest.
- Bidirectional linkage between each AIP and its associated descriptive information.
- Compliance with Access Policies.
- Policies and procedures that enable the dissemination of digital objects that are traceable to the "originals," with evidence supporting their authenticity.
- Procedures that require documentation of actions taken in response to reports about errors in data or responses from users.

Technical Infrastructure and Security Risk Management Primary Elements[10] include:

- Technology watches or other monitoring systems that track when hardware and software is expected to become obsolete.
- Procedures, commitment, and funding when it is necessary to replace hardware.
- Procedures, commitment, and funding when it is necessary to replace software.
- Adequate hardware and software support for backup functionality sufficient for preserving the repository content and tracking repository functions.
- Effective mechanisms that identify bit corruption or loss.
- Documentation captures of all incidents of data corruption or loss, and steps taken to repair/replace corrupt or lost data.
- Defined processes for storage media and/or hardware change (e.g., refreshing, migration).
- Management of the number and location of copies of all digital objects.
- Systematic analysis of security risk factors associated with data, systems, personnel, and physical plant.
- Suitable written disaster preparedness and recovery plan(s), including at least one off-site backup of all preserved information together with an offsite copy of the recovery plan(s).

ISO 16363 represents the "gold standard" of audit and certification for trustworthy digital repositories. In some instances the resources available to a trusted repository may

ISO 16363 represents the "gold standard" of audit and certification for trustworthy digital repositories.

not support full implementation of the audit and certification specifications. Decisions about where full and partial implementation is appropriate should be based on a risk-assessment analysis.

PREMIS Preservation Metadata Standard

ISO 14721 specifies that preservation metadata associated with all Archival Storage Activities (e.g., generation of hash digests, normalization/transformation, and media renewal) should be captured and stored in Preservation Description Information (PDI). *This is a high-level guidance requirement that demands greater specificity in an operational environment.*

Toward this end, the U.S. Library of Congress and the Research Library Group supported a new international working group called PREservation Metadata Information Strategies (PREMIS)[11] to define a core set of preservation metadata elements with a supporting data dictionary that would be applicable to a broad range of digital preservation activities and to identify and evaluate alternative strategies for encoding, managing, and exchanging preservation metadata. Version 2.2 was released in June 2012.[12]

PREMIS enables designers and managers of digital repositories to have a clear understanding of the information that is required to support the "functions of viability, renderability, understandability, authenticity, and identity in a preservation context." PREMIS accomplishes this through a Data Model that consists of five "semantic units" (think of them as high level metadata elements, each of which is decomposed into subelements) and a Data Dictionary that decomposes these "semantic units" into a structure hierarchy. The five "semantic units" and their relationships are displayed in Figure 17.2.[13]

Note the arrows that define relationships between the following entities:

- **Intellectual Entities** are considered a single intellectual unit such as a book, map, photograph, database, or records (e.g., an Archival Information Package).
- **Objects** are discrete units of information in digital form that may exist as a bit stream, a file or a representation.
- **Events** denote actions that involve at least one Digital Object and/or Agent known to the repository. Events may include the type of event (e.g., media renewal), a description of the event, and the agents involved in the event. Events support the chain of custody of digital objects.
- **Agents** are actors in digital preservation that have roles. An agent can be an individual, organization, or a software application.
- **Rights** involve the assertion of access rights and access privileges that relate to intellectual property, privacy, or other related rights

The PREMIS Data Dictionary decomposes Objects, Events, Agents, and Rights into a structured hierarchical schema. In addition, the PREMIS Data Dictionary

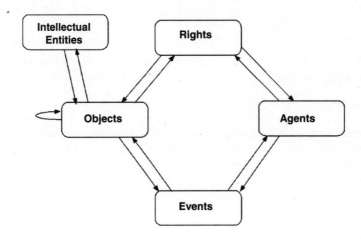

Figure 17.2   PREMIS Data Model

contains semantic units that support documentation of relationships between Objects. An important feature of the PREMIS is an XML schema for the PREMIS Data Dictionary. The primary rationale for the XML schema is to support the exchange of Metadata Information, which is crucial in Ingest and Archival Storage. The XML schema enables automated extraction of preservation related metadata in Submission Information Packages (SIP) and population of this preservation metadata into Archival Information Packages (AIP). In addition, the XML schema can enable automatic capture of preservation Events that are foundational for maintaining a chain of custody in Archival Storage.

Recommended Open-Standard Technology-Neutral Formats

A digital file format specifies the internal logical structure of digital objects (i.e., binary bits of 1s and 0s) and signal encoding (e.g., text, image, sound, and the like). File formats are crucial to long-term preservation because a computer can open, process, and render file formats that it recognizes and can open. *Many file formats are proprietary* (also known as "native"), *meaning that digital content can be opened and rendered only by the software application used to create, use, and store it.* However, as information technology changed some software vendors introduced new products that no longer support earlier versions of a file format. In such instances these formats become "legacy" format and digital content embedded in them can only be opened with computer code written expressly for this purpose. Other vendors, such as Microsoft, support backward compatibility across multiple generations of technology so Microsoft Word 2010 can open

The PREMIS standard defines a core set of preservation metadata elements with a supporting data dictionary applicable to a broad range of digital preservation activities.

> Many digital file formats are proprietary, meaning that content can be viewed and controlled only by the software application used to create, use, and store it.

and render documents in Microsoft Word 95. Nonetheless, it is unrealistic to expect any software vendor to support backward compatibility for its proprietary file formats for digital content that will be preserved for multiple decades.

In the late 1980s an alternative to vendor-supported backward compatibility emerged to mitigate dependence on proprietary file formats through open-system interoperable file formats. Essentially, this meant that digital content could be exported from one proprietary file format and imported to one or more other proprietary file formats. Over time, interoperable file formats evolved into open-standard technology-neutral formats that today have these characteristics:

- **Open** means that the process is transparent and that participants in the process reach a consensus on the properties of the standard.
- **Standard** means that a recognized regional or international organization (e.g., ISO) published the standard.
- **Technology-neutral** means that the standard is interoperable on almost any technology platform that asserts conformance to the standard.

Even open-standard technology-neutral formats are not immune to technology obsolescence so the selection of open-standard technology-neutral formats must take into account their technical sustainability and implementation in digital repositories. The PRONON program of the National Archives of the United Kingdom and long-term sustainability of file formats of the U.S. Library of Congress assess the sustainability of open-standard technology-neutral formats.

The recommended open-standard technology-neutral formats for nine content types listed in Table 17.1 are based upon this ongoing work along with preferred file formats supported by Library and Archives Canada and other national archives. Unlike PDF/A several of these file formats (e.g., XML, JPEG 2000, and SVG) were not explicitly designed for digital preservation. Nonetheless, *it cannot be emphasized too strongly that this list of recommended open-standard technology-neutral formats or any other comparable list is not static and will change over time as technology changes.*

ISO 19005 (PDF/A)—Document Management—Electronic Document File Format for Long-Term Preservation (2005, 2011, and 2012)

PDF/A is an open-standard technology-neutral format that enables the accurate representation of the visual appearance of digital content without regard for the proprietary

> The PDF/A file format was specifically designed for digital preservation.

Table 17.1   Recommended Open-Standard Technology-Neutral Formats

	PDF/A	XML	TIFF	PNG	JPEG 2000	SVG	MPEG-2	BWF	WARC
Text	√	√							
Spreadsheets	√								
Images (raster)	√		√	√					
Photographs (digital)					√				
Vector Graphics						√			
Moving Images							√		
Audio								√	
Web									√
Databases		√							

format or application in which it was created or used. PDF/A is widely used in digital repositories as a preservation format for static textual and image content. Note that PDF/A is agnostic with regard to digital imaging processes or storage media. PDF/A supports conversion of TIFF and PNG images to PDF/A. There are two levels of conformance to PDF/A specifications. PDF/A-1a references the use of a "well-formed" hierarchical structure with XML tags that enable searching for a specific tag in a very large digital document. PDF/A-1b does not require this conformance and as a practical matter it does not affect the accurate representation of visual appearance.

Since its publication in 2005 there have been two revisions of PDF/A. The first revision, PDF/A-2, was aligned with the Adobe Portable Document Format 1.7 published specifications, which Adobe released to the Public Domain in 2011. The second revision, PDF/A-3, supports embedding documents in other formats, such as the original source document, in a PDF document.

Extensible Markup Language (XML)—World Wide Web Consortium (W3C) Internet Engineering Group (1998)

XML is a markup language that is a derivative of **Standard General Markup Language** (SGML) that logically separates the rendering of a digital document from its content to enable interoperability across multiple technology platforms. Essentially XML defines rules for marking up the structure of content and its content in ASCII text. Any conforming interoperable XML parser can render the original structure and content. XML-encoded text is human-readable because any text editor can display the marked-up text and content. XML is ubiquitous in information technology environments because many communities of users have developed Document Type Definitions (DTD) unique to their purposes, including Genealogy, Math, and relational databases. Structure data elements work with relational databases, so this enables relational database portability.

Tagged Image File Format: 1992

Tagged Image File Format (TIFF) was initially developed by the Aldus Corporation in 1982 for storing black-and-white images created by scanners and desktop publishing applications. Over the following years several new features were added, including a wide range of color images and compression techniques, including lossless compression. The most recent version of TIFF 6.0 was released by Aldus in 1992. Subsequently, Adobe purchased Aldus and chose not to support any further significant revisions and updates. Nonetheless, TIFF is widely used in desktop scanners for creating digital images for preservation. With such a large base of users it is likely to persist for some time, but Adobe's decision to discontinue further development of TIFF means that it will lack features of other current and future image file formats. Fortunately, there are tools available to convert TIFF images to PDF and PNG images.

ISO/IEC 15498: 2004—Information Technology-Computer Graphics and Image Processing-Portable Network Graphics (PNG): Functional Specifications

The W3C Internet Engineering Task Force supported the development of PNG as a replacement for Graphics Image Format (GIF) because the GIF compression algorithm was protected by patent rights rather than being in the public domain as many believed. In 2004 PNG became an international standard that supports lossless compression, grayscale, and true-color images with bit depths that range from 1 to 16 bits per pixel, file integrity checking, and streaming capability.

Scalable Vector Graphics (SVG): 2003. W3C Internet Engineering Task Force

Vector graphics images consist of two-dimensional lines, colors, curves, or any other geometrical shapes and attributes that are stored as mathematical expressions, such as where a line begins, its shape, where it ends, and its color. Changes in these mathematical expressions will result in changes in the image. Unlike raster images, there is no loss of clarity of a vector graphics image when it is made larger. SVG images and their behavior properties are defined in XML text files, which means any named element in a SVG image can be indexed and searched. SVG images also can be accessed by any text editor, which minimizes on a specific software application to render and edit the images.

ISO/IEC 15444:2000—Joint Photographic Engineers Group (JPEG 2000)

JPEG 2000 *is an international standard for compressing full-color and grayscale digital images* and rendering them as full-size images and thumbnail images. Unlike JPEG, its predecessor, which supported only lossy compression, JPEG 2000 supports both lossy and lossless compression. Lossy compression means that during compression bits that are considered technically redundant will be permanently deleted. Lossless compression means no bits are lost or deleted. *The latter is very important for long-term digital preservation because lossy compression is irreversible.* JPEG 2000 is widely used in producing digital images in digital cameras and is an optional format in many digital scanners.

PNG replaced GIF as an international standard for grayscale and color images in 2004.

JPEG 2000 is an international standard for compressing and rendering full-color and grayscale digital images in full size or as thumbnails.

ISO/IEC 13818–3: 2000—Motion Picture Expert Group (MPEG-2)

MPEG-2 is an international broadcast standard for lossy compression of moving images and associated audio. The major competitor for MPEG-2 appears to be Motion JPEG 2000, which is used in small devices such as cell phones.

European Broadcasting Tech 3285: 2011—Broadcast Wave Format (BWF)

Broadcast Wave Format (BWF), Tech 3285. First issued by the European Broadcasting Union in 1997 and revised in 2001 (v1) and 2011 (v2), BWF is a file format for audio data that is an extension of the Microsoft Wave audio format. Its support of metadata ensures that it can be used for the seamless exchange of audio material between different broadcast environments and between equipment based on different computer platforms.

ISO 28500: 2009—WebARChive (WARC)

WebARChive (WARC) is an extension of the Internet Archive's ARC format to store digital content harvested through "web crawls." WARC was developed to support the storage, management, and exchange of large volumes of "constituent data objects" in a single file. Currently, WARC is used to store and manage digital content collected through "web crawls" and data collected by environmental sensing equipment, among others.

Digital Preservation Requirements

Implementing a sustainable LTDP program is not an effort that should be undertaken lightly. Digital preservation is complex, costly, and requires collaboration with all of the stakeholders who are accountable for or have an interest in ensuring access to usable, understandable, and trustworthy electronic records for as far into the future as may be required.

As noted earlier, ISO 14721 and ISO 16363 establish the baseline functions and specifications for ensuring access to usable, understandable, and trustworthy electronic records, whether this involves regulatory and legal compliance for a business entity, vital records, or accountability for a government unit, or cultural memory for a public or private institution. Most first-time readers who review the functions and specifications of ISO 14721 and ISO 16363 are likely to be overwhelmed by the detail and complexity of almost 150 specifications.

Long-Term Digital Preservation Capability Maturity Model®

A useful approach that both simplifies these specifications and provides explicit criteria regarding conformance to ISO 14721 and ISO 16363 is the Long-Term Digital Preservation Capability Maturity Model® (DPCMM).[14] The DPCMM, which is described in some detail in this section, draws upon functions and preservation services identified in ISO 14721("OAIS"), as well as attributes specified in ISO 16363, Audit and Certification of Trustworthy Repositories. It is important to note that the DPCMM is not a "one size fits all" approach to ensuring long-term access to authentic electronic records. Rather, it is a flexible approach that can be adapted to an organization's specific requirements and resources.

DPCMM can be used to identify the current state capabilities of digital preservation that form the basis for debate and dialogue regarding the desired future state of digital preservation capabilities and the level of risk that the organization is willing to take on. In many instances, this is likely to come down to the question of what constitutes digital preservation that is "good enough" to fulfill the organization's mission and meet the expectations of its stakeholders. The DPCMM has five incremental stages, which are depicted in Figure 17.3. In Stage 1 a systematic digital preservation program has not been undertaken or the digital preservation program exists only on paper, whereas Stage 5 represents the highest level of sustainable digital preservation capability and repository trustworthiness that an organization can achieve.

The DPCMM is based on the functional specifications of ISO 14721and ISO 16363 and accepted best practices in operational digital repositories. The DPCMM is a systems-based tool for charting an evolutionary path from disorganized and undisciplined management of electronic records, or the lack of a systematic electronic records management program, into increasingly mature stages of digital preservation capability.

The goal of the Digital Preservation Capability Maturity Model (DPCMM) is to identify at a high level where an electronic records management program is in relation to optimal digital preservation capabilities, report gaps, capability levels, and preservation performance metrics to resource allocators and other stakeholders to establish priorities for achieving enhanced capabilities to preserve and ensure access to long-term electronic records.

Stage 5: Optimal Digital Preservation Capability

Stage 5 is the highest level of digital preservation readiness capability that an organization can achieve. It includes a strategic focus on digital preservation outcomes by continuously improving the manner in which electronic records lifecycle management is executed. Stage 5 digital preservation capability also involves benchmarking the digital preservation infrastructure and processes relative to other "best in class" digital preservation programs and conducting proactive monitoring for breakthrough technologies that can enable the program to significantly change and improve its digital preservation performance. *In Stage 5 few if any electronic records that merit long-term preservation are at risk.*

The Long-Term Digital Preservation Capability Maturity Model (DPCMM) simplifies conformance to ISO 14721 and ISO 16363.

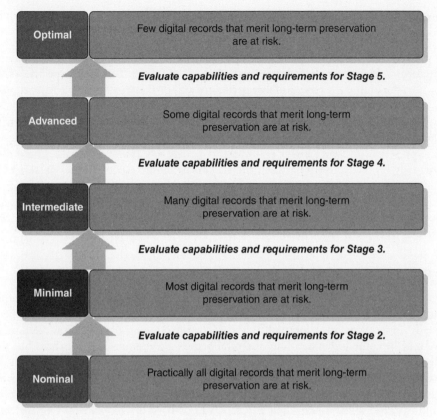

Figure 17.3   Five Levels of Digital Preservation Capabilities

Stage 4: Advanced Digital Preservation Capability

Stage 4 capability is characterized by an organization with a robust infrastructure and digital preservation processes that are based on ISO 14721 specifications and ISO 16363 audit and certification criteria. At this stage the preservation of electronic records is framed entirely within a collaborative environment in which there are multiple participating stakeholders. Lessons learned from this collaborative framework serve as the basis for adapting and improving capabilities to identify and proactively bring long-term electronic records under lifecycle control and management. *Some electronic records that merit long-term preservation may still be at risk.*

Stage 3: Intermediate Digital Preservation Capability

Stage 3 describes an environment that embraces the ISO 14721 specifications and other best practice standards and schemas and thereby establishes the foundation for sustaining an enhanced digital preservation capability over time. This foundation includes successfully completing repeatable projects and outcomes that support the enterprise digital preservation capability and enables collaboration, including shared resources, between record producing units and entities responsible for managing and maintaining trustworthy digital repositories. *In this environment many electronic records that merit long-term preservation are likely to remain at risk.*

Stage 2: Minimal Digital Preservation Capability

Stage 2 describes an environment where an ISO 14721-based digital repository is not yet in place. Instead a surrogate repository for electronic records is available to some records Producers that satisfies some but not all of the ISO 14721 specifications. Typically, the digital preservation infrastructure and processes of the surrogate repository are not systematically integrated into business processes or universally available so the state of digital preservation is somewhat rudimentary and lifecycle management of the organization's electronic records is incomplete. There is some understanding of digital preservation issues but it is limited to a relatively few individuals. There may be virtually no relationship between the success or failure of one digital preservation initiative and the success or failure of another one. Success is largely the result of exceptional (perhaps even heroic) actions of an individual or a project team. Knowledge about such success is not widely shared or institutionalized. *Most electronic records that merit long-term preservation are at risk.*

Stage 1: Nominal Digital Preservation Capability

Stage 1 describes an environment in which the specifications of ISO 14721 and other standards may be known, accepted in principle, or under consideration, but have not been formally adopted or implemented by the record-producing organization. Generally, there may be some understanding of digital preservation issues and concerns but this understanding is likely to consist of ad hoc electronic records management and digital preservation infrastructure, processes, and initiatives. Although there may be some isolated instances of individuals attempting to preserve electronic records on a work station or removable storage media (e.g., DVD or hard drive), *practically all electronic records that merit long-term preservation are at risk.*

Scope of the Capability Maturity Model

This capability maturity model consists of 15 components, or key process areas, that are necessary and required for the long-term preservation of usable, understandable, accessible, and trustworthy electronic records. Each component is identified and is accompanied by explicit performance metrics for each of the five levels of digital preservation capability.

The objective of the model is to provide a process and performance framework (or benchmark) against best practice standards and foundational principles of digital preservation, records management, information governance, and archival science. Figure 17.4 displays the components of the DPCMM.

Scope notes for each of the graphic elements in Figure 17.4 are provided below for additional clarity. Numbered components in the model are associated with performance metrics and capability levels described in the next section.

- **Producers and Users**
  - **Records creators and owners** are stakeholders who have either the obligation or the option to transfer permanent and long-term (10+ year retention) electronic records to one or more specified digital repositories for safekeeping and access.

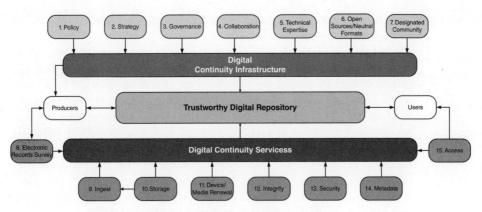

Figure 17.4   Digital Preservation Capability Maturity Model

- **Users.** Individuals or groups that have an interest in and/or right to access records held in the digital repository. These stakeholders represent a variety of interests and access requirements that may change over time.
- **Digital preservation infrastructure.** Seven key organizational process areas required to ensure sustained commitment and adequate resources for the long-term preservation of electronic records are:
  1. **Digital preservation policy.** The organization charged with ensuring preservation and access to long-term and permanent legal, fiscal, operational, and historical records should issue its digital preservation policy in writing including the purpose, scope, accountability, and approach to the operational management and sustainability of trustworthy repositories.
  2. **Digital preservation strategy.** The organization charged with the preservation of long-term and permanent business, government, or historical electronic records must proactively address the risks associated with technology obsolescence, including plans related to periodic renewal of storage devices, storage media, and adoption of preferred preservation file formats.
  3. **Governance.** The organization has a formal decision-making framework that assigns accountability and authority for the preservation of electronic records with long-term and permanent historical, fiscal, operational, or legal value, and articulates approaches and practices for trustworthy digital repositories sufficient to meet stakeholder needs. Governance is exercised in conjunction with information management and technology functions and with other custodians and digital preservation stakeholders such as records producing units and records consumers, and enables compliance with applicable laws, regulations, record retention schedules, and disposition authorities.
  4. **Collaboration.** Digital preservation is a shared responsibility so the organization with a mandate to preserve long-term and permanent electronic business, government, or historical records in accordance with accepted digital preservation standards and best practices is well served by maintaining and promoting collaboration among its internal and external stakeholders. Interdependencies between and among the operations of records producing units, legal and statutory requirements, information

technology policies and governance, and historical accountability should be systematically addressed.

5. **Technical expertise**. A critical component in a sustainable digital preservation program is access to professional technical expertise that can proactively address business requirements as well as respond to impacts of evolving technologies. The technical infrastructure and key processes of an ISO 14721/ISO 16363 conforming archival repository requires professional expertise in archival storage, digital preservation solutions, and lifecycle electronic records management processes and controls. This technical expertise may exist within the organization, be provided by a centralized function or service bureau, or by external service providers, and should include an in-depth understanding of critical digital preservation actions and their associated recommended practices.

6. **Open-standard technology-neutral formats.** A fundamental requisite for a sustainable digital preservation program that ensures long-term access to usable and understandable electronic records is mitigation of obsolescence of file formats. Open-standard platform-neutral file formats are developed in an open public setting, issued by a certified standards organization, and have few or no technology dependencies. Current preferred open-standard technology file format examples include:
   - XML and PDF/A for text
   - PDF/A for spreadsheets
   - JPEG 2000 for photographs
   - PDF/A, PNG, and TIFF for scanned images
   - SVG for vector graphics
   - BWF for audio
   - MPEG-4 for video
   - WARC for web pages

   Over time new digital preservation tools and solutions will emerge that will require new open-standard technology-neutral standard file formats. Open-standard technology-neutral formats are backwardly compatible so they can support interoperability across technology platforms over an extended period of time.

7. **Designated community.** The organization that has responsibility for preservation and access to long-term and permanent legal, operational, fiscal, or historical government records is well served through proactive outreach and engagement with its Designated Community. There are written procedures and formal agreements with records producing units that document the content, rights, and conditions under which the digital repository will ingest, preserve, and provide access to electronic records. Written procedures are in place regarding the ingest of electronic records and access to its digital collections. Records Producers will submit fully conforming ISO 14721/ISO 16363 Submission Information Packages (SIPs) while Dissemination Information Packages (DIPs) are developed and updated in conjunction with its user communities.

- **Trustworthy digital repository.** The integrated people, processes, and technologies committed to ensuring the continuous and reliable design, operation, and management of digital repositories entrusted with long-term and permanent electronic records. A trustworthy digital repository may range from a simple system that involves a low-cost file server and software that provide nonintegrated preservation services to complex systems comprising data centers and server farms, computer hardware and software, and communication networks that interoperate.

The most complete trustworthy digital repository is based on models and standards that include ISO 14721, ISO 16363, and generally accepted best digital preservation practices. The repository may be managed by the organization that owns the electronic records or may be provided as a service by an external third party. It is likely that many organizations initially will rely on surrogate digital preservation capabilities and services that approximate some but not all of the capabilities and services of a conforming ISO14721/ISO 16363 trustworthy digital repository.

■ **Digital preservation processes and services**. Eight key business process areas needed for continuous monitoring of the external and internal environments in order to plan and take actions to sustain the integrity, security, usability and accessibility of electronic records stored in trustworthy digital repositories.

1. **Electronic records survey**. A trustworthy repository cannot fully execute its mission or engage in realistic digital preservation planning without a projected volume and scope of electronic records that will come into its custody. It is likely that some information already exists in approved retention schedules but may require further elaboration as well as periodic updates, especially with regard to preservation ready, near preservation ready, and legacy electronic records held by records producing units.

2. **Ingest**. A digital repository that conforms to ISO 14721/ISO 16363 has the capability to systematically Ingest (receive and accept) electronic records from records producing units in the form of Submission Information Packages (SIPs), move them to a staging area where virus checks and content and format validations are performed, transform electronic records into designated preservation formats as appropriate, extract metadata from SIPs, and write it to Preservation Description Information (PDI), creates Archival Information Packages (AIPs), and transfers the AIPs to the repository's storage function. This process is considered the minimal workflow for transferring records into a digital repository for long-term preservation and access.

3. **Archival storage**. ISO 14721 delineates systematic automated storage services that support receipt and validation of successful transfer of AIPs from ingest, creation of Preservation Description Information (PDI) for each AIP that confirms its "fixity"[15] during any preservation actions through the generation of hash digests, capture and maintenance of error logs, updates to PDI, including transformation of electronic records to new formats, production of Dissemination Information Packages (DIPs) from Access, and collection of operational statistics.

4. **Device and media renewal**. No known digital device or storage medium is invulnerable to decay and obsolescence. A foundational digital preservation capability is ensuring the readability of the bit streams underlying the electronic records. ISO 14721/ ISO 16363 specify that a

trustworthy digital repository's storage devices and storage media should be monitored and renewed ("refreshed") periodically to ensure that the bit streams remain readable over time. A projected life expectancy of removable storage media does not necessarily apply in a specific instance of storage media. Hence, it is important that a trustworthy digital repository have a protocol for continuously monitoring removable storage media (e.g., magnetic tape, external tape drive, or other media) to identify any that face imminent catastrophic loss. Ideally, this renewal protocol would automatically execute renewal after review by the repository.

5. **Integrity**. A key capability in conforming ISO 14721/ISO 16363 digital repositories is ensuring the integrity of the records in its custody, which involves two related preservation actions. The first action generates a hash digest algorithm (also known as a Cyclical Redundancy code) to address a vulnerability to accidental or intentional alterations to electronic records that can occur during device/media renewal and internal data transfers. The second action involves integrity documentation that supports an unbroken electronic chain of custody captured in Preservation Description Information (PDI) in AIPs.

6. **Security**. Contemporary enterprise information systems typically execute a number of shared or common services that may include communication, name services, temporary storage allocation, exception handling, role-based access rights, security, backup and business continuity, and directory services, among others. A conforming ISO 14721/ISO 16363 digital repository is likely to be part of an information system that may routinely provide some or perhaps all of the core security, backup, and business continuity services, including firewalls, role-based access rights, data-transfer-integrity validations, logs for all preservation activities, including failures and anomalies to demonstrate an unbroken chain of custody.

7. **Preservation metadata**. A digital repository collects and maintains metadata that describes actions associated with custody of long-term and permanent records, including an audit trail that documents preservation actions carried out, why and when they were performed, how they were carried out, and with what results. *A current best practice is the use of a PRE-MIS-based Data Dictionary to support an electronic chain of custody that documents authenticity over time as preservation actions are executed.* Capture of all related metadata, transfer of the metadata to any new formats/systems, and secure storage of metadata are critical. All metadata is stored in the Preservation Description Information (PDI) component of conforming AIPs.

8. **Access**. Organizations with a mandate to support access to permanent business, government, or historical records are subject to authorized restrictions. A conforming ISO 14721/ISO 16363 digital repository will provide consumers with trustworthy records in "disclosure free" Dissemination Information Packages (DIPs) redacted to protect privacy, confidentiality, and other rights where appropriate, and searchable metadata that users can query to identify and retrieve records of interest to them. Production of DIPs is tracked, especially when they involve extractions, to verify their trustworthiness and to identify query trends that are used to update electronic accessibility tools to support these trends.

Digital Preservation Capability Performance Metrics

Digital preservation performance metrics for each level of the five levels of the model have been mapped to each of the 15 numbered components described in the previous section. The performance metrics are explicit empirical indicators that reflect an incremental level of digital preservation capability. The digital preservation capability performance metrics for Digital Preservation Strategy listed in Table 17.2 illustrate the results of this mapping exercise.[16]

Conducting a gap analysis of an organization's digital preservation capabilities using these performance metrics enables the organization to identify both its current state and desired future state of digital preservation capabilities. In all likelihood this desired future state will depend upon available resources, the mission of the organization, and expectations of stakeholders. "Good enough" digital preservation capabilities will vary by organization; what is "good enough for one organization" is unlikely to coincide with what is "good enough" for another organization.

Digital Preservation Strategies and Techniques

Any organization with long-term or permanent electronic records in its custody must ensure that the electronic records can be read and correctly interpreted by a computer application, rendered in an understandable form to humans, and trusted as accurate representations of their logical and physical structure, substantive content, and context. To achieve these goals, a digital repository should operate under the mandate of a digital preservation strategy that addresses 10 digital preservation processes and activities:

1. **Adopt preferred open-standard technology-neutral formats.** An earlier section in this chapter recommended nine open-standard technology-neutral

Table 17.2   Digital Preservation Performance Metrics

Level	Capability Description
0	A formal strategy to address technology obsolescence does not exist.
1	A strategy to mitigate technology obsolescence consists of accepting electronic records in their native format with the expectation that new software will become available to support these formats. During this interim period viewer technologies will be relied on to render usable and understandable electronic records.
2	Electronic records in interoperable "Preservation-ready"[17] file formats and transformation of one native file format to an open-standard technology-neutral file format are supported. Changes in information technologies that may impact electronic records collections and the digital repository are proactively and systematically monitored.
3	The organization supports transformation of selected native file formats to preferred/supported preservation file formats in the trustworthy digital repository. Records producing units are advised to use preservation-ready file formats for permanent or indefinite long-term (e.g., case files, infrastructure files) electronic records in their custody.
4	Electronic records in all native formats are transformed to available open-standard technology-neutral file formats.

file formats that covered text, images, photographs, vector graphics, moving images, audio, and web pages. Adoption of these file formats means that the digital repository will support their use in its internal digital preservation activities and notify the producers of records of the preferred formats for preservation-ready electronic records to be transferred to the repository's custody.

2. **Acquire electronic records in preservation-ready formats.** It is likely that many born digital electronic records along with scanned images will be created or captured in a preservation-ready format. Acquisition or ingest of electronic records already in preservation-ready formats can significantly reduce the workload of the repository because it will not be necessary to convert or "normalize" records to open-standard technology-neutral formats.

3. **Acquire and normalize electronic records in near preservation-ready formats.** Near preservation-ready formats are native proprietary file formats that can be easily normalized to preservation-ready file formats through software plug-ins that are widely available. Ideally, over time the volume of near preservation-ready records will diminish as records producers increasingly convert records scheduled for long-term retention in preservation-ready formats before they are transferred to the repository.

4. **Acquire legacy electronic records.** Legacy electronic records were initially created in a proprietary file format that is obsolete and no longer supported by a vendor. In most instances electronic records embedded in legacy file formats can only be recovered and saved in a Preservation-ready format if special computer code is written to extract the records from their legacy format. Once extracted from the legacy format they can be written to a contemporary format. Niche vendors provide this kind of service but it tends to be relatively expensive and perhaps beyond the resources of many repositories.

   An alternative is to forego this costly process in the hope that a future technology such as Emulation will be widely available and relatively inexpensive. Meanwhile, the repository would rely on a file viewer technology such as Inside Out to render legacy electronic records into human understandable format with the exact logical and physical structure and representation at the time they were created and used.

5. **Maintain bit streams readability through device/media removal.** No known digital storage device or media is exempt from degradation and technology obsolescence. Consequently, the bit streams of 1s and 0s that underlie electronic records are stored on media that are vulnerable to degradation and technology obsolescence. Technology obsolescence may occur when a vendor introduces a new form factor for storage device/media, such as the transition from 5.25-inch disk drives and disks to 3.5-inch disk drives and media to thumb drives. In other instances the form factor, such as a tape cartridge, may not change but an increased storage capacity means a different recording of 1s and 0s is introduced and there is no backward compatibility between the old and the new. Periodic device/medial renewal is the only known way with today's technology to keep bit streams available. *A rule of thumb is to renew storage device/media at least every 10 years.* Failure to maintain the readability of bit streams over time is an absolute guarantee the electronic records cannot be recovered and for all practical purposes the records will be permanently lost.

6. **Migrate to new open-standard technology-neutral formats.** Open-standard technology-neutral formats are not immune to technology obsolescence. The inevitable changes in information technology mean that new open-standard technology formats will be created that displace current ones. The solution to this issue is migration from an older or current open-standard technology-neutral format to newer ones. Seamless migration from old to new open-standard technology-neutral formats is made possible through backward compatibility. Backward compatibility means that a new standard can interpret digital content in an old standard and then save it in the new format standard. Migration is the most widely used tool to mitigate file format obsolescence.

7. **Protect the integrity and security of electronic records.** Imperfect information technologies inevitably have glitches that, along with accidental human error and intentional human actions, can corrupt or otherwise compromise the trustworthiness of electronic records though some alteration in the underlying bit stream. Accidental alteration occurs when preservation actions are initiated for electronic records. These actions may occur during normalization migration, media renewal, accessions to digital records, and relocation of electronic records from one part of the repository to another. The most effective tool for validating that no unauthorized changes to electronic records occur is to compute a hash digest before a preservation action occurs and after the action is completed. If there is change of only one bit a comparison of the two will identify it. Capturing these pre- and posthash digests and saving them as preservation description information can contribute to an electronic chain of custody.

   A robust firewall that blocks unauthorized access with tightly controlled role-based permission rights will help protect the security of records in the custody of the repository.

   A further enhancement to protect against a cataclysmic natural or man-made disaster is maintaining a backup copy of the repository's holdings at an off-site facility.

8. **Capture and save preservation metadata.** Preservation metadata, which consists of tracking, capturing, and maintaining documentation of all preservation actions associated with electronic records, involves identifying these events, the agents that executed the actions, and the results of the actions, including any corrective action taken. Saving this metadata along with the hash digest integrity validations discussed above enables robust electronic chain of custody and establishes a strong basis for the trustworthiness of electronic records in the custody of the digital repository.

9. **Provide access.** *Access to usable and trustworthy records is the ultimate justification for digital preservation.* In some respects this may be the most challenging aspect of digital preservation because user expectations for customized retrieval tools, access speed, and delivery formats of electronic records may exceed the current resources of a trusted digital repository. Nonetheless, some form of user access, through replication of records in a single open-standard technology format such as PDF/A for text and scanned images and JPEG 2000 for digital photographs would be a major accomplishment and form the basis for a more aggressive access program over time.

10. **Engage proactively with records producers and other stakeholders.** *The traditional notion of an archives being in a reactive mode with regard to records producers and other stakeholders in long-term access to usable, understandable, and trustworthy electronic records simply will not work in today's world.* Proactive engagement with records producers about how capturing electronic records in open-standard technology-neutral formats can support both current business operation requirements and long-term requirements for usable, understandable, and trustworthy records and can be a "win-win" for the digital repository and the records producers. Equally important is the notion of pro-active engagement with all of the stakeholders in ensuring long-term access to usable, understandable, and trustworthy electronic records. Gaining the support of other stakeholders can be leveraged to gain broad organizational support for the digital repository.

Evolving Marketplace

The design and implementation of a digital repository that operates under this digital preservation strategy can be carried out in several different ways. One way is to use internal expertise to build a standalone repository that conforms to these digital preservation strategy requirements. Typically, an internally built repository is costly, takes considerable time to implement, and may not meet all expectations because of technical inexperience. An alternative is to use the services and/or solutions offered by an external institution or supplier. A third-party solution is offered by Archivematica, a Vancouver, British Columbia company that specializes in the use of open-source software and conformance to the specifications of ISO 14721. "Archivematica is a free and open-source digital preservation system that is designed to maintain standards-based, long-term access to collections of digital objects."[18] Another company, Tessella Technology & Consulting,[19] has an ISO 14721 conforming digital preservation solution called Safety Deposit Box that has been implemented in a number of national archives. In June 2012 Tessella introduced Preservica,[20] a cloud-based implementation of their Safety Deposit Box that runs on Amazon Web Services (AWS). *It is likely that other repository solutions and preservation services and cloud-based digital preservation services will emerge over the next few years.* The digital preservation strategy discussed earlier can be used to assess the capabilities of these solutions.

Looking Forward

Organizations face significant challenges in meeting their LTDP needs, especially those whose primary mission is to preserve and provide access to permanent records. They must collaborate with internal and external stakeholders, develop governance policies and strategies to govern and control information assets over long periods of time, inventory records in the custody of Records Producers, monitor technology changes and evolving standards, and sustain trustworthy digital repositories. The most important consideration is to determine what level of LTDP maturity is appropriate, achievable, and affordable for the organization, and to begin working methodically toward that goal for the good of the organization and its stakeholders over the long term. In addition, organizations should focus on what is doable over the next 10 to 20 years rather than the next 50 or 100 years.

CHAPTER SUMMARY: **KEY POINTS**

- Digital preservation is defined as: long-term, error-free storage of digital information, with means for retrieval and interpretation, for the entire time span the information is required to be retained.

- Digital preservation applies to content that is born digital as well as content that is converted to digital form.

- Capabilities for properly ensuring access to authentic electronic records over time, regardless of the challenges of technological obsolescence, are a sophisticated combination of policies, strategies, processes, specialized resources, and adoption of standards.

- Most records are useful for only a short period of time, but some may need to be retained for long periods or permanently. For those records, organizations will need to plan for their preservation to ensure that they remain accessible, trustworthy, and useful.

- Electronic records are being created at rates that pose significant threats to our ability to organize, control, and make them accessible for as long as they are needed.

- Threats to LTDP of records can be internal or external, from natural disasters, computer or storage failures, and even the financial viability of an organization.

- Building and sustaining the capability to manage digital information over long periods of time is a shared responsibility among all stakeholders.

- ISO 14721 is the "lingua franca" of digital preservation as the international digital preservation community has embraced it as the framework for viable and technologically sustainable digital preservation repositories.

- An ISO 14721 (OAIS)-compliant repository is the best way to preserve an organization's long-term digital assets.

- ISO 18492 provides practical methodological guidance for the long-term preservation of e-documents, when the retention period exceeds the expected life of the technology that created it.

- ISO 16363 is an audit and certification standard organized into three broad categories: Organization Infrastructure, Digital Object Management, and Technical Infrastructure and Security Risk Management.

- ISO 16363 represents the "gold standard" of audit and certification for trustworthy digital repositories.

- The PREMIS standard defines a core set of preservation metadata elements with a supporting data dictionary applicable to a broad range of digital preservation activities.

(Continued)

(Continued)

- Many digital file formats are proprietary, meaning that content can viewed and controlled only by the software application used to create, use, and store it.

- The digital preservation community recognizes that open-standard technology-neutral standards play a key role in ensuring that digital records are usable, understandable, and reliable for as far into the future as may be required.

- The PDF/A file format was specifically designed for digital preservation of electronic documents.

- PNG replaced GIF as an international standard for grayscale and color images in 2004.

- JPEG 2000 is an international standard for compressing and rendering full-color and grayscale digital images in full size or as thumbnails.

- The Long-Term Digital Preservation Capability Maturity Model® (DPCMM) simplifies conformance to ISO 14721 and ISO 16363.

- Migration, refreshment, and replication are examples of specific preservation techniques.

- It is likely that new third-party repository solutions and preservation services, including cloud-based offerings, will emerge over the next few years.

Notes

1. Consultative Committee for Space Data Systems, *Reference Model for an Open Archival Information System (OAIS)*, (Washington, DC: CCSDS Secretariat, 2002), 1-1.
2. Kate Cumming, "Metadata Matters," in *Managing Electronic Records*, ed. Julie McLeod and Catherine Hare (London: Facet Publishing, 2005), 48.
3. David Rosenthal et al., Stanford University Libraries, "Requirements for Digital Preservation Systems: A Bottom-Up Approach," *D-Lib Magazine*, November 2005, www.dlib.org/dlib/november05/rosenthal/11rosenthal.html.
4. Ibid.
5. International Organization for Standardization, "ISO 14721:2003, Space Data and Information Transfer Systems—Open Archival Information System—Reference Model," www.iso.org/iso/catalogue_detail .htm?csnumber=24683 (accessed May 21, 2012).
6. ISO 14721:2003(E), 4.1.
7. ISO 14721:2003(E), 5-4.
8. See ISO 16363:2012 (E), Sections 3.1-3.5.2.
9. See ISO 363: 20012 (E), Sections 4.1-4/6/2/1.
10. See ISO 16363: 20012 (E), Sections 5.1-5.2.3.
11. For a useful overview of PREMIS see Priscilla Caplan, "Understanding PREMIS," Library of Congress (February 2009) at www.loc.gov/standards/premis/understanding-premis.pdf.
12. The Library of Congress, "PREMIS Data Dictionary Version 2.2: Hierarchical Listing of Semantic Units," September 13, 2012, www.loc.gov/standards/premis/v2/premis-dd-Hierarchical-Listing-2-2 .html.

13. Library of Congress, *PREMIS Data Dictionary for Preservation Metadata*, Version 2.1 (January 2011).
14. Charles Dollar and Lori Ashley are codevelopers of this model. Since 2007 they have used it successfully in both the public and private sectors. The most recent instance is a digital preservation capability assessment for the U.S. Council of State Archivists (CoSA). For more information about the model see "Digital Preservation Capability Maturity Model" at www.savingthedigitalworld.com.
15. ISO 1472 uses fixity to express the notion that there have been no unauthorized changes to electronic records and associated Preservation Description Information in the custody of the repository. See ISO 14721:2003 (E): 1.6.
16. For information about digital preservation capability performance metrics visit "Digital Preservation Capability Maturity Model" at www.savingthedigitalworld.com.
17. "Preservation-ready" file formats refer to open-standard technology-neutral formats that the organization has identified as preferred for long-term digital preservation.
18. "What Is Archivematica?," October 15, 2012, www.archivematica.org/wiki/Main_Page.
19. Tessella, www.tessella.com/tag/safety-deposit-box (accessed June 28, 2012).
20. Tessella, "Preservica: Digital Preservation as a Service," January 2011, www.digital-preservation.com/wp-content/uploads/Paas-Description-V3-Alternate-Web.pdf.

CHAPTER 18

Storage and Hardware Considerations

When considering the fact that information is estimated to be doubling approximately every two years, and that more data has been generated in the past three years than in all of time, the massive amounts of data that organizations are struggling to manage becomes readily apparent. It's a crushing amount, and it increases in volume daily.

The Onslaught of "Big Data"

In today's environment, it is not feasible for humans to review each and every document or record to determine its final disposition; there is simply too much information being generated for this approach to be practical and cost-effective. Some fundamental changes are needed in the records management industry to allow for information governance (IG) rules to be set, retention schedules developed and agreed upon, and then to allow for the systematic auto-classification of documents and records according to document type.

Larger organizations that are being choked with this onslaught of "big data" are beginning to realize that they do not need to keep probably 50 to 80 percent of the information that they are keeping, it is simply "data debris," so massive savings in hardware, labor, and maintenance costs can be had by gaining control over the information and distilling it down to only what is needed, and then managing it according to a policy-based retention schedule. *Also, the data itself is all discoverable, and represents an avoidable legal risk.*

It really all boils down to correct classification of the data, according to IBM's Craig Rhinehart. This will allow organizations to sort out what information they need, and what they can dispose of.[1] This cuts down the mountains of useless data, which helps to posture an organization more agilely, and, combined with robust search

> Organizations are being deluged with information, yet upon examination it is clear that only 10 to 20 percent of what is being kept is truly essential.

tools, helps to improve the findability of information and therefore the productivity of knowledge workers. In addition, it cuts exposure to business and legal risk.

Basic Types of Computer Storage

Storage devices and methods for maintaining permanent copies of electronic records have evolved substantially over the decades; just as records stored on microfilm went through legal challenges and were accepted, e-records, and more broadly, **electronically stored information** (ESI), had to be proven to be authentic and reliable to be accepted during e-discovery by the courts.

The primary legal focus has been in determining whether or not the records stored electronically were, in fact, unalterable, and whether the policies and methods used to handle the e-records could demonstrate a protected chain of custody to ensure the authenticity of the records.

E-records cleared a number of legal hurdles along the way, but formally were recognized into the mainstream legally with the changes in the U.S. Federal Rules of Civil Procedure (FRCP) in 2006, which set out a number of conditions for the legal acceptance of ESI, and its exchange between opposing parties in civil litigation.

There are several primary types of storage media used to store data electronic records.

Magnetic disk drives have been the main storage device used in data centers for over a half-century, and they provide very fast, online access to e-records. Their capacities and speeds have steadily improved, while prices per megabyte have declined.

The desktop or portable personal computer (PC) most people use today has a fixed magnetic disk drive, or "hard disk," although with the advent of tablet PCs, more and more tablets are using faster and more reliable (and expensive) **solid state disks,** which have no moving parts and are made of semiconductor materials, just as **computer memory** is. Memory sticks and removable USB "thumb" or flash drives are also solid state technology.

An analogy from years past may be useful in showing how computer memory and hard disk interoperate: The paperwork your grandfather was working on on his desk is analogous to computer memory, where active files are being viewed and processed; but when he finished his paperwork he stored it in his desk drawer in folders, which is analogous to your computer's disk drive.

Magnetic tape drive technologies have been around the longest, and are typically used for backing up data and records. Tape used to be deployed in commercial environments as simple tape reels (similar to reel-to-reel audio tape used for high-end stereos in the 1960s to 1970s), but today cartridges and cassettes are used. For higher volumes, tape autoloaders and tape libraries help to manage larger volumes of data. *The disadvantage of tape is that access to its contents is linear, and accessing it is slower than with hard disk. But the advantage is cost: tape is inexpensive when compared to other storage media.*

The high volumes and density of scanned images of records (versus simple data) required much greater storage capacities, and the need to store e-records permanently, so magneto **optical disc** drives and media began to be used. Optical drives use lasers to record and retrieve information, and optical media has a much longer useful life (some purported to be 100 years or more).

There are three basic types of storage media for e-records: (1) magnetic, (2) solid state, and (3) optical. Magnetic is the least expensive, solid state is the fastest, and optical offers reliability and long-term permanence.

Although they were developed in the late 1970s, different types of optical storage technologies entered the mainstream in the 1980s when retail consumers where able to buy compact disc players which offered much greater fidelity and permanence, versus vinyl records or cassette tapes. Their use for document imaging, in the form of 12-inch and 14-inch optical platters (by manufacturers such as Sony, Philips, and Kodak), became prevalent in the late 1990s. They came as standalone drives and also in large, refrigerator-sized optical disc autochanger units, which were dubbed a **jukebox** (for its similarity in mechanics to jukebox units for playing vinyl records, and later, CDs). The move to more compact 5.25-inch optical discs occurred when storage densities were significantly increased. The smaller form factor allowed much faster exchange times in jukebox units when compared to its larger-sized predecessors.

Today's E-Records Storage Solutions

Today, organizations deploying major e-records implementations have mostly moved away from the slower and more cumbersome optical disc units to magnetic, using software and firmware (fixed instruction sets on a chip) to enforce **write once read many** (WORM) protocols. WORM technology began with magneto optical disc drives and then the capability was developed for magnetic drives. *WORM disk technology helps to prove that e-records have not been altered, overwritten, or erased.*

According to Rhinehart, "Any optical disc jukeboxes still in production today are legacy systems."[2] The information held on them is expiring as each year progresses, so the units will be phased out over time.

Nonerasable Nonrewritable Requirement for Securities Broker-Dealers

As the result of a Securities and Exchange Commission (SEC) rule, the use of the term **nonerasable nonrewritable** (NENR) for storage technologies arose. NENR refers to multiple types (e.g. optical, magnetic) of media that, once written, do not allow for erasure or overwriting of the original data. The SEC spelled out its key requirements

Magnetic WORM disk drives are the most frequently used storage medium for e-records. Optical disc jukeboxes are still in use in legacy systems, and are still being used for archival purposes.

and concerns, stating that the choice of media does not matter, but that, under 17 CFR part 241, *"electronic records must be preserved exclusively in a nonrewriteable and nonerasable format."*[3]

"Rule 17a-3 requires broker-dealers to make certain records, including trade blotters, asset and liability ledgers, income ledgers, customer account ledgers, securities records, order tickets, trade confirmations, trial balances, and various employment related documents. Rule 17a-4 specifies the manner in which the records created in accordance with Rule 17a-3, and certain other records produced by broker-dealers, must be maintained. It also specifies the required retention periods for these records. For example, many of the records, including communications that relate to the broker-dealer's business as such, must be retained for three years; certain other records must be retained for longer periods."[4]

Beyond unalterable records retention, the SEC required certain audit procedures be in place. "Under the final rule amendments, users of electronic storage media must have in place an audit system that provides for accountability regarding inputting of records required to be maintained and preserved pursuant to Rules 17a-3 and 17a-4 to electronic storage media and inputting of any changes made to every original and duplicate record maintained and preserved thereby.[5] Although the Commission is not specifying the contents of each audit system, data automatically or otherwise stored (in the computer or in hard copy) regarding inputting of records and changes to existing records will be part of that system. The Commission envisions that names of individuals actually inputting records and making particular changes, and the identity of documents changed and the identity of new documents created, are the kind of information that automatically would be collected pursuant to the audit system requirement. The results of the audit system must be available for examination by the staffs of the Commission and the appropriate SROs and must be preserved for the time required for the audited records.

In addition, the entity employing the electronic storage media must organize and index all information maintained on both original and duplicate electronic storage media, and each index must be duplicated. The entity employing the technology must also maintain, keep current, and provide promptly upon request by the Commission or SROs all information necessary to access records and indexes stored on electronic storage media, or escrow and keep current a copy of the physical and logical file format, the field format of all different information types written on the electronic storage media and the source code, together with appropriate documentation and information necessary to access records and indexes."[6]

Nonalterable Media Helps Meet Regulations in Healthcare and Other Industries

Certain other regulations and legal requirements may be met using WORM and other NENR storage technologies, such as the Health Insurance Portability and Accountability Act (HIPAA), which specifies not only privacy requirements but also records retention and preservation periods for patients' clinical and financial information.[7]

CHAPTER SUMMARY: **KEY POINTS**

- Organizations are being deluged with information, yet upon examination it is clear that only 10 to 20 percent of what is being kept is truly essential.

- There are three main types of storage media for e-records: (1) magnetic, (2) solid state, and (3) optical. Optical offers the greatest storage capacity and permanence, yet is slower to access and retrieve records.

- Magnetic WORM drives are the most frequently used storage medium for e-records. Optical disc (OD) jukeboxes are still in use in legacy systems, and OD is still being used for archival purposes, yet will continue to be phased out.

- The SEC requires that broker-dealers keep certain records for stated retention periods and that they be preserved using media that is nonerasable, nonrewritable (NENR). Other industries such as health care can meet certain retention and preservation regulations with the support of WORM and NENR storage technologies.

Notes

1. Craig Rhinehart, IBM Software Solutions Group, telephone interview with author, August 7, 2012.
2. Ibid.
3. U.S. Securities and Exchange Commission, "SEC Interpretation: Electronic Storage of Broker-Dealer Records," May 20, 2003, www.sec.gov/rules/interp/34-47806.htm.
4. Ibid.
5. U.S. Securities and Exchange Commission, "Reporting Requirements for Brokers or Dealers under the Securities Exchange Act of 1934," January 31, 1997, www.sec.gov/rules/final/34-38245.txt.
6. Ibid.
7. Storage Quest, "Optical Storage Overview," 2012, www.storagequest.com/894.

PART FIVE
Project and Program Management Issues

CHAPTER 19

E-Records Project Planning and Program Management Issues

Robert Smallwood; edited by Monica Crocker, CRM, PMP

Implementing technology for technology's sake is never a good idea. To be successful, projects focused on managing electronic records, like all projects, must have some compelling **business driver** in a crucial area that makes it imperative for the organization to tackle and solve a problem.

This business driver should align with one or more of the organization's **business objectives**. Implementing technology to achieve business objectives and move the organization forward and improve its competitive posture is good business.

The primary business driver for an **electronic records management** (ERM) project or program could be one of several things. Here are a few examples:

- A new regulation or law can be met only by automating records management in a target area.
- The loss of a legal case due to the lack of formal, defensible records management policies, or the inability to produce electronic records in a timely and cost-effective manner to meet e-discovery requirements.
- Compliance sanctions are suffered by the organization and it must improve its ability to maintain, preserve, and produce e-records.
- Major productivity gains and possibly a competitive advantage can be gained by automating a key business area or by extending the business process outside the walls of the organization.
- Auditors find that information governance (IG) and records management policies are undeveloped, outdated, or inadequate, and recommend changes.
- Knowledge workers consistently cannot find the documents and records they need to perform their job duties in a timely fashion.
- It takes too long to bring new staff up to speed in their positions.
- Lack of process reporting tools and transparency into the process.
- A desire to improve customer service or customer retention.
- A significant number of holders of corporate knowledge are preparing to retire and there is no means to categorize or store their information.[1]
- After a merger or acquisition, one organization has automated their records management function and the other needs to be brought up to the same level of automation to streamline and integrate operations.

> A key business driver is required to fuel a project or program forward.

So, the first step is to identify a key business driver that causes the project to gain interest, executive sponsorship, allocated budget, management time, and implementation resources.

Avoiding Problems

According to various studies and anecdotal project evidence, often ERM implementations do not meet their planned expectations, due to lack of attention to, or underestimation of key issues, such as:

- **Underestimating the business process redesign effort.** Often quite significant changes in the way people work with records is required to achieve significant improvements in productivity, auditability, compliance capabilities, and organization development.
- **Lack of training or poor training plan.** Affected staff must be trained not only on the fundamentals of the new ERM system, but also, a plan for continuous training and updates must be in place to allow for those workers to more fully exploit the new system's capabilities. In addition, as turnover occurs, new hires must be trained on system use to bring them up to speed and maximize their productivity and value to the organization.
- **Lack of proper and complete IG efforts.** Changes to internal policy to improve management and control of information must be made. The ERM system can help enforce these IG guidelines, but IG must be continually monitored and fine-tuned to provide maximum effectiveness.
- **Internal power struggles.** If basic project management (PM) best practices are not followed (such as having a clear business objective, budgeted funds, and a formal project charter signed by an executive sponsor who is actively involved and has the budget authority and political power to carry the project through to completion), then the project is subject to political infighting and budget battles.
- **Underestimation of the records conversion or migration effort.** Paper documents may have to be scanned and electronic files may have to be converted to allow for full implementation of the ERM system. This is a challenging, time-consuming, and costly process that must be gauged properly by an experienced team.
- **Unplanned project expansion.** Or "scope creep" beyond the original defined project risks the possibility of not completing the initial project phase soon enough to show real results to senior management, and potentially risks killing the project altogether.
- **Lack of attention to search structure detail.** If taxonomy and metadata issues are not addressed properly, then users will not be able to derive the maximum benefit the ERM can provide as they will not be able to perform as complete or rapid searches.
- **Lack of user acceptance.** There is an adage in the IT industry that says, "The perfect system will fail without user acceptance." This is usually attributed to

> Often ERM implementations do not meet their planned expectations due to underestimation of the business process redesign effort, training needs, IG requirements, and other critical issues.

lack of consultation with users and stakeholders in the early phases of the project, and, as a result their needs and concerns are not reflected in the final system design, so they may reject it.

It is also worth noting that ERM systems can (and should) have high visibility in the organization. And they can have high impact (and associated risk). By their nature, they also require support from the users and other stakeholders. Lack of user buy-in can easily derail an ERM system, as they can (possibly subconsciously) make the system appear less efficient than the "old way." As a result, even more so than with a typical project, communication is a key component to project success.[2]

Communication Is Key

Your executive (or project) sponsor and PM must:

- *Communicate strategically*—and be thinking several steps ahead so that the project can stay on track, on time, and on budget.
- *Communicate politically*—remembering that political infighting is a real risk and it can jeopardize a project.
- *Communicate within the project team*—develop a close business relationship with team members and work to keep them communicating between each other.
- *Communicate tactically (with users)*—bear in mind that changing the way users work upsets their normal routine and way of doing things and that there is going to be resistance. Do not be condescending or authoritative, but strive to be inclusive, consultative, and yet lead the project with a firm hand.
- *Communicate with other organizations/users*—keep those who need to know in the know for long-term success.
- *Communicate with the vendor(s)*—let vendors know of festering problems so they can apply resources to assist. Keep the vendors on your side, you are in a business marriage, and it behooves all parties to make it work.
- *Communicate with others who may threaten the project's success*—such as anyone who might be creating a "content silo." Do not let users run off and create new problems while you are trying to solve old ones.[3]

Getting an Early Win

It is crucial to demonstrate the benefits of an ERM system implementation and supporting IG polices early on. This will help to maintain the support of senior management, assure the required level of resources to continue the roll-out of the project,

> The selection of the pilot area or key business process is a critical decision point.

and the transition into an ongoing program. That means *success must be shown within months, not years.*

So when scoping the initial or pilot implementation, the selection of that departmental area or key business process is a critical decision point.

There may be several candidate areas vying for the business resources needed to implement ERM, so some preliminary analysis must take place to prioritize and roughly rank the possible implementation areas based on the projected benefit and ease of implementation. Other factors come into play, such as budget realities, cultural resistance, and management availability, but *the ideal application to pilot is one that is fairly simple or straightforward, and involves a limited number of users* (typically less than 25 to 30). It is best if, during initial inquiries with software providers, it is found that similar types of implementations have been successfully completed.

The pilot project should be one that is able to demonstrate significant gains in efficiencies and productivity (i.e., "low-hanging fruit") as well as improved completeness and accuracy of searches, and faster retrieval of records. But more important, where the payback period or return on investment (ROI) is readily calculable. This provides fodder for the business case to move forward, and justifies the initial investment. (For more detail on developing the business case, see Chapter 20 on this topic.)

It is important to select a simple pilot area, *but not too simple*, that is, this author has seen major organizations conduct an incomplete software evaluation and successfully pilot an application, only to find out that the software was incapable of handling more challenging applications that the organization needed to address down the road. The question arose, "We spent a million dollars on *this*?" It ended in litigation, but didn't have to, if they had done their homework.

A judicious and thorough request for proposal (RFP) process would have been able to smoke out these types of deficiencies (see Chapter 22 on procurement governance for more detail). This requires that you have a long-term plan/strategy for ERM throughout the enterprise, but start with one implementation.

Also a key consideration is gaining an executive sponsor in the target area (see Chapter 21 on securing executive sponsorship). If there is no available executive sponsor, or the best person for that role is simply unwilling to lead the effort, another area must be considered that gives the initial launch a better chance for success.

Another consideration for candidate pilot areas is the basic makeup of a business unit; if the unit is comprised mostly of employees nearing retirement age, for instance, they are naturally going to be more resistant to change.

> The pilot area should be one that is fairly simple to automate yet can show a significant benefit. A modest number of users should be included.

Selecting the Right Team Members

Project team members should be stakeholders who represent a cross-section of functional areas that must be involved for the project to succeed. At a minimum, for an ERM system implementation, project members must come from the target application area, as well as records management, information technology (IT), business analysis, legal, compliance, and risk management. These last areas are often combined in organizations or grouped such as "records management and compliance" or "risk management and compliance" but in any case, you will need records management expertise, IT expertise, business application expertise, legal expertise, and project management expertise to keep the project on track, on time, and on budget.

Project Charter

The first step in all quality methodologies (e.g., Six Sigma, TQM) is to establish a **project charter**.[4] *The project charter is a document that will formally authorize the project to move forward*, once it is signed by the executive sponsor (or project sponsor). It defines the scope of the project, names the **project manager** (PM), and launches the **project plan**.[5] "A project charter dramatically reduces the risk of a project being cancelled due to lack of support or perceived value to the company. It documents the overall objectives of the project and helps manage the expectations."[6]

The project plan includes a schedule, cost estimates, and more scoping detail. It must be approved by the executive/project sponsor, who releases budgeted funds, and the project tasks can commence.

In the scope statement, the ultimate deliverable (e.g., "ERM system implementation and live operation of 25 users in the tax department by June 30") is specified, and it is tied to business needs and objectives. It must be clearly shown *how* the project meets business objectives and *why* it is a business necessity. More detailed deliverables should be broken out that support the accomplishment of the ultimate deliverable of the project.

The PM is the primary facilitator and communicator of project progress. (See Chapter 21 on executive sponsorship for details on PM tasks and responsibilities throughout the project.) They must develop and update the project plan, inform stakeholders (including project contractors or subcontractors) of progress, request resources, and make change order requests for any project changes outside the original scope. The PM must control and manage the project, measure its progress, and take corrective action to address any lags, conflicts, or other barriers to implementation.

The PM must develop a summary of critical milestones to measure progress on the project, and they must "obtain approval from the Project Sponsor for any schedule changes that impact the project completion milestone."[7]

A project budget must be created by the PM and approved by the executive/project sponsor. It should show where the budget money comes from and what it will be

The project charter defines the scope of the project, names the project manager, and, once signed by the executive sponsor, formally authorizes a project.

spent on. Any variances must be documented and justified, and submitted to the executive sponsor for approval.

Standards in Project Management

Two committees have been formed by the International Organization for Standardization (ISO) to pursue development of standards for project management: PC236 Project Management and TC258 Project, Programme, and Portfolio Management.[8]

Project Management Methodologies

There are several well-established approaches to project management. These can be used as a framework for managing the initial project. When the project becomes an ongoing *program*, its maintenance and execution will become more complex, and will require additional monitoring and controls.

Project Management Body of Knowledge

Project Management Body of Knowledge (PMBOK), from the U.S.-based Project Management Institute (PMI),[9] describes the sum of codified knowledge and best practices in the project management field. It is available in book form, spanning over 400 pages. Originally released as a white paper in 1983, it is in its fourth edition, and has been translated into more than 10 languages.

PMBOK divides project management knowledge into nine distinct areas:

Project Integration Management—ensures the project is "properly coordinated" and includes the key processes of Project Plan Development and Execution, and Overall Change Control

Project Scope Management—Scope Planning, Definition, Verification, and Change Control to ensure that the size and breadth of the project is proper to achieve successful implementation

Project Time Management—managing project time and milestones to keep the project on schedule

Project Cost Management—managing financial and physical resources (people, materials) to stay within the planned budget

Project Quality Management—meet internal and external customer and stakeholder expectations and requirements

Project Human Resource Management—effectively leveraging the time and talents of all stakeholders, including the executive sponsor and project team, and any outside contractors or consultants

Project Communications Management—communicating progress and project needs in a cyclic, regular, and businesslike fashion to all stakeholders

Project Risk Management—identifying, analyzing, and countering potential project risks

Project Procurement Management—controlling the processes for acquiring software, hardware, materials, and human resources. Includes "Procurement Planning, Solicitation Planning, Solicitation [of bids], Source Selection, Contract Administration, and Contract Close-Out"[10]

The nine cited knowledge areas operate in parallel throughout the duration of the project. Not all projects will require full use of all these areas, and some areas will be more heavily utilized than others.

Once executive sponsorship and budget are obtained, and the project charter is signed off on, *the biggest keys to project success are leadership and communication.* This requires regular status meetings that have a planned agenda are led authoritatively and expediently by the PM; progress is documented and outstanding "to do" items are addressed.

There are five groups of processes that PMBOK presents that are core project management processes:

1. *Initiating processes*—to start a project or project phase;
2. *Planning processes*—to plan costs, human resource needs, timelines, milestones, etc. Pervasive and very important processes throughout the project;
3. *Executing processes*—includes "core processes" to execute tasks like project plan and team development;
4. *Controlling processes*—to meet time and budget constraints;
5. *Closing processes*—closure of phases and the project itself (e.g., signoff of completion by executive sponsor).[11]

MIKE2.0 Enterprise Information Management Methodology

MIKE2.0 (Method for an Integrated Knowledge Environment) is an established framework and delivery methodology for information management best practices tied to technology-specific solutions and common business issues. It covers the entire information supply chain from creation, through access and presentation, storage, security and ultimately, final disposition (which may include archival or destruction). Although it began as an approach to information management for structured data, its goal is to provide a general model that includes unstructured data (such as e-records). It was originally developed by Bearing Point, a major global consulting firm with European roots.[12]

In 2006, the MIKE2.0 methodology was released to the public and became an open source methodology that allows input from interested parties. The MIKE2.0 Governance Association (MGA) took over governance in 2009. The content has continued to evolve and become more sophisticated and mature.[13] AIIM International used MIKE2.0 as the basis for their Enterprise 2.0 training certificate program.

MIKE2.0 is a vertical market-agnostic methodology that can be applied to the private and public sector.[14]

What MIKE2.0 Offers

The MIKE2.0 methodology is a comprehensive approach for improving how information is managed across the enterprise by providing a common business strategy, technology architecture, and delivery methodology for information management projects. To summarize, "MIKE2.0 provides the following characteristics:

Established—our Enterprise Information Management Methodology derives from successful client implementations.

Tool-enabled—utilizes tools, techniques and templates for Information Management engagements

Comprehensive—takes into consideration all factors contributing to data issues by considering people, process, organisation, technology and strategy.

Modular—the overall methodology is composed of a number of smaller parts that are targeted at specific business problems. A governing framework provides continuity to the overall MIKE2.0 methodology.

Enterprise capable—by providing a cornerstone approach, the Enterprise Information Management Methodology provides reusable assets that can be used to build solutions at the Enterprise level.

Actionable—can be used to create a vision and an action plan that incorporates policies, practice, standards and the system components to address business priorities as a continuous improvement effort instead of as a one-time event.

ROI-driven—can be used to build a business case that is used to guide the implementation program and measure targeted benefits and benchmark realized benefits."[15]

MIKE2.0 Project Phases

There are five phases in the MIKE2.0 methodology; not all tasks and activities within each phase are required, as they depend on the project at hand:

Phase 1: Business Assessment and Strategy Definition Blueprint. This initial phase includes education and communication about information management, a rapid assessment of the state of information management in the target implementation area, painting a vision of the "after" state of the newly automated area, developing a business strategy for the project, calculating the return on investment (ROI) to make the business case, and other related project initiation and planning activities.[16]

Phase 2: Technology Assessment and Selection Blueprint. In this phase, strategic requirements for the project are laid out, the present technological environment is documented, the "future state" view of the targeted area (postimplementation) is created, and a "technology blueprint" for getting there is fleshed out. This phase also includes establishment and/or communication of data governance polices and standards, metadata architecture strategy is developed, standards are reviewed and considered, and preparations are made for the software development lifecycle.

Phase 3: Information Management Roadmap and Foundation Activities. The planned information management roadmap/blueprint is reviewed, a testing and deployment plan is created, detailed business requirements are gathered, governance metrics are agreed upon, the taxonomy is designed and metadata structure is developed, revisions are made and the new information management solution is prototyped.

Phase 4: Design Increment. In this phase, information security and business intelligence (if needed) schemes are designed, along with process design, user interfaces, and service-oriented architecture (SOA), if needed, and physical and logical data integration issues are resolved, followed by testing.

Phase 5: Incremental Development, Testing, Deployment, and Improvement. Operational and user guides are created to assist in user training and support, functional and system integration testing commences, live benchmarks and stress testing is performed to see if the solution can scale and perform with live data loads, users and system administrators are trained, the system is deployed into production, evaluations and adjustments are made, and the move to continuous improvement as an ongoing *program* is made. MIKE2.0 features continuous improvement in this phase for compliance auditing; standards, policies, and processes; data quality; and infrastructure and information management development. The project should be closed out and signed off on by the executive sponsor before it is elevated to an ongoing program with all its associated requirements and complexities.[17]

PRINCE2™

Whereas PMBOK is a collection of project management knowledge and best practices for guidance, MIKE2.0 and **Pr**ojects **IN C**ontrolled **E**nvironments (PRINCE2) are project management methodologies.

PRINCE2 was originally developed within the U.K. government by the Central Computer and Telecommunications Agency (CCTA) as a project management standard for IT projects.[18] Now, it is widely used and is the de facto standard for managing all types of projects in the United Kingdom. PRINCE2 "is a process-based approach for project management, providing an easily tailored and scaleable project management methodology for the management of all types of projects."[19]

PRINCE2 principally focuses on five key areas: (1) business case/justification, (2) project management team structure, (3) planning approach that is product-based (and focused on resulting deliverables), (4) segmenting the project into "manageable and controllable" stages, and (5) flexibility that can be applied according to project-specific needs.[20]

In the PRINCE2 methodology, projects are justified on the business case, which is regularly reviewed during the project to ensure focus on achieving project business objectives.

In 2009, a "refresh" or update was performed on PRINCE2.[21] This is done every few years by the UK's Cabinet Office, which owns the methodology. The biggest change to come out of the updating process is that now there are two books, *Managing Successful Projects Using PRINCE2* and *Directing Successful Projects Using PRINCE2*, which are presented in a format that makes them easier to navigate and understand. The latter manual is for executives and board members directing projects.

Individuals and groups may take PRINCE2 training courses online or in classroom sessions. There are two "qualification" levels that may be achieved, which require a competency examination. The first level is PRINCE2 Foundation, which is a three-day course, and the more advanced PRINCE2 Practitioner, which is a five-day course that includes the PRINCE2 Foundation.[22]

There are eight component areas to the PRINCE2 methodology:[23]

1. **Business case.** The most important part of any PRINCE2 project. If at any time during the project the business case cannot justify the project, it should be halted. In the Business Case, a detailed business rationale including the projected benefits and costs, and potential risks, is presented.
2. **Organization.** This component is focused on creating an effective and workable project organization structure. It is based on the traditional "customer/supplier relationship model", which places the project board, PM, and project team members on the supplier side, and the customer can be either internal or external to the organization.
3. **Plans.** Planning takes place throughout the different stages of the project, and in PRINCE2, projects have a defined beginning, middle, and end. There are three plan levels: Project Plan, Stage Plan, and Team Plan. Plans must include the specifics of deliverables to be produced, and the required activities and resources (i.e., money, people, time) to achieve those aims. If plans exceed their budgeted resource levels, then an Exception Plan (similar to a change order) can be produced to modify the plan.
4. **Controls.** These are used to keep a project on schedule and on budget, and controls are in place throughout the life of the project, many being event-driven. Controls in place for the project board include Project Initiation, End Stage Assessments, Highlight Reports, Exception Reports, Exception Assessments, and Project Closure.
5. **Management of risk.** Begins with Identifying and Evaluating Risks, and then this process monitors and tracks risks in a formal Risk Log. PRINCE2 uses the concept of "risk ownership" to tie an owner directly to a risk, which should be the person who can best monitor, evaluate, and control the risk (typically Project Board members).
6. **Quality in a project environment.** Quality Management in PRINCE2 is made up of four components: Quality System, which are the processes and procedures to implement Quality Management; Quality Assurance, which is the method used to ensure acceptable levels of quality are achieved for the customer (e.g., end users); Quality Planning, which is used to plan for and check quality and document customer expectations of quality; and Quality Control, which is actual inspection of products (or outputs) to see if they meet stated quality criteria.
7. **Configuration management.** Concerns the methods used in controlling and managing projects, such as version control. When a product or deliverable is created, it is archived or "frozen" to establish a baseline product for that particular phase. There are five basic components to this area: Planning, Identification, Control, Status Accounting, and Verification.
8. **Change control.** This is the approach to managing change and change order requests, which must be managed once they arise. This helps the project stay on track and also provides a business rationale for each change that deviates from the original plan. The change request risk is logged and tracked as well.

PRINCE2 provides an excellent and proven methodology for project management, with ample opportunities for training to achieve competence, particularly in the United Kingdom and Europe.

PMBOK is a project management knowledge base, and MIKE2.0 and PRINCE2 are framework methodologies that can help to guide the planning and implementation of ERM systems.

Determining the Best Approach

Which is the best approach and methodology to use? This will depend on your organization, its culture, and the unique requirements of your project. At a basic level, it is true that many projects have been managed successfully with a simple timeline and pen and paper at status meetings, addressing outstanding "to do" items. The three PM approaches overviewed certainly have commonalities and provide a framework for reference that should improve the odds for success and reduce risks. The proper and most appropriate approach for your project depends on a number of factors. Survey the methodologies and body of knowledge and draw the best practices and steps that best fit your implementation scenario. Utilize the methodology or combination of methodologies that you feel is most appropriate, if one is not specified for you, with the knowledge of the available resources and guides that you have at your disposal based on the experience of practitioners in thousands of projects.

Moving to an Ongoing Program

Implementing ERM is an iterative process that requires regular updating and fine-tuning to maintain effectiveness. This means that once your initial project is complete, signed off, and closed out, you may kickoff another project in another area, or move to supporting an ongoing program. *Administering a program is more complex and challenging, as there is no end to it.* You will need to develop or update IG policies, and put in place audits and checkpoints to ensure that IG policies are enforced on an ongoing basis so that records are managed efficiently and effectively.

Also, *consider that the processes of taxonomy and metadata development and strategy will be ongoing*—they must continue to be adapted for new document and record types, new user demands, and to improve the organization and findability of documents and records. If your implementation is in a fast-changing area, such as one that deals with social media or cloud computing, continual changes are needed to keep pace with technological changes and to take advantage of new capabilities. Retention schedules will need updating, as new regulations are brought online and requirements change.

Monitoring and Accountability

This requires a continuous tightening down and expansion of the new capability brought into the organization by the implementation of newer, strategic ERM-related technologies. IT developments and innovations that can foster the effort must be steadily monitored and evaluated, and those technology subsets that can assist in providing improved ERM and improved user experience need to be incorporated into the mix.

> Maintaining a program for ERM requires that someone is accountable for continual monitoring and refinement of policies and tools.

The policies themselves must be reviewed and updated periodically to accommodate changes in the business environment, laws, regulations, and technology. Program gaps and failures must be addressed and the effort should continue to improve and adapt as the context and characteristics of records and the business environment itself continue to evolve and change.

Effective program management requires *accountability*—some individual must remain responsible for an IG policy's administration and results[24]—perhaps the executive sponsor for the project becomes the chief records officer (CRO); or the project manager for the initial target area becomes the chief IG officer or IG Czar; or the chief executive officer (CEO) continues ownership of the project and drives its active improvement. The organization may also decide to form an IG board, steering committee, or team with specific responsibilities for monitoring, maintaining, and advancing the program.

However it takes shape, a program to implement ERM must be ongoing, dynamic, and aggressive in its execution in order to remain effective.

Continuous Process Improvement

Program management requires implementing principles of continuous process improvement (CPI). CPI is a "never-ending effort to discover and eliminate the main causes of problems. It accomplishes this by using small-steps improvements, rather than implementing one huge improvement. In Japan, the word kaizen reflects this gradual and constant process, as it is enacted throughout the organization, regardless of department, position, or level."[25] To remain effective, the program must continue using CPI methods and techniques.

Maintaining and improving the program requires monitoring tools, periodic audits, and regular meetings for discussion and approval of changes to improve the program. It requires a cross-section of representatives from IT, legal, records management, compliance, risk management, and functional business units participating actively and citing possible threats and sources of information leakage. It also requires ongoing technical and financial resources to implement system modifications, enhancements, and upgrades.

Why Continuous Improvement Is Needed

While the specific drivers of change are always evolving, the reasons that organizations need to continuously improve their program for managing electronic records are relatively constant, and include:

- **Changing technology**. New technology capabilities need to be monitored and considered with an eye to improving, streamlining, or reducing the cost of managing electronic records. The program to manage e-records needs to anticipate new types of threats and also evaluate adding or replacing technologies to continue to improve it.

- **Changing laws and regulations**. Compliance with new or updated laws and regulations must be maintained.
- **Internal information governance requirements**. As an organization updates and improves its overall IG, the program elements that concern critical electronic records must be kept aligned and synchronized.
- **Changing business plans**. As the enterprise develops new business strategies and enters new markets, it must reconsider and update its program for managing electronic records. If, for instance, a firm moves from being a domestic entity to a regional or global one, new integration challenges will exist and new threats will arise so new strategies must be developed.
- **Evolving industry best practices**. Best practices change and new best practices arise with the introduction of each successive wave of technology, and with changes in the business environment. The program should consider and leverage new best practices.
- **Fixing program shortcomings**. Addressing flaws in the program that are discovered through testing, monitoring, and auditing; or addressing an actual regulatory violation; or a legal sanction imposed due to noncompliance are all reasons why a program must be revisited periodically and kept updated.[26]

Maintaining the program requires that a senior level officer of the enterprise continues to push for enforcement, improvement, and expansion to manage records and documents which are crucial information assets. This requires leadership, and a consistent and clear message to employees. The organization and management of information assets must be on the minds of all members of the enterprise; it must be something they are aware of and think about daily. They must be on the lookout for ways to improve it, and they should be rewarded for those contributions.

Gaining this level of mindshare in employees' heads will require follow-up messages in the form of personal speeches and presentations, newsletters, corporate announcements, e-mail messages, and even posters placed at strategic points (e.g., near the shared printing station). Everyone must be reminded that managing records and documents is everyone's job, and that they are valuable information assets.

CHAPTER SUMMARY: **KEY POINTS**

- A key business driver is required to drive a project or program forward.
- Often ERM implementations do not meet their planned expectations due to underestimation of the business process redesign effort, training needs, IG requirements, and other critical issues.
- The selection of the pilot area or key business process is a critical decision point.

(Continued)

(Continued)

- The pilot area should be one that is fairly simple to automate yet can show a significant benefit. A modest number of users should be included.

- The project charter defines the scope of the project, names the project manager and, once signed by the executive sponsor, formally authorizes a project.

- Two committees have been formed by ISO to pursue development of standards for project management.

- PMBOK is a project management knowledge base, and MIKE2.0 and PRINCE2 are framework methodologies that can help to guide the planning and implementation of ERM systems.

- Maintaining a program for ERM requires that someone is accountable for continual monitoring and refinement of policies and tools.

Notes

1. Monica Crocker, e-mail to author, August 2, 2012.
2. Ibid.
3. Ibid.
4. iSixSigma, "Six Sigma Project Charter," www.isixsigma.com/tools-templates/project-charter/six-sigma-project-charter/ (accessed July 20, 2012).
5. Project Management Docs, www.projectmanagementdocs.com/templates/project-charter-template-verbose.html (accessed July 20, 2012).
6. Rita Mulcahy, "Project Management Crash Course: What Is a Project Charter?," October 28, 2009, www.ciscopress.com/articles/article.asp?p=1400865.
7. Ibid.
8. Project Management Institute, "PMBOK Guide and Standards," www.pmi.org/PMBOK-Guide-and-Standards.aspx (accessed July 20, 2012).
9. Project Management Institute, "Library of PMI Global Standards," www.pmi.org/PMBOK-Guide-and-Standards/Standards-Library-of-PMI-Global-Standards.aspx (accessed July 20, 2012).
10. Azad Adam, *Implementing Electronic Document and Record Management Systems* (Boca Raton, FL: Auerbach Publications, 2008), 140–141, 143–148.
11. Ibid., 142.
12. Mike2.0, "BearingPoint," http://mike2.openmethodology.org/wiki/BearingPoint (accessed July 24, 2012).
13. "The History of Mike2.0," http://mike2.openmethodology.org/wiki/The_History_of_MIKE2.0 (accessed July 24, 2012).
14. Mike2.0, "FAQs," http://mike2.openmethodology.org/wiki/MIKE2:FAQs (accessed July 24, 2012).
15. Mike2.0, "Executive Summary," http://mike2.openmethodology.org/wiki/Executive_Summary (accessed July 24, 2012).
16. Mike2.0, "Structural Overview of Mike2.0," http://mike2.openmethodology.org/wiki/Structural_Overview_of_MIKE2.0 (accessed July 24, 2012).
17. Ibid.
18. Adam, *Implementing Electronic Document and Record Management Systems*, 127.
19. www.prince2.com/ (accessed July 26, 2012).
20. "What is Prince2? Prince2 Definition," www.prince2.com/what-is-prince2.asp (accessed July 26, 2012).

21. Prince2, "Manual Managing Successful Projects with Prince2," 2009 ed., www.prince2.com/ prince2-2009.asp (accessed July 26, 2012).
22. "What is Prince2? Prince2 Definition."
23. Adam, *Implementing Electronic Document and Record Management Systems*, 135–140.
24. Mark Woeppel, "Is Your Continuous Improvement Organization a Profit Center?" June 15, 2009, www.processexcellencenetwork.com/process-management/articles/is-your-continuous-improvement-organization-a-prof.
25. Donald Clark, "Big Dog and Little Dog's Performance Juxtaposition," March 11, 2010, www.nwlink .com/~donclark/perform/process.html.
26. Blair Kahn, *Information Nation: Seven Keys to Information Management Compliance* (Silver Spring, MD: AIIM International, 2004), 242–243.

CHAPTER 20

Building the Business Case to Justify an ERM Program

I mplementing a successful **electronic records management** (ERM) program to meet **information governance** (IG) demands requires all the essentials of any successful project, from setting program objectives and building the **business case,** to securing executive sponsorship in the early stages, to formal analysis and design of the ERM system, testing, implementation, and user training.

Determine What Will Fly in Your Organization

The requirements for a business case to justify a project vary by organization, culture, and management style. Some require a strict **internal rate of return** (IRR), hurdle rate, or **return on investment** (ROI) to be calculated before moving forward. Others require justification of hard costs, then look at these alongside the intangible, soft benefits of the automation to complete the justification. Yet other organizations understand the inherent efficiencies of automation and their impact on labor costs, especially with the added advantages of security and risk reduction, and base a management decision on intuition or gut feel. Finally, there are organizations that base the decision on a purely budgetary or tax basis; that is, they have determined the capital budget and which projects to compete for using those allocated funds.

There are clear tangible and intangible benefits to implementing ERM, but fears of compliance violations, spiraling e-discovery costs, or lost and misfiled records may be sufficient to justify the ERM program. Critical questions to raise during the decision-making process include: What would happen if our internal documents and e-mail messages are not organized and retained in accordance with an established, legally defensible schedule? What if we are not able to meet legal demands for records production during litigation? What would happen if auditors or regulators investigated our recordkeeping practices? These types of serious questions must be asked and can only be addressed with a successful ERM implementation managed and controlled by IG.

> The approach to project justification varies by organization, but with ERM, there are clear tangible and intangible benefits.

And just as the September 11th attacks and Hurricane Katrina changed the realities of disaster recovery and business continuity plans, and the WikiLeaks scandal changed the realities of e-document security, *one major adverse event can change the way your organization thinks about managing documents and records.*

The first step in launching an ERM program is to understand what key factors qualify a project as viable in a particular organization. Once that is known, steps to build the business case that satisfy or exceed those requirements can be taken.

Strategic Business Drivers for Project Justification

A fully implemented program for managing electronic records must necessarily be guided and monitored by IG policies, which, in turn, must have built-in controls and audit processes to enforce policy. *ERM technologies will allow the organization to manage its records throughout their lifecycle, from creation to archiving or destruction, but solid IG is what legally defensible records management programs are built upon.*

A robust ERM program enables the organization to capture and declare information and documents as official business records. The records are maintained with accurate and secure metadata and audit trails to provide context along with the content. The ERM software locks the records, preventing modifications, changes, or accidental file deletion, thereby protecting them and ensuring authenticity, a great benefit in legal matters. Records are maintained in the software until the retention period has been met, which further assists in meeting regulatory and legal requirements. Once the retention requirements have passed, the disposition process is initiated, according to the records' retention policy, which means that some may be scheduled to be destroyed. This qualifies as *defensible disposition*, which reduces the organization's risk of keeping records that could be detrimental in future legal or regulatory proceedings. Any records placed on legal or audit hold are suspended from the disposition process until the hold has been removed, which helps ensure compliance with IG policies in the e-discovery and auditing process.[1]

Forming and enforcing the IG policies developed during the ERM project will help transform the corporate culture into one of greater records management awareness and compliance. More concretely, though, following these IG guidelines and policies will boost knowledge worker productivity and help the organization business-wise in all its pursuits. Any business documents or records that are utilized in social media, mobile computing, e-mail, IM, or web applications, whether running internally or externally, will be governed appropriately by rational, prudent business methods. *This will bring the organization a wealth of benefits in business agility, compliance, litigation readiness, and competitiveness, while protecting information assets from erosion, misuse, or theft.*

With the full implementation of an ERM program, *a standard classification system* is used to standardize naming conventions for electronically stored information (ESI).

> Solid IG is what legally defensible records management programs are built upon.

This classification must be in place before any automated system can be implemented. Physical records are generally filed following standard alphabetic, numeric, or alphanumeric filing rules, but e-records are rarely filed consistently (in the Windows directory format); most are filed on an ad hoc basis.

Most organizations have a number of automated business processes in areas such as accounting, human resources (HR), and customer relationship management (CRM). In instances where software applications have replaced manual processes, the data is maintained within the applications. *These systems typically do not include records management features.* The data in these systems is dynamic, so changes to the system can change the representation of the records. For example: The name of a general ledger account on the chart of accounts is changed. Any reports or statements printed after the change, including reports from before the change, may reflect the change rather than the original. The records contained within the application remain in the system until IT purges the data from the database.[2]

Often an organization may create e-records but not manage them properly. Physical records are being replaced by scanned versions, without allowing for the e-records' lifecycle management according to a standard retention and disposition schedule. Organizations often scan records using digital printers and desktop scanners for ease of access. The physical records are usually filed and retained in addition to the electronic copy, creating duplicate copies of the same record. This causes confusion over the authenticity of the records and adds to labor and production costs during litigation or regulatory proceedings.

In addition, if retention periods are not consistently applied to the same types of records across the organization, compliance with IG policies cannot be tracked. It is nearly impossible to identify electronic records holdings or ESI in compliance with legal statutes, as applicable.

When electronic records are not tracked using a central or systematic process, organizations cannot prove compliance with the records retention policy. In the event of a discovery request in the case of litigation, audit, or investigation, the organization has no mechanisms to indicate what records existed or if they have been destroyed in compliance with the records retention schedule. Organizations that do not track their records or the e-record destruction process are at risk of noncompliance.

In the event of litigation, investigation, or audit, this noncompliance could result in adverse actions if requested records cannot be located, regardless of whether they were destroyed following the records retention schedule or simply lost. When organizations do not have a systematic process for tracking records and their authorized destruction, compliance with current regulations and IG policies cannot be proven. A robust IG program, including the implementation of an automated ERM software application, provides this evidence with reports and audit logs.

The regular use of *digital signatures* to safeguard e-documents helps reduce business process cycle times by avoiding the disruptions that occur waiting for signature approvals. This enables business to be carried on in a much more geographically dispersed manner, both within and between organizations. But more important to the security aspect is that the *attached e-documents can confidently be certified as authentic, and the signer's identity is assured, and the chain of custody of these e-records is verifiable and secure.*

Benefits of Electronic Records Management

Implementing ERM represents a significant investment. An investment in ERM is an investment in business process automation and yields document control, document integrity, and security benefits. The volume of records in organizations has often exceeded the employees' ability to manage them. ERM systems do for the information age what the assembly line did for the industrial age. The cost/benefit justification for ERM is sometimes difficult to determine, but there are real labor and cost savings. ERM also provides a number of intangible benefits, while the requirements are clearly justified. There are many ways in which an organization can gain significant business benefits, tangible and intangible, with ERM.[3]

Tangible Financial Benefits

- **Space savings**. The financial benefits for ERM are often difficult to quantify. While saving space is a significant financial benefit, the space used for physical records storage is usually unusable as office space. Organizations often store records in basements or warehouses, where they are vulnerable to water, mildew, dust, and other environmental threats, as well as rodents and insects. During the records survey process, studies often find many records are copies of records maintained by other departments or are duplicated electronically. To fully assess the space savings of implementing ERM, a records inventory would be required to identify all of the records, whether they are originals or duplicates, if they can or are being stored electronically, and if they have met their retention requirements. Without a tracking system for these records, it is not impossible to accurately estimate the space savings.
- **Additional office cost savings.** Additional cost savings can be realized through reduction in printing, postage, faxing, filing, and archiving costs. With ERM, the records in off-site storage would be scheduled for destruction in a timely manner.
- **Disposal of furniture and filing consumables**. A small benefit may be expected in cost avoidance of additional filing cabinets, and the disposal of obsolete filing cabinets. There will be decreased expenditure on file folders and other filing supplies, and so on; however, this savings is minor.
- **Hardware savings**. Implementing an ERM system will result in reduced costs for network and shared drives, including the cost for maintenance. When employees store their documents and records on the repository, the requirement for the network and shared drives will be reduced.

Intangible, Nonfinancial Benefits

- **Information governance over business documents and records.** By using an ERM repository for documents and records, costs are saved through easier access to accurate information, reduced maintenance, handling, and physical storage costs, and gaining full control over the lifecycle of information, documents, and records. Records need to be securely managed, while being made easily accessible to those who have a valid business need and right of access. Plainly, there are benefits to the enterprise, yet they are not readily calculable.

- **Reduced risk**. Organizations can reduce the risk of adverse actions and financial penalties resulting from litigation, government investigation, or audit, by implementing ERM. Through company-wide ERM implementation, the organization can identify ESI and records. ERM provides organizations with tools to systematically identify, manage, protect, and dispose of records and information in the normal course of business, and also engage in audits to provide proof of compliance with legal and regulatory requirements including records management policy and records retention schedule. ERM provides legal departments with search tools to locate ESI required for litigation, sequester or protect ESI, and prepare ESI for discovery according to the document retention order.
- **Productivity benefits**. *ERM provides productivity benefits by enabling employees to work more efficiently and accomplish more with the same staffing levels.* This is achieved by reducing the time spent copying paper records (for ease of access), looking for lost or misfiled records, and recreating records. It also increases productivity by making the records needed by employees instantly available. Also, customer service (both external and internal) is usually improved.
- **Legislative and regulatory compliance**. Organizations are increasingly being required to conform to new regulations that effectively mandate the use of enterprisewide ERM. Specific legislation and guidelines are designed to protect the public and govern records management in organizations, setting the standards for the highest level of security and transparency.

   From a simple browser interface employees will have access to the declaration of records, disposal and retention schedules, authentication and audit features, security, search and retrieval functionality, and the storage of contextual metadata.

   By providing an up-to-date, relevant, accurate, and more complete set of records, ERM will provide increased document auditability, which can be used to justify an organization's past actions and decisions.
- **Higher evidential weight**. With ERM, records presented as evidence in support of litigation will be complete, accurate, and credible. By comparison, collections of paper records and unstructured electronic records seem incomplete, unreliable, and not closely tracked or audited. In any future litigation, there will be processes for identifying the electronically stored information and protecting required records by placing them under a legal hold. The integrity of electronic records may also be used to facilitate complete discovery of evidence.
- **Record security**. ERM provides a highly secure, flexible framework, including options to protect against unauthorized access, accidental deletion, overwriting and version-control issues, and physical storage device failure. ERM provides protection through the full lifecycle management of records from creation to disposal.
- **A structured and trusted information base**. A properly configured ERM system can provide information that is reliably up-to-date and complete. Effective ERM ensures that all users who need access to information, regardless of where it is held and maintained, can access it in a timely and simple manner. This results in avoiding duplication of records. ERM will allow rapid storage and retrieval of information to support a more effective decision-making cycle.

- **Better decision making**. Many benefits of ERM combine to facilitate the making of decisions more quickly, *and the decisions will be based on better information*. Better decision making can be extremely valuable, although the value cannot be quantified.
- **Improved search capability**. Records would be available across departments and functional areas. With the records being stored in their native formats or as PDFs, they can be searched via full-text search capabilities. Additionally, more granular, refined searches are available. Keep in mind that images (scanned or otherwise) not converted by optical character recognition (OCR) software cannot be searched for keywords.

  Storing the records in a searchable format can provide employees with research opportunities that rely on textual searches. Often, specific industries, such as health care and legal, require industry-specific dictionaries to be loaded so industry terms and jargon are recognized correctly.

  For employees, searches can be tailored to a specific set of data and saved. Saved searches are used by employees who search for the same information often. A saved search could recall specific search requirements so the user only needs to enter minimal criteria rather than start from scratch. The time savings can be substantial over the long term.

Presenting the Business Case

Timing is everything. Once a team understands what their organization requires to prioritize and fund a project, then they must work toward fulfilling those requirements. The business case will be different for each organization, as the business environment, corporate culture, funding process, and competitive position varies between organizations.

The project can begin with a broad justification based on a key business driver, something that compels the organization to move forward. Then, as the actual implementation costs become known—including computer hardware, software, training, management time, and maintenance fees—a specific business case can be drawn to implement.

CHAPTER SUMMARY: **KEY POINTS**

- The first step to launching an ERM program is to understand what key factors qualify a project as viable in a particular organization.
- A fully implemented ERM program managed by IG provides a legally defensible posture for e-discovery, legal claims, and compliance inquests.

(Continued)

(*Continued*)

- Tangible financial benefits derived from the implementation of an ERM system include: hardware savings, disposal of furniture and consumables, and space savings. Intangible benefits include: reduced risk, improved search capability, better decision making, a structured and trusted information base, record security, stronger legal evidence, legislative and regulatory compliance, and productivity benefits.

- Timing is everything. Funding an ERM project using IG principles requires developing a solid business case and presenting it at the right time.

Notes

1. Charmaine Brooks, CRM, e-mail to the author, August 21, 2011.
2. Ibid.
3. Ibid.

CHAPTER 21

Securing Executive Sponsorship

Securing an executive sponsor at the senior management level is always crucial to projects and programs. It is not possible to require managers to take time out of their other duties to participate in a project if there is no executive edict. It is a best practice and supports the Generally Accepted Recordkeeping Principles® principle of Accountability.[1]

The higher your executive sponsor is in the organization, the better. The implementation of an ERM program with information governance (IG) principles may be driven by the chief compliance officer, CIO, or ideally, the CEO. With CEO sponsorship come many of the key elements needed to complete a successful project, including allocated management time, budget money, and management focus.

It is important to bear in mind that this ERM/IG effort is truly a *change management* effort, in that it aims to change the structure, guidelines, and rules within which employees operate. *The change must occur at the very core of the organization's culture.* It must be embedded permanently, and to do so, the message must be constantly and consistently reinforced. To achieve this kind of change requires commitment from the very highest levels of the organization.

If the CEO is not the sponsor, then another high-level executive must lead the effort and be accountable for meeting milestones as the program progresses. *"Executive Sponsorship is one of those project success factors that are required for any project to succeed. An absent Executive Sponsor greatly increases the likelihood of project failure."*[2] It will fade, fizzle out, or be relegated to the back burner.[3] Without strong high-level leadership, when things go awry, finger pointing and political games may take over, impeding progress and cooperation.

The executive sponsor must be actively involved, tracking project objectives and milestones on a regular, scheduled basis. He or she must be aware of any obstacles or disputes that arise, take an active role in resolving them, and push the project forward. Absent this and the ERM/IG initiative will not survive competition with other projects when budgeting priorities are pressured.

> Executive sponsorship is critical to project success. There is no substitute.

Executive Sponsor Role

The role of an executive sponsor is high-level, which requires periodic and regular attention to the status of the project, particularly with budget issues, staff resources, and milestone progress. The role of a project manager (PM) is more detailed and day-to-day, tracking specific tasks that must be executed to make progress toward milestones. Both roles are essential, and the savvy PM brings in the executive sponsor to push things along when more authority is needed, but reserves such project capital for those issues that absolutely cannot be resolved without executive intervention. It is best for the PM to keep the executive sponsor fully informed, but to ask for assistance only when absolutely needed.

At the same time the PM must manage the relationship with the executive sponsor, perhaps with some gentle reminders, coaxing, or prodding, to ensure that the role and tasks of executive sponsorship are being fulfilled. "More importantly, the successful Project Manager knows that if those duties are not being fulfilled, it's time to call a timeout and have a serious conversation with the Executive Sponsor about the viability of the project."[4]

The executive sponsor serves six key purposes on a project:

1. **Budget.** Ensures an adequate financial commitment is made to see the project through, and lobbies for additional expenditures when change orders are made or cost overruns occur.
2. **Planning and control.** Sets direction and tracks accomplishment of specific, measureable business objectives.
3. **Decision-making.** Makes or approves crucial decisions and resolves issues that are escalated for resolution.
4. **Manages expectations.** Since success is quite often a stakeholder perception.
5. **Anticipates.** Every project that is competing for resources can run into unforeseen blockages and objections. Executive sponsors run interference and provide political might for the project manager to lead the project to completion, through a series of milestones.
6. **Approves.** Signs off when all milestones and objectives have been met.

An eager and effective executive sponsor makes all the difference, if properly managed by the PM. It is a tricky relationship, since the PM is always below the executive sponsor in the organization's hierarchy, yet the PM must coax the superior into tackling certain high-level tasks. Sometimes a third-party consultant who is an expert in the project at hand can provide the initiative and support for requests made of the sponsor and provide a solid business rationale.

Project Manager: Key Tasks

Here are four fundamental steps a successful PM will need to take to ensure an executive sponsor rises to the role and advances the project toward a successful conclusion:

1. **Expectation management.** The PM should meet with the executive sponsor and review expectations not only for the resources required but the impact the project's completion will have on the organization's operations. In addition, *it is critical that the ground rules are laid out up front as to what the project manager*

expects of the executive sponsor—and vice versa. Clear lines of communication need to be established. One way to address this need is to schedule weekly status meetings between the PM and executive sponsor to review progress and resource needs. "Like managing the expectations of any stakeholder, the successful Project Manager will want to identify the Executive Sponsor's interests and expectations in the project up front, and ensure those align with the goals of the project."[5] *The aforementioned six executive sponsor role points are a good place to start the conversation.*

The discussions should also include working out the game plan for updating the executive sponsor on project status, tackling thorny issues, and communicating requests for more time and resources.

2. **Approvals: Obtain acceptance on objectives and metrics**. "The Executive Sponsor should approve the objectives and measurement metrics for project completion, normally outlined in the Project Charter."[6] The program objectives should directly align to the executive sponsor's own objectives; for instance, reducing the resources needed to respond to compliance requests in order to cut variable expense levels in their functional area by a targeted percentage. The acceptance criteria should be definitively measurable, meaning it should have measureable objectives (e.g., reduce the cost of file production requests for litigation by 20 percent), and be time constrained (e.g., by fiscal year end) so that it is very clear when the project has achieved those objectives and can be declared complete. By ensuring the objectives are tied to the executive sponsor's objectives, "the successful Project Manager will be assured to get the Sponsor's attention when the project objectives are in jeopardy of being attained."[7]

3. **Engage.** During initial discussions when expectations are hammered out until they are clear, the guidelines for communication between the PM and executive sponsor should be laid out. The executive sponsor should be appropriately engaged, but not *overly* so. Certain types of tasks must be owned by the PM, and high-level guidance and support is owned by the executive sponsor. This means the latter must also communicate the project's progress to C-level peers. In other words, a steady stream of supportive and firm memos should be issued by the sponsor to keep executive-level peers and the CEO (if appropriate) apprised of the project's needs and progress. The successful PM will attempt to manage the sponsor's input by including in their status updates whether or not assistance is being requested. It should be spelled out clearly.

It is a balancing act. The successful PM keeps the executive sponsor in the loop but does not waste precious political capital requesting assistance for issues that can be solved without it. And when the executive sponsor *is* asked to address a thorny issue, the PM should prepare several alternative approaches and stand ready to make a recommendation.

4. **Final approval.** This should be a logical and simple step, provided approvals of a sequence of milestone accomplishments have been made by the executive sponsor. But it is *critically important*. Once the PM can check off completion of the pre-established acceptance criteria, "the Executive Sponsor should be able to sign off on project completion without hesitation."[8]

So why is it extremely important to gain final sign-off? Sign-off means more than completing the project (or major phase) and releasing resources. "Signoff says there is no more work to be completed, the project has met its objectives and delivered on its expected value, and that all stakeholders identified needs from the project have been met. It means that the successful Project Manager has met his or her obligations to the organization."[9]

In the case of an ongoing effort, such as an ERM program to manage e-records that utilizes IG principles to reduce risk and cost, there will be a series of sign-offs as major milestones are accomplished and new business processes and technologies are put into production. Resources will be shifted accordingly as the program progresses and matures.

It's the Little Things

There are some additional smaller tasks and activities that the project manager can ask the executive sponsor to take up to improve the project's odds of success. Here are some little things an executive sponsor can do to push the project to success:

- **Coach.** Show active support and involvement—perhaps by dropping in on project status meetings and inserting some nuggets of advice and encouragement.
- **Cheerlead.** Make sure that project wins, however small, are celebrated and recognized.
- **Commend.** Take the time to single out personal contributions and reward team members in some way—be it with a half-day off or free lunch—to show that efforts are noticed and appreciated.
- **Communicate.** Keep executive levels apprised of progress and laud the project's progress in other meetings, newsletters, and internal memos.

There are many other small ways an executive sponsor can positively impact a project, and they can be encouraged by a proactive PM. "It never hurts to ask, and a successful PM is always looking for ways to leverage every resource on the project team roster, [including] the executive team sponsor."[10]

Active, engaged, and fully invested executive sponsors are "paramount to project success," according to Roger Kastner. In order to be successful, the PM must constantly communicate, court, and interact with the executive sponsor to ensure they fulfill their role in the project for task awareness and "willingness to participate when necessary."[11]

Evolving Role of the Executive Sponsor

The role of the executive sponsor necessarily evolves and changes over the life of the initial ERM project effort, during the implementation phases, and on through the continued ERM/IG program.

To get the project off the ground, he or she must make the business case and get adequate budgetary funding. But an effort such as this takes more than money—it takes *time*. Not just time to develop new policies and implement new technologies, but the time of the designated PM, program leaders, and needed program participants.

In order to get this time set aside, the program must be made a top priority of the organization. It must be recognized, formalized, and aligned with organizational objectives. All this up-front work is the responsibility of the executive sponsor.

Once the program team is formed, team members must clearly understand why the new program is important, and how it will help the organization meet its business objectives. This message must be regularly reinforced by the executive sponsor; he or she must not only paint the vision of the future state of the organization but articulate the steps in the path to get there.

When the formal program effort commences, the executive sponsor must remain visible and accessible. They cannot disappear into their everyday duties and expect the program team to carry the effort through. They must be there to help the team confront and overcome business obstacles as they arise, and they must hail the successes along the way. This requires active involvement and a willingness to spend the time to keep the program on track and focused.

The executive sponsor must be the lighthouse that shows the way even through cloudy skies and rough waters. They are the captain that must steer the ship, even if the first mate (PM) is seasick and the deckhands (project team) are drenched and tired.

After the program is implemented, the executive sponsor is responsible for maintaining its effectiveness and relevance. This is done through periodic checks, audits, and testing, and scheduled meetings with the ongoing program manager.

CHAPTER SUMMARY: **KEY POINTS**

- Engaged and vested executive sponsors are necessary for ERM project success. It is not possible to require managers to take time out of their other duties to participate in a project if there is no executive edict or allocated budget.

- The executive sponsor must be: (a) directly tied to the success of the project, (b) fully engaged and aware in the project, and (c) actively eliminating barriers and resolving issues.

- The role of the executive sponsor evolves over the life of the ERM project, and IG program effort. Initially, the focus is on garnering the necessary resources, but as the program commences, the emphasis is more on supporting the IG program team and clearing obstacles. Once implemented, the responsibilities shift to focusing on maintaining the effectiveness of the program through testing and audits.

Notes

1. ARMA International, "How to Cite GARP," www.arma.org/garp/copyright.cfm (accessed June 19, 2012).
2. Roger Kastner, "Why Projects Succeed—Executive Sponsorship," February 15, 2011, http://blog.slalom.com/2011/02/15/why-projects-succeed-%E2%80%93-executive-sponsorship/.
3. Ibid.
4. Ibid.
5. Ibid.
6. Ibid.
7. Ibid.
8. Ibid.
9. Ibid.
10. Ibid.
11. Ibid.

CHAPTER 22

Procurement Governance: The Buying Process

Creating an open and transparent process for evaluating and selecting potential solution providers is in keeping with the Generally Accepted Recordkeeping Principles® ("GAR Principles") principle of Transparency, meaning the processes and activities of the project team are "documented in a manner that is open and verifiable."[1]

Getting a good start is important. In sum, always begin an ERM project or program based on a *clearly defined business need or business objective.* The potential benefits to the organization must be articulated and consistently communicated, particularly throughout the planning and implementation phase. (See Chapter 20 on "Building the Business Case" for more detail.)

Next, determine the potential business impact of solving the need. This is where cost justification and a return on investment (ROI) come into play. Many times it is best to use ranges, as it is difficult to make exact ROI projections. The project team may have several scenarios, based on differing assumptions.

Then you must secure an executive sponsor. This helps support the GAR Principles' principle of accountability,[2] and is the only way the project will have the steam to carry through to completion. Someone must lead the charge, marshal the resources, make the case to upper management, and delegate responsibilities. An executive sponsor helps keep a project's momentum when obstacles come in its path or competition for budget and resources heats up. (See Chapter 21, Securing Executive Sponsorship, for more detail.)

Evaluation and Selection Process: RFI, RFP, or RFQ?

For a foundation understanding of the business and technical requirements that form the basis for your buying decision process, see the chapters on inventorying e-records, developing retention and disposition schedules, taxonomy design, business process improvement (BPI), metadata, and standards for details on developing ERM system requirements. This will provide detailed guidance on developing business and technical requirements as the basis for your buying decision.

If you are including social media, cloud computing, mobile computing, or other platform requirements, then, of course, they must be addressed in your requirements documents. *Your requirements development effort will be unique to your organization*, depending on volumes, document types, taxonomy, and metadata needs, the department or business unit, IT infrastructure, application software needs and other factors unique to your organization's project, including its corporate culture.

This chapter will summarize that requirements development process, and cover the methods for procuring ERM systems and some **information governance** (IG) recommendations to keep the buying process open, transparent, and effective.

What you are looking to do when procuring an ERM system from a vendor is to find a new business partner who can meet not only your immediate system and training requirements, but also anticipated future needs. So it is critically important that you invest time and resources on the front-end so that your potential new business partner(s) have a clear understanding of your needs and your organization, including its direction and possible future needs.

Start with a clean slate and inventory all document types and records in the target area (organization-wide efforts are rare, but the scope of the initiative can be that broad).

Aim to keep the focus narrow, begin by piloting a small representative area to gain an early success and incorporate some lessons learned, and do not expand the scope as the project progresses, unless absolutely necessary. And in that case, document the need for the expanded scope in a formal **change order** or change request document, which specifies the need and business rationale for the change. Otherwise, the project will suffer from "scope-creep" and may become unwieldy and suffer cost overruns, increasing the risk of failure or abandonment.

In developing the requirements for vendors to formulate proposals, some redesign of document-based business processes is almost surely required, irrespective of technologies or vendor offerings. Ask the question, "What is the absolute best way to conduct this process?" Once you have collaborated with staff and **subject matter experts** (SME) to document current business processes, document types, and volumes, address any apparent process bottlenecks or redundancies by drafting an optimized or "Should-Be" process using BPI techniques. Then consider available information technologies (IT) that can speed up processes, and facilitate IG efforts that increase security and control, and help in meeting legal and regulatory demands.

Then, take this inventory of documents and records—including volumes, file-size estimates, projected increases, and basic business process steps—and fold it into a requirements document that any vendor must meet to successfully implement it. These requirements will become the basis for evaluating potential solutions.

There are several ways to approach the procurement process. The one that is the best fit for your organization will depend on its timeframe, budget, corporate culture, and the nature of the project itself. Although issuing a **request for proposal** (RFP) is the most common procurement approach, there is not necessarily a preferred approach. The one that suits your organization and its situation may not be the RFP route and, in fact, may end up combining several methods.

In this chapter several basic approaches to procuring software, hardware, and professional services are reviewed and key caveats and tips are provided.

> Never begin a project or program without a clearly defined business need.

Request for Information

Although it is not a required first step, often, a good way to start the buying process is with a **request for information** (RFI). It is a way to gather information, explore solutions, see what offerings vendors have that may meet your needs, and to see whether your requirements and specifications are realistic and appropriate.[3] *Encourage your supplier respondents to provide input to see if your technology aspirations are realistic, and your project objectives and timeframes are reasonable.*

An RFI is a simple, short request sent to potential bidding vendors to gather basic information about their firms and solution offerings. An RFI can also help you gather ballpark pricing information that will help you establish your budget or consider alternative solutions if the pricing is much higher than expected. An RFI lets these companies know that your organization is entering the sales cycle and allows them to plan for the resources they will need to address the opportunity.

One thing that most buying organizations don't realize is that these potential bidders have a choice: They do not have to respond to information requests. And if a supplying organization makes the determination early on that the deal is biased or "wired" for another vendor, or that they have little chance in winning the business, their management may make the decision not to compete. So it is important to maintain an unbiased approach to keep the vendors' interest and arrive at the best solution at the best price.

It is critical not to waste vendor resources in the evaluation phase as vendors can *and will* refuse to compete. This can lead to an embarrassing situation (e.g., not enough bidders) for the project team and can lead to a project failure or nondecision. You cannot implement a solution to improve your organization if vendors refuse to bid!

A basic RFI should be simple and straightforward, and contain only 15 to 20 general questions. It should let the vendor know when to expect an RFP document that provides the details needed to supply a suitable bid. It also helps to winnow out the vendors to determine which are viable and which are not.

Basic RFI questions could be:

- How long has your firm been in business?
- What were the last two years' revenues and profit/loss overall? In the e-records software division?
- Describe your ERM and related product/solution offerings and provide detailed data sheets.
- Provide at least two profiles of major customers of yours related to our project. They do not have to be named but rather can be referred to in general terms.
- Does your firm focus on particular vertical markets? What about ours?
- How many employees do you have? How many did you have three years ago?
- Is there any pending litigation with existing customers? If so, please explain.
- How is your support structured and staffed?

An RFI is a good way to see what suppliers offer and if your requirements are reasonable.

- What are your support escalation mechanisms and timeframe triggers for solving customer problems?
- Can your firm provide or make arrangements for escrow of software source code in the event of financial default or bankruptcy?
- What is your pricing structure and cost per user? Is pricing for concurrent users or dedicated seats? Do you offer enterprise licensing?
- What types of training do you offer, both pre- and postinstallation? What are the costs?
- What is the cost of support? When do support costs commence?
- How often are software upgrades made? Are they included in support costs?

Additional technical and support questions specific to the project should also be included, but the RFI should not exceed 20 questions and should not ask for much detail. Make sure that enough information about your upcoming project is provided to give the vendors the opportunity to respond with salient answers, and to pique their interest. Also, provide enough information about the number of archived documents, daily incoming documents, and the number of users so that bidders can provide ballpark pricing. The bidder should understand that you are trying to develop a project budget and need their estimates to do this.

Again, *be sure to ask them for any comments or input that can help you improve your RFP and test to see if your expectations are realistic.*

RFI responses can help your team learn: (1) whether the technology solutions you are seeking are available in the marketplace; (2) whether the solutions are affordable and within your budget expectations; and (3) whether your requirements are clear enough for vendors to respond properly.[4]

What motivation do vendors have for taking the time and investing the resources to respond to the RFI? Especially when they have real bids and RFPs to respond to? The answer is that they have an opportunity to get in early and influence the formation and strategic direction of the RFP, to stress features that they offer and make the case for them. It also allows them the opportunity to educate the project team on their company and products.[5]

If you are successful at getting vendors to respond to your RFI, these requirements and additional information gathered are used as input into the RFP. Many organizations do not use an RFI, but go straight to developing a detailed RFP document to solicit bids and proposals.

Request for Proposal

A request for proposal (RFP) is used to make a major business purchase (e.g., software, hardware, professional services) when it is clear that many vendors can provide a solution. It may be the next step after an RFI, which provides input and direction. Project requirements and specifications are clearly defined in an RFP,

> An RFI should be limited to 20 questions or less. It is used create a snapshot of potential vendors and to provide more information for an RFP.

meaning the buyer is looking for the best fit, as determined by a vendor's total response and bid.

Frequently, an RFP is the best approach when price is not the leading factor in the organization's decision. Also, an RFP is helpful since cross-functional skill sets from the issuing organization must be considered, and a range of departments (e.g., IT, records management, human resources, legal, risk management, purchasing, and others) are consulted. If a third-party consultant is used, they will solicit input from these groups and develop the detailed questions and rating system for the RFP.

It is considered a best practice to include the vendor RFP responses into the final contract as an addendum.[6] "This procedure allows the company [or organization] to obligate the supplier contractually to comply with statements made in the proposal, and to seek legal recourse if the supplier cannot meet the requirements as stated."[7] If vendors know their responses are legally binding in the event of a contract award, they are much less likely to "fudge" or stretch representations of their capabilities.

The key RFP benefits of producing an RFP are:

- Requiring the RFP team to analyze its business problem and sharpen the focus of its business objectives.
- Requiring in-depth analysis of project challenges, obstacles, and issues.
- Requiring in-depth technical analysis of requirements and possible solutions.
- Allowing vendors to not only address the basic requirements of the RFP but to be creative in proposing new approaches that may add value to the project.
- Evaluating vendors in a fair and unbiased way, regardless of past business relationships or ties to the buying organization.
- Evaluating vendors using common requirements and rules, yielding a better understanding of the proposed solutions and clarifying their differences.[8]

The RFP process can be costly and time-consuming and may not always produce the expected results—not only can a poor RFP and poor governance of the procurement process discourage vendor participation—but even if the process is followed through, with extensive vendor evaluations, software demonstrations, customer site reference checks, and revisions to both the RFP and resultant proposals, the outcome can be unsatisfactory and result in a "nondecision." If so, having the original RFP and original vendor responses allows buyers and bidders to review the process based on the documentation and determine what may have gone wrong.

The RFP process also serves the purpose of educating the purchasing organization's project team on a technology they are not familiar with, and that can be a moving target, since information technology (IT) changes rapidly and implementation issues are unique. For the vendors, the RFP provides a detailed set of specifications for customizing the bid.

The RFP provides a common blueprint for both sides to understand the project needs, and it aims to provide a fair and objective way to evaluate the bids. The RFP is the beginning of what will be a long-term relationship with the winning vendor. It provides

An RFP is issued when requirements are clearly defined and there is a field of qualified vendors to select from.

an open forum so bidding firms may ask questions about requirements and specifications in the RFP. At times, the vendors may question some of the requirements.

Providing a **bidders' conference** to allow for questions is a good way to keep the process open and transparent while allowing an RFP to be fine-tuned and clarified, based on vendors' feedback. A bidders' conference is normally held within a few weeks of the issuance of the RFP, and it allows an open forum for vendors to ask questions and get clarification on issues.

Once the RFP responses are in from the bidding vendors, the buying organization may need to question vendor responses to gain clarification and request a revised response and quote. For instance, if one vendor has bid very little training compared to the other vendors, their proposal team would need to address that issue and the buying organization could then take the revised response into consideration.

The final RFP and final winning proposal will often change in the course of evaluation. An RFP can be a significant undertaking that require resources from different departments. E-documents and records span across all departments and the procurement process will include the end user area representatives, along with representatives from several key departments, such as IT, legal, records management, risk management, purchasing, and possibly human resources.

Creating an RFP for an ERM (and/or) IG project will require time and resources from multiple departments.

The seven key steps in writing an RFP are:

1. **Identify need.** This may be spurred by a negative compliance action, a lost lawsuit, new regulations, or as the result of an organizational initiative. In the early stages of development, some initial analysis will be required to get the funding and operational priority for the project. The initial high-level analysis should focus on risk/return and delineate the broad-based benefits to the organization. This step may be undertaken by a small project team, possibly made up of employees from the end user department driving the project, IT, records management, finance, and the legal department.

2. **Recruit or endorse an executive sponsor.** This person provides the management wherewithal to overcome obstacles or political hurdles, helps to keep communications about the project's progress going consistently and clearly, trumpets small successes and milestones, and supports the project team with advice and encouragement. Mostly, though, they provide a single point of accountability.

3. **Allocate budget.** This is crucial to get the project moving. Underfunded projects die and waste management time and resources. There must be a hard number allocated to the project, as well as the commitment to dedicate management time.

4. **Select and formalize the project team.** This should include individuals from key departments as well as those who will be responsible for implementing and supporting the new technologies. The basic team should include individuals from the aforementioned departments, as well as corporate communications, education, and operations, and any other teams that manage efficiency or business process optimization.

5. **Undertake a detailed analysis of requirements.** This will include historical, current, and projected document and records transaction volumes, business process analysis, and technological requirements. Also, include any legal

requirements or regulatory directives that the ERM project will address, and their (potential) impact.

6. **Survey the marketplace.** Look for a broad range of vendors that may satisfy the buying organization's requirements.
7. **Solicit basic information from vendors.** Usually in the form of an RFI or query letter sent ahead of an RFP. This will give the buying organization information as to technological capabilities, ballpark pricing, and additional ideas for the RFP. If the RFP is the first formal contact with the organizations, there is a risk of not identifying the correct individuals to send it to.

Don't drag the process out and drain vendor resources. A long, drawn-out process with an overly complex RFP *is not recommended.* Ask the relevant questions and get to the short list as fast as you can, usually within 90 days. See the demonstrations and presentations, do your reference checks, and narrow the list to two to three viable competitors. Then, the competition heats up.

If the decision has already been made and the executive sponsor or project manager (PM) are trying to justify it through a RFP process, the vendors will soon sniff this out, and the project team will be sitting there with no valid competitors to compare.

Request for Quote

A **request for quote** (RFQ) is used to solicit bids when detailed requirements are known or a project is relatively straightforward. Often this applies to adding disk drive capacity, buying additional PCs, or expanding networks. It can also apply to buying an enterprise license for ERM software once a pilot has been conducted, or there is another source of confidence about a particular vendor (e.g., that is the vendor of choice for other enterprise-wide solutions).

Negotiated Procurement

A **negotiated procurement** is a way to acquire a new system when the buying organization wants to make a rapid decision and requirements are known. Often a trusted consulting firm will be engaged to solicit bids, negotiate with vendors, and make a recommendation for procurement. This approach can be a better fit than issuing an RFP when cost and time are leading issues.

Evaluating Software Providers: Key Criteria

Sometimes project teams focus on a detailed list of features when evaluating and selecting software and hardware. They create a complex matrix of priorities and weights to score the vendors and *voilà*: A winner emerges.

There are two main problems with this approach:

1. The manipulation of weights and scoring values can skew an evaluation toward a bias that some members of the team may hold.
2. It fails to aptly consider the big picture and the long term, which may be the most important considerations.

Often, project teams focus on a detailed list of features when evaluating and selecting vendors; this may skew the evaluation and overlooks critical long-term factors.

There are at least 10 key issues that must be considered when evaluating software and hardware vendors:

1. **Technological fit.** Does the vendor have the right type of solution considering the business needs and technological infrastructure environment? Can they integrate with the current and planned IT infrastructure (including operating systems, databases, e-mail systems, hardware platform support, line of business systems, and legacy systems)?
2. **Company viability.** What are the vendor's financial strengths, operating history, and culture? It is safe to rely on them for the long term?
3. **Track record.** What is the vendor's history of implementation success and ongoing service? Has the software and hardware been reliable in the past? What do their references say?
4. **Support.** Does the vendor offer adequate staffing, response time, and service-level agreements?
5. **Access to senior management.** Are clients and prospects able to communicate with senior management, as needed? Is senior management involved enough in the purchase and support processes?
6. **Partnerships.** Does the vendor have partnerships or strategic alliances with third parties that present a particular value or hindrance?
7. **Technology architecture and scalability.** What is the architecture and scalability of the vendor's service? How well does it mesh with the needs of the buyer's organization?
8. **Total cost of ownership (TCO).** What will the purchase cost? Be sure to understand up-front costs, as well as software and support fees. Calculate the TCO over a three- to five-year period.
9. **Ease.** How easy is the system to implement? How easy is it to use? Remember that complicated processes often result in failure of adoption at the knowledge-worker level.
10. **Training.** Does the vendor offer training recommendations and capabilities that meet the buying organization's needs? Do they have sufficient training resources?

In addition, you will want to consider criteria such as: experience level, credentials, and quality of implementation personnel; demonstrations or product stress testing; site visits to customers of the finalists to see a live example of the software in action; overall quality of RFP response; and the ability to work with the project team.[9]

Technological Fit

This comes down to the basic technological suitability of the vendor. Most vendors in a particular market segment have the tendency to say they can essentially be all things to all organizations, but this is fundamentally untrue. There are always *basic* scenarios where they fit best.

If your need for features requires a lot of customization to the software, it may not be the right solution. Generally, *the more out-of-the-box capabilities offered that meet your requirements, the better.* But often vendors will profess to be able to *integrate* when they really mean *interface*. Interfacing involves writing some custom software code that makes your organization a one-of-a-kind installation and therefore more difficult to support.

If your business scenario is one that stretches their capabilities, or their basic architecture conflicts with the direction your organization is moving, it may not be a fit. Suppose your organization is an all-IBM shop planning to move to all Microsoft platforms within two years. Some of the vendors on your short list might have tight integration with Microsoft, and perhaps even some helpful conversion tools. The decision must lean toward those vendors.

Other details will need to be negotiated, such as recourse in the event of default and gross performance guarantees. The result both parties are looking to avoid is for the buyer to be so disappointed in the system after implementation, they want to give it back after it has been installed and entrenched into daily operations. Try to work things out.

Often, an outside consultant can bring the pressure to bear since they hold the keys to the vendor's future successes, and the vendor does not want their failure widely reported. Again, litigation with the software vendor should be considered the last line of defense.

Company Viability

Once the field of prospective vendors has been narrowed down to a possible three or four, the project team should look closely at each prospective vendor's current financial statements. If the vendor is privately held, sometimes this information is difficult to obtain from them directly. But usually they will release it if they are a finalist and your financial and legal representatives sign a nondisclosure agreement.

They may be hiding something or they may, in fact, have nothing to hide. Additional information about financial strength can be found from services like Hoover's and Dun & Bradstreet. Also, some assumptions can be made if the vendor will reveal their current and historic staffing levels, as workforce growth can be an indicator of financial strength and stability. The rate at which they are adding installed customers can also be considered when financials are not available.

The business viability evaluation should necessarily consider the number of years the vendor has been in business. There is not much difference in a vendor that has been operating for 10 years and one that has been operating for 20—in fact, the older organization may be more wedded to older technologies. But if one firm has been operating for five years or less, they should be scrutinized more closely. The project team may want to ask for a software escrow agreement that can be invoked in the event the vendor becomes financially unstable or goes out of business.

> Keep proposed custom software development to a minimum. It introduces complexity and risk.

Some vendors may tout their rapid growth as a sign of their success and viability. But it depends on *how* they supported that growth. Companies that have been funded with venture capital or have gone public through an initial public offering (IPO) will be pressured to grow top-line revenues by investors seeking a greater return. Often, this is not healthy for the company. The amalgamation of technologies and corporate cultures can quickly cause real problems in integration and performance, both from a technology and human standpoint. Too many competing technical architectures and fiefdoms can spell risk for customers.

Organic, controlled growth is usually the sign of a healthy, stable company. Overall, look at viability as a big-picture evaluation that considers more than just current financial statements or number of installed customers.

Track Record

This may seem obvious but it is not as easy to evaluate as it may seem. Vendors will provide the project team with a host of press releases and contact information from happy customers. What is needed to complete an evaluation on this measure is to find out what has happened in the trenches. Yes, call the organizations and contacts provided—but go further. Ask those references for names that are not on the list, both inside their organization and at other recent clients. *Most vendors have had some projects that have gone wrong. What is important is how they handled those challenges and how satisfied the customer ended up being.*

Support

Support is absolutely crucial. Since most vendors typically charge 18 to 20 percent of the initial software/hardware purchase price *each year* in support, this is their bread and butter. Good support is also critical for the success of your project. Check into response times, escalation procedures, and contractual obligations the vendor makes to supporting installations. Also, check the credentials and resumes of those who will be assigned to supporting your project.

Although most software and hardware diagnostics are performed online today, *geographic proximity helps.* The closer the planned installation is to the headquarters of the vendor, the better the support will be. They can quickly dispatch a top expert, or you can have lunch with the CEO. There is simply more access to more resources. Even a nearby branch office will help.

This does not mean you exclude vendors from out of your state or region. A lot can be accomplished with remote diagnostics. But certainly, the first line of support should not be located in India or Malaysia if your organization is based in the United States.

Service-level agreements (SLAs) will delineate hours that support is available, guaranteed response time (and that return phone call is different from actually solving your problem), escalation procedures (which deal with how and when the service problem is sent up the chain of command), and other support details. The project team

> Most vendors have *some* projects that have gone awry. Dig into the causes and find out how they handled the situation.

may also want to specify the level of credentials and experience for those responding when there is a serious problem. And, if a problem lingers, resulting in system downtime, the client and vendor can negotiate gross performance guarantees and specific financial penalties to be paid to the client organization. A daily rate of $1,000 is a good place to begin negotiations since the vendor will never agree to be responsible for any damages caused by their lack of support or software performance. That takes litigation, which all parties want to avoid if at all possible.

Access to Senior Management

This is particularly important in large projects, or in the pilot stage of potentially large projects. It is always a good idea to negotiate the final terms and conditions of a contract with an executive who is at least two to three levels above the field-level salesperson. *The higher the level, the better.* Of course, the CEO is the ideal choice. High-level executives feel valuable when they walk out of a meeting with a signed contract. This establishes a base for a strong relationship between the client and the executive, which can help an organization achieve a priority status in the future.

Try to schedule the meeting for 10:30 or 11:00 A.M. so there might be the possibility of spending more time with the executive at lunch. When assurances are gained from an executive, and business cards and handshakes are exchanged, the project gains extra leverage and this improves its chances for success. If things start to go awry, it is time to pick up the phone and make any issues known to that key vendor executive.

Partnerships

Strong vendors have strong strategic alliances with third-party vendors. These alliances allow them to capitalize on an exchange of technology or services while minimizing costs. Alliances create leverage. Often these third-party relationships can spell the difference in project success. Suppose that your vendor-of-choice is a small integrator, yet they have an alliance with IBM, HP, EMC, Oracle, or Microsoft. The project team may want to negotiate for the larger vendor to be the prime vendor (like a general contractor) on the project to ensure its success. The smaller integrator will then work as a subcontractor and the project risk is reduced. Of course, it will cost more for a larger vendor to assume this risk.

Technology Architecture and Scalability

The project team will need to look at more than just pretty demonstrations of user interfaces. *Demonstrations always look nice.* What is needed is to look "under the hood" to see how the software was designed, and evolved. Often, systems are interfaced to add functionality. There is a big difference in interfacing disparate systems, integrating different systems, and a single system that was designed holistically from the ground up. In each case, vendors will claim their system is seamlessly integrated. But if their original product was designed to be optimized for, say, the IBM OS/400 operating system running a proprietary database, and then years later they made it work with IBM AIX, and now they have reworked it for the Microsoft SharePoint platform without rewriting the system from the ground up, there will be system overhead created from inefficient software design. This means that as your project increases in number of users, the system performance will lag. So it is just as important *how* a vendor arrives at a particular solution as getting there itself.

Total Cost of Ownership

Most inexperienced IT buyers can be easily fooled by savvy software salespeople. It is not just the sticker price that your team must consider but the total cost of ownership (TCO) over the life of the installed system, usually considered over a range of three to five years. TCO includes not only initial implementation price but also change orders (and the change order approval process), which occur when changes to the project are made outside of the original proposal. This can be a real *gotcha*.

Timing and pricing of software support fees are also critical. Questions to ask include: Is there a 90-day or one-year warranty period with no support fees? What percentage are the fees of the list price? (As previously stated, an annual rate of 18 to 20 percent is average.) What are the planned increases and maximum annual increases? What are the costs of hardware maintenance, increases, and trade-in/upgrade costs? All these questions must be asked to gain a true picture of the TCO.

Ease of Implementation and Use

Some systems are commercial off the shelf (COTS) and are easily implemented without customization. There will be a number of parameters to set up but these are like simple switches or selections you can turn on or off. Other systems are very complex and require much custom IT development work and additional training. These work well when your organization has very complex requirements and the IT staff to support them, but the implementation is difficult, time consuming, and costly. And ongoing support is also costly, since you will have installed a one-off system. These are trade-offs that your organization will want to consider.

Remember also that systems that are easier to use succeed more readily because knowledge workers adopt them more readily. This can be the difference between a project's success or failure.

Training

If a vendor does not include training, or if training is grossly under bid (less than 10 percent of the system implementation cost), *it is telling*. Often, they are cutting back to compete on price. The project will suffer. You'll pay for it later when your choices are limited. Sometimes, vendors just don't understand how crucial training is to implementation success. The client organization should consider the training staff's credentials, processes, and availability when making software and hardware purchase decisions. *The perfect system won't work without user acceptance, and user acceptance depends on training.*

Negotiating Contracts: Ensuring the Decision

Poorly crafted contracts are harbingers of project failure.

Unfortunately, when problems arise in mid-implementation, it is often too late. The key principle to keep in mind is that litigation or arbitration is *never* the preferred way to clarify a contract: It should be so clearly written that both sides understand its terms and they never have to go back to the contract to enforce it.

There is an odd incongruity: *It seems that the larger the organization, the worse it is at negotiating contracts.* Maybe that is due to the layers of bureaucracy, but more likely it comes down to contract negotiators' failing to respect expenditures outside their area. If contracts are considered with the scrutiny of a small business owner who is very cautious with money, many potential problems can be avoided.

First, when negotiating a major contract, understand the company's motivations. Remember, the salesperson has a boss, and that boss has a boss, and so on, so there is built-in pressure to sign deals as large as possible, as fast as possible, and without giving up a lot of unusual contract terms that will be difficult to get approved or achieve.

Similar to car dealers, *IT vendors feel more pressure at the end of each fiscal quarter, and that pressure is at a fevered pitch in the final month of the vendor's fiscal year*. Their performance will determine annual bonuses, promotions, and quota performance. Many times, someone's job is on the line. No deal equals a loss of employment and a whole collection of personal and financial problems. Sign the deal this month and the salespeople are heroes, don't sign the deal, they lose their jobs. This is reality. As a buyer of technology, the best shot at a good deal is available at these times. *So make sure to find out how the vendor's fiscal year runs and when it ends.*

Secondly, gauge the strategic importance of the project to the vendor. If it is the deployment of a relatively new product or technology set, the vendor is more highly motivated to agree to terms that are advantageous to the client organization. This is because racking up sales and references is the surest way to make the new technology sell faster. If the current project makes the client organization the first or second customer, there is much greater leverage than if it might be customer number 52. That's a fact, and it can be used as leverage to get performance guarantees, price concessions, and additional add-on products and services.

Third, and related to the previous point, is the potential for future revenue for the vendor. This could mean the project at hand or from the greater marketplace. If the current project is a $300,000 pilot project to prove a concept, and the carrot at the end is a $3 million enterprise wide deal, the vendor is going to be more flexible in initial negotiations, in order to establish a beachhead. In like manner, if the project is the first in a key industry segment the vendor wants to penetrate, and he or she can see the additional revenue a signed contract will bring, the vendor will again be more flexible in negotiations.

Typically customers/end users are perfectly willing to sign a standard contract. *Never do this.*

Standard contracts are heavily weighted in the vendor's favor. Decipher every phrase and dig into the contract language at a detailed level. This doesn't mean starting from scratch—a very difficult thing to do—but consider negotiation of performance warranties, service-level agreements, and prescribed penalties in the case of nonperformance.

It is a recommended best practice that the vendor's response to the RFP be folded into the contract, so that its official responses are contractually binding. If a vendor claims to have a feature or functionality, it should be able to contractually stand by its contention. This prevents vendors from responding with anything to get the deal and holds them legally accountable if they do.

> Never sign a vendor's standard contract without modifying the terms and conditions to include some specific assurances.

Once the project team gets to the contract negotiation stage, it should have a very detailed project plan with a timeline and specific milestones along that timeline. Include this in the contract. As a practical matter, it is best to tie payments to milestone achievements. So when the project is halfway done, they have been paid half the money. This sounds like common sense, but we have found many examples of naive negotiations by end-user organizations. Here are a few:

- A large southern U.S. nuclear power facility wanted to replace its existing document imaging and workflow system with a more advanced one. It started by conducting a small pilot in a relatively obscure area—stockholder services—at around $200,000. That seems like a good move. But the requirements were so light it didn't make for a good trial run (for the purchasing organization). Then, for whatever reason, the vendor convinced the purchaser to pay the entire next phase of the project—a $1 million license fee—up front. The problem was that when the implementation got into the engineering areas of the company with more complex requirements, it became painfully clear that the software had a fundamental architectural weakness: It could not handle subindexes beneath the primary indexes. The software couldn't be completely redesigned and the vendor had received all the money, so the deadlock ended in litigation. This could have been avoided by a more relevant pilot area selection and progress payments tied to milestone successes.
- Years ago, AT&T's tax department called on IMERGE Consulting to review a document management system decision it was making. It had a proposal on the table from a Big 5 consulting firm (which was also their audit firm in the pre-Sarbanes-Oxley days), but something didn't seem right. The business need was there. They were duplicating efforts when presenting their business case to states and municipalities to minimize AT&T's tax burden. They could save millions in taxes and penalties by forming expeditious and detailed responses. In evaluating the proposal, we found that no monthly maintenance fees were included, no Oracle database license fees were included (and they would be required), and the proposed solution was overpriced and not a good fit. We brought in a couple of viable competitors, negotiated the cost down by more than $1 million, and forced the Big 5 consultants to render a complete proposal. AT&T's staff voted for the recommended alternative solution, which had two CEOs from different parts of the world flying in to agree to terms. Despite this, the staff was overruled by a distant manager with ties to a West Coast Big 5 firm, justifying the contract by saying "we have such a good business relationship with them anyway." Of course, people got promoted, quit, or otherwise moved on, and the project was fraught with problems in implementation.
- The City of New Orleans had negotiated an outsourcing contract for $25 million annually with a major provider. The Civil Service Commission felt that something was amiss since the contract would displace the entire IT staff, yet no IT staffers were slated to be laid off. When inspecting the contract, it took less than five minutes for this author to determine some major flaws, the biggest of which was that the contract could be modified with the stroke of a pen by one person to increase it to over $50 million a year. Also, the outsourcing company could not be held liable for any damages in the event of a problem; service levels were not defined; and no training was included. In fact, the contracting company did not have to achieve any milestones at all and it would be entitled to payments

of more than $400,000 per month—retroactively for six months! A public hearing ensued, where Robert Smallwood testified regarding the extensive problems in the contract, which proved somewhat embarrassing to city officials, but they ignored Smallwood's advice and the contract was amended to include training to appease the Civil Service Commission, and the project moved forward, ultimately toward disaster. *Within less than four years, the City's CIO and the crooked contractors plead guilty to corruption and bribery charges and were sent to federal prison.*

- A state agency decided to bring in a specific best-of-breed software vendor, to cure its IT ills. It confected a process whereby the business processes of the organization would be redesigned to fit the software functionality—the exact opposite of normal best practice approaches. In evaluating consultants, it was determined that the project evaluation was biased and incomplete, and the entire bid process had to be halted while a best practices review took place. A year later, nothing had moved forward toward implementation.

More Contract Caveats

What will vendors *not* agree to under any circumstances? They will not agree to guarantee to save the enterprise time or money on a certain task. They will not agree to a performance guarantee that involves interaction or interfaces with another vendor's product. *But if pressed hard, they will agree to warrant that their software performs as advertised, and with reasonable performance response times.*

What if the vendor goes out of business? The client organization normally would get the vendor to agree to put the software source code into escrow, in the event they go bankrupt. But that is not good enough. A case in point: IBM owned 25 percent of Image Business Systems (IBS), an early document-imaging entrant. No one thought it could fail. Its customers had the escrow provision in their contracts, but it could be invoked only in the event of a formal bankruptcy. The financially ailing IBS downsized to just two employees, then it held up its customers by forcing them to pay $200,000 each to get the source code—and it later went out of business anyway. To avoid this situation, you can negotiate escrow provisions that are invoked when certain liquidity or other financial ratios indicate a company is on the rocks.

In summary, do the required homework, justify the project based on business need, and use both carrots and sticks to formulate a contract that enforces achievement of milestones and software performance. Then move forward with the enterprise's new partner into an era of productivity and results.

How to Pick a Consulting Firm: Evaluation Criteria

If the client organization chooses to engage a consulting firm to assist in making ERM or IG project decisions (or any IT-related decision), there are some key criteria to consider:

- **Are they vendor-independent?** You must find a consulting firm without economic ties to a particular vendor or vendors, as these ties—and financial pressures—necessarily color their evaluation. Some firms will say, "We have ties to all the major vendors, so we know them and we'll select the best one for you." This doesn't wash, since each vendor agreement has certain quota levels, commission levels, bonus levels, and payment terms. So naturally, the consulting company (really an integrator or reseller) and salesperson will tend to maximize their profits by selecting the system that is best for them, not your organization.

There must be no economic interest tied to the recommendations.

- **Will they live with their recommendations?** Some consulting firms are independent, but they won't see a project to fruition. They will help you generate an RFP, but they won't evaluate the vendors, assist in negotiation, and oversee the project implementation successfully. This way, they can never be blamed for making poor decisions.

  Firms like this don't have the real-world expertise that is derived from actual project implementations. There are problems that do not manifest themselves until the project proceeds. Napoleon said, "No battle plan ever survives an encounter with the enemy." This means that things change once you are engaged in a project implementation. For instance, software documentation is not always correct, and there are other nuances that are found only during implementation. So, you must ask if they are able to go beyond the theoretical to the real and willing to be held accountable for their recommendations.

- **Do they have the breadth of knowledge required?** Many firms in the IT consulting marketplace focus on skill sets and technologies that have become out-of-date. So their recommendations will reflect this focus, and they won't have the current experience in IT to make sound recommendations. They are likely to go with whichever firm they have established a relationship with, rather than the optimum choice for the implementing organization.

  When beginning a project, it is advisable to delve further and determine if the consulting firm has expertise in not only ERM and IG, but also in newer or emerging technologies like cloud computing, social media (SM), document lifecycle security (DLS), information rights management (IRM), and other related e-document technologies. Many firms get stuck in technologies of the past and do not have broad multidisciplinary expertise in areas like records management, document management, DLS, business process management, long-term digital preservation (LTDP), knowledge management, and change management.

  The key to the decision is: Does the consulting firm have the independence and expertise in the breadth of methodologies and technologies to determine a truly optimal solution?

- **What related work have they done?** Look at specific application areas, industry vertical markets, and project-specific business process and technological requirements. The more closely related the firm's experience, the more relevant, and the more likely the firm will perform well.

- **How many top-notch, experienced people does the firm have?** Often firms will parade out a few top people to impress you and close the deal, then you won't see them again as underlings are thrown at your project. So ask, "Who will be assigned to this project? Can you contractually guarantee these people and suitable replacements in the event of illness or other factors?"

- **What do their clients say about them?** Good, strong firms will have no trouble providing references to call to verify their credentials—as many as needed to make the project team comfortable. To really do the required homework, dig deeper and contact others in the end-user organization that worked on the project (who were *not* named by the consulting firm) to determine a consensus.

- **What do their peers say about them (i.e., what is their reputation in the industry?)** Determine this by looking at how many presentations the firm gives at major conferences, how many articles they have written as experts on related topics, and by asking disinterested third parties about the firm's reputation.
- **How stable are they?** This comes down to how long they have been established, and how long top people stay at the firm.

Consider all the previous factors and make an overall judgment as to whether a third-party consulting firm is needed, and then find the one that best fits your project.

When making a software/system decision, determine whether a vendor can meet your requirements and whether or not the bidding firm would be a good partner over the long term. After all, it's a marriage of sorts.

CHAPTER SUMMARY: **KEY POINTS**

- A *request for information* (RFI) is a simple, short request sent to potential bidding vendors to gather basic information about their firms and solution offerings.

- A *request for proposal* (RFP) is used to purchase software and hardware when it is clear that many vendors can provide a solution, project requirements and specifications can be determined, and price is not the leading factor in the organization's decision.

- It is recommended that the vendor's response to the RFP be folded into the contract, so that its official responses are contractually binding.

- A *request for quote* (RFQ) is used to solicit bids when detailed requirements are known or the project is very simple.

- A *negotiated procurement* is a way to acquire a new system when the buying organization wants to make a rapid decision and requirements are known. Often a trusted consulting firm will be engaged to solicit bids, negotiate with vendors, and make a recommendation for procurement at a discounted price.

- At least ten key issues that must be considered when evaluating vendors are: (1) technological fit, (2) company viability, (3) track record, (4) support levels, (5) access to senior management, (6) partnerships, (7) technology architecture and scalability, (8) total cost of ownership (TCO), (9) ease of implementation and use, and (10) training.

(Continued)

(Continued)

- Poorly crafted contracts are the harbingers of failed projects. There is an odd incongruity: It seems that the larger the organization, the worse it is at negotiating contracts.

- Never sign a vendor's standard contract. Always add additional assurances.

- Financial and career pressure builds for vendors to a greater intensity at the end of each fiscal quarter, and is at a fevered pitch in the final month of the vendor's fiscal year end. This is the best time to negotiate contracts.

- Vendors will not agree to guarantee to save the enterprise time or money on a certain task. They will not agree to a performance guarantee that involves interaction or interfaces with another vendor's product. But if pressed hard, they will agree to warrant that their software performs as advertised.

Notes

1. ARMA International, "How to Cite GARP," www.arma.org/garp/copyright.cfm (accessed June 19, 2012).
2. Ibid.
3. Bud Porter-Roth, *Request for Proposal: A Guide to Effective RFP Development* (Indianapolis: Addison-Wesley, 2002), 6.
4. Ibid., 7.
5. Ibid, 8.
6. Ibid, 10.
7. Ibid.
8. Ibid., 12.
9. Ibid, 15.

CHAPTER 23

Best Practices for Electronic Records Management

Although electronic records management (ERM) is an evolving field that is still formulating industry *best practices* and accommodating rapid changes in the information technology (IT) and information governance (IG) landscapes, there are some key best practices you should keep in mind while managing and implementing ERM projects and programs:

1. *IG is a key underpinning for a successful ERM program*—Practicing good IG is the essential foundation for building a legally defensible records management program; it provides the basis for consistent, reliable methods for managing documents and records. Having trusted and reliable records, reports, and databases allow managers to make key decisions with confidence.[1] And accessing that information and business intelligence in a timely fashion can yield a long-term sustainable competitive advantage, creating more agile enterprises.

   To do this, enterprises must standardize and systematize their handling of information, and most especially their formal business records. They must analyze and optimize how information is accessed, controlled, managed, shared, stored, preserved, and audited. They must have complete, current, and relevant policies, processes, and technologies to manage and control information, including *who is able to access* what *information*, and *when*, to meet external legal and regulatory demands and internal governance requirements. This, in short, is IG.

2. *IG is not a project but rather an ongoing program* that provides an umbrella of rules and policies, monitored and enforced with the support of information technologies to manage and control information output and communications. Since technologies change so quickly, it is necessary to have overarching "technology agnostic" policies that can manage the various information technology (IT) platforms that an organization may use.

   Compare it to a workplace safety program; every time a new location, team member, piece of equipment, or toxic substance is acquired by the organization, the workplace safety program should dictate how that is handled and, if it doesn't, the workplace safety policies/procedures/training that are part of the workplace safety program need to be updated. And you conduct regular reviews to ensure the program is being followed and make adjustments based on your findings. *The effort never ends.*[2]

3. *Using an IG framework or maturity model is helpful in assessing and guiding IG programs*—various models are offered, such as the Generally Accepted Record-keeping Principles ("The Principles") from ARMA International; the Information Governance Reference Model (IGRM) which grew out of the Electronic Discovery Reference Model (found at EDRM.net)[3] or MIKE2.0, which was developed by Bearing Point and released to the public domain. Another tool that is used particularly in the Australian market for records management projects is Designing and Implementing Recordkeeping Systems (DIRKS).

4. *For electronic records, inventory at the computer systems level, rather than by records series*—according to recommendations by the U.S. National Archives and Records Administration (NARA).

5. *Taxonomies need to be considered from two main perspectives: Navigation and Classification*—most people consider the former, but not the latter. The navigational construct that is represented by a taxonomy is evident in most file structures and file shares—the nesting of folders within folders—and in many web applications where users are navigating hierarchical arrangements of pages or links. However, classification is frequently behind the scenes. A document can "live" in a folder that the user can navigate to. *But within that folder, the document can be classified in different ways through application of metadata.* The metadata is also part of the taxonomy or related to the taxonomy. In this way, usability can be impacted by giving the user *multiple ways* to retrieve their information.[4]

6. *Retention schedules are developed for records not individually, but rather, by records series, categories, functions or systems.* Ideally, they include all of the record series in an organization, although they may be broken down into smaller subset schedules, such as by business unit. For e-records, NARA recommends inventorying by system.

7. *An enterprise-wide retention schedule is preferable because it eliminates the possibility that different business units will be following conflicting records retention periods.* For example, if one business unit is discarding a group of records after five years, it would not make sense for another business unit to keep the same records for 10 years. Where enterprise-wide retention schedules are not possible, then smaller business units, such as divisions or regions, should operate under a consistent retention schedule.

8. *Senior management must set the tone and lead sponsorship for vital records program governance and compliance.* Although e-records are easier to protect and back-up, most vital records today are e-records, and without them, an organization cannot continue operations.

9. *Business processes must be redesigned to improve the management of electronic records or implement an **electronic records management** (ERM) system.* Using ERM fundamentally changes the way people work, and greater efficiencies can be gained with business process redesign (versus simply using ERM systems as an electronic filing cabinet).

10. *E-mail messages, both inbound and outbound, should be archived automatically, and in real-time.* This ensures that spoliation does not occur, that is, the loss of proven authenticity of an e-mail. This preserves legal validity and forensic compliance. Additionally, e-mail should be indexed to facilitate the searching process, and all messages should be secured in a single location. With these measures, e-mail records can be assured to be authentic and reliable.

11. *Personal archiving of e-mail messages should be disallowed.* Although users will want to save certain e-mail messages for their own reasons, control and management of e-mail archiving must be at the organization level, or as high of a level as is practical, such as division or region.

12. *Destructive retention of e-mail helps to reduce storage costs and legal risk, while improving "findability" of critical records.* It makes good business sense to have a policy to, say, destroy all e-mail messages after 90 or 120 days that are not flagged as potential records (which, for instance, help document a transaction or that document a situation that may come into dispute in the future) or those that have a legal hold.

13. *Take a practical approach and limit cloud use to documents that do not have long retention periods and carry a low litigation risk*—this will reduce the risk of compromising or losing critical documents and e-records. Some duplicate copies of vital records may be stored securely in the cloud to help the organization recover in the event of a disaster.

14. *Social media content must be managed by IG policies and monitored with controls that ensure protection of critical information assets, and preservation of business records.* Your organization must state clearly what content and tone is acceptable in social media use, and it must retain records of that use, which should be captured in real-time.

15. *A SharePoint governance model that states which documents and records will be managed needs to be tailored to your organization.* It will not work if it does not fit with your culture and resources. There is no such thing as one set of SharePoint governance best practices that every organization can adopt.[5] Rather, developing SharePoint governance involves a series of questions you need to answer in the context of your organization's constraints and goals, and validated against a broad sample of use cases for the system.

16. *International and national standards provide effective guidance for implementing ERM.* Although there are no absolutes, researching and referencing ISO and other standards must be a part of any ERM effort.

17. *Creating standardized metadata terms should be part of an IG effort that enables faster, more complete, and more accurate searches and retrieval of records.* This is important not only in everyday business operations, but also when delving through potentially millions of records during the discovery phase of litigation. Good metadata management also assists in the maintenance of corporate memory, and improving accountability in business operations.[6] Using a standardized format and controlled vocabulary provides a "precise and comprehensible description of content, location, and value."[7] Using a controlled vocabulary means your organization has standardized a set of terms used for metadata elements describing records. This "ensures consistency across a collection" and helps with optimizing search and retrieval functions and records research, as well as meeting e-discovery requests, compliance demands, and other legal and regulatory requirements.

18. *Some digital information assets must be preserved permanently as part of an organization's documentary heritage.*[8] Long-term digital preservation (LTDP) applies to content that is born digital as well as content that is converted to digital form. Digital preservation is defined as: long-term, error-free storage of digital information, with means for retrieval and interpretation, for the entire time

span that the information is required to be retained. Dedicated repositories for historical and cultural memory such as libraries, archives, and museums, need to move forward to put in place trustworthy digital repositories that can match the security, environmental controls, and wealth of descriptive metadata that these institutions have created for analog assets (such as books and paper records). Digital challenges associated with records management affect all sectors of society—academic, government, private, and not-for-profit enterprises—and ultimately all citizens of all developed nations.

19. *Executive sponsorship is crucial.* Securing an executive sponsor at the senior management level is key to successful ERM projects and programs. It is not possible to require managers to take time out of their other duties to participate in a project if there is no executive edict. It is a best practice and supports the Generally Accepted Recordkeeping Principles® principle of Accountability.[9]

20. *ERM system procurement must be researched and governed using transparency and accountability, the first two of the GAR Principles.* The appropriate vehicle (e.g., RFI, RFP, RFQ) for developing requirements and evaluating a complete set of vendors must be governed appropriately using an open, unbiased process.

Detailed ERM Best Practices

Some additional detailed ERM best practices for managing electronic files have been developed by IMERGE Consulting:[10]

1. **Keep names short.** When naming folders and files, try to:
   - Use abbreviations that are common or well-known.
   - Use meaningful terms such as subject, date, or status.
   - Do not use employees' names.
2. **State dates as year-month-day.** Date files using the four-digit year, followed by the two-digit month and then the two-digit day. *This allows you to sort chronologically.*

   NO: 24March2005 Minutes.doc

   YES: 20050324 Minutes.doc
3. **Avoid using symbols.** Symbols will lead to inconsistencies, making it difficult to locate and identify files.

   NO: Monthly $ Reports!!!!.xls

   YES: 200701 Expense Report.xls
4. **Use spaces to separate words.** Spaces are easier on the eye than underscore marks and other symbols. Using spaces makes file names easier to scan and identify.

   NO: OGA_Bulletin—Sum—July_2_08.pdf

   YES: Bulletin Sum 20080702.pdf
5. **Show the file status.** To help keep track of files, place its status at the end of the file name:
   - For drafts, write "draft."
   - For versions, write a "V" followed by the version number.

- When the document is final, write "final."
- Delete drafts and versions that have no real value.

6. **Use file names that make sorting easy.** In MS Windows™, you can sort files alphabetically, numerically or chronologically. When naming files, think about how others will search for them.

   For example, if you are naming files in an events folder, you may want to put the event name first rather than at the date.

   NO: May 1 04 HR Training.doc

   YES: HR Training 20040501.doc

   If you are naming a collection of invoices, you may want to name them chronologically.

   NO: Visa Invoice Jan 01 06.xls

   YES: 20060106 Invoice Visa.xls

7. **Divide top folders by function.** Divide top folders by your business unit's primary function. Then divide each primary function by each subfunction and so on.

8. **Do not keep files at the top two folder levels.** Top-level folders are very general. They should be used only as a way to organize information. Every file belongs somewhere and should be placed in a subject-specific folder.

   NO: T:\OGAGEN\FBC Invoice.doc

   YES: G:\Finance\Invoices\FBC

9. **Do not have more than nine primary folders or five sublevels in each primary folder:**
   - Our brains can only process so many items in a list. In general, we can handle seven items, plus or minus two.
   - Think of the best way to divide information using this guideline. It will be easier to find files and for you to remember where you put them.

10. **Do not repeat the folder name.** Do not repeat the information in the file name that is already in the folder name. This will reduce the length of the file path.

    NO: TST\Minutes\Minutes2007.doc

    YES: TST\Minutes\2007.doc

Using these detailed best practice recommendations in naming files and folders will facilitate search and retrieval in the future, which can provide a host of benefits including improved knowledge worker productivity, improved decision support, improved information confidence, and improved litigation and e-discovery capabilities.

Conclusion

In summary, implementing ERM is on ongoing effort that requires a solid IG underpinning and using an IG framework or reference model can assist and guide organizations in their ERM implementations and program management.

Some newer technologies are available that impact records management policies and practices. For cloud use, limit the storage of documents in the cloud to those that do not have long retention periods and carry a low litigation risk. If your organization is utilizing social media, be sure to establish and communicate a clear social media policy, and to capture records of social media posts in real-time.

When inventorying e-records, do so at the system level, not by record series, and in developing your taxonomy strategy, consider both navigation *and* classification. The inventory feeds into retention schedule development. Retention schedules should, ideally, be developed at the enterprise level, or at the highest business unit level possible.

Capturing accurate and reliable e-mail records requires that that they be archived in real-time (both inbound and outbound) at the organizational level, and personal e-mail archiving should be disallowed. A policy that implements destruction of e-mail after a stated period (e.g., 90 days) is a legally defensible approach, so long as e-mail items flagged as records or potential records, and those placed under a legal hold, are preserved intact.

If your organization utilizes SharePoint, be sure to customize your SharePoint governance model and project charter to state exactly which types of documents the system will be managing, and who is responsible for specific project or program duties.

Where possible, research and refer to industry standards when considering an ERM program implementation. Industry standards are not absolutes, and they are maturing in the ERM space, but standards are helpful, especially in areas such as metadata design and LTDP.

Use LTDP methods, best practices, technologies and standards when preserving digital assets over the long term. These records are critical to maintaining organization heritage and corporate memory.

Executive sponsorship and accountability are key in implementing ERM programs and in setting the tone for records management programs. Bear in mind that business process redesign is essential to gaining real productivity benefits, and it is a challenging task, as it requires workers to adapt to new, streamlined business processes and to change the way they work with records, which can get personal. So it must be driven and supported by an executive sponsor who clearly and regularly communicates the business objectives and scope of the program.

When making ERM system procurements, keep the process open, and transparent, and draw clear lines of accountability. You should have a clear executive sponsor and a designated project manager, with distinct roles and responsibilities.

Notes

1. The Economist Intelligence Unit, "The Future of Information Governance," www.emc.com/leadership/business-view/future-information-governance.htm (accessed March 10, 2012).
2. Monica Crocker, e-mail to author, June 21, 2012.
3. www.edrm.net/resources/guides/igrm (accessed Nov. 30, 2012).
4. Seth Earley, e-mail to author, September 10, 2012.
5. Monica Crocker, e-mail to author, June 21, 2012.
6. Kate Cumming, "Metadata Matters," in *Managing Electronic Records*, ed. Julie McLeod and Catherine Hare (London: Facet Publishing, 2005), 34.
7. Minnesota State Archives, "Electronic Records Management Guidelines," March 12, 2012, www.mnhs.org/preserve/records/electronicrecords/ermetadata.html.
8. Charles Dollar and Lori Ashley, e-mail to author August 10, 2012.
9. ARMA International, "How to Cite GARP," www.arma.org/garp/copyright.cfm (accessed June 19, 2012).
10. Paula Lederman, e-mail to author, October 2, 2012.

Laws and Major Regulations Related to Records Management

United States

Records management practices and standards are delineated in many federal regulations. Also, there are a number of state statutes that have passed and in some cases they actually supersede federal regulations; therefore it is crucial to understand compliance within the state or states where an organization operates.

On the federal level, public companies must be vigilant in verifying, protecting, and reporting financial information to comply with requirements under Sarbanes-Oxley and the Gramm-Leach-Bliley Act (GLBA). Healthcare concerns must meet the requirements of HIPAA, and investment firms must comply with a myriad of regulations by the Securities and Exchange Commission (SEC) and National Association of Securities Dealers (NASD).

Following is a brief description of current rules, laws, regulators, and their records retention and corporate policy requirements. *(Note: This is an overview, and firms should consult their own legal counsel for interpretation and applicability.)*

Gramm-Leach-Bliley Act

The Financial Institution Privacy Protection Act of 2001 and Financial Institution Privacy Protection Act of 2003 (Gramm-Leach-Bliley Act) was amended in 2003 to improve and increase protection of nonpublic personal information. Through this Act, financial records are to be properly secured, safeguarded, and eventually completely destroyed so that the information cannot be further accessed.

Healthcare Insurance Portability and Accountability Act of 1996 (HIPAA)

HIPAA requires that security standards be adopted for: (1) controlling who may access health information; (2) providing audit trails for electronic record systems; (3) isolating health data, making it inaccessible to unauthorized access; (4) ensuring the confidentiality and safeguarding of health information when it is electronically transmitted to ensure it is physically, electronically, and administratively secure; and (5) meeting the needs and capabilities of small and rural healthcare providers.

PATRIOT Act (Uniting and Strengthening America by Providing Appropriate Tools Required to Intercept and Obstruct Terrorism Act of 2001)

The PATRIOT Act: (1) requires that the identity of a person opening an account with any financial institution is verified by the financial institution, and they must implement reasonable procedures to maintain identity information; and (2) provides law enforcement organizations broad investigatory rights, including warrantless searches.

Sarbanes-Oxley Act (SOX)

The key provisions of SOX require that: (1) public corporations implement extensive policies, procedures, and tools to prevent fraudulent activities; (2) financial control and risk mitigation processes be documented and verified by independent auditors; (3) executives of publicly traded companies certify the validity of the company's financial statements; and, (4) business records must be kept for not less than five years.

SEC Rule 17A-4

SEC Rule 17A-4 requires that: (1) records that must be maintained and preserved be available to be produced or reproduced using either micrographic media (such as microfilm or microfiche) or electronic storage media (any digital storage medium or system); and (2) original copies of all communications, such as interoffice memoranda, be preserved for no less than *three* years, the first two in an easily accessible location.

CFR Title 47, Part 42—Telecommunications

CFR Title 47, Part 42 requires that telecommunications carriers keep original records or reproductions of original records, including memoranda, documents, papers, and correspondence that the carrier prepared or that were prepared on behalf of the carrier.

CFR Title 21, Part 11—Pharmaceuticals

CFR Title 21, Part 11 requires: (1) controls are in place to protect content stored on both open and closed systems to ensure the authenticity and integrity of electronic records; and (2) generating accurate and complete electronic copies of records so that the Food and Drug Administration (FDA) may inspect them.

U.S. Federal Authority on Archives and Records: National Archives and Records Administration (NARA)

The National Archives and Records Administration (nara.gov):

- Oversees physical and electronic recordkeeping policies and procedures of government agencies, requiring adequate and proper documentation on the conduction of U.S. government business;
- Defines formal e-records as machine-readable materials created or received by an agency of the U.S. federal government under federal law or in the course of the transaction of public business;
- Requires that organized records series be established for electronic records on a particular subject or function to facilitate the management of these e-records.

NARA regulations affecting Federal agencies and their records management programs are found in Subchapter B of 36 Code of Federal Regulations Chapter XII.[1,2]

- Part 1220—Federal Records; General
- Part 1222—Creation and Maintenance of Records
- Part 1223—Managing Vital Records
- Part 1224—Records Disposition Program
- Part 1225—Scheduling Records
- Part 1226—Implementing Disposition
- Part 1227—General Records Schedule
- Part 1228—Loan of Permanent and Unscheduled Records
- Part 1229—Emergency Authorization to Destroy Records
- Part 1230—Unlawful or Accidental Removal, Defacing, Alteration, or Destruction of Records
- Part 1231—Transfer of Records from the Custody of One Executive Agency to Another
- Part 1232—Transfer of Records to Records Storage Facilities
- Part 1233—Transfer, Use, and Disposition of Records in a NARA Federal Records Center
- Part 1234—Facility Standards for Records Storage Facilities
- Part 1235—Transfer of Records to the National Archives of the United States
- Part 1236—Electronic Records Management
- Part 1237—Audiovisual, Cartographic, and Related Records Management
- Part 1238—Microform Records Management
- Part 1239—Program Assistance and Inspections
- Part 1240–1249—[Reserved]

U.S. Code of Federal Regulations

In the **Code of Federal Regulations** there are over 5,000 references to retaining records. It can be found online at: www.ecfr.gov.

Canada*

The National Standards of Canada for electronic records management are: (1) *Electronic Records as Documentary Evidence* CAN/CGSB-72.34–2005 ("72.34"), published in December 2005; and, (2) *Microfilm and Electronic Images as Documentary Evidence* CAN/CGSB-72.11–93, first published in 1979 and updated to 2000 ("72.11").[3] 72.34 incorporates all that 72.11 deals with and is therefore the more important of the two. Because of its age, 72.11 should not be relied upon for its "legal" content. However, 72.11 has remained the industry standard for "imaging" procedures—converting original paper records to electronic storage. The Canada Revenue Agency has adopted these standards as applicable to records concerning taxation.[4]

72.34 deals with these topics: (1) management authorization and accountability; (2) documentation of procedures used to manage records; (3) "reliability testing" of electronic records according to existing legal rules; (4) the procedures manual and the chief records officer; (5) readiness to produce (the "prime directive"); (6) records recorded and stored in accordance with "the usual and ordinary course of business" and "system integrity," being key phrases from the Evidence Acts in Canada; (7) retention and disposal of electronic records; (8) backup and records system recovery; and, (9) security and protection. From these standards practitioners have derived many specific tests for auditing, establishing, and revising electronic records management systems.[5]

The "prime directive" of these standards states: "An organization shall always be prepared to produce its records as evidence."[6] *The duty to establish the "prime directive" falls upon senior management:*[7]

5.4.3 Senior management, the organization's own internal law-making authority, proclaims throughout the organization the integrity of the organization's records system (and, therefore, the integrity of its electronic records) by establishing and declaring:

   a. The system's role in the usual and ordinary course of business.
   b. The circumstances under which its records are made.
   c. Its prime directive for all RMS [records management system] purposes, i.e., an organization shall always be prepared to produce its records as evidence. This dominant principle applies to all of the organization's business records, including electronic, optical, original paper source records, microfilm, and other records of equivalent form and content.

Being the "dominant principle" of an organization's electronic records management system, the duty to maintain compliance with the "prime directive" should fall upon its senior management.

Because an electronic record is completely dependent upon its ERM system for everything, compliance with these National Standards and their "prime directive" should be part of the determination of the "admissibility" (acceptability) of evidence and of electronic discovery in court proceedings (litigation) and in regulatory tribunal proceedings.[8]

---

* This section was contributed by Ken Chasse JD, LLM, member of the Law Society of Upper Canada (Ontario) and of the Law Society of British Columbia, Canada.

There are 14 legal jurisdictions in Canada: 10 provinces; 3 territories; and the federal jurisdiction of the Government of Canada. Each has an Evidence Act (the Civil Code in the province of Quebec[9]), which applies to legal proceedings within its legislative jurisdiction. For example, criminal law and patents and copyrights are within federal legislative jurisdiction, and most civil litigation comes within provincial legislative jurisdiction.[10]

The admissibility of records as evidence is determined under the "business record" provisions of the Evidence Acts.[11] They require proof that a record was made "in the usual and ordinary course of business," and of "the circumstances of the making of the record." In addition, to obtain admissibility for electronic records, most of the Evidence Acts contain electronic record provisions, which state that an electronic record is admissible as evidence on proof of the "integrity of the electronic record system in which the data was recorded or stored."[12] This is the "system integrity" test for the admissibility of electronic records. The word "integrity" has yet to be defined by the courts.[13]

However, by way of sections such as the following, the electronic record provisions of the Evidence Acts make reference to the use of standards such as the National Standards of Canada:

> For the purpose of determining under any rule of law whether an electronic record is admissible, evidence may be presented in respect of any standard, procedure, usage or practice on how electronic records are to be recorded or stored, having regard to the type of business or endeavor that used, recorded, or stored the electronic record and the nature and purpose of the electronic record.[14]

There are six areas of law and records and information management (RIM) applicable to paper and electronic records:

1. The laws of evidence applicable to electronic and paper records.[15]
2. The National standards of Canada concerning electronic records.[16]
3. The records requirements of government agencies, such as the Canada Revenue Agency.[17]
4. The electronic commerce legislation.[18]
5. The privacy laws.[19]
6. The guidelines for electronic discovery in legal proceedings.[20]

These six areas are closely interrelated and are based upon very similar concepts. They all make demands of records systems and of the chief records officer or others responsible for records. *Therefore, a failure to satisfy the records management needs of any one of them will likely mean a failure to satisfy all of them.* Agencies that manage these areas of law look to the decisions of the courts to determine the requirements for acceptable records.

Each of these areas of law affects records and information management, just as they are affected by the laws governing the use of records as evidence in legal proceedings—the laws of evidence. These relationships make mandatory compliance with the "prime directive" provided by the national standards, which states: "an organization shall always be prepared to produce its records as evidence."[21]

United Kingdom

Regulations and Legislation Impacting Records Retention

"The following Acts and Statutory Instruments of the UK and Scottish Parliaments contain provisions that are relevant to records retention and disposal:"[22]

Acts of the UK Parliament

1957 c31 Occupiers Liability Act 1957

1969 c57 Employers' Liability (Compulsory Insurance) Act 1969

1970 c41 Equal Pay Act 1970

1970 c9 Taxes Management Act 1970

1973 c52 Prescription and Limitations (Scotland) Act 1973

1974 c37 Health and Safety at Work (etc.) Act 1974

1975 c65 Sex Discrimination Act 1975

1976 c74 Race Relations Act 1976

1980 c58 Limitation Act 1980

1992 c4 Social Security Contributions and Benefits Act 1992

1994 c30 Education Act 1994

1994 c23 Value Added Tax Act 1994

1995 c50 Disability Discrimination Act 1995

1998 c29 Data Protection Act 1998

Acts of the Scottish Parliament

2002 asp13 Freedom of Information (Scotland) Act 2002

Statutory Instruments of the UK Parliament

SI 1977/500 The Safety Representatives and Safety Committees Regulations 1977

SI 1981/917 The Health and Safety (First Aid) Regulations 1981

SI 1982/894 The Statutory Sick Pay (General) Regulations 1982

SI 1986/1960 The Statutory Maternity Pay (General) Regulations 1986

SI 1989/1790 The Noise at Work Regulations 1989

SI 1989/635 The Electricity at Work Regulations 1989

SI 1989/682 The Health and Safety Information for Employees Regulations 1989

SI 1991/2680 The Public Works Contracts Regulations 1991

SI 1992/2792 The Health and Safety (Display Screen Equipment) Regulations 1992

SI 1992/2793 The Manual Handling Operations Regulations 1992

SI 1992/2932 The Provision and Use of Work Equipment Regulations 1992

SI 1992/2966 The Personal Protective Equipment at Work Regulations 1992

SI 1993/3228 The Public Services Contracts Regulations 1993

SI 1993/744 The Income Tax (Employments) Regulations 1993

SI 1995/201 The Public Supply Contracts Regulations 1995

SI 1995/3163 The Reporting of Injuries, Diseases and Dangerous Occurrences Regulations 1995

SI 1996/1513 The Health and Safety (Consultation with Employees) Regulations 1996

SI 1996/341 The Health and Safety (Safety Signs and Signals) Regulations 1996

SI 1996/972 The Special Waste Regulations 1996

SI 1997/1840 The Fire Precautions (Workplace) Regulations 1997

SI 1998/1833 The Working Time Regulations 1998

SI 1998/2306 The Provision and Use of Work Equipment Regulations 1998

SI 1998/2307 The Lifting Operations and Lifting Equipment Regulations 1998

SI 1998/2573 The Employers' Liability (Compulsory Insurance) Regulations 1998

SI 1999/3242 The Management of Health and Safety at Work Regulations 1999

SI 1999/3312 The Maternity and Parental Leave (etc.) Regulations 1999

SI 1999/584 The National Minimum Wage Regulations 1998

SI 2002/2675 The Control of Asbestos at Work Regulations 2002

SI 2002/2676 The Control of Lead at Work Regulations 2002

SI 2002/2677 The Control of Substances Hazardous to Health Regulations 2002

Other Provisions

HMCE 700/21 HM Customs and Excise Notice 700/21: Keeping [VAT] records and accounts

IR CA30 Statutory Sick Pay Manual for Employers CA30

Australia

Archives Act

The Archives Act 1983 empowers the Archives to preserve the archival resources of the Australian government—those records designated "national archives." Under the Act, it is illegal to destroy Australian government records without permission from the Archives unless destruction is specified in another piece of legislation or allowed under a normal administrative practice.

The Act also establishes a right of public access to nonexempt Commonwealth records in the "open access period" (transitioning from 30 years to 20 years over the period 2011 to 2021 under amendments to the Act passed in 2010). Different open access periods exist for Cabinet notebooks (transitioning from 50 years to 30 years over the period 2011 to 2021) and records containing Census information (99 years).

Freedom of Information Act

The Freedom of Information Act 1982 gives individuals the legal right to access documents held by Australian government ministers, departments, and most agencies, including Norfolk Island government agencies. From November 1, 2010, the FOI Act also applies to documents created or held by contractors or subcontractors who provided services to the public or third parties on behalf of agencies.

The FOI Act applies to records that are not yet in the open access period under the Archives Act unless the document contains personal information (including personal information about a deceased person). The Archives Act regulates access to records in the open access period.

When a member of the public requests information, your agency must identify and preserve all relevant sources, including records, until a final decision on the request is made. The FOI Act also sets out how agencies may correct, annotate, or update records if a member of the public shows that any personal information relating to them is incomplete, incorrect, out of date, or misleading.

The FOI Act also establishes the Information Publication Scheme (IPS), which requires agencies subject to the FOI Act to take a proactive approach to publishing a broad range of information on their website. The IPS does not apply to a small number of security and intelligence agencies that are exempt from the FOI Act.

Australian Information Commissioner Act

The Australian Information Commissioner Act 2010 established the Office of the Australian Information Commissioner. The OAIC has three sets of functions. These are:

1. Freedom of information functions—protecting the public's right of access to documents under the amended *Freedom of Information Act* and reviewing decisions made by agencies and ministers under that Act.
2. Privacy functions—ensuring proper handling of personal information in accordance with the *Privacy Act 1988*.
3. Government and information policy functions, conferred on it by the *Australian Information Commissioner Act 2010*—these include strategic functions relating to information management and ensuring maximum coordination, efficiency and transparency in government information policy and practice.

As part of its government and information policy function, the OAIC is committed to leading the development and implementation of a national information policy framework to promote secure and open government. It aims to achieve this by driving public access to government information and encouraging agencies to proactively publish information.

Privacy Act

The Privacy Act 1988 regulates the handling of personal information by Australian government agencies, ACT government agencies, Norfolk Island Government agencies, and a range of private and not-for-profit organizations. The *Privacy Act* regulates the way in which personal information can be collected, its accuracy, how it is kept secure, and how it is used and disclosed. It also provides rights to individuals to access and correct the information that organizations and government agencies hold about them. Records in the open-access period as defined in the *Archives Act 1983* are not covered by the Privacy Act. The Privacy Act also sets out requirements that may apply when an agency enters into a contract under which services are provided to the agency.

Evidence Act

The Evidence Act 1995 defines what documents, including records, can be used as evidence in a Commonwealth court.[23]

All agencies need to take account of evidence legislation. A court may need to examine records as evidence of an organization's decisions and actions. General advice on the impact of the *Evidence Act* is given in the publication Commonwealth Records in Evidence (pdf, 418kb).

Electronic Transactions Act

The Electronic Transactions Act 1999 encourages online business by ensuring that electronic evidence of transactions is not invalidated because of its format. This Act does not authorize the destruction of any Australian government records, whether originals or copies. The obligations placed on agencies under the *Archives Act 1983* for the preservation and disposal of Commonwealth records continue to apply.

Financial Management and Accountability Act

The Financial Management and Accountability Act 1997 states that an APS employee who misapplies, improperly disposes of, or improperly uses Commonwealth records may be in breach of the *Financial Management and Accountability Act* (s. 41). Regulation 12 of the Act requires that the terms of approval for a proposal to spend money be recorded in writing as soon as practicable.

Australian government records fall within the meaning of "public property" as defined in this Act.

Crimes Act

The Crimes Act 1914 outlines crimes against the Commonwealth. Several parts of the Act relate to records. For example, section 70 prohibits public servants (or anyone working for the Australian government, including contractors and consultants) from publishing or communicating facts, documents, or information that they gain access to through their work unless they have permission to do so. This includes taking or selling records that should be destroyed.

This Act also makes it an offence for someone to intentionally destroy documents that they know may be required as evidence in a judicial proceeding.

Identifying Records Management Requirements in Other Legislation

Your agency [or business] needs to be aware of the legislation governing its own records practices.

Some legislative requirements apply to many agencies [and businesses]. For example, occupational health and safety legislation requires an organization to keep certain types of records for prescribed periods of time. Requirements that apply to all agencies are included in the National Archives' Administrative Functions Disposal Authority.

Other legislative requirements may apply only to the particular business of one or a number of agencies.

Recordkeeping requirements may be stipulated in your agency's enabling legislation (legislation that established the agency) or in specific legislation that your agency is responsible for administering.[24]

Notes

1. NARA Records Management Guidance and Regulations, www.archives.gov/records-mgmt/policy/guidance-regulations.html (accessed October 17, 2012).
2. NARA Records Management Guidance and Regulations, www.archives.gov/about/regulations/subchapter/b.html (accessed October 17, 2012).
3. These standards were developed by the CGSB (Canadian General Standards Board), which is a standards-writing agency within Public Works and Government Services Canada (a department of the federal government). It is accredited by the Standards Council of Canada as a standards development agency. The Council must certify that standards have been developed by the required procedures before it will designate them as being National Standards of Canada. 72.34 incorporates by reference as "normative references": (1) many of the standards of the International Organization for Standardization (ISO) in Geneva, Switzerland. ("ISO," derived from the Greek word *isos* (equal) so as to provide a common acronym for all languages); and, (2) several of the standards of the Canadian Standards Association (CSA). The "Normative references" section of 72.34 (p. 2) states that these "referenced documents are indispensable for the application of this document." 72.11 cites (p. 2, "Applicable Publications") several standards of the American National Standards Institute/Association for Information and Image Management (ANSI/AIIM) as publications "applicable to this standard." The process by which the National Standards of Canada are created and maintained is described within the standards themselves (reverse side of the front cover), and on the CGSB's website (see, "Standards Development"), from which website these standards may be obtained; online: www.ongc-cgsb.gc.ca.
4. The Canada Revenue Agency (CRA) informs the public of its policies and procedures by means, among others, of its *Information Circulars* (IC's), and *GST/HST Memoranda*. (GST: goods and services tax; HST: harmonized sales tax, *i.e.*, the harmonization of federal and provincial sales taxes into one retail sales tax.) In particular, see: *IC05-1*, dated June 2010, entitled, *Electronic Record Keeping*, paragraphs 24, 26 and 28. Note that use of the National Standard cited in paragraph 26, *Microfilm and Electronic Images as Documentary Evidence* CAN/CGSB-72.11-93 is mandatory for, "Imaging and microfilm (including microfiche) reproductions of books of original entry and source documents. . . ." Paragraph 24 recommends the use of the newer national standard, *Electronic Records as Documentary Evidence* CAN/CGSB-72.34-2005, "To ensure the reliability, integrity and authenticity of electronic records." However, if this newer standard is given the same treatment by CRA as the older standard, it will be made mandatory as well. And similar statements appear in the GST Memoranda, *Computerized Records* 500-1-2, *Books and Records* 500-1. IC05-1. *Electronic Record Keeping*, concludes with the note, "Most Canada Revenue Agency publications are available on the CRA website, www.cra.gc.ca, under the heading 'Forms and Publications.'"
5. There are more than 200 specific compliance tests that can be applied to determine if the principles of 72.34 are being complied with. The analysts—a combined team of records management and legal expertise—analyze: (1) the nature of the business involved; (2) the uses and value of its records for its various functions; (3) the likelihood and risk of the various types of its records being the subject of legal proceedings, or of their being challenged by some regulating authority; and, (4) the consequences of the

unavailability of acceptable records—for example, the consequences of its records not being accepted in legal proceedings. Similarly, in regard to the older National Standard of Canada, 72.11, there is a comparable series of more than 50 tests that can be applied to determine the state of compliance with its principles.

6. *Electronic Records as Documentary Evidence* CAN/CGSB-72.34-2005 ("72.34"), clause 5.4.3 c) at p. 17; and, *Microfilm and Electronic Images as Documentary Evidence* CAN/CGSB-72.11-93 ("72.11"), paragraph 4.1.2 at p. 2, *supra* note 49.

7. Ibid., 72.34, Clause 5.4.3.

8. "Admissibility" refers to the procedure by which a presiding judge determines if a record or other proffered evidence is acceptable as evidence according the rules of evidence. "Electronic discovery" is the compulsory exchange of relevant records by the parties to legal proceedings prior to trial. As to the admissibility of records as evidence see: Ken Chasse, "The Admissibility of Electronic Business Records" (2010), 8 Canadian Journal of Law and Technology 105; and, Ken Chasse, "Electronic Records for Evidence and Disclosure and Discovery" (2011) 57 The Criminal Law Quarterly 284. For the electronic discovery of records see: Ken Chasse, "Electronic Discovery—*Sedona Canada* is Inadequate on Records Management—Here's *Sedona Canada* in Amended Form," *Canadian Journal of Law and Technology* 9 (2011): 135; and Ken Chasse, "Electronic Discovery in the Criminal Court System" *Canadian Criminal Law Review* 14 (2010): 111. See also note 18 *infra*, and accompanying text.

9. For the province of Quebec, comparable provisions are contained in Articles 2831-2842, 2859-2862, 2869-2874 of Book 7 "Evidence" of the Civil Code of Quebec, S.Q. 1991, c. C-64, to be read in conjunction with, An Act to Establish a Legal Framework for Information Technology, R.S.Q. 2001, c. C-1.1, ss. 2, 5-8, and 68.

10. For the legislative jurisdiction of the federal and provincial governments in Canada, see The Constitution Act, 1867 (U.K.) 30 and 31 Victoria, c. 3, s. 91 (federal), and s. 92 (provincial); at online: www.canlii.org/en/ca/laws/stat/30—31-vict-c-3/latest/30—31-vict-c-3.html.

11. The two provinces of Alberta and Newfoundland and Labrador do not have business record provisions in their Evidence Acts. Therefore "admissibility" would be determined in those jurisdictions by way of the court decisions that define the applicable common law rules; such decisions as, *Ares v. Venner* [1970], S.C.R. 608, 14 D.L.R. (3d) 4 (S.C.C.), and decisions that have applied it.

12. See for example, the Canada Evidence Act, R.S.C. 1985, c. C-5, ss. 31.1-31.8; Alberta Evidence Act, R.S.A. 2000, c. A-18, ss. 41.1-41.8; (Ontario) Evidence Act, R.S.O. 1990, c. E.23, s. 34.1; and the (Nova Scotia) Evidence Act, R.S.N.S. 1989, c. 154, ss. 23A-23G. The Evidence Acts of the two provinces of British Columbia and Newfoundland and Labrador do not contain electronic record provisions. However, because an electronic record is no better than the quality of the record system in which it is recorded or stored, its "integrity" (reliability, credibility) will have to be determined under the other provincial laws that determine the admissibility of records as evidence.

13. The electronic record provisions have been in the Evidence Acts in Canada since 2000. They have been applied to admit electronic records into evidence, but they have not yet received any detailed analysis by the courts.

14. This is the wording used in, for example, s. 41.6 of the Alberta Evidence Act, s. 34.1(8) of the (Ontario) Evidence Act; and, s. 23F of the (Nova Scotia) Evidence Act, *supra* note 10. Section 31.5 of the Canada Evidence Act, *supra* note 58, uses the same wording, the only significant difference being that the word "document" is used instead of "record." For the province of Quebec, see sections 12 and 68 of, An Act to Establish a Legal Framework for Information Technology, R.S.Q., chapter C-1.1.

15. *Supra* notes 54 to 59 and accompanying texts.

16. *Supra* notes 49 and 52 and accompanying texts.

17. *Supra* note 50 and accompanying text.

18. All 14 jurisdictions of Canada have electronic commerce legislation except for the Northwest Territories. See for example, the Personal Information Protection and Electronic Documents Act, S.C. 2000, c. 5, Parts 2 and 3; Ontario's Electronic Commerce Act, 2000, S.O. 2000, c. 17; and, British Columbia's Electronic Transactions Act, R.B.C. 20001, c. 10. The concept of "system integrity" in the Evidence Acts (*supra* note 58 and accompanying text), is also found in the electronic commerce legislation. See for example, s. 8 of the Ontario Electronic Commerce Act, 2000, under the heading, "Legal Requirement re Original Documents."

19. For example, Part 1, "Personal Information Protection," of the federal Personal Information Protection and Electronic Documents Act (PIPEDA), S.C. 2000, c. 5, which applies within provincial legislative jurisdiction as well as federal, until a province enacts its own personal information protection Act (a PIPA"), which displaces it in the provincial sphere. British Columbia, Alberta, and Quebec are the only provinces that have done so.

20. The dominant guideline for electronic discovery in Canada is *The Sedona Canada Principles—Addressing Electronic Discovery*; online: The Sedona Conference, Canada, January 2008: www.thesedonaconference .com/content/miscFiles/canada_pincpls_FINAL_108.pdf or www.thesedonaconference.org/dltForm? did=canada_pincpls_FINAL_108.pdf. See also E-Discovery Canada website, hosted by LexUM (at the University of Montreal), online: www. lexum.umontreal.ca/e-discovery; and, the law journal articles concerning electronic discovery cited in note 54 *supra*.

21. *Supra* notes 52 and 53 and accompanying texts.

22. "Information Governance Record Retention Guidance," www.rec-man.stir.ac.uk/rec-ret/legislation. php (accessed October 17, 2012).

23. http://www.comlaw.gov.au/Details/C2012C00518 (accessed Nov. 30, 2012).

24. National Archives of Australia, www.naa.gov.au/records-management/strategic-information/standards/ recordslegislation.aspx (accessed October 17, 2012).

Listing of Technology and Service Providers

Electronic Records Management

Autonomy/HP (HP acquired in 2012)
U.S. Headquarters
One Market Plaza
Spear Tower, Suite 1900
San Francisco, CA 94105
(415) 243-9955
www.autonomy.com

EMC
176 South Street
Hopkinton, MA 01748
(866) 438-3622
www.emc.com

File Trail
111 North Market Street, Suite 715
San Jose, CA 95113-1108
(408) 289-1300
http://filetrail.com/FT_Home/Index.asp?gclid=

GimmalSoft
Three Galleria Tower
13155 Noel Road, 9th Floor
Dallas, TX 75240
(214) 800-2300
www.gimmalsoft.com/Pages/default.aspx

Hyland
28500 Clemens Road
Westlake, OH 44145
(888) HYLAND-8
www.hyland.com

Infolinx
10800 Connecticut Avenue
Kensington, MD 20895
(800) 251-8399
http://infolinx.com/

IBM
1 New Orchard Road
Armonk, NY 10504-1722
(800) 426-4968
www.ibm.com/us/en/

Integro
88 Inverness Circle East, Suite N106
Englewood, CO 80112
(888) 575-9300
www.integro.com

Iron Mountain
745 Atlantic Ave
Boston, MA 02111
(800) 899-4766
www.ironmountain.com

Laserfiche
3545 Long Beach Blvd.
Long Beach, CA 90807
(800) 985-8533
www.laserfiche.com/en-US

OmniRIM
39 Plymouth Street
Fairfield, NJ 07004
(800) 899-3975
www.archivesystems.com/products/omnirim-records-management.aspx

Open Text
275 Frank Tompa Drive
Waterloo, Ontario
(800) 499-6544
www.opentext.com/2/global.htm

Oracle
500 Oracle Parkway
Redwood Shores, CA 94065
(800) 392-2999
www.oracle.com

RecMan for Google Apps
555 California Street, Suite 4925
San Francisco, CA 94104
(415) 659-1521
http://recman.net/

E-Mail Archiving
Autonomy/HP
U.S. Headquarters
One Market Plaza
Spear Tower, Suite 1900
San Francisco, CA 94105
(415) 243-9955
www.autonomy.com

AXS-One/Unify
301 Route 17 North
Rutherford, NJ 07070-2581
(201) 935-3400
http://axsone.com/

C2C
134 Flanders Road
Westborough, MA 01581
(508) 870–2205
www.c2c.com

CommVault
2 Crescent Place
Oceanport, NJ 07757
(888) 746-3849
www.commvault.com

CA
One CA Plaza
Islandia, NY 11749
(800) 225-5224
www.ca.com

Critical Technologies
3601 S Broadway, Suite 1400
Edmond, OK 73013
(405) 650-1234
www.criticaltech.com

Dell MessageOne
1 Dell Way
Round Rock, TX 78682
(888) 782-3355
www.dellmodularservices.com

EMC
176 South Street
Hopkinton, MA 01748
(866) 438-3622
www.emc.com

Forsythe
7770 Frontage Road
Skokie, IL 60077
(800) 843-4488
www.forsythe.com/na/

Proofpoint
892 Ross Drive
Sunnyvale, CA 94089
(408) 517-4710
www.proofpoint.com

GFI
15300 Weston Parkway, Suite 104
Cary, NC 27513
(888) 243-4329
www.gfi.com

GlobalRelay
286 Madison Avenue, 7th Floor
New York, NY 10016-6368
(866) 484-6630
www.globalrelay.com

GWAVA
100 Alexis Nihon Suite 500
Montreal, Quebec, Canada
(866) 464-9282
www.gwava.com

HP
Hewlett-Packard Company
3000 Hanover Street
Palo Alto, CA 94304-1185
(650) 857-1501

IBM
1 New Orchard Road
Armonk, NY 10504-1722
(800) 426-4968
www.ibm.com/us/en/

MessageSolution
1851 McCarthy Blvd., Suite 105
Milpitas, CA 95035
(408) 383-0100
www.messagesolution.com

Messaging Architects
180 Peel Street, Suite 333
Montreal, QC Canada H3C 2G7
(866) 497-0101
www.messagingarchitects.com

Metalogix
1601 Trapelo Road
Waltham, MA 02451
(877) 450-8667
metalogix.com

Open Text
275 Frank Tompa Drive
Waterloo, Ontario
(800) 499-6544
www.opentext.com/2/global.htm

Oracle
500 Oracle Parkway
Redwood Shores, CA 94065
(800) 392-2999
www.oracle.com

Overtone Software
44 Montgomery St., Suite 2040
San Francisco, CA 94104
(866) 517-4100
www.overtone.com

Postini/Google
1600 Amphitheatre Parkway
Mountain View, CA 94043
(650) 253-0000
www.google.com/postini/

Quest Software
5 Polaris Way
Aliso Viejo, CA 92656
(800) 306-9329
www.quest.com

Sherpa Software
456 Washington Ave, Suite 2
Bridgeville, PA 15017
(800) 255-5155
www.sherpasoftware.com

Symantec
350 Ellis Street
Mountain View, CA 94043
(424) 750-7580
www.symantec.com

Waterford Technologies
19700 Fairchild, Suite 300
Irvine, CA 92612
(949) 428-9300
www.waterfordtechnologies.com

ZL Technologies
2000 Concourse Drive
San Jose, CA 95131
(408) 240-8989
www.zlti.com

ZyLab
7918 Jones Branch Drive, Suite 530
McLean, VA 22102
(866) 995-2262
www.zylab.com

Trends in Electronic Medical Records Technology

John W.Orth

While the first **electronic medical record** (EMR) implementations began in the 1990s, they only become truly clinically viable after the year 2000. Clinicians and medical informatics experts have attributed the rise in adoption to more sophisticated software, improved computer literacy of the younger clinicians, and, in the United States, financial incentives that the federal government has provided to speed the implementation of EMR technology.

According to the 2012 Healthcare Information Management Systems Society (HIMSS) Leadership Survey, governmental initiatives including the 2009 Health Information Technology for Economic and Clinical Health Act (HITECH) provision in the American Recovery and Reinvestment Act (ARRA), and the Patient Protection and Affordable Care Act (PPACA) of 2010, "have challenged providers to enhance their IT capabilities like never before."[1]

The 2012 survey indicated that over 65 percent of hospitals and 80 percent of physicians are now using EMRs. This does not mean that all medical records are in electronic form because the historic paper records still exist and many clinical procedures are still creating paper records.

Previously the industry differentiated between electronic medical records (EMRs) for physicians and clinics and electronic Health records (EHRs) for hospitals. Since the software vendors now have different versions for each medical discipline with integration to a hospital electronic records system, the terms have become interchangeable.

As discussed later in this appendix, the new term *personal health record* (PHR) is required by the HITECH "Meaningful Use (MU)" rules and is designed to provide a simplified version of the patient's records for direct access by patients. The MU rules in general are being defined to establish "best practices" guidelines and are being implemented in three stages. Stage 1 began in 2011, Stage 2 was recently deferred to 2014, and Stage 3 has not yet been scheduled.

Diagnostic Support Intelligence

One of the most common reasons cited for implementing EMRs is that they include built-in intelligence to assist the clinician to diagnose a patient's condition as well as identify any high-risk therapies based on a patient's medical history, allergies, or preferences. Most physicians will tell you that the symptoms of many diseases are very common and identifying the exact patient condition or disease can often be very confusing. Today's EMR technology contains access to many medical databases and drug side-effects that suggest possible diagnoses for the physician to consider. The development of new therapies and recognition of rare symptoms will frequently improve the quality of patient care, and also identify the correct condition and therapy faster, to minimize trial and error medicine.

Continuous updates in EMR software allow the user to be aware of new clinical results and therapies reported in medical journals, especially in EMR applications for specialists like neurologists, cardiologists, orthopedics, oncologists, and so on.

The implementation of clinical intelligence in today's EMR systems not only makes them more valuable and effective in providing better patient care, but also improves outcomes.

Another interesting side effect of the new EMR technology is that the physicians that utilize this new tool can decrease their risk of making an error in diagnosis or therapy that could result in a malpractice case. See the section on drug alerts for an example of how an EMR saved a physician from prescribing a drug that the patient was allergic to.

One of the most promising technologies for the future of EMRs is the recent IBM announcement of a project utilizing the WATSON computer system and software to assist with the diagnoses and management of cancer patients, partnering with the Sloan Kettering Cancer Center.[2]

This state-of-the-art digital intelligence technology should lead the way to more meaningful use of medical information and successful clinical therapies.[3]

Computerized Physician Order Entry (CPOE) Facilitation

Something as simple as writing a prescription has resulted in so many medical errors, whether due to sloppy handwriting or misinterpretation by the pharmacist, that the new Meaningful Use rules from the U.S. Health and Human Services (HHS) requires that physicians enter their prescriptions via computer and have them transmitted direct to the patient's pharmacy to eliminate these errors. While the technology to implement this practice has been around for years, less than 25 percent of physicians were using it until EMR software was made available for their use. The database of approved pharmaceuticals is also embedded in the EMR software to make the choices available to the physician appear on his or her computer screen so that he or she needs only to click on the right drug and dose to eliminate the risk of a typing error.

In addition to reducing prescription errors, the software provides a wide selection of lab tests, radiology procedures, and other diagnostic procedures available for the physician to order.

As with all digital recordkeeping systems, the physician's orders are then permanently recorded in the patient's medical record, thereby generating an audit trail and time line for later recall and analysis.

A 2012 HIMSS survey found that 65 percent of hospitals and 80 percent of physicians use some form of EMR technology.

New Meaningful Use rules from the U.S. HHS require that prescriptions are entered directly into a computer for transmission to a pharmacy. The Meaningful Use terms can be found at the website: www.healthit.gov/buzz-blog/.

Drug Alerts

Today's practice of medicine is facilitated not only with the use of thousands of different pharmaceuticals, but also complicated by the implementation of too many and often detrimental interactions. The typical patient today is frequently being treated with more than three drugs, sometimes up to 12 different drugs simultaneously. Because not all of the drugs are being prescribed by the same physician it is vital for the patient's benefit that all of the clinicians treating the patient know all of the different drugs the patient is taking and frequently a list of vitamin supplements as well. For this reason the EMR system being used by the patient's general practitioner (GP) should be made available to all physicians treating the same patient. Since this is not currently the case for most medical practices, patients are forced to reproduce their list of prescribed drugs and vitamin supplements for every new physician they visit. The new incentives to participate in Health Information Exchanges should make the sharing of patient's EMRs more common and efficient.

Today's EMR technology and pharmaceutical databases allow the software to watch for the potential of drug interactions that may not be recognized by the prescribing physician. When the potential for such an event exists, the software will issue an *alert* to the physician cautioning of the potential for an adverse reaction.

A similar alert capability exists to identify allergies to specific drugs that the prescribing physician may not be aware of.

A classic case has been cited by a physician in which he was about to prescribe a sulfur drug for a patient without knowing that she had a strong allergy to that drug. He makes the case that the *Drug Alert* feature in his EMR software probably saved his medical career that day by flashing a *red alert* on his computer screen.

Charting Patient Vital Signs and Significant Indicators

Under the old paper medical records practice it was not easy for clinicians to recognize trends in patient vital signs and monitoring of patient responses to various therapies. With the current EMR software, ***trend charts*** *are automatically displayed on the monitor to give the physician and other clinical staff a quick graphical view* of the patient's responses. In some of the more sophisticated applications for intensive care the software has built-in alarms to alert the clinicians when the patient is exceeding the desired vital sign values.

EMR technology is helpful in alerting physicians of possible drug interactions.

> EMR software automatically displays vital signs trend charts to assist caregivers.

Charting of patient data can also be very valuable in creating reports for the patient to explain how their therapy is working and/or how some behavior of the patient is adversely affecting their condition. The Meaningful Use rules now require that physicians provide their patients with written reports describing the results of their diagnostic testing and the use of charting from the software can make the reports much more meaningful to the patient. For example, the tabular report of a blood test might list the patient's current readings, but a chart can show them how they have changed in time as well as superimpose the normal values on the same chart to give the patient an indication of how their current condition is progressing or regressing.

Patient Compliance Support

Many physicians will report that the biggest reason why their patients do not respond to their prescribed therapies is that they do not comply with them. Whether it is a drug therapy or physical therapy, diet or exercise regimen, the typical physician has little control over the patient's compliance with their advice.

The latest EMR software now includes the ability to send e-mail, text messages, and/or telephone reminders to patients to assist them with compliance and has been shown to improve the patient's participation as well as positive response to the prescribed therapy. Some EMR applications also allow the patients to submit vital signs data into their EMR over the Internet so the physician can monitor their daily condition. Any significant changes in the data can be flagged on the physician's computer so he does not have to monitor every patient's records daily for signs of a problem. Patient follow-up data is also recorded in their EMR to document the result of a recent surgery or change in drug therapy. Meaningful Use rules require that clinicians do follow-up checks to validate compliance as well as document their quality of care.

Improved Organization of Clinical Data for Improved Access

The EMR systems of today store patient data in a structured database that allows clinicians to access relevant data for multiple patients without having to access each patient's record independently. With the older paper record systems there was no practical method of identifying all of the patients in a physician's practice that might be allergic to a specific drug or at risk for a specific disease. An example of this capability is currently being used in hospitals with EMR systems to identify patients in

> EMR software can now send patient alerts via e-mail, text messages, or telephone to assist them in complying with doctor's orders.

their database with a specific health condition that would place them at risk for a new disease or make them a logical client for a new drug.

Using this feature allows physicians to be proactive in treating patients and protecting them from increased risks.

Connectivity with Existing Digital Technologies

Current EMR software is capable of utilizing the industry standard Health Level Seven (HL7) interface technology to connect directly to patient monitoring devices such as holter counters, pacemakers, blood pressure monitors, and glucose monitors to record patient information directly into their EMR. This eliminates the tedious and error-prone process of manually keying in vital signs information.

Other digital technologies also include recording of digital EKG information, pulse oximetry, laboratory reports, and dozens of other reports of clinical information that were previously hand-recorded.

Improved Workflow for Added Efficiency and Status Tracking

Today's EMR systems have workflow features that automatically transmit a clinician's orders to their lab or additional clinical department to formally request more diagnostic tests as well as to identify other patient-related activity, such as orders for physical therapy, referral to another specialist, or even a follow-up order for home care or medical devices.

EMR systems of the future will be implementing tracking features that will alert a clinician when a requested lab report is ready or display an alert that a scheduled event has not occurred. The latest Meaningful Use requirements require follow-up contact with patients that can be scheduled and logged in as part of the patient's EMR record.

Another feature of EMR systems, similar to most electronic record systems is the ability to store an audit trail of all entries into a patient's medical records. This complete history accounts for all contacts of the patient with a clinician, any medical procedures provided, as well as the identification of the person making the entry as well as the time and date of all entries. This unambiguous and secured information is not subject to editing, so that it is not possible for anyone to delete or change an entry to cover up a mistake or fraudulent event.

Mobile Technologies More Easily Integrated

One of the most recent upgrades of EMR systems is their ability to communicate directly with the new mobile devices to make patient data available to physicians on their smart phones and tablets. The most advanced EMR systems will also allow physicians to input data and prescriptions and therapy instructions into the patient's EMR remotely.

> EMR software today connects directly to patient monitoring devices through the industry standard HL7 interface.

Newer EMR software is designed to support mobile devices like smart phones and tablets, keeping physicians in touch.

The new HIPAA rules for security and privacy of patient data put some significant restrictions on the networking of patient data through these mobile devices but the modern encryption technology is able to provide the security necessary to comply. The new HIPAA security rules are built on the best practices of the banking industry with added factors to confirm the identification of the person accessing the information.

The primary risk still resides in storing this information in the mobile device that then exposes it to easier fraudulent access through theft and other unauthorized access. Security safeguard similar to the HIPAA requirements are now being implemented for mobile devices, but they do not replace good physical security of any device storing patient data.

Compatibility with Radiology Picture Archiving and Communication Systems (PACS) Networks for Access to Diagnostic Images

One of the first open standards for electronic medical records was the DICOM standard that allowed competitive imaging devices to share a common format so that they could all be stored and viewed on a single computer and monitor. Now the electronic medical records systems for storing patient data are faced with a similar problem that will allow different EMR systems to share patient data to achieve the interoperability required in the Meaningful Use rules. One of the most common pieces of medical information utilized by clinicians today are the medical images and therefore easy access to these images is an essential tool to facilitate accurate and efficient patient management. The current EMR certification requirements require EMR systems to provide access to available PACS networks so they can be distributed to any workstation available to the clinicians and viewed alongside the patient's medical records. The newest EMR systems will also store links to the PACS networks to identify all of the potential diagnostic imaging studies available for that patient together with the radiologists interpretations. One of the issues this presents is that radiology images are frequently much higher resolution (frequently 2,000 × 2000 pixels or larger) and do not fit on the average EMR monitor. In most cases the software will automatically compress the images to fit the monitor resolution being used, but in the process compromise the diagnostic quality of the image. Some newer EMR systems will flag these images as compressed to alert the clinician. To compensate the clinician may roll and zoom into an image to recall and view a portion at a time in the native resolution.

Enables Patient Remote Access to Their Medical Records

Under the Meaningful Use rules medical providers must make a patient's medical records available to each patient or their authorized representative. This version of the patient's electronic medical record is known as the personal health record or PHR. It may represent a printed report of a patient's latest visit to their physician's office, or a scheduled surgery at their hospital or any other abstract from their complete EMR.

Most medical providers are making portals available on the Internet for patient's to access their PHR information on line.

While this seems like a potential security risk the portals must be encrypted and monitored for security breaches to protect patient data. Under the HIPAA rules for securing patient data any patient can opt out of making their data available through a public portal if they do not feel the risk of loss is greater than they are comfortable.

Recent studies have confirmed that easy access to a patient's PHR enables them to monitor the information and report any errors. One study confirmed that 64 percent of patients viewing their PHR data found one or more errors either by omission or false entry.

A new recommendation of the Society for Participatory Medicine is to create a personally controlled health record or PCHR. The PCHR differs from the PHR in that it will be interactive, allowing the patient to correct any errors they find, which would then be stored along with the original data for a clinician to review and confirm.[4]

Interoperability with Multiple Clinicians and Medical Providers to Optimize and Coordinate Patient Care

Today's clinical practices are structured into many specialties and historically each specialty maintained a medical record for each patient with thousands of items repeated in every physician's records. A single consolidated, master EMR may now be maintained by their medical provider and shared by all physicians and clinicians treating that patient. In order to facilitate access to one master EMR all of the clinicians must be using an EMR system that is "interoperable" or in other words able to communicate with multiple brands of EMR software and accessing the same patient's information. While this may seem to be simple on the surface it is complicated by dozens of formatting and identification issues. To provide an initial method of communication, the HHS/FDA has specified a document format called a coordinated care document or CCD.

This consolidated record must contain all of the vital information from a patient's EMR for a selected period of time and distributed by secure e-mail or fax. In return all physicians treating the same patient are expected to update the master EMR with similar communications to maintain a current set of the patient's records.

All Certified EMR Vendors Must Implement the Health Information Exchange Protocols for Interoperability

As part of the Stage 3 implementations of the Meaningful Use rules, all EMR vendors will be required to adopt the open standards that will be specified by their local Health Information Exchange. The most complete standard currently available for this purpose is the Integrated Health Enterprise (IHE) protocols adopted by the RSNA and HIMSS professional organizations.

The IHE protocols provide an indexing system that categorizes all clinical information by its medical specialty, such as CATH for a Cardiac Cath lab study or ECED for eye care reports, and so on. In the terms of conventional electronic records it is an ideal *taxonomy* for electronic medical records, but more important, it is a common taxonomy for an entire industry, allowing the accurate access to a patient's medical records by multiple medical providers without having to make translations and conversions from multiple vendors EMR terminologies. This is the goal of "interoperability."

Electronic Master Patient Index

Another one of the issues of sharing patient medical records is the unambiguous identification of the patient. All EMR systems currently establish a patient number when they are first logged into that EMR software and it is unique to that EMR system. When there is a need to share that information with another EMR system there must be a method of correctly identifying the patient. The ideal solution to this issue is to have one Master Patient Index. In the case of all electronic medical records systems, the Electronic Master Patient Index is known as the "e-MPI."

The IHE standards[5] have resolved this issue with the identification of a PIX layer or indexing system that identifies each patient with a unique number and nine other identification factors that can be compared if necessary to confirm the patient's true identity. While most EMR vendors have participated in a test of the IHE protocols through an annual "Connectathon" the technology is not in wide use because the health information networks to provide the sharing pathways are just getting organized. We expect this to become much more common when Stage 3 becomes required.

Public Health Access to Patient Data

The advent of EMR patient information and shared health information networks will make reporting of public-related information faster and more automated. Another expected advantage is that local, state, and national public health alerts can be transmitted through the HIE networks and instantly distributed through each EMR system. State and national databases, such as the Centers for Disease Control (CDC), will become more integrated with local health care organizations for more effective use of the data.

Provides Better and Faster Data for Epidemiology Studies and Drug Efficacy

With easy access to the EMR information for millions of patients, sanitized without patient identification, epidemiology studies will be more effective and statistically more meaningful. The electronic access to such large quantities of patient medical information will significantly expand the field of epidemiology and its clinical usefulness, especially regarding drug efficacy and identifying patients who are at risk for new diseases and viruses.

EMR Technology for the 2012 U.S. Olympic Team

The U.S. Olympic Committee (USOC) used a new state of the art EMR system to monitor the health and performance of over 700 athletes and 3,000 staff members at the 2012 Summer Olympics.[6] Among the many medical benefits they saw are the prompt access to any athlete's complete medical history and pharmaceutical records as well as any injury reports and therapy plans used in the past. Some of the major challenges they faced were to assemble all of this data on 3,700 people from thousands of existing medical records and familiarize more than 100 USOC medical personnel with the EMR system in a relatively short (90-day) time period. The USOC medical staff had the advantage of an EMR system integrated with a PACS network to have medical image history for all athletes, as well as prompt access to new diagnostic imaging on site at the Olympic village.

More significantly from the USOC's point of view was the potential to optimize performance of athletes in the future by using the power of the EMR analytics capability. Since they will be recording details of every athlete's therapy, clinical, and athletic performance as well as nutritional information, they expect to be able to use this information to improve training and performance practices with future USOC athletes. The power of having access to this epidemiology data in an organized database should create a great opportunity to impact the future of athletic performance as well as medical therapy information in general.

HIMSS EMR Adoption Model

The HIMSS EMR Adoption model is an 8-level scale for measuring the extent to which medical providers are utilizing their EMR systems. Table C.1 diagrams and defines the eight levels of adoption as well as records the percentage of providers that have been certified at each level.[7]

The EMR Adoption chart is being updated on a monthly basis and is an elegant measure of how rapidly medical providers are implementing the benefits of their EMR systems. Currently providers must be at the Stage 4 level to qualify for the Meaningful Use rewards because the CPOE requirements are one of the features that must be utilized.

Implementation of New ICD-10 Codes to Automate Medical Billing and Manage Costs

Today's medical billing procedures are very manually intensive and are a significant cost of hospital and physician practice administration. The next generation of EMR systems will be able to implement the new ICD-10 codes, due to be adopted in 2014, and automatically generate a billing event or identify a cost for the administration software to import and process for each patient. As more of the medical payers also adopt this same coding system the exchange of patient data thru the EMR systems will become more effective and more efficient.

United States EMR Adoption Model℠

Stage	Cumulative Capabilities	2012 Q2	2012 Q3
Stage 7	Complete EMR; CCD transactions to share data; Data warehousing; Data continuity with ED, ambulatory, OP	1.7%	1.8%
Stage 6	Physician documentation (structured templates), full CDSS (variance & compliance), full R-PACS	6.5%	7.3%
Stage 5	Closed loop medication administration	11.5%	12.0%
Stage 4	CPOE, Clinical Decision Support (clinical protocols)	13.3%	14.2%
Stage 3	Nursing/clinical documentation (flow sheets), CDSS (error checking), PACS available outside Radiology	42.4%	41.3%
Stage 2	CDR, Controlled Medical Vocabulary, CDS, may have Document Imaging; HIE capable	11.7%	11.2%
Stage 1	Ancillaries - Lab, Rad, Pharmacy - All Installed	5.1%	4.8%
Stage 0	All Three Ancillaries Not Installed	7.9%	7.4%

N = 5,303   N = 5,319

Table C.1   United States EMR Adoption Model℠
Data from HIMSS Analytics® Database © 2012.

Accountable Care Organizations

The latest direction now being promoted to reduce the cost of medical care is to convert from a fee for service billing intensive method of delivering health care to a fixed fee per patient that will be paid to a combined healthcare provider and payer organization now called an **Accountable Care Organization**, or ACO. There are working examples of this today, such as the Kaiser Permanente healthcare system in western U.S. states. Another similar approach is the Medicare Advantage program in which Medicare pays a fixed fee per patient to the provider to provide all Medicare approved care necessary.

While this may take a few years to become a reality in most health-care markets the accurate accounting of costs and analysis of medical information required to manage an ACO can best be provided with access to the EMR data. Therefore we can predict that the EMR of the future will become more integrated with the hospital information systems to provide access to the best information necessary to optimize and manage an ACO.

APPENDIX SUMMARY: **KEY POINTS**

- A 2012 HIMSS survey found that 65 percent of hospitals and 80 percent of physicians use EMR technology.

- New Meaningful Use rules from the U.S. HHS require that prescriptions are entered directly into a computer for transmission to a pharmacy.

- EMR technology is helpful in alerting physicians of possible drug interactions.

- EMR software automatically displays vital signs trend charts to assist care givers.

- EMR software can now send patient alerts via e-mail or telephone to assist them in complying with doctor's orders.

- EMR software today connects directly to patient monitoring devices through the industry standard HL7 interface.

- Newer EMR software is designed to support mobile devices like smart phones and tablets, keeping physicians in touch.

- IBM Watson technology now being tested to assist in cancer diagnoses and patient therapy management.

- The ICD-10 coding system will be integrated into the EMR systems of the future.

- EMR systems will improve the patient's access to their medical records.

- The Accountable Care Organization concept will become very dependent on continuous availability of electronic medical records and cost data.

Notes

1. Details for both the ARRA and HITECH acts can be found at http://healthit.hhs.gov/programs/REC.
2. The IBM Watson and Sloan Kettering Cancer Institute announcement can be found at: www-148.ibm.com/tela/webmail/Newsletter/10527/37258.
3. More details on the advantages of using EMR for public health applications can be found at: www.medicalnetsystems.com/index.php/public-health.
4. The PCHR concept is recommended and defined in more detail by the Society for Participatory Medicine. A link to their website can be found at: http://participatorymedicine.org.
5. Additional details on the IHE standard protocols may be found at: www.IHE.net.
6. The USOC application of EMR was announced in the press release at: www.healthcareitnews.com/news/ge-brings-emrs-analytics-london-2012-olympics?topic=08,19,20.
7. The HIMSS Analytics EMR Adoption Model was created by the HIMSS organization and is now maintained by their HIMSS Analytics affiliate. Their home page can be found at: www.himssanalytics.org/home/index.aspx.

GLOSSARY

access control list In systems, such as ERM, EDRMS, or document management systems, a list of individuals authorized to access, view, amend, transfer, or delete documents, records, or files. Access rights are enforced through software controls.

application programming interface (API) A way of standardizing the connection between two software applications. They are essentially standard hooks that an application uses to connect to another software application.

archival information package (AIP) One of three types of information packages that can be submitted in the OAIS preservation model for long-term digital preservation (LTDP).

archive Storing information and records for long-term or permanent preservation. With respect to e-mail, in a compressed and indexed format to reduce storage requirements and allow for rapid, complex searches (this can also done for blogs, social media, or other applications). Archiving of real-time applications like e-mail can only be deemed reliable with record integrity if it is performed immediately, in real time.

ARMA Association for Records Managers and Administrators, the U.S.-based nonprofit organization for records managers with a network of international chapters.

authentication, authorization, and audit (or accounting) (AAA) A network management and security framework that controls computer system log-ons and access to applications that enforces IG policies and audits usage.[1]

authenticity of records Verified content and author information as original for the purposes of electronic records management (ERM); in a legal context, proof that the e-document is what it purports to be when electronically stored information (ESI) is submitted during the e-discovery process.

auto-classification Setting predefined indices to classify documents and records and having the process performed automatically by using software, rather than human intervention. A strong trend toward auto-classification is emerging due to the impact of "Big Data" and rapidly increasing volumes of documents and records.

backup A complete spare copy of data for purposes of disaster recovery. Backups are nonindexed mass storage and cannot substitute for indexed, archived information that can be quickly searched and retrieved (as in archiving).

best practices Those methods, processes, or procedures that have been proven to be the most effective, based on real-world experience and measured results.

bidders conference A formal meeting where vendors bidding on a request for proposal (RFP) can ask questions and raise issues about the RFP, proposal requirements, and the procurement process.

business activities The tasks performed to accomplish a particular business function. Several activities may be associated with each business function.

business case A written analysis of the financial, productivity, auditability and other factors to justify the investment in software and hardware systems, implementation, and training.

business classification scheme Also referred to as a BCS, the overall structure an organization uses for organizing, searching, retrieving, storing, and managing documents and records in ERM. The BCS must be developed based on the business functions and activities. A file plan is a graphic representation of the BCS, usually a "hierarchical structure consisting of headings and folders to indicate where and when records should be created during the conducting of the business of an office. In other words *the file plan links the records to their business context.*"

business driver A compelling business reason that motivates an organization to implement a solution to a problem. Business drivers can be based on financial, legal, or operational gaps or needs.

business functions Basic business units such as accounting, legal, human resources, and purchasing.

business process A coordinated set of collaborative and transactional work activities carried out to complete work-steps.

business process improvement (BPI) Analyzing and redesigning business processes to streamline them and gain efficiencies, reduce cycle times, and improve auditability and worker productivity.

business process outsourcing (BPO) Contracting out a third party to perform specific business processes. One example could be using a customer service center taking inbound telephone calls from U.S. customers and handling customer requests and complaints from a service center located offshore, in locations such as India, where labor costs are lower.

business process management Managing the work-steps and business activities of an organization's workers in an automated way.

business process management system (BPMS) A superset of workflow software, and more: BPMS software offers five main capabilities:[2]

1. Puts existing and new application software under the direct control of business managers.
2. Makes it easier to improve existing business processes and create new ones.
3. Enables the automation of processes across the entire organization, and beyond it.
4. Gives managers "real-time" information on the performance of processes.
5. Allows organizations to take full advantage of new computing services.

capture Capture components are often also called input components. There are several levels and technologies, from simple document scanning and capture to complex information preparation using automatic classification.

case records Case records are characterized as having a beginning and an end, but are added to over time. Case records generally have titles that include names, dates, numbers, or places.

change management Methods and best practices to assist an organization and its employees in implementing changes to business processes, culture, and systems.

classification Systematic identification and arrangement of business activities and/or records into categories according to logically structured conventions, methods, and procedural rules represented in a classification system. A coding of content items as members of a group for the purposes of cataloging them or associating them with a taxonomy.

cloud computing Cloud computing refers to the provision of computational resources on demand via a network. Cloud computing can be compared to the supply of electricity and gas, or the provision of telephone, television, and postal services. All of these services are presented to the users in a simple way that is easy to understand without the users' needing to know how the services are provided. This simplified view is called an abstraction. Similarly, cloud computing offers computer application developers and users an abstract view of services, which simplifies and ignores much of the details and inner workings. A provider's offering of abstracted Internet services is often called The Cloud.

Code of Federal Regulations "The Code of Federal Regulations (CFR)" annual edition is the codification of the general and permanent rules published in the Federal Register by the departments and agencies of the federal government. It is divided into 50 titles that represent broad areas subject to federal regulation. The 50 subject matter titles contain one or more individual volumes, which are updated once each calendar year, on a staggered basis."[3]

cold site A cold site is simply an empty computer facility or data center that is ready with air-conditioning, raised floors, telecommunication lines, and electric power. Backup hardware and software will have to be purchased and shipped in quickly to resume operations. Arrangements can be made with suppliers for rapid delivery in the event of a disaster.

compliance monitoring Being regularly apprised and updated on pertinent regulations and laws and examining processes in the organization to ensure compliance with them. In a records management sense, this involves reviewing and inspecting the various facets of a records management program to ensure it is in compliance. Compliance monitoring can be carried out by an internal audit, external organization, or records management and must be done on a regular basis.

computer memory Solid state volatile (erasable) storage capability built into central processing units of computers. At times memory size can be increased by expanding it to the computer's hard drive or external magnetic disks.

content In records, the actual information contained in the record; more broadly, content is information; for example, content is managed by ECM systems, and may be e-mail, e-documents, web content, report content, and so on.

controlled vocabulary Set, defined terms used in a taxonomy.

corporate compliance The set of activities and processes that result in meeting and adhering to all regulations and laws that apply to an organization.

data loss prevention (DLP)   Data loss prevention (DLP; also known as data *leak* prevention) is a computer security term referring to systems that identify, monitor, and protect data in use (e.g., endpoint actions), data in motion (e.g., network actions), and data at rest (e.g., data storage) through deep content inspection, contextual security analysis of transaction (attributes of originator, data object, medium, timing, recipient/destination, and so on) and with a centralized management framework. Systems are designed to detect and prevent unauthorized use and transmission of confidential information.

declaration   Assignment of metadata elements to associate the attributes of one or more record folder(s) to a record, or for categories to be managed at the record level, providing the capability to associate a record category to a specific record.

designing and implementing recordkeeping systems (DIRKS)   An Australian framework or methodology consisting of eight steps developed by the Archives Authority of New South Wales, included in ISO 15489, the international standard for records management. Roughly analogous to the Generally Accepted Recordkeeping Principles® developed later by ARMA in the United States.

destruction   The process of eliminating or deleting records, beyond any possible reconstruction.

destruction certificate   Issued once the destruction of a record is complete, which verifies it has taken place, who authorized the destruction, and who carried it out. May include some metadata about the record.

destructive retention policy   Permanently destroying documents or e-documents (such as e-mail) after retaining them for a specified period of time.

disaster recovery (DR)/business continuity (BC)   The planning, preparation, and testing set of activities used to help a business plan for and recover from any major business interruption, and to resume normal business operations.

discovery   May refer to with the process of gathering and exchanging evidence in civil trials; or, to discover information flows inside an organization using data loss prevention (DLP) tools.

dissemination information package (DIP)   One of three types of information packages that can be submitted in the OAIS preservation model for LTDP.

disposition   The range of processes associated with implementing records retention, which can be destruction, transfer, or archiving decisions, which are documented in disposition authorities or other instruments.

document   Recorded information or object that can be treated as a unit.

document analytics   Detailed usage statistics on e-documents, such as time spent viewing, which pages were viewed and for how long, number of documents printed, where printed, number of copies printed, and other granular information about how and where a document is accessed, viewed, edited, or printed.

document imaging   Scanning and digitally capturing images of paper documents.

document lifecycle   The span of a document's use, from creation through active use, storage, and final disposition, which may be destruction or preservation.

document lifecycle security (DLS)   Providing a secure and controlled environment for e-documents. This can be accomplished by properly implementing technologies, including information rights management (IRM) and data loss prevention (DLP), along with complementary technologies like digital signatures.

document management   Managing documents throughout their life cycle from creation to final disposition, including managing revisions. Also called document lifecycle management.

document type   A term used by many software systems to refer to a grouping of related records.

e-document   An electronic document, that is, a document in digital form.

electronic code of regulations (e-CFR)   "It is not an official legal edition of the CFR. The e-CFR is an editorial compilation of CFR material and Federal Register amendments produced by the National Archives and Records Administration's Office of the Federal Register (OFR) and the Government Printing Office."[4]

electronic document and records management system (EDRMS)   Software that has the ability to manage documents and records. Sometimes referred to as ERM as well (see next).

electronic records management (ERM)   Electronic records management is the management of electronic and nonelectronic records by software, including maintaining disposition schedules for keeping records for specified retention periods, archiving, or destruction. (*For* enterprise rights management, *see* information rights management [IRM].)

electronic record   Information recorded in a form that requires a computer or other machine to process and view it and that satisfies the legal or business definition of a record.

electronic records repository   A direct access device on which the electronic records and associated metadata are stored.

electronically stored information (ESI)   A term coined by the legal community to connote any information at all that is stored by electronic means; this can include not just e-mail and e-documents but also audio and video recordings, and any other type of information stored on electronic media. ESI is a term that was created in 2006 when the U.S. Federal Rules of Civil Procedure (FRCP) were revised to include the governance of ESI in litigation.

e-mail and e-document encryption   E-mail and e-document encryption refers to encryption or scrambling (and often authentication) of e-mail messages, which can be done in order to protect the content from being read by unintended recipients.

enterprise content management (ECM)   Software that manages unstructured information such as e-documents, document images, e-mail, word processing documents, spreadsheets, web content, and other documents; most systems also include some records management capability.

enterprise process analytics Detailed statistics and analysis of business process cycle times and other data occurring throughout an enterprise. This business intelligence can help spot bottlenecks, optimize workflow, and improve worker productivity while improving input for decision-making.

event-based disposition A disposition instruction in which a record is eligible for the specified disposition (transfer, archive, or destroy) when or immediately after the specified event occurs. No retention period is applied and there is no fixed waiting period as with timed or combination timed-event dispositions. Example: *Destroy when no longer needed for current operations.*

faceted search Faceted search (sometimes referred to as faceted navigation or faceted browsing) is where, for instance, document collections are classified in multiple ways, rather than in a single, rigid taxonomy.

faceted taxonomy Faceted taxonomies allow for multiple organizing principles to be applied to information along various dimensions. Facets can contain subjects, departments, business units, processes, tasks, interests, security levels and other attributes used to describe information. There is never really one single taxonomy but rather collections of taxonomies that describe different aspects of information.

Federal Rules of Civil Procedure (FRCP)—Amended 2006 In U.S. civil litigation, the FRCP governs the discovery and exchange of electronically stored information (ESI), which includes not only e-mail but all forms of information that can be stored electronically.

file plan A file plan is a graphic representation of the business classification scheme (BCS), usually a "hierarchical structure consisting of headings and folders to indicate where and when records should be created during the conducting of the business of an office. In other words *the file plan links the records to their business context.*"

file transfer protocol (FTP) File transfer protocol (FTP) is a standard network protocol used to copy a file from one host to another over a TCP-based network, such as the Internet. FTP is built on a client-server architecture and utilizes separate control and data connections between the client and server. FTP users may authenticate themselves using a clear-text sign-in protocol but can connect anonymously if the server is configured to allow it.

folksonomy The term used for a free-form, social approach to metadata assignment. Folksonomies are not an ordered classification system; rather, they are a list of keywords input by users that are ranked by popularity.[5]

functional retention schedule Groups records series based on business functions, such as financial, legal, product management, or sales. Each function or grouping is also used for classification. Rather than detail every sequence of records, these larger functional groups are less numerous, and are easier for users to understand.

Generally Accepted Recordkeeping Principles® A set of eight Generally Accepted Recordkeeping Principles®, also known as "Gar Principles" or "The Principles" within the records management community,[6] published in 2009 by U.S.-based ARMA International to foster awareness of good recordkeeping practices and to provide guidance for records management maturity in organizations.

These principles and associated metrics provide an information governance (IG) framework that can support continuous improvement.

governance model   A framework or model that can assist in guiding governance efforts. Examples include using a SharePoint governance model, the information governance reference model (IGRM), MIKE2.0, and others.

guiding principles   In developing a governance model, for instance for a Share-Point deployment, the basic principles used to guide its development. May include principles such accountability (who is accountable for managing the site, who is accountable for certain content), who has authorized access to which documents, and wheter or not the governance model is required for use, or to be used optionally as a reference.

HIPAA   The Healthcare Insurance Portability and Accountability Act (HIPAA) was enacted by the U.S. Congress in 1996. According to the Centers for Medicare and Medicaid Services (CMS) website, Title II of HIPAA, known as the administrative simplification (AS) provision, requires the establishment of national standards for electronic health care transactions and national identifiers for providers, health insurance plans, and employers.

hot site   A hot site is one that has identical or nearly identical hardware and operating system configurations, and copies of application software, and receives live, real-time backup data from business operations. In the event of a business interruption, the IT and electronic vital records operations can be switched over automatically, providing uninterrupted service.

information governance (IG)   IG is a subset of corporate governance and is an all-encompassing term for how an organization manages the totality of its information. IG "encompasses the policies and leveraged technologies meant to dictate and manage what corporate information is retained, where and for how long, and also how it is retained (e.g., protected, replicated, and secured). Information governance spans retention, security and life cycle management issues."[7] IG is an ongoing program that helps organizations meet external compliance and legal demands and internal governance rules.

information life cycle   The span of the use of information, from creation through active use, storage, and final disposition, which may be destruction or preservation.

information map   A graphic diagram that shows where information is created, where it resides, and the path it takes.

information rights management (IRM)   Information rights management (IRM) is often referred to as enterprise rights management. IRM applies to a technology set that protects sensitive information, usually documents or e-mail messages, from unauthorized access. IRM is technology that allows for information (mostly in the form of documents) to be remote controlled. This means that information and its control can be separated, and rights such as viewing, editing, and forwarding, can be controlled. IRM is also sometimes also referred to as enterprise digital rights management (E-DRM). This can cause confusion because digital rights management (DRM) technologies are typically associated with business-to-consumer systems designed to protect rich media such as music and video.

information technology   Technologies used to manage digital information.

inherited metadata   Automatically assigning certain metadata to records based on rules that are established in advance and set up by a system administrator.

inventorying records   A descriptive listing of each record series or system, together with an indication of location and other pertinent data. It is not a list of each document or each folder but rather of each series or system."[8]

jukebox (optical disk jukebox)   Optical disc autochanger units for mass storage that use robotics to pick and mount optical disks and remove and replace them after use; dubbed a "jukebox" for their similarity in mechanics to jukebox units for playing vinyl records and, later, CDs.

knowledge management (KM)   The accumulation, organization, and use of experience and "lessons learned," which can be leveraged to improve future decision-making efforts. Often involves listing and indexing subject matter experts, project categories, reports, studies, proposals, and other intellectual property sources or outputs that is retained to build corporate memory. Good KM systems help train new employees and reduce the impact of turnover and retirement of key employees.

limitation period   The length of time after which a legal action cannot be brought before the courts. Limitation periods are important because they determine the length of time records must be kept to support court action [including subsequent appeal periods]. It is important to be familiar with the purpose, principles, and special circumstances that affect limitation periods and therefore records retention."[9]

long term digital preservation   The managed activities, methods, standards, and technologies used to provide long-term, error-free storage of digital information, with means for retrieval and interpretation, for the entire time span the information is required to be retained.

magnetic disk drives   A common data storage device using erasable magnetic media. Magnetic disk drives are common peripherals and inbuilt storage devices in desktop PCs and mini- and mainframe computers.

master retention schedule   A retention schedule that includes the retention and disposition requirements for records series that cross business unit boundaries. *The master retention schedule contains all records series in the entire enterprise.*

metadata   Data about data, or detailed information describing context, content, and structure of records and their management through time. Examples may be the author, department, document type, date created, length, and so forth.

migration   The act of moving data or records from one system to another while maintaining their authenticity, integrity, reliability, and usability.

negotiated procurement   A way to acquire a new system or components when the buying organization wants to make a rapid decision and requirements are known, such as making a bulk purchase of additional workstations or tablet computers that will be added to an existing network. Often a trusted consulting firm will be engaged to solicit bids, negotiate with vendors, and make a recommendation for procurement. This approach can be a better fit than issuing an RFP when cost and time are leading issues.

NENR   Non-erasable, non-rewritable media (e.g., optical, magnetic) that, once written, do not allow for erasure or overwriting of the original data.

OAIS   Reference model for an Open Archival Information System, describes how to prepare and submit digital objects for long-term digital preservation (LTDP) and retrieval but does not specify technologies, techniques, or content types. The OAIS reference model defines an archival information system as an archive, consisting of an organization of people and systems that has accepted the responsibility to preserve information and make it available and understandable for a Designated Community (i.e., potential users or consumers), who should be able to understand the information. Thus, the context of an OAIS-compliant digital repository includes producers who originate the information to be preserved in the repository, consumers who retrieve the information, and a management/organization that hosts and administers the digital assets being preserved. The OAIS Information Model employs three types of information packages: A **Submission Information Package** (SIP), an **Archival Information Package** (AIP), and a **Dissemination Information Package** (DIP). An OAIS-compliant digital repository preserves AIPs and any PDI associated with them. A Submission Information Package encompasses digital content that a Producer has organized for submission to the OAIS. After the completion of quality assurance and normalization procedures, an Archival Information Package is created, which as noted previously is the focus of preservation activity. Subsequently, a Dissemination Package is created that consists of an AIP or information extracted from an AIP that is customized to the requirements of the Designated Community of users and consumers.

optical character recognition (OCR)   A visual recognition process that involves photo-scanning text character-by-character.

Optical disk   Round, platter-shaped storage media written to using laser technologies. Optical disk drives use lasers to record and retrieve information, and optical media has a much longer useful life (some purported to be 100 years or more) than magnetic.

phishing   Phishing is a way of attempting to acquire sensitive information such as user names, passwords, and credit card details by masquerading as a trustworthy entity in an electronic communication. Communications purporting to be from popular social websites, auction sites, online payment processors, or IT administrators are commonly used to lure the unsuspecting public. Phishing is typically carried out by e-mail or instant messaging, and it often directs users to enter details at a fake website that looks and feels almost identical to the legitimate one. Phishing is an example of social engineering techniques used to fool users, and it exploits the poor usability of current web security technologies.

preservation description information (PDI)   In the LTDP process, adhering to the OAIS reference model, description information such as provenance, context, and fixity.

process-enabled technologies   Information technologies that automate and streamline business processes. Process-enabled technologies are often divided into two categories: workflow automation or business process management. The two technologies have a significant amount in common. Indeed it is fair to say that a good deal of the technology that underpins business process management concepts has its roots in the late 1980s and early 1990s and stems from the early efforts of the workflow community.

project charter   A document that formally authorizes a project to move forward. "A project charter dramatically reduces the risk of a project being cancelled due to lack of support or perceived value to the company. It documents the overall objectives of the project and helps manage the expectations."[10]

project management   The process of managing required project activities and tasks in a formal manner to complete a project; performed primarily by the project manager.

project manager   The person primarily responsible for managing a project to its successful completion.

project plan   Includes the project charter and project schedule and a delineation of all project team members and their roles and responsibilities.

project schedule   A listing of project tasks, subtasks, and estimated completion times.

policy   A high-level overall plan, containing a set of principles that embrace the general goals of the organization and are used as a basis for decisions. Can include some specifics of processes allowed and not allowed.

preservation   The processes and operations involved in ensuring the technical and intellectual survival of authentic records through time. Record information created, received, and maintained as evidence and information by an organization or person, in pursuance of legal obligations or in the transaction of business.

provenance   In records management, provenance is information about who created a record and what it is used for.

records appraisal   The process of assessing the value and risk of records to determine their retention and disposition requirements. Legal research is outlined in appraisal reports. This may be accomplished as a part of the process of developing the records retention schedules, as well as conducting a regular review to ensure that citations and requirements are current.

record category   A description of a particular set of records within a file plan. Each category has retention and disposition data associated with it, applied to all record folders and records within the category.

records integrity   Refers to the accuracy and consistency of records, and the assurance that they are genuine and unaltered.

records management (RM) or records and information management (RIM)   The field of management responsible for the efficient and systematic control of the creation, receipt, maintenance, use, and disposition of records, including processes for capturing and maintaining evidence of and information about business activities and transactions in the form of records. A set of instructions allocated to a class or file to determine the length of time for which records should be retained by the organization for business purposes, and the eventual fate of the records on completion of this period of time.

records retention schedule   A records retention schedule spells out how long different types of records are to be held, and how they will be archived or disposed of at the end of their life cycle. It considers legal, regulatory, operational, and historical requirements.[11]

record series   A group or unit of identical or related records that are normally used and filed as a unit and that can be evaluated as a unit or business function for scheduling purposes.[12]

refreshment   The process of copying stored data or e-records to new copies of the same media, to extend the storage life of the record by using new media.

return on investment (ROI)   "A performance measure used to evaluate the efficiency of an investment. . . . To calculate ROI, the benefit (return) of an investment is divided by the cost of the investment; the result is expressed as a percentage or a ratio."[13]

secure sockets layer (SSL)/transport layer security (TLS)   Secure sockets layer (SSL) and transport layer security (TLS) are cryptographic protocols that provide communications security over the Internet. SSL and TLS encrypt the segments of network connections above the transport layer, using symmetric cryptography for privacy and a keyed message authentication code for message reliability.

senior records officer (SRO)   The leading records manager in an organization; may also be titled chief records officer or similar.

service level agreement (SLA)   The service or maintenance contract that states the explicit levels of support, response time windows or ranges, escalation procedures in the event of a persistent problem, and possible penalties for nonconformance in the event the vendor does not meet its contractual obligations.

service oriented architecture (SOA)   An IT architecture which separates infrastructure, applications, and data into layers.

Six Sigma   A highly structured approach for eliminating defects in any process, whether from manufacturing or transactional processes. It can be applied to a product or a service-oriented process in any organization. Further, Six Sigma is "a statistical term that measures how far a given process deviates from perfection." The goal of Six Sigma is to systematically measure and eliminate defects in a process, aiming for a level of less than 3.4 defects per million instances or "opportunities."

social tagging   A method that allows users to manage content with metadata they apply themselves using keywords or metadata tags. Unlike traditional classification, which uses a controlled vocabulary, *social tagging keywords are freely chosen by each individual.* This can help uncover new categories of documents that are emerging, and helps users find information using their terms they believe are relevant.

solid state disk drive Storage devices that can be inbuilt or external that have no moving parts and are made of semiconductor materials. Being used more often in tablets computers as they are faster and more reliable than magnetic disk drives, although also more expensive. Memory sticks and removable USB "thumb" or flash drives are also solid state technology.

spoliation The loss of proven authenticity of a record. Can occur in the case of e-mail records if they are not captured in real-time, or they have been edited in any way.

structured data/records A collection of records or data that is stored in a computer; records maintained in a database or application.

subject matter expert (SME) A person with deep knowledge of a particular topical area. SMEs can be useful in the consultation phase of the taxonomy design process.

subject records Subject records (also referred to as topic or function records) "contain information relating to specific or general topics and that are arranged according to their informational content or by the function/activity/transaction they pertain to."[14]

Submission Information Package (SIP) One of three types of information packages that can be submitted in the OAIS preservation model for LTDP.

synonym ring (or synset) Denotes that no synonym is preferred and all have equal weight. For instance, "human resources" may be the same term as "personnel." Various (agreed-on) synonyms may be displayed to the user when making searches in the ERM/EDRMS system. The taxonomist or taxonomy team may designate a "preferred" term among synonyms.

taxonomy A hierarchical structure of information components, for example, a subject, business-unit, or functional taxonomy, any part of which can be used to classify a content item in relation to other items in the structure.

text mining Performing detailed full-text searches on the content of document.

thesaurus In taxonomies, a thesaurus contains all synonyms and definitions, is used to enforce naming conventions in a controlled vocabulary, for example, *invoice* and *bill* could be terms that are used interchangeably.

time- /date-based disposition A disposition instruction specifying when a record shall be cut off and when a fixed retention period is applied. The retention period does not begin until after the records have been cut off, for example: Destroy after two years.

time-, date-, and event-based A disposition instruction specifying that a record shall be disposed of after a fixed period of disposition time after a predictable or specified event. Once the specified event has occurred, then the retention period is applied. Example: Destroy three years after close of case. In this example, the record does not start its retention period until after the case is closed—at that time its folder is cut off and the retention period (three years) is applied.

total cost of ownership (TCO) All costs associated with owning a system over the life of the installation and implementation—usually considered over a range of three to five years. TCO includes implementation price and change orders (and the change order approval process), which occur when changes to the project are made outside of the original proposal. Timing and pricing of the software support fees are also critical TCO components, and may include warranty periods, annual fees, planned and maximum increases, trade-in and upgrade costs, hardware maintenance costs, and other charges that may not be immediately apparent to buyers.

transfer   Moving records from one location to another, or change of custody, ownership, and/or responsibility for records.

unstructured records   Records that are not expressed in numerical rows and columns but rather, are objects such as image files, e-mail files, Microsoft Office files, and so forth. Structured records are maintained in databases.

usage (records)   The purpose a record is used for; i.e., its primary use.

vital records   Vital records are mission-critical records that are necessary for an organization to continue to operate in the event of disruption or disaster and cannot be recreated from any other source. Typically, they make up about 3 percent to 5 percent of an organization's total records. They are the most important records to be protected, and a plan for disaster recovery (DR)/business continuity (BC) must be in place to safeguard these records.

warm site   A warm site may have all (or mostly all) identical hardware and operating systems, such as a hot site does, and software licenses for the same applications, and needs only to have data loaded to resume normal operations. Internal IT staff may have to retrieve magnetic tapes, optical disks, or other storage media containing the most recent backup data, and some data may be lost if the backup is not real-time and continuous.

workflow, workflow automation, and workflow software   Software that can route electronic folders through a series of worksteps to speed processing and improve auditability. Not to be confused with business process management systems (BPMS), which have more robust capabilities.

WORM   Write Once Read Many optical disk storage media that is nonerasable and can be written to only one time.

Notes

1. TechTarget.com, "Authentication, Authorization, and Accounting," http://searchsecurity.techtarget .com/definition/authentication-authorization-and-accounting (accessed Dec. 5, 2012)
2. John O'Connell, Jon Pyke, and Roger Whitehead, *Mastering Your Organization's Processes* (Cambridge, UK: Cambridge University Press, 2006), 14.
3. The U.S. Government Printing Office (GPO), "Code of Federal Regulations," www.gpo.gov/help/ index.html#about_code_of_federal_regulations.htm (accessed) April 22, 2012).
4. National Archives and Records Administration, "Electronic Code of Federal Regulations," October 2, 2012, http://ecfr.gpoaccess.gov/cgi/t/text/text-idx?c=ecfr&tpl=%2Findex.tpl.
5. Tom Reamy, "Folksonomy Folktales," *KM World*, September 29, 2009, www.kmworld.com/Articles/ Editorial/Feature/Folksonomy-folktales-56210.aspx.
6. ARMA International, "How to Cite GARP," www.arma.org/garp/copyright.cfm (accessed May 8, 2012). Chapter 3 was contributed by Charmaine Brooks, CRM.

7. Kathleen Reidy, "The Rise of Information Governance," *Too Much Information: The 451 Take on Information Management* (blog), August 5, 2009, http://blogs.the451group.com/information_management/2009/08/05/the-rise-of-information-governance/

8. U.S. National Archives and Records Administration, "Disposition of Federal Records: A Records Management Handbook," www.archives.gov/records-mgmt/publications/disposition-of-federal-records/chapter-3.html (accessed April 3, 2012).

9. Government of Alberta, "Developing Retention and Disposition Schedules," 122.

10. Rita Mulcahy, "Project Management Crash Course: What Is a Project Charter?" October 28, 2009, www.ciscopress.com/articles/article.asp?p=1400865.

11. National Archives, "Frequently Asked Questions about Records Scheduling and Disposition," updated June 6, 2005, www.archives.gov/records-mgmt/faqs/scheduling.html#whysched.

12. University of Toronto Archives, "Glossary," www.library.utoronto.ca/utarms/info/glossary.html (accessed September 10, 2012).

13. Investopedia website, "Return on Investment," http://www.investopedia.com/terms/r/returnoninvestment.asp#axzz2E6SXDDOc, (accessed December 4, 2012).

14. Ibid.

ABOUT THE AUTHOR

Robert F. Smallwood is a founding partner of IMERGE Consulting and heads up its E-Records Institute, a specialty consulting practice, as executive director. Mr. Smallwood has over 25 years of experience in the information technology industry focusing on e-document and e-records management, and has been recognized as one of the industry's "25 Most Influential People" and "Top 3 Independent Consultants" by *KM World* magazine. He was a chapter founder and president, and has served on the Executive Committee of the Board of Directors of AIIM International. Smallwood consults with Fortune 500 companies and governments to assist them in making technology decisions and implementations. Some of his past research and consulting clients include the World Bank, Johnson & Johnson, Apple, Miller-Coors, AT&T, the Supreme Court of Canada, Xerox, and IBM. He has published more than 100 articles and given more than 50 conference presentations on documents, records, and content management. He is the author of *Safeguarding Critical E-Documents, Managing Social Media Business Records, Taming the Email Tiger,* and several other books, including a novel, a theatrical play, and the first published personal account of Hurricane Katrina.

ABOUT THE MAJOR CONTRIBUTORS

Lori J. Ashley is a Wisconsin-based consultant, writer, and educator dedicated to helping clients improve the performance of their record and information management (RIM) practices and controls. An experienced business strategist and organizational development specialist, she has codeveloped four continuous improvement methodologies aimed at jumpstarting collaboration among stakeholders who share accountability for effective and efficient life-cycle management of valued records and information assets.

Barbara Blackburn, CRM, is an electronic records management consultant who assists organizations in defining, researching, selecting, and implementing cost-effective solutions. She assists clients in preparing for technology deployment by providing strategic planning and developing recordkeeping programs and taxonomies. Ms. Blackburn has expert taxonomy design skills and has taught AIIM's Electronic Records Management and Electronic Content Management (ERM and ECM) certification classroom courses.

Charmaine Brooks, CRM, is a principal with IMERGE Consulting, Inc., and has over 25 years of experience in records and information management (RIM) and content management. Ms. Brooks is a certified trainer and has taught AIIM classroom courses on ERM, and provided many workshops for ARMA. Ms. Brooks was records manager for a leading worldwide provider of semiconductor memory solutions; a records management software development company manager; and today provides clients, small and large, public and private, with guidance in developing records management and information governance (IG) programs.

Monica Crocker, CRM, PMP, is the corporate records manager for Land O'Lakes, Inc. Ms. Crocker has also been an information management consultant for 20 years, defining content and records management best practices for organizations across the United States. Her expertise includes SharePoint governance, enterprise strategies for content management, records management, electronic discovery, taxonomy design, project management, and business process redesign. Ms. Crocker is a recipient of AIIM's Distinguished Service Award.

Charles M. Dollar is an internationally recognized archival educator, consultant, and author who draws upon more than three decades of knowledge and experience in working with public and private sector organizations to optimize the use of information technologies to satisfy legal, regulatory, business, and cultural memory recordkeeping requirements for digital preservation. He is codeveloper of a Capability Maturity Model (CMM) for long-term digital preservation (LTDP) that incorporates the specifications of ISO 15489, ISO 14721, ISO 18492, and ISO 16363.

Stephen Goodfellow, CRM, CDIA, is a nationally recognized consultant, author, and speaker in records and information management, process improvement, and disaster preparedness. As president of Access Systems Consulting, he has advised Global 1000 firms, leading universities and numerous government agencies. Mr. Goodfellow is a Certified Records Manager, a Certified Document Imaging Architect, and a recipient of the AIIM Laureate of Information Technology designation. He is also an adjunct professor at Syracuse University's School of Information Studies.

Paula Lederman is a leading information management consultant in records management, information governance, classification/taxonomy development, and electronic records management systems with IMERGE Consulting. She holds degrees in computer science, an MBA, and a Masters of Library/Information Science. These have provided a basis for many years of consulting, teaching, and publishing in this field including assignments for large government agencies, the private sector, and international businesses. Ms. Lederman's approach moves theoretical concepts to cost-effective, practical, and user-friendly implementation.

John W. Orth, BSME, MBA, CDIA+ has had a successful career of over 35 years in the medical instrument field, including nuclear imaging and patient monitoring systems. He participated in the original health-care DICOM imaging standards and is currently working with the IHE standards group to facilitate the sharing of electronic medical records through Health Information Exchanges. Mr. Orth is principal consultant with IMERGE Consulting, Inc., specializing in the selection and implementation of electronic medical records.

Jon Pyke, FBCS, CITP, has more than 30 years of experience in the field of software product development. He was personally responsible for defining many of the key software metaphors that enable business process management (BPM) to work, and as chair of the Workflow Management Coalition (WfMC), he has also overseen the development of standards. He can truly claim to be one of the founders of BPM. Mr. Pyke was past CTO of Staffware, Plc, and is now CEO of CIMtrek, a cloud migration company, in the United Kingdom.

INDEX

434 INDEX